Alex Wade's
GUIDE TO AFFORDABLE HOUSES

Other Books by Alex Wade

Low-Cost, Energy-Efficient Shelter for the
Owner and Builder (coauthor)

30 Energy-Efficient Houses . . . You Can Build
(coauthor)

A Design and Construction Handbook for
Energy-Saving Houses

Alex Wade's GUIDE TO AFFORDABLE HOUSES

Ingenious ideas for keeping new house costs down without sacrificing looks or comfort, plus plans and photographs of over 30 new, affordable, family homes.

 Rodale Press, Emmaus, Pennsylvania

Printed in the United States of America on recycled paper containing a high percentage of de-inked fiber.

Front cover photographs (clockwise from top): Weiss remodeling, upstate New York 1780–1984; Wade restoration, Mount Marion, New York; Howard house, upstate New York, photographer Howard Dratch; Knopf house, upstate New York.

Back cover photographs (counterclockwise from top): Knopf house, upstate New York; Grant house, Connecticut; 1971 prototype panelized house, Hilton Head Island, South Carolina; Civic panelized house, New England.

All photographs by Alex Wade unless otherwise noted.

Library of Congress Cataloging in Publication Data

Wade, Alex.
    Alex Wade's Guide to affordable houses.

    Includes index.
    1. House construction. 2. Dwellings. I. Title.
II. Title: Guide to affordable houses.
TH4811.W23 1984   690'.837   84–9990

ISBN   0-87857-511-1   hardcover
ISBN   0-87857-512-X   paperback

2 4 6 8 10 9 7 5 3 1   hardcover
2 4 6 8 10 9 7 5 3 1   paperback

Contents

Acknowledgments

Thousands of people from all parts of the world have contributed directly or indirectly to this book. A select few have made major contributions without which the book would not exist. Carol Hupping, my editor at Rodale Press, sold a new book on housing to a doubtful management in the midst of our country's most severe housing depression and then coordinated the transformation from manuscript to finished book. Elizabeth Groeneman worked as my personal editor and smoothed out many of the wrinkles in my text. Mike Saporito developed and printed most of the photographs on a rush basis, giving me the highest quality in the shortest possible time. Ed Landrock of Rodale's Photography Department was instrumental in reviewing all of the photographs and in helping with the printing. Graphics Assistant Elvira Wolven; Designers Tom Chinnici, Linda Jacopetti, and Anita G. Patterson; Editorial Assistant Cheryl Winters Tetreau; and Copyeditor Dolores Plikaitis all contributed their individual talents to produce the final product.

I also wish to thank my hosts in foreign countries, Fredrick Hundertwasser and Noriko Yamamoto, and the many clients who contributed their experiences and house designs to this book. The names and specific locations of these clients have been changed to protect their privacy.

Since the houses here involve new construction techniques, the contractors who helped develop and refine the system deserve special mention. Kevin Berry and Jeff Seeley of Kevin Berry Builders helped build the majority of the houses in the book. Peter McNaull of Vermont Laminates and Bob Dakin of Essex Timber Frames supplied panels and frames for several of the houses.

Finally, there are those dedicated workmen who went to the aid of the owner-builders and helped them over the rough spots: Harry Rustad, Kevin Conner, Jeff Seeley, Joe Ventulith, and George Steckler.

To all of you who helped with this project, my sincerest thanks.

AW
April, 1984

Introduction

The American housing industry is in serious trouble. Runaway construction costs and high interest rates have combined to force most low- and middle-income families out of the housing market. The National Association of Home Builders (NAHB) 1982 Home Builder's profile revealed that the median price of a new home in 1982 was $74,790, and that the household income of families able to afford a new house had risen to $37,131. Since the average family income for 1982 was some $15,000 less than this figure, it is obvious that the average American family can no longer afford the average American house. 1982 was bad, but 1983 was even worse; according to the NAHB, the average new house in 1983 cost $98,000. This drastic increase far outstripped the inflation rate and suggests that new houses are primarily purchases for those in the highest income brackets. Although price tags on today's houses are higher than ever, the number of housing starts and the total dollar volume are far less than the levels needed to sustain a healthy industry and provide adequate housing for our country.

The easy solution to our housing predicament is for federal or state governments to subsidize interest rates or legally cap (limit) them, since the high cost of borrowing the money to buy these new houses is a big source of the problem. But by using tax dollars for such purposes, we effectively make all taxpayers subsidize the costs of new houses for a relatively small number of people who buy new houses each year. A second, much more logical solution is to get to the heart of the matter—cut the cost of houses by building smaller, "no frills" houses. Unfortunately, there is a limited market for such houses because they are usually very poorly designed and totally lacking in visual appeal. Detroit has found, much to its sorrow, that there is absolutely no market for shrunken, stripped-down versions of its big cars. Japanese companies that offer elegantly designed, efficiently packaged cars are so deluged with orders that "voluntary import quotas" have been imposed to save Detroit from the onslaught of these imports. While a few home builders are having success marketing well-designed small houses, the vast majority have failed to learn anything from their Detroit brethren. I have made a major effort in this book to assemble a unique collection of new designs that make houses lower in cost and more pleasant to live in. For years I have specialized in compact, low-cost houses, and I've found that interest in these houses has been tremendous. Since I wrote my first book, *30 Energy-Efficient Houses... You Can Build* (Rodale Press, 1977), I have received letters from literally thousands of people from all parts of the world who ask questions and want to share ideas.

While in New Zealand doing research for this book, I read an article describing how a group of Australian naturalists had successfully saved several members of a school of beached whales by rocking them back and forth to reestablish their sense of direction so that they could swim back to sea at high tide. Shortly after my return to the United States, there was an article in the *New York Times* reporting that an entire school of beached whales had died on the coast near Boston because "there is no known technique for saving them." New, improved construction methods do exist; unfortunately, neither the public nor builders is aware of them. These new methods drastically reduce both construction and operating costs and can make good housing available to many more people. By implementing some of these changes, we all can hope to rescue our own "beached whale" of a housing industry and reopen the housing market to people of limited means.

The houses featured in this book use a relatively new construction system of prefabricated wall panels attached to a structural wood frame. This system is much superior to conventional house construction for many reasons. Construction is easier and quicker because fewer building materials are used; panelization makes it simple to do a first-rate job of insulating and weathersealing the structure. Since energy costs have escalated rapidly in the last decade, most builders spend much more money now on insulation than was formerly the custom. It is quite expensive to insulate a conventionally framed, stud-wall house and do a good job. Every gap between hundreds of wooden pieces has to be filled. With the panelized system I feature in this book, the insulation itself becomes part of the structure. Large structural panels enclose the house quickly and economically and leave little chance for air leaks. Since no wooden frame members penetrate the insulation barrier, the house is more effectively insulated from the effects of heat and cold.

J-Deck, a Columbus, Ohio, company, has been building houses using this technique for over 10 years. They have documented proof that this system reduces fuel consumption to less than 15% of the amount required for houses conforming to the usual construction standards. Jim Jackson of J-Deck has even convinced skeptical Ohio officials of the efficiency of this system, and they have made exceptions to the state code to permit installation of a heating system much smaller than that required for conventional houses because the heating requirements in J-Deck panelized homes are so much less.

Rather than a sprawling, one-story plan with its long axis parallel to the road, my basic panelized houses are compact and multilevel. By facing a short elevation to the street, these houses can be built on smaller lots to save on land costs. If constructed on larger lots, they can be readily duplexed. Instead of drastically reducing room sizes I've eliminated unnecessary, duplicate spaces to get overall size and costs down. Room sizes and shapes and traffic flow patterns have been carefully considered so that all of the space built is truly usable.

A comparison between a typical builder's ranch house and my two-story Civic house will give you some idea of the kinds of savings that are possible. Let us consider a typical three-bedroom ranch house measuring 28 by 48 feet, with a crawl space and 4-on-12 roof trusses. I compare this to my 24-foot-square two-story Civic house with sleeping lofts. Both houses have almost exactly the same amount of usable floor area; the ranch house is framed conventionally with stud frame and roof trusses, and the Civic uses a lightweight post-and-beam frame with fabricated wall and roof panels. When I put together a materials list for each house, I see that there are six times as many pieces of wood in the ranch house and that it consumes 2½ times as much board footage of lumber. If one were to assume that all new houses in this country were to be panelized houses, the lumber savings would be staggering. The labor savings that would result from handling substantially fewer pieces of lumber is equally impressive.

The key to this drastic reduction in construction costs is the use of prefabrication. We are virtually the only major country in the world that makes limited use of prefabrication for residential construction. Fortunately, this is changing. Prefabricated panelization is starting to sweep the country. One post-and-beam contractor in New England has built 50 houses with prefabricated panels in the past three years; J-Deck has built several hundred.

My strong interest in this field goes back to my college days, when I did my thesis project using prefabrication techniques. Upon graduating, I spent several years designing dreary hospitals and schools until I got a chance to visit Finland. I stayed several weeks to study their innovative architecture. The strikingly versatile buildings constructed by the Finnish architects using standardized building components quickly rekindled my interest in techniques of prefabrication. A few years later, I landed a job with a firm of architects that specialized in designing prefabricated structures, and I was soon in charge of a prefabricated dormitory project. Later, I transferred to another firm to work on precast concrete apartment buildings that were constructed for the New York State Urban Development Corporation. All these systems were doomed to failure, largely due to their complexity and the substantial capital costs required to produce the components. Added complications were intransigent labor unions and widely varying building code requirements that prevented true mass production. In 1971, I successfully prefabricated panelized walls for a house and shipped them several hundred miles for erection. This easy house panelization system worked out very well and was the forerunner of the system used to build many of the houses in this book.

The components of the panels are so simple that a potential homeowner can even build them in the backyard or garage. A small contractor who only builds a few houses a year can use the system to slash construction costs and extend the work season. Since the components go up quickly and the shell is completely insulated upon erection, many cold-weather construction problems are eliminated. The design key to my version of this system is a lightweight post-and-beam frame based upon an 8-foot module. Perimeter post spacing is standardized at 8 feet, and all wall and roof panels are 8 feet square. The coordinated post- and-panel dimension plus the new urethane foam sealant materials eliminate the expensive and unsightly panel joints that are the Achilles' heel of earlier prefabricated building systems. Mechanical trades have been simplified and organized in interior core areas to prevent complications with the prefab panels. Electrical wiring is concentrated in inside walls where possible. On the exterior walls, the wiring is installed in surface raceways so that construction is speeded and there are no penetrations of the exterior insulating skin to increase heat losses.

Obviously, this panelized building system is not the only way to save money in new construction. Careful organization, modular construction, and efficiently planned houses can reduce costs significantly even when conventional construction is used, and I go into all these areas, plus some others that are bound to save you money. But in addition to this book, the crisis in the building industry has produced several worthwhile publications aimed at making conventional construction procedures more cost-effective. The best of these is a U.S. Department of Housing and Urban Development (HUD) manual, *Building Affordable Homes—A Cost Savings Guide for Builder/ Developers.* A second, slightly older publication, also by HUD, is *Reducing Home Building Costs with OVE Design and Construction* (HUD-PDR 505). It is claimed that OVE (Optimum Value Engineering) saves 15% over the cost of conventional construction just by eliminating wasteful practices. The manual was produced for HUD by the National Association of Home Builders Research Foundation and was published in 1978. While it is not as up-to-date as *Building Affordable Homes,* both have good ideas.

If you are interested in saving money and having a cost- and energy-efficient small house, I highly recommend another new book, *The Compact House Book,* edited by Don Metz (Garden Way Publishing Company, 1983). The book is the result of a competition held jointly by Garden Way and the National Association of Home Builders for a 1000-square-foot maximum, energy-efficient, two-bedroom house. Thirty-three winning house designs were selected for publication. While the book has a great deal going for it, it has some drawbacks. Most of the houses are illustrated by the competition drawings, which are variable in quality. It may be hard to visualize just how the house will look when completed. And because these are just plans and not constructed houses, some of the designs may not work very well when completed, either.

Another drawback is inherent in the rules of the competition: a lack of variety. What we have are 33 houses of 998 square feet, each with two bedrooms, usually on two stories. This is not bad if this is exactly the type of house you are looking for. I think it would have been nice to have had three categories of size represented in the competition, or at least a variation in the number of bedrooms. All in all, many of the designs are splendid, and there is good geographic diversity. There are several nice designs for the South and Southwest, areas that are usually overlooked by other designers.

In Chapter 12 I list sources of plans for houses I think have particular merit. I have included several of the winning designers in the Garden Way competition who have indicated that they have plans available for their houses.

In addition to prefabricated panels and the other cost-cutting measures, the book explores several other systems from all parts of the world that save labor and materials. Unfortunately, many of them use such unconventional techniques and materials that they will be difficult to implement on a widespread basis. Most truly innovative systems will have trouble with conservative building codes, banks, and contractors. Although I know that many people interested in pursuing them will run into financial and legal stumbling blocks, I present them in detail anyway, in hopes of encouraging our conservative building industry to try some new ideas. For owner-builders in noncode areas of the country, some of these systems may be just the ticket.

Code acceptance is a problem for any new technique. The vast majority of the land area of this country is unregulated as far as single-family houses are concerned. Electrical and waste systems tend to be regulated, but not the house proper. Fortunately, for those of us who advocate the panelized system illustrated in this book, much of the work has already been done to break down resistance from code officials. The largest manufacturer of the panels, J-Deck, has put its panels through exhaustive tests and conforms with three of the major recognized building codes. I have encountered skepticism, but no direct opposition, from building officials in the areas where my panelized houses have been erected.

I present 14 different examples of houses using post and beam or post and beam with panels, all with detailed drawings. I made the selection as diverse as possible in order to show that the system can be adapted to a wide variety of houses and to give you as much choice as possible. Plans for all the houses featured in the book are available; see Appendix C for an order blank.

In addition to a listing of architects and contractors and some publications that I think are particularly good, Appendix A contains a detailed source list for materials to build the houses I feature. Frames, panels, and the materials to make them yourself are listed, as are lists of construction materials and energy- and cost-saving products from around the world that I think are especially good and that have appeal for the American market. Finally, there are detailed construction drawings in Appendix B.

Every possibility for cost savings, from land selection and financing to cabinetwork and trim, must be taken advantage of in order to build an affordable house today. In this book I take you through all the steps and show you how they can be interconnected. The ranch house I used for comparison a little while back wastes a cubic foot of space in both its attic and crawl space for each square foot of its living area. We can't afford to build any more of these inefficient monsters. I hope this book will open your eyes to the alternatives and lead the way to a new resource-consciousness in the construction industry.

Part I

Preliminary Considerations

1 Financing Options

Back in the good old days of double-digit inflation and single-digit interest rates, financing was relatively simple. Most people could afford to take out a mortgage for the major portion of the cost of a new house; virtually all banks offered similar fixed-rate, 30-year mortgages. Banks tended to quibble over the number of bedrooms and the design of the house (conform, conform), but you could usually find a house you liked that the bank would finance. Back in those days, the banks had a hard, fast rule that your yearly housing costs could not exceed 25% of your annual household income. After deregulation allowed banks to raise their investment rates to compete with the money markets, the banks discovered that they had to raise their mortgage rates to stay in business; you can't last long paying out 17% on interest and only charging 8% for mortgages. The steep increase in mortgage rates caused the banks to forget their old 25% rule—now 32% is the norm.

Even though the banks will let you use up a much larger percentage of your income for a mortgage, I strongly recommend the lower limit. Interest rates have gotten so high that you are paying considerably more for the use of the bank's money than the amount of money itself. My objective is to show you how you can reduce the cost of building a house so that you can reduce the amount you have to borrow. According to the United States League of Savings Associations, a 14% fixed-rate, 30-year mortgage for $60,000 costs $902.92 per month and requires a house-

hold income of $33,860. These figures include $192 per month for taxes, utilities, and home insurance (the national average) and assume that these costs will equal 32% of your yearly household income. If you build a more economical house and save more money toward construction, you can take out a smaller mortgage. The table below compares the payments required for smaller mortgages:

Amount of Mortgage at 14% Interest	Monthly Payment Required at 14% Interest	Required Annual Household Income (assuming 25% of income for housing)
$30,000	$548	$26,300
$20,000	$429	$20,592

Mortgages

The other loophole that was created by the banks to escape from the bind caused by the high interest rates and limited consumer incomes is called a variable-rate mortgage. These come in a bewildering array. As I write this, over 150 different types of mortgages of both fixed and variable rate are available; in practice, only a dozen are actually in common use. State banking laws vary considerably, so you will have to check locally to see what is available.

The majority of the mortgages written in this country are still of the fixed-rate variety. Unless you are reasonably assured of a continually esca-

materials, you could eliminate
gether. Automobile insurance
state to state. Think about tha
on a home site. If you pay cash
have to insure the car itself; a
big savings.

The key to lowering medica
dentistry and eye care, is the
ailment before it happens. Mc
sionals are still usually indiffe
to this approach, even though
shown that life-style, nutrition
self-awareness and self-care (
cant impact upon one's health
zine, published by Rodale Pre
advice on the subject. While
extreme and unproven by sor
regard the advice given in the
Now by Jon N. Leonard (Gross
as excellent. Much of the adv
sense; some of the dietary me
seem severe, but the directio

I was most fortunate to have b
preventive dentistry and eye
About 20 years ago, I had a pr
bration done to my teeth; it im
reduced pressure on my mout
The dentist who did the wor
rigorous brushing and flossing
my teeth are in perfect shape. I
I recommend *How to Save Yo*
B. Marshall (Penguin Books
preventive care of the eyes is
highly effective technique. Th

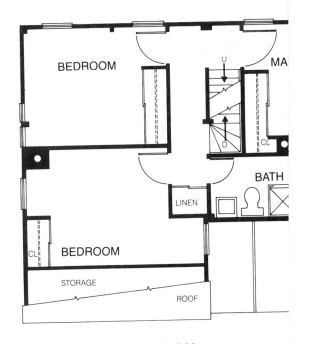

SECOND FLOOR PLAN

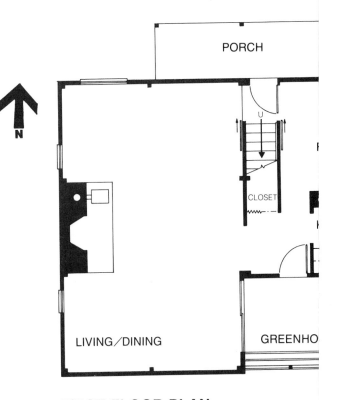

FIRST FLOOR PLAN

As funds permit, the basic structure can be expanded into a
house. A small mortgage can be taken on the originally con
the addition. Note that the house has been carefully design
with virtually no changes to the original structure.

Alt
cor
har
cus
ene
lati
var
and
ma
sm
Mil
kits
the
Ev
fie
of t
ave
cor
hai
mu

Th
cal
sid
yo
wh
Ba
a n
wh
bo
ba
fre
of
frie
are
ma
inç
a 1
co
Th
yo
a l

Ba
fur
lo
yo
to
for
to
ch
Th
sp
sp
Yo
bc
th
qu

lating income, I would not consider anything but
a fixed-rate mortgage. Traditional fixed-rate mortgages are sometimes written so that they are
assumable by a new owner and usually do not require a penalty payment if you prepay the mortgage. Obviously, if you took out a mortgage when
the rates were 17% and the rates drop to 11%, you
will want to pay off your old mortgage and re-
finance. If you are holding an old 6% mortgage
on your present house, it will be much easier to
sell if the buyer can assume your mortgage at the
same rate. Since the banks turn around and sell
your mortgage to other financial institutions, obviously they would prefer that mortgages not be
assumable and that they have a penalty clause for
prepayment. So-called reform movements are
afoot to allow banks to write different combinations of the features discussed above. Presum-
ably, the banks could offer lower rates on a basic,
fixed-rate mortgage with no options and charge
more for optional features—just like Detroit does
with cars. Most thoughtful consumers would opt
for a basic, fixed-rate mortgage, even without
the assumability or prepayment option, over the
highly risky adjustable-rate mortgages.

For many people, the adjustable-rate mortgage
may be the only solution, particularly if you are
buying a house at a non-negotiable price that's
out of your reach with a conventional mortgage.
All these mortgages are tricky, and you should
examine the "worst-case" possibilities very carefully. We are in a situation where the major banks
in this country have decided to make a killing on
Poland and Brazil, thereby starving the domestic
credit markets. The situation is aggravated by
senseless government policies of spending bil-
lions of dollars we don't have on additional arma-
ments we don't need. Given these realities, we
are unlikely to ever see any significant permanent
drop in interest rates short of a total collapse of
the free-world economy. Adjustable-rate mortgages are promoted on the dubious proposition
that high interest rates are a temporary phenomenon that will soon go away, and that the rates
will then return to "normal."

The most insidious of the adjustable-rate mortgages is called a negative amortization mortgage.
This mortgage is likened to swimming upstream
against a heavy current that continues to carry
you downstream. In this mortgage, the initial
payments are too low to cover the interest, so
that the total amount of the mortgage increases
rather than decreases. Technically, this thing can't
properly be called a mortgage, as the meaning of
the word mortgage comes from the French "to
kill a debt." Very few people would be foolhardy
enough to take out such a mortgage if they under-

stood exactly how it works. I mention this type
because there is a real danger that a more conventional graduated-rate mortgage could turn into
such an animal if the interest rates continue to
rise steeply. Although there is usually a limit of
one to two percentage points per year to which
the adjustable rate mortgage can rise (or fall),
there is no total limit to how much it can eventually rise (or fall). Even though you may be saving
quite a bit in initial monthly payments, you could
be wiped out by several years of escalating interest rates. The banks are protecting themselves
against such an eventuality and giving you a break
on your current payments. Of course, you are
taking a risk of losing your house to the bank if
interest rates go through the roof. For older
people or those on fixed incomes, adjustable
rates are a modified form of Russian roulette; I
do not recommend them at all.

Veterans Administration (VA) and Federal Housing Authority (FHA) mortgages are a lower-cost
alternative to high-priced, fixed-rate mortgages
that do not entail the risks of the adjustable variety. Unfortunately, their availability is somewhat
limited, and the VA and FHA attach strings to the
design of your house. Both these mortgages are
government sponsored and are aimed at the
lower end of the housing market. VA mortgages
are by definition available only to veterans. If you
are a veteran, they are well worth looking into.
The restrictions can be difficult if you are buying
an existing house, but you can tailor a new house
to meet their requirements. The FHA requirements are a bit stiffer than the VA ones, but are
still fairly reasonable. Passive solar or open-
plan houses for hot climates may run into trouble
because there are requirements for full walls
separating all spaces. Similarly, the requirements that call for thermostatically controlled
heat sources for each room can be difficult to
meet in superinsulated houses that have only a
single, central source of backup heat such as a
wood stove. A few used electric baseboard heaters
can solve the heating problem if necessary, but
you will have to plan ahead. Not all banks can
arrange these mortgages, so you may have to
shop around for the best deal. See the box on the
next page for a summary of common mortgage
types.

Other Financial Sources

The extraordinary rise in interest rates in recent
years has caused a considerable upheaval in the
traditional financial markets. In years gone by,
you were limited to a commercial or savings bank
as a source of funds; other avenues were closed
to the general public. Now, the banking industry
is being stood on its head because higher interest

Mortg

Fixed-
with a s
type. E
agenci
gages,
able wi
are 15,
mortga
over th

Adjusta
to a fix
tions. T
below t
gage af
vals of
at one-y
top inte
quite d

Negativ
a mortg
never a
mortga
be avoic
circums
will onl
because
poratior
rent. If t
your ho
actually
limited
renovati
may be

Gradua
of the b
ments o
with the
initial pa
The amc
each ye
portion
mortgag
years of
faster th
you can
the type

---

rates have
attractive
mortgage
investors,
you are h
from a ban

---

mate use for an emergency, but you pay a high price for that convenience on a day-to-day basis. Vegetable and poultry proteins are vastly cheaper than grain-fed beef. I stock my freezer in season with locally grown fruits, vegetables, and turkey, and I save a great deal by purchasing such staples as potatoes, onions, and soybeans in bulk from local producers, and I make soups and casseroles from leftovers rather than discarding them. Restaurant foods have a high markup and are usually not at all nutritious, so rather than eating out regularly, I save by doing so only on special occasions. Our society throws away more food than some people have to live on.

Other societies place a high value on sewing machines. Many Americans wouldn't know how to use one. Typical Americans have many more clothes than they can ever use. New wardrobes are bought for reasons of style rather than practicality. Mending or altering clothes is seldom a solution we're willing to live with. The Chinese have a saying, "three years new, three years old, patch and wear for three years more." Clothes are regularly discarded and sold at yard sales, second-hand stores, or at the Salvation Army, usually for a tiny fraction of their cost when new. In an emergency, most of us could get by for several years with what we already own.

Rental payments are a permanent drain on finances; they are like money thrown away. A large number of my clients have saved this cost by camping out on their sites while their houses were under construction. For some who wouldn't consider camping, living in small temporary structures on the sites made more sense, especially to those who were doing all the work themselves and planned to spend a long time in construction. Other possibilities might be to build a small section of your house and expand as you save the necessary funds. The plans shown here are for an expandable house under construction by Carl and Angela Herrington. By using their own lumber and doing most of the labor, they have built a small starter house using only savings of less than $10,000.

Transportation costs offer one of the biggest areas of all for large savings. Everyone is aware that Japanese cars cost less to buy and run and are virtually maintenance free, but few are aware of the staggering cost differences over the lifetime of a car. Several years ago, I seriously considered buying a new American car called the X-car. To this end, I rented one on several occasions to make a 100-mile trip to a job site. Although the general concept of the car was fine, construction

---

CLOSET

STUDY

DESK

SECO

↑
N

CLOSET

DINING

FIRST

0

This 16-foot-square h
young family and can
taking out a mortgage
panelized walls and ro

---

quality was abysmal and the gas n
short of advertised claims. Sever
X-car confirmed my original inclin
new Subaru. I kept full records an
document the exact costs of runnir
for 105,000 miles. The gasoline cost
have paid the entire $6000 purchas
car. Maintenance costs were virtu
tent: a couple of sets of brake pads
drive shaft boot. Nothing broke, no
nothing wore out; even at more
miles, oil consumption was not meas
Trend magazine and *Consumer Rep*
reported very high repair costs fo
has been subjected to the most rec
ever produced. *Motor Trend's* ve
almost $2000 in repair costs in only
Subaru's unlimited mileage warran
covered most of these costs.

It is the rolling realization of that
impossible dream, a really good c
age guy can afford to buy. It is sim
well built, comprehensively equip
does things two-wheel-drive cars c
to do. The Subaru is superior be
ideas that led to its creation wer
General Motors and Ford have sp
time and money telling us about "w
Subaru has built one.

David E. Davis, Jr.,
editor and publisher,
Car and Driver magazine.

I just made a comparison of the pu
for the lowest-priced hatchback ve
X-car and Subaru; the difference is a
base price of the American car is
than the Japanese car. But this is ju
ning; when one adds a spare tire, t
tinted glass, and a maintenance
standard on the Subaru) to the X-c
difference leaps to $2600.

Overall, I think it is realistic to proje
savings with the Subaru in 100,0
driving. Subarus are rugged, noisy,
durable basic transportation—the Vo
the 1980s. New or used, they are a
buy. They are also available in an arr
durable four-wheel-drive models. S
American company that imports ve
Japan; its stock is highly recommer
lysts. All other foreign cars are sold di
foreign company or by an American c

---

2 Recycling for Major Savings

In case you are discouraged after reading what I had to say about building costs and financing, cheer up; there are ways to sidestep much of the bank problem. Ours is a throwaway society; automobiles, houses, furniture, and other possessions are routinely discarded by the rich when they need repairs or when they are no longer in fashion. If you are on a strictly limited budget or just abhor banks and wastefulness, you can readily take advantage of this bad habit of our society.

One of the easiest ways to acquire a home and save money is to recycle an existing one. By this, I do not mean just buying a used house from your local real estate broker. Thousands and thousands of perfectly serviceable old houses are abandoned and falling into decay in this country. These houses are rarely listed by real estate agents, except as "worthless" adjuncts to a piece of property up for sale. A solid building shell in suitable condition for rehabilitation can save you many thousands of dollars. Finding such a shell may take months or years, so if you are in a hurry, you may have to forgo this option. Some parts of the country simply do not have such houses available no matter how hard you search. Chapter 13 gives more detail on where and how to locate low-cost property. The same tips will apply when looking for an old house.

Criteria

In these days of energy shortages, just any old shell will not do. The house should have a long

axis and the high side facing south. Old-timers knew a lot more about siting houses than do modern developers, so you may be lucky. You are more likely to find a suitably sited house that was built in the 1800s than you are to find one of more recent vintage. You are much better off if you can find a house that has not been "modernized." By this, I mean wiring, plumbing, and a central heating system. Most of these systems will have to be removed or considerably disrupted in order to insulate the exterior walls properly. Obviously, if the seller hasn't spent a great deal of money on mechanical systems for the house, he or she is not likely to pass on these costs to you. Make sure that the main center core of the old structure is solid and free from rot and termites; otherwise, it may be virtually worthless. Old houses are notorious for having poorly built later additions. Frequently, these are in the process of collapse, giving the whole structure a worthless look. Keep your eyes peeled and you may pick up a rare bargain. Even if you have to dismantle an old house, a good well and septic system or a solid foundation may make the project quite worthwhile.

The ideal structure for renovation would be a small- to medium-size house, but don't limit yourself to this category. A large white elephant in very good shape can sometimes be bought quite cheaply just because of its size. One local group has bought a 50-acre estate with just such a large house. They have subdivided the house into six apartments. These apartments provide living

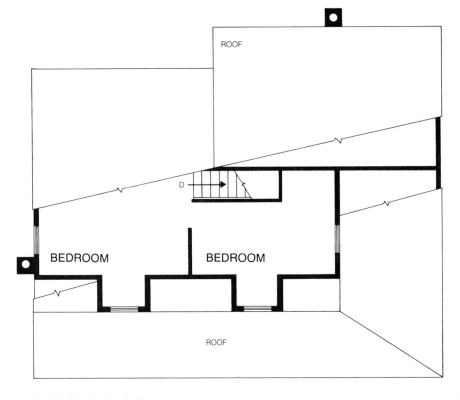

SECOND FLOOR PLAN (BEFORE)

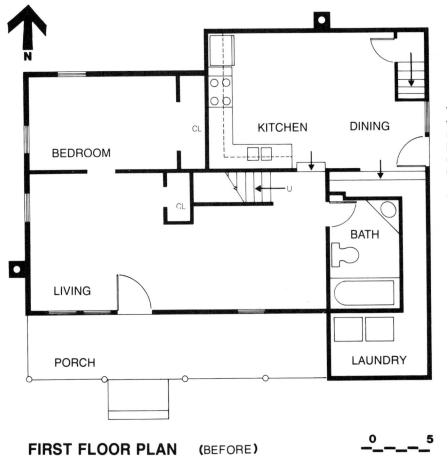

Tiny, dark rooms with poor traffic flow made the house virtually unusable. The ceilings were so low that most people advised demolition. The bathroom opened directly into the living room, and basement stairs chopped up the only nice room, the kitchen.

FIRST FLOOR PLAN (BEFORE)

0 ___ 5

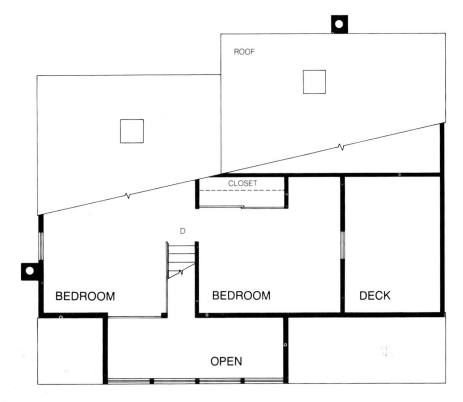

Major changes involved enclosing
the porch and adding a sloped-
glass dormer. The stairs were
relocated to their original 1780
location. The bath and laundry
were kept in their existing location
to save money.

ROOF

CLOSET

D

BEDROOM   BEDROOM   DECK

OPEN

SECOND FLOOR PLAN (AFTER)

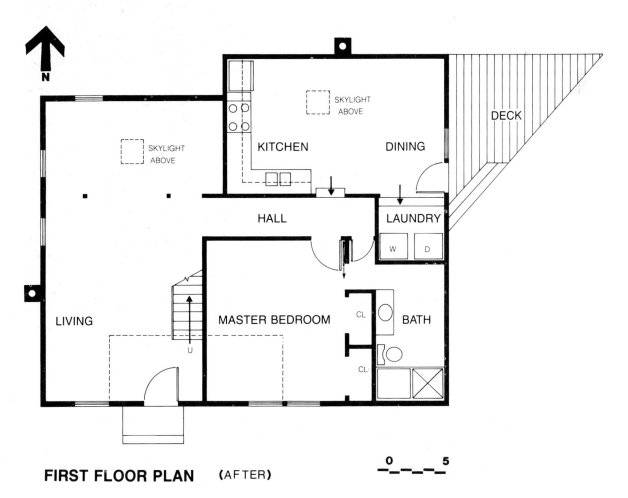

N

SKYLIGHT
ABOVE

KITCHEN   DINING

DECK

SKYLIGHT
ABOVE

HALL   LAUNDRY

W   D

LIVING   MASTER BEDROOM   CL   BATH

U

CL

0   5

FIRST FLOOR PLAN (AFTER)

The Weiss house before renovation. The southeast porch darkens the interior and wastes space. Tiny dormers provide no headroom upstairs in the original scheme.

The porch was enclosed by the remodeling. A slanting skylight provides light to both floors. The roof lines were unified.

houses that were designed completely from scratch, and one of my clients is so fond of the house that he has requested plans for an essentially identical new house. Since this was a major renovation, I have been able to utilize many of the same techniques and materials on my new

houses. For a more complete description of materials and techniques that are mentioned here in passing, see Part III.

About three years ago, the Weisses paid around $15,000 for a small south-facing house set against

The east corner of the house was a hodgepodge of conflicting shapes. An awkward parapet at the kitchen emphasized the effect.

By extending the parapet to meet the new roof line, we eliminate the conflicting shapes. A new deck and door complete the change.

a rock cliff on a 1½-acre lot. The house is jammed tightly to one corner of the lot, giving complete privacy from the street. It is undesirably close to a neighboring house and shares a driveway with two other houses. The dark, unappealing nature of this house, coupled with the access problems, accounted for the low sale price. Most people re-

garded the house as hopeless and recommended bulldozing it and building anew elsewhere on the property. Fortunately for the old house, the tight money market precluded such an option. After the baseboard hot water heating system froze and burst, Barry and Marcia turned to me for help with renovation. They reasoned that the

house, as it was designed, was not worth the installation of a replacement heating system and they should incorporate any new system into a remodeled, fully insulated house.

The house contained about 1100 square feet of badly organized space with painfully low ceilings (less than 6 feet in some cases). A narrow porch along the south wall obstructed what little light might have otherwise filtered into the downstairs rooms. The second floor contained two tiny bedrooms with sloping ceilings and one small dormer per room. There was standing room only at the ridge and in the dormers. Many houses of this general description were built in the 1800s, and another wave occurred in the 1920s. Since this is a common building type with typical problems, I spent more time than I usually do solving the problems because I assumed these problems would come up again with other clients.

My solution involved the creation of a sunspace by enclosing the porch, removing the south-facing

roof and the existing dormers, and constructing a new "solar dormer," which spans the width of the old dormers plus the space between them. Our new dormer has 60-degree sloping windows that start at the eave of the original porch and slope upward to meet the new dormer roof. The dormer roof extends past the ridge line and creates a small north-facing clerestory for much-needed ventilation. The original porch was incorporated into the downstairs living areas, and the upper part of the porch space was left open to the sloping windows on both floors. The original south wall of the second floor was exactly the proper height for a railing and was left in place and refurbished.

Privacy was maintained to the south while still admitting light, air, and selected views. Furthermore, this was accomplished with very slight structural modifications to the house. A small ridge beam was installed in the area of the dormer, and a supporting post was placed in the center of the ridge beam. Then we framed the dormer;

A view from the west end of the porch shows wasted space and a dark roof overhang.

The porch has now become a part of the living room with a glass ceiling. A corner of the original porch roof remains at the upper right.

Note how a simple sloping-glass dormer ties the porch to the existing roof without major structural changes. The dotted lines show the profile of the original dormers and porch roof. This dormer is applicable to many old houses.

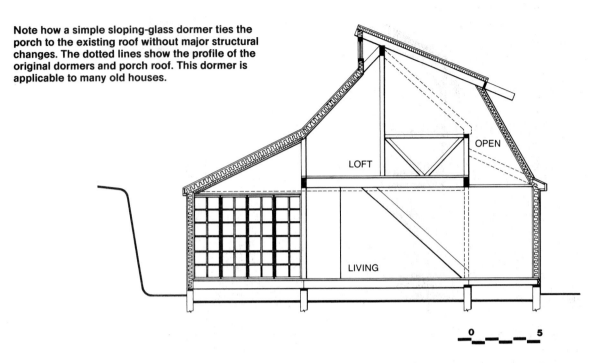

LOFT

OPEN

LIVING

0 _ _ _ 5

The other end of the porch has become part of the master bedroom. The original wall of the house is to the right of the chest.

that's all. We were extremely lucky in that the north face of the roof had been completely resheathed and reroofed. We were even luckier in that there is no conceivable way to view the north roof except from the top of the cliff. That way, we could put on a decent-looking roof without worrying about matching the dirty white shingles on the back of the house. I was fortunate to be able to obtain some Onduline roofing that had been removed from a new building to correct a defect in installation. The material was in mint condition, except that the manufacturer voided the guarantee. It is a very handsome, dark-brown, corrugated material, which completely transforms the appearance of the house. For $200 we picked up enough to reroof the south face and cover the new dormer with several sheets to spare. For a complete description of this lifetime roofing material, see Chapter 21.

The dormer solved our second-floor headroom problem nicely, and the first floor miraculously solved itself. The interior of the house was tastelessly finished in 1960s middle-American doctor's office style; that is, cheap plywood paneling, cardboard ceiling tiles, and dirty "sculptured" carpeting. There was no hint of any character or anything whatsoever of historical value. We knew that the town was 200 years old, but the house seemed to date to the late 1800s. The hand-hewn roof rafters pegged together at the ridge were the first clue that we had a treasure. Stripping the stained ceiling tiles revealed furring strips and a rat's nest of armored electric cables. It also re-

The upstairs was low ceilinged, dark, and hot. The original staircase opening was boarded over. Note the missing board at the center of the photo.

The staircase was relocated to its original position. Tiny dormers were replaced by a large glass dormer. Vent windows are just above the ridge beam at the center of the photo.

vealed magnificent chestnut beams topped by wide-plank flooring. Down came the cheap paneling to reveal a pegged and braced oak timber frame. Due to the porch extension and an earlier extension on the back, two of the original walls are now inside the house and the frame is exposed as a historical artifact.

The gold carpeting covered a plywood subfloor, which in turn covered two layers of strip flooring; each with furring strips. Each layer of flooring got wider. On the bottom, in the living room, we found 12-inch-wide virgin pine planks. These were in the original portion of the house which, it turns out, was built in the late 1700s. The floor

The new living room is brightened by a slanting dormer. The original beamed ceiling was restored. The open stair makes the room seem larger.

had some serious defects, but by scavenging from the second-floor planking, we were able to patch it as well as extend it into the new area created by the porch enclosure. Between the floor and ceiling we gained over a foot in ceiling height!

Since the budget was extremely limited, I declared the kitchen off limits (it was by far the nicest room in the house). We contented ourselves with removing the black and white checkered floor tiles, sanding the floor, and painting the paneling and ceiling white. The bathroom was an interior room finished in several garish patterns of yellow. We enlarged it so that we could have an outside window, but left it in the same location so that the supply and waste system could be reused. A Swedish water-saving toilet and a Japanese soaking tub complete the bathroom. I designed and fabricated a combination tub and shower stall from wood lined with sheet neoprene. In proper Japanese fashion, you wash yourself before you enter the bath; hence, a tub *and* a shower side by side. Such tub and shower units sell for almost $900; materials for the job-fabricated setup cost less than $200. In the bathroom and other additions of the house, we removed the ceiling joists and applied a new wood ceiling directly to the bottom of the rafters. Thus, the remaining 6-foot ceilings were wiped out.

The budget for the house was severely constrained by the state of the U.S. economy. The bank was ecstatic over the new plans; they took one look at them and granted the loan the same day. The catch was that they were limiting all their construction loans to $10,000. That was just the beginning of the trouble. I pointed out

that even the most economical remodeling would easily cost double the bank figure. Barry and Marcia decided to add some savings and squeeze the balance from their income by stretching out the project. Then came the companion problem of finding a contractor who could do the work for the limited budget and also provide a written budget for Barry and Marcia to show to the bank and prove that it could be done. I was fortunate in locating an eager, inexperienced contractor who was willing to give it a try.

He turned out to be the strongest asset and worst enemy all rolled up in one. The job was started with great enthusiasm and fine workmanship. The contractor generally worked by himself and was a speed demon. The initial phases of stripping and reconstructing the shell of the house flew by. As the house was magically transformed, the clients became so happy they would have granted any wish. Unknown to me, the contractor was requesting (and getting) advances on the work yet to be done. He quickly sided the house and finished the transformation of the exterior. Then came disaster—Sheetrock. Everything he used was old and of odd sizes. I have cautioned many times against letting a carpenter hang Sheetrock. The contractor assured us that he was a master taper and there would be no problem. He may have been a master taper, but he couldn't begin to fit the material properly. The relationship slid rapidly downhill. Suddenly, there wasn't any money for materials; the contractor demanded more money to continue the job. Alas, all available funds had been spent. Fortunately, the bulk of the work had been completed. All expensive items had been purchased, and the really im-

portant work was completed. The clients and the contractor parted ways—bitterly.

We were lucky that the contractor had done a careful job of salvaging materials. All the trim and finish materials came from the salvage pile. Strip flooring became baseboards and trim. Scrap siding became interior paneling. The old plywood was used for underlay in the bathroom and to construct the tub. Salvaged hinges were used to hang the insulated front door, which was itself made from scrap cedar boards.

The heating system, which triggered the whole project, was replaced with a simple wood stove (Vermont Castings' Vigilant) and a Sears oil-fired space heater as a backup unit; total cost, $900. That was just $1800 less than the heating contractor wanted to replace the defunct oil-fired, baseboard hot water system. We were able to make this saving by spending money on super-insulating and by weather-stripping the house. I must note that this is only possible in a complete renovation. We were also very lucky; there was an almost-new chimney hidden behind the paneling just where we wanted a wood stove, and the flue and oil supply for the old boiler hooked right up to the new space heater. The transformation in comfort levels was every bit as dramatic as the visual changes. Now the house is cool in summer and warm in winter with very little in the way of artificial heating and cooling. The old house took $2000 in oil for winter heating and was unbearable in the summer. Now the oil bill is closer to $200, and the summer coolness elicits amazed comments. The solar dormer actually creates a chimney effect, sucking, and thereby circulating, air up and through the house.

The total cost for the house, including original purchase, all renovation costs, and architect's fees, was a bit less than $34,000. The bank sent an insurance appraiser by the house when it was nearing completion to assess the value of the improvements. He insisted that the house be insured for a minimum of $75,000. That's quite a good deal, to double your money in one year. Of course, that's a paper figure and the actual sales figure might be something else; but still, it's a better deal than you get through any normal investment these days.

This solution is a natural for almost any house with a south-facing front porch and second-floor dormers. If you plan to follow this scheme, you should check the structure very carefully. We were very lucky in that the loads from the second floor and roof of the original south wall of the Weiss house were carried by the post-and-beam frame and not the exterior wall. This made enclosing the porch very easy. If you have a more typical structure with framing members supported by this wall, you will have to install heavy beams to support the weight. This will require the services of a knowledgeable builder or structural engineer. When all is said and done, however, it is a fine way to update an old house and well worth the extra trouble.

Obviously, you need to know much more than this to adequately remodel a house, and full details on the subject are beyond the scope of this book. *Old Houses, A Rebuilder's Manual* by George Nash (Prentice-Hall, 1980) is a dandy reference on the subject. George's book is comprehensive and very well illustrated. Another book on a related topic is also highly recommended: *Salvaging Old Barns & Houses, Tear it Down and Save the Pieces* by Lawrence and Kathleen Abrams (Sterling Publishing Company, 1983).

Salvaged Materials

Salvaged materials are frequently an even better bargain than salvaged houses. This is because you can often get the materials in return for the labor of demolishing the building. The Abramses give full instructions on how to proceed in their book. Virtually everything you need to build a house can be salvaged. Notable exceptions are such easily damaged items as asphalt shingles, Sheetrock, insulation, and electrical wiring. Even in these days of runaway inflation, I have had several clients who have built their own houses of salvaged materials for less than $10,000. One even managed on less than $5000. Obviously, if most materials are free in return for your salvage labor and you then supply the actual construction labor, your actual out-of-pocket expenses are quite low. The house does have its price, however, in thousands of hours of back-breaking labor by you or others. Salvaging materials is not easy, and reusing them takes more time than building with all new materials. You might also live in one of those rare areas where the building codes actually forbid the use of used materials; check before you jump into a salvage job. On the positive side, many old materials are of much better quality and much more handsome than their modern counterparts. This is particularly true in the case of doors, cabinetwork, millwork, hardware, and plumbing fixtures. Whether you salvage a whole building or just the materials from one, you will be making an important contribution to energy conservation. Good hunting!

Part II

Exploring New Techniques

SOLUTIONS IN OTHER COUNTRIES

3 China

Several years ago, I was invited by Ken Butti, coauthor of *The Golden Thread, 2,000 Years of Solar History* (Van Nostrand-Reinhold, 1980) to join him on a solar tour of China. The tour was to be a special custom tour especially for architects and sounded like a dream come true. Unfortunately, Ken found that architects were either too busy or didn't have the money. I signed on for his tour even though I fell into both categories. I figured that this was just too fine an opportunity to pass up. Sadly, Ken wound up with only two architects for the tour and had to fill the remaining spaces with tourists. Fortunately, two of the other members of the tour had excellent solar qualifications, and as a group we were reasonably able to discuss solar developments with the Chinese. For their part, the Chinese were blissfully unaware of the skimpiness of our credentials and responded by treating us as visiting royalty. Ken's unceasing efforts and the perseverance of our national tour guide gained us access to many installations hitherto unseen by foreigners. This was despite damage from severe floods, which had washed out many major roads and bridges.

Even though the Chinese government mandates clearance for all travel points in advance of a visit to China, most of our wishes were accommodated. We were not allowed to change the cities, their order, or the duration of our stay, but we were freely allowed to add or subtract specific points of interest. This is a courtesy almost never extended to foreigners. Much of the reason for this rigidity seems to lie in the meager nature of the transportation system. Intercity trains and airplanes have to be booked months in advance, and all seats are reserved. There are no empty seats in China.

China, with its 1-billion-plus population, has energy and food supply problems that would stagger the rest of the world. This has prompted the government to work very hard to develop alternatives to conventional sources of energy. They have in operation the world's largest hydroelectric facility and are now at work constructing another one that will be even larger. A total of 3.2 million people use solar cookers to prepare their food. Conventional residential hot water heaters are virtually unknown; what hot water there is is usually heated on a stove. The government actually encourages the use of solar water heaters by giving buyers a 40% rebate on the purchase price. Thus, a 30-gallon batch-type heater that sells for the equivalent of $40 is knocked down to a staggering $25 with the rebate. I wonder where they got that idea?

Our guide, Chou Lin, even arranged a private meeting with the Chinese Minister of Energy. Chou Lin would try anything for her American charges. She got in a cab and visited the minister at his home and persuaded him to accompany her to our hotel where we discussed the energy

A Chinese apartment building with gravity-feed solar water heaters attached to balcony railings. Note the vertical row at left and two in the center of the photo.

A prototype solar power station. Hot water from flat-plate collectors is boosted to steam by tracking collectors at the top of the roof; the steam then turns a generator.

priorities of our respective countries for a couple of hours. Since China has no national power grid like that of other large countries, their emphasis is upon localized sources of power. In order to conserve fossil fuels, renewable resources play a major role in Chinese planning. Small local hydroelectric stations, tidal power, and solar electrical plants are given top priority. Methane, solar cells, and wind power are being tested in rural communes. The few existing conventional generating stations are usually coal fired. China canceled its order to France for two nuclear power plants shortly after the debacle at Three Mile Island. The Chinese government officially denies any construction activity involving nuclear power, but outside sources report that they are constructing one small plant in the southern provinces.

All the major buildings in Bejing (formerly called Peking) have electric sockets built into the perimeter of their facades. Three times a year, on ceremonial occasions, the skyline is illuminated. It was a fascinating experience for us to gather in the tallest building in the city and observe this electrical extravaganza while discussing China's limited energy resources.

During our tour we got to observe firsthand some of the projects described by the minister. We visited a prototype solar generating station that produces enough power to supply 10,000 Chinese homes. The station uses tracking solar collectors to produce steam and run a generator. Coal is used as a backup for cloudy days. Six more such stations are planned for construction in the near

Experimental solar water heaters at a self-sufficient commune.

future. We also bucked the bureaucracy and got to travel into the remote hinterlands to see a totally self-sufficient commune. The trip itself was almost as fascinating as the commune. Since all major roads in the area were closed, we traveled about 150 miles over back roads where no foreigners had been seen for years.

The commune was directed by a young, bearded solar activist who responded to our unannounced visit with great enthusiasm. Even though he spoke no English, he eagerly unfurled the engineering drawings for the solar water heaters, the solar grain dryer, and the central methane-generating system. Of all the houses, 40% are now equipped with batch-type solar water heaters of several different designs. Four people are occupied full-time constructing solar devices and the goal is to equip 100% of the houses in the commune with solar water heaters. Virtually all the 1500 people in the village are connected to the large central methane system. Bamboo pipes distribute gas to each kitchen for cooking, and there are occasional gas lights. The methane also fires a generating station, which supplies a limited amount of electricity to all of the houses. Animal, human, and vegetable wastes are collected to produce the methane. As we were leaving, we passed a young worker building masonry shading screens to help cool the houses. He was wearing a T-shirt with an inscription in English, "Detect the Universe."

Chinese Houses

We architects were particularly insistent about getting to see typical Chinese housing. We were not disappointed. Several times we halted the tour bus abruptly and piled out to explore a remote village. At all our meetings with Chinese architects, we huddled and drew sketches. As Chou Lin realized our sincere interest, she began to help in our quest. If we admired a particular

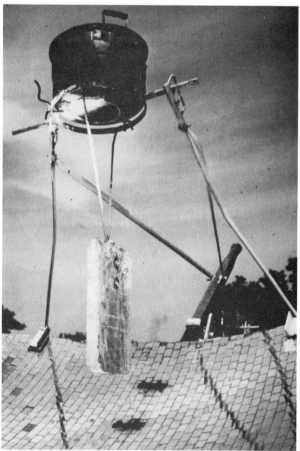

A solar collector heats a pot of food for a rural commune. More than 3 million people eat food prepared in these cookers.

house, she would march up to the door, knock, and inquire if we were welcome to see the interior. Many of the occupants declined, although we got to see at least half the houses that interested us.

One of the communes we visited in Shanghai contained a development of new owner-built houses. These were well-constructed, two-story

Modern owner-built houses still feature south orientation with deep overhangs and balconies. Houses are usually duplexed or built in rows for economy of land use.

Soochow tile roofs surround a private courtyard. Note the glass skylight in the roof at right.

masonry duplex houses, carefully oriented to face south. Generous overhangs and second-floor balconies shaded the south-facing windows in this semitropical climate. The kitchen, where the charcoal-fired stove was located, was placed on the cool north side of the house. I calculated that the house contained about 900 square feet —we were told that it cost about $2000 for materials and land for the owner to construct this house.

We had all heard of the legendary Chinese "court-yard houses" and were quite anxious to see a good example of this type. Unfortunately, we were usually in cities, where pressures of population had encroached upon the original houses. It was easy to get a general idea of how they were supposed to work, and our Chinese colleagues sketched examples for us, complete with dimensions. (They were even able to mentally convert from meters to feet and inches, quickly.) Basically,

This drawing shows an award-winning duplex house design featuring a modernized version of the traditional Chinese courtyard design.

the courtyard houses consist of a walled compound 40 to 50 feet square, with rooms around two or three sides. Small farm animals, a vegetable garden, well, and privy are physically and visually protected from invasion by neighbors or hostile outsiders. The major rooms of the house are placed along the north wall of the compound, facing south. Outbuildings are placed along the west wall; any expansion takes place along the east wall. Entrance is through the center of the south courtyard wall, usually through a double-gated, roofed structure.

The basic courtyard design has endured for centuries. Even though the government encourages building up, not out, the first-prize winner in a rural housing competition was the nice variation on the courtyard scheme shown here. This duplex scheme was published in *China Reconstructs,* a monthly magazine distributed in the United States by China Books and Periodicals (2929 24th Street, San Francisco, CA 94110). A wide variety of books and magazines is available from this firm at reasonable prices. I recommend them highly.

China is densely populated, making all services, including housing, constant crises. The area of China is almost exactly the same as the United States, but where we have only 62 people per square mile, China has 256. Of course, Japan has 805 people per square mile, but it is one of the wealthiest countries in the world, while

China is one of the poorest. Despite the extreme population pressures, China manages rather well by severely limiting the living space allotted per family. Usually, each family is allowed two rooms to itself and shares the use of kitchen, bath, and toilet facilities with other families. Single-family units are frowned upon by the authorities, but I saw a number of new one- or two-family houses in my travels. The standard government solution to the housing problem in the cities is precast concrete apartment buildings. These are oppressive, five- or six-story walk-up affairs housing 50 to 60 families. They do have single-loaded corridors with all rooms facing south, sheltered by balconies. Ironically, in our country, balconies and single-loaded corridors would be considered luxury housing but, of course, we don't design two-room apartments nor provide only stairs for access. China claims to be constructing new housing at the rate of 3.5 million square meters per year, about 20 times the construction rate in the United States. Labor is virtually free, since the army does most of the heavy construction work in China.

Underground Housing

When people in the United States talk about underground housing, they mean building a house and berming earth up around it; possibly putting a few inches on the roof itself. The Chinese, on the other hand, actually excavate a house out of

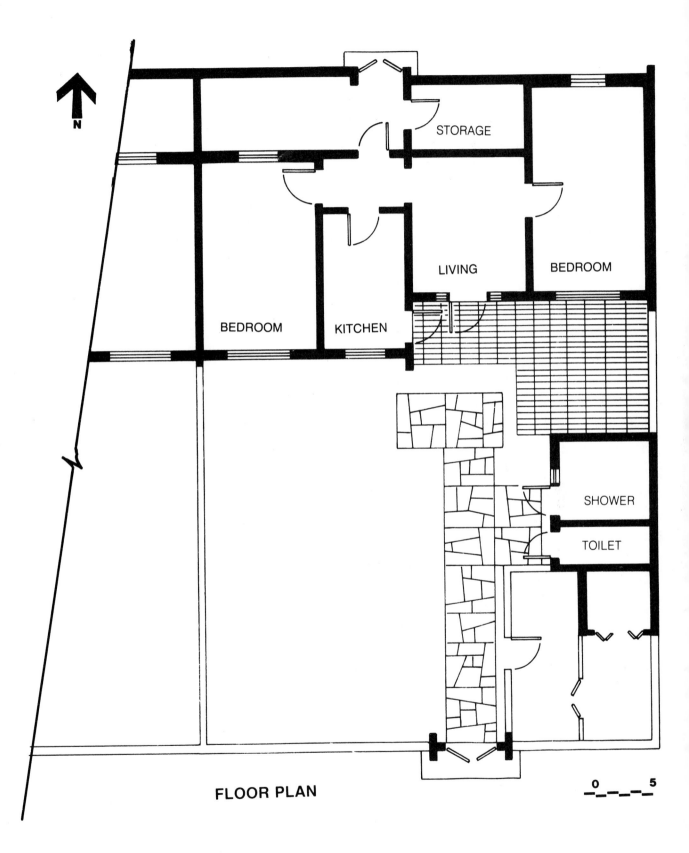

N

STORAGE

LIVING

BEDROOM

BEDROOM   KITCHEN

SHOWER

TOILET

FLOOR PLAN

0 _ _ _ _ 5

This south-facing courtyard provides garden space and security. A composting toilet is combined with a solar shower in the courtyard.

A street scene in Soochow shows overhanging second stories that gain living space and shade windows below.

Wide overhangs protect the open doors and windows in the rainy season. This wall of openings abuts on yet another courtyard.

Ferrocement boats serve both as home and workplace for many. River traffic is brisk in Soochow.

The Great Wall of China is seen vanishing in the distance from one of the guard towers in the restored portion.

the side of a cliff in somewhat similar fashion to early American cliff dwellers. These Chinese cliff houses are quite famous and, of course, the American architects I traveled with were anxious to see them. Alas, the storms that played havoc with the rest of our trip had washed out the roads, so we had to make do with descriptions and sketches from our Chinese hosts. Only embankments facing east or south are used for these dwellings. Several cavelike rooms are usually excavated facing a courtyard on the south. A light/ventilation shaft is sunk from the top of the cliff to the back of the largest room to provide cross ventilation and a bit of extra light. The interiors of the cave rooms are plastered with a cement-clay mixture to provide a durable, waterproof surface. I hasten to add that these houses are located in a relatively dry part of China; in a wet area, this technique could spell disaster.

A traditional Chinese "moon gate" opens to a courtyard at army headquarters.

This traditional Chinese house facade shows windows and overhang facing to the south for winter heat gain and summer blockage.

The sketch shown was provided by one of our hosts and shows an elaborate two-story cliff dwelling. In this case, the builders have cheated a bit, as one of the rooms is constructed in front of the original cliff wall. The front structure with a man standing in the doorway is a courtyard that leads to the main living rooms.

Chinese Geomancy *(feng shui)*

"Geomancy" is defined as the art of divining the future, good or ill fortune, from the figure suggested by dots or lines placed at random on the earth's surface. It has been said that the fortunes of men depend on how well their ancestors were buried with respect to geomancy and also on how correctly their own dwellings were built with respect to orientation, planning, construction, and so on, according to *feng shui* or geomancy. The words *feng shui* literally mean the winds and the water. Actually, *feng shui* is related to all geographical features where a tomb is situated and in many aspects is related to building and architectural features. "*Feng shui* stands for the power

This sketch by P. Zhou, G. Yang, and B. Li shows renovation of an old cliff dwelling.

of the natural environment—the wind and the air of the mountains and hills; the streams and the rain; and the composite influence of the natural process." (From the dust jacket of a fascinating book, *Chinese Geomancy,* by Evelyn Lip [Times Books International, Singapore, 1979].)

Mrs. Lip has a master's degree in architecture and is a senior lecturer at the University of Singapore. Her book is the only work in English on this fascinating subject. Private architects are virtually nonexistent in China, and most people who build engage the services of a geomancer. This is an ancient and highly secret art that appears to be part tradition, part superstition, with a large measure of common sense. For instance, geomancers recommend placing a house into the south face of a hill with a body of water at the bottom. The house should face south with no doors or windows facing north to admit evil spirits. Trees should be placed on the northwest, but not

on the south. Buildings should be constructed on high ground rather than in a valley prone to flooding. A house without a second exit spells death and misfortune. All this is good common sense and would be highly welcome in the United States, if builders and architects could assimilate these principles.

Other principles of geomancy are not so obvious. Geomancers identify 27 different types of sand and 9 types of water and assign good or bad luck to each. A house with three, four, or eight bedrooms symbolizes ill fortune. There are even good luck and bad luck dimensions for a house.

The basic tool of a geomancer is a compass, called a *luopan.* Traditional *luopans* are circular boards set in a square base with up to 34 rows of concentric figures. In the center is a compass. Two strings at 90-degree angles are stretched across the compass. Each row of figures has a

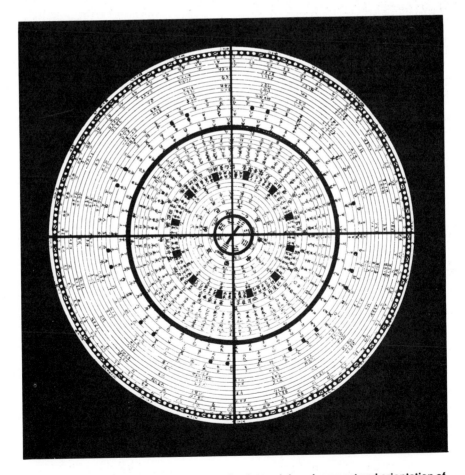

A *luopan*—an ancient Chinese instrument for determining placement and orientation of a house. This is a modern version. North (*Kan*) is black, water, winter, midnight, mourning and calamity. East (*Zhen*) is green, wood, spring, morning, posterity and harmony. South (*Li*) is red, fire, summer, midday, joy and festivity. West (*Dui*) is white, metal, autumn, evening and purity.

specific meaning regarding the siting of the house or good or bad luck for the owners. To use the *luopan,* one starts by placing the base parallel to one of the sides of a proposed building and rotating the compass to align with the strings. Then the various attributes of the site are read off the intersection points of the strings and the concentric circles.

The center row of all *luopan*s is a set of eight trigrams representing eight points on the compass: north, northeast, east, southeast, and so on. These trigrams are highly regarded in China as good luck symbols; one sees them frequently on banners and as good luck signs to ward off evil spirits. I have designed an octagonal window incorporating the eight trigrams for clients with an octagonal house. Traditional trigram elements have either a mirror or a stylized *yin-yang* symbol in the center. Various circles represent the 12 months of the year, the 24 hours of the day, and so forth. Each direction has a color, an animal, an element, a season, time of day, and other meanings associated with it.

For further reading, Mrs. Lip's book has an excellent bibliography of books in English on Chinese culture. For those who want to make further study of China and can't visit personally, I highly recommend the *Encyclopedia of China Today* by Fredrick M. Kaplan and Julian M. Sobin (Eurasia Press, 1982; available in Canada through Fitzhenry and Whiteside). This is a large-format, 450-page monster that has been constantly updated with revised editions. It contains most major vital statistics for the country. There is even an extensive chapter describing procedures for doing business with the People's Republic of China.

China is rapidly becoming used to foreign visitors, and I would not hesitate to travel there without a guide now. The Chinese even invite foreigners who have had a year of basic Chinese language instruction to come to China for a year to continue their language studies, and the cost is borne by the Chinese government. At our farewell banquet we learned that the Chinese government had asked one member of our group to return to teach a solar course at Bejing University. We learned, too, that Boston University had accepted Chou Lin for its graduate study program in solar energy.

4 Finland

I have included Finland in my select group of countries primarily to show off some of the fine designs by Finnish architects. Unlike the United States, where most architects put themselves on a pedestal and price themselves out of the residential market, the Finns enthusiastically design everything. Architecture is virtually a national preoccupation. Most foreigners who visit Finland come away with a feeling of being rebuffed by the gruff Finns. Indeed, I felt the same coolness; that is, until I said I was an architect. Suddenly, doors opened, red carpets rolled out and invitations to visit were proffered from every side. In the world-famous Stockmanns Department Store, I was ushered in to meet the architectural staff—12 architects for one department store. The architects design the furniture and light fixtures, arrange the store windows and help select beautiful merchandise. Perhaps this helps explain why Stockmanns is able to sell its merchandise worldwide.

On my first of several visits to Finland, I went to study their residential architecture. Most architects who visit Finland go to study their striking contemporary commercial buildings and don't even see the private houses. Indeed, you will see very few private houses, as the Finns are primarily apartment dwellers. In this highly socialized country, employers of any size provide housing for their employees. The country is sparsely populated; there are only 37 persons per square mile. Despite this low population density, most Finns live in apartment complexes near the cities of Helsinki and Turku. Unlike the United States, the apartments are situated outside the cities, with parks and wilderness surrounding them. The Finnish ideal is to have an apartment in the city and a hideaway in the country.

House plans in Finland are much more open and flexible than in the United States; privacy is of little concern. One of the Finnish architects chided me, "You Americans are taught to be ashamed of your bodies, we're taught to be proud of ours." I had expressed shock that my host had stopped to chat with his wife's bridge club on the way back from the sauna clad only in a towel, which happened to be draped across his shoulder.

Some of my favorite pieces of architecture in the United States were designed by Finnish architects. Eero Saarinen's graceful terminal buildings at Dulles Airport in Washington, D.C., and for TWA at Kennedy Airport in New York are almost more sculpture than buildings. The Saint Louis arch, Ingalls rink at Yale, and the Milwaukee War Memorial building are other striking designs by Saarinen. While beautiful buildings such as these are rare in the United States, they are common in Finland. In fact, everywhere you look in Finland, you see beauty. The countryside is glorious; houses and commercial buildings are simply and tastefully furnished. Store windows are composed to show the merchandise in a nice setting rather than to cram as much junk as possible into a window.

An example of dramatic Finnish architecture in which the entire building is cantilevered on posts surrounding an open courtyard.

There is something in the temperament of the Finnish people that seems to inspire good design. Glassware, china, silver, furniture, rugs, and fabrics are all of the highest quality. (The world-famous Finnish Arabia china and glassware started as a small sideline for a large plumbing fixture manufacturer; plumbing fixtures are still their major product despite the popularity of their artware.) Strangely, the Finns do rather poorly in such art fields as painting and sculpture. They seem to require a direct practical application before they are inspired to creativity.

> There is no beauty that does not arise from a functional requirement; it is a mistake to add or take away features for no other reason than to make a change or to make a new impression on the eye. . . . It does not matter what the commodity is—houses, furniture, clothing, or machinery—the things that do best what they are supposed to do are by that very fact the most beautiful things.
>
> *Henry Ford*

The Finnish government has sponsored low-cost designs for energy-efficient houses for a very, very cold climate. These houses are designed to be fabricated from 8- by 16-inch concrete planks that are cast in a factory. Since these dimensions are the same as our concrete blocks, the designs can be readily translated to this country. Either of the two designs shown in the illustrations would be suitable for owner-built houses using the surface-bonding technique described in Chapter 19.

The exterior insulation system shown in the same chapter should be used in cold climates.

Since similar precast concrete planks are used in this country for floors in commercial buildings, it would be very easy for a contractor to adapt our planks to this building system. Further details can be obtained from the Finnish manufacturer. The trade name of the product is Siporex, and the manufacturer is Oy Saseka Ab (Erottajankatu 1, Helsinki, Finland).

I have selected two of the many Siporex designs that I felt would be adaptable to American tastes. The Finnish architects Ole and Bertel Gripenberg have done an extraordinary job of packing a great deal of living space into compact houses. The 822-square-foot, two-bedroom model has great potential for the United States. This house has a center bearing wall with cathedral ceilings throughout. It would work very nicely as a plan for factory-built modular houses; any construction technique could be used. The dimensions are such that it fits exactly our panelized system described in Chapter 11. Notice the sliding door between the master bedroom and the living room; with the door open, the entire 32-foot expanse becomes one living area. This is the type of flexibility that we should build into our houses. You will also notice that there is virtually no space consumed by hallways in this house. The only possible drawback to this plan is a slight lack of privacy. In such a small house, though, this isn't likely to matter.

The second design is 28 feet square and contains four bedrooms in its 1280 square feet of space.

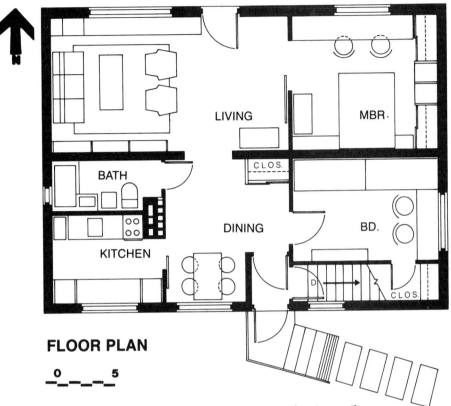

FLOOR PLAN

0 ___ 5

This is a one-story house using the same structural system as the house shown on the next page.

An exterior view of a wall-bearing masonry house. The floor plans are on the next page.

Three of these are tucked up under the steeply pitched roof. As in the smaller house, there is a center bearing wall for economy of construction. This design also borrows space with sliding doors and gives up none to wasted circulation. Again, the construction technique does not have to be limited to precast concrete.

Contraflow Heaters

Both of the Siporex houses have prominent chimneys with multiple flues. The Finnish government actually requires that houses built in the countryside have a built-in wood heating system. Several different types of wood heating systems have been developed. My favorite is the contra-

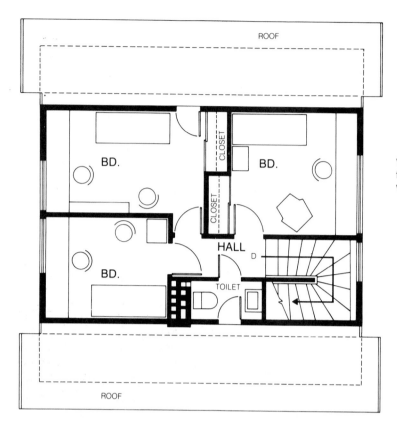

SECOND FLOOR PLAN

Wall-bearing masonry houses are well-suited to cold climates. These designs would work well in the northern United States and Canada.

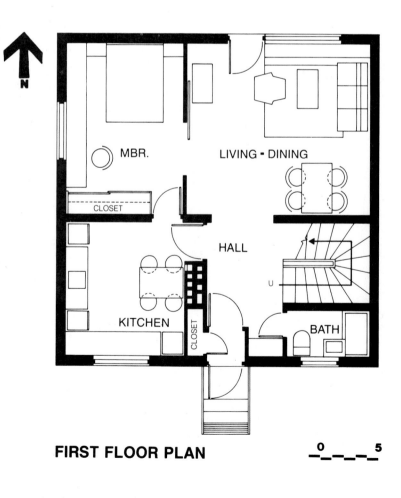

FIRST FLOOR PLAN

0 _ _ _ _ 5

flow heater, which is used extensively in Finland. The Siporex plans apparently show the more common Russian fireplace with the firebox located in the basement. Both the contraflow and the Russian fireplace are actually masonry stoves that burn wood at extremely high temperatures for complete combustion. The large mass of masonry allows the great quantity of heat generated to be stored, and then released gradually over many hours. The results are very low pollution levels and minimal wood consumption, hence the Finnish government's strong support of them.

I have used the contraflow masonry heater in several of my larger designs, and I am delighted with the results. The Russian fireplaces, which I have also used (and have recommended in my earlier books), have turned out to be too expensive and too large, and there have been problems in one of my houses due to cracking. There also appears to be a problem with materials and workmanship. The contraflow heater was developed in Sweden in the 1850s and has been popular in the Scandinavian countries ever since. In recent years, Finnish designers have improved upon the design by developing operable glass doors that allow a view of the fire and that can also be opened to allow the heater to be used as a fireplace in mild weather. This last feature is the one that has attracted so many of my clients.

We owe the development of the Finnish contraflow heaters in the United States to Albie Barden of Norridgewock, Maine. He has done extensive research in Finland so that the necessary modifications could be made to bring the heaters to this country. Since the heaters are designed in such a way that they don't build up dangerous creosote, they are normally built with only a single layer of brick. That method may be fine for Scandinavia, but we require either double-layer brick or a flue liner. Albie experimented with flue liners and rejected them because they tend to crack under the intense heat.

The Finns use a clay-based mortar that stays elastic and minimizes cracking. Albie's firm, Maine Wood Heat Company (RFD 1, Box 640, Norridgewock, ME 04957) imports the special clay mortar from Finland. The trade name for the mortar is Uunilaasti. I can vouch for it as a fine material that limits cracking to almost nothing. Albie is attempting to have a similar mortar made under license in this country. Fireplace doors, bypass dampers, mortar and other heater supplies are available from Maine Wood Heat. Plans are available from Albie at the same address for $12 per set.

I cannot emphasize enough the importance of proper materials and workmanship for all masonry heaters. Do not attempt to have materials fabricated locally for the doors or bypass damper. One of my clients did this, and the result was unmitigated disaster. The plans for such heaters are far more complicated than the limited abilities of most masons. I would only consider using a mason who has actually built one of them before. Barden gives classes on the fine art of building masonry heaters. Either go take the class or write to him for a recommendation of a mason in your area. He does have associates who travel, and my clients who have used them have been delighted with the work, as well as their pleasant attitude.

The firebox of a massive Russian fireplace under construction. The outlet at the rear of the firebox leads to a heat exchange labyrinth that distributes heat for many hours.

Summer Cottage

During my stay in Finland I was invited to spend the night with a family in their summer cottage. This cottage represents the most aesthetically pleasing low-cost structure I have ever seen in any part of the world. The house is cleverly

This Finnish contra-flow fireplace not only is the main heat source for the house, but also is an attractive open fireplace. The glass doors are shown in the open position.

arranged so that it can sleep seven people. One couch is built into the wall of the living room and opens into a double bed. Two tiny bedrooms have five double-decker bunks between them. The floor space in the kitchen doubles as a hallway for access to the bunkrooms. Each bunkroom has a combination door-window opening directly outside, which prevents the kitchen-hallway from getting too congested. Each of the exterior doors has a casement sash built right into the top half of

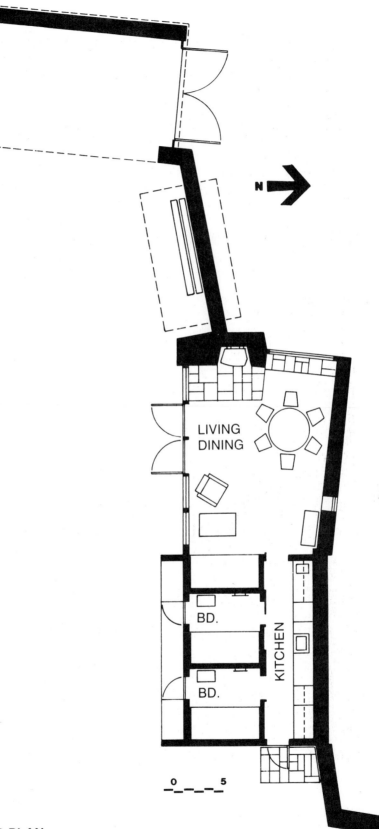

N →

LIVING
DINING

BD.

BD.

KITCHEN

0 — 5

FLOOR PLAN

The summer cottage shown here and on the next page makes the best use of space inside and out. The staggered bunks provide sleeping space for a maximum number of people in a minimum of space. The open-sided garage and covered seating area serve to define an elegant outdoor courtyard.

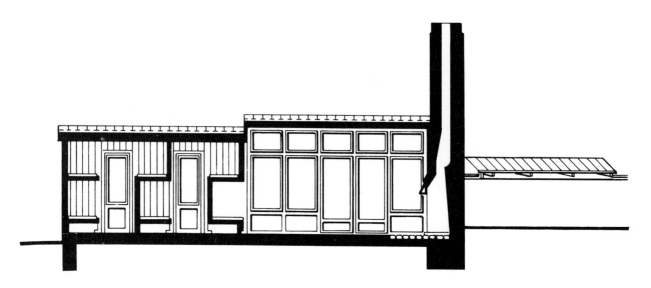

SECTION

the door that hinges open. In mild weather, you open the window; in hot summer weather, you open the door. The living room has a door separating it from the kitchen-hallway, and it doubles as the master bedroom. Even though the living room is rather small, it has a slight taper to the fireplace end which makes it seem larger than it really is.

There is no running water or electricity, as both are rare in remote rural Finland. A conventional outhouse is provided for sanitation, and a sauna with a shower takes care of bathing needs. Water is carefully collected from both of the sloping roofs: One roof serves the kitchen sink, the other the sauna. If you were building the house in this country, it would be very easy to add a bathroom and vestibule on the kitchen end.

The house feels much more spacious than its 480 square feet would suggest. An integrated wall and outside courtyard enhance this effect. A carport is part of the complex. It has doors on the street side so that the courtyard is completely private and, when not occupied by the car, the carport becomes a large, outdoor living area. This house could be easily manufactured by one of our trailer manufacturers for a modest sum. You could also build it yourself. Smallplan, my own house plans service, will prepare plans (see address in Appendix C) if there is enough interest.

My hosts had a surprise for me as I was leaving. They pressed a book into my hand that contained plans for the original house, which was built in Sweden. I have included those plans here.

5 Japan

As an added incentive to attract more people to his China tour, Ken Butti persuaded his friend Noriko Yamamoto to be our guide for a brief tour of solar architecture and manufactured housing in Japan. Although the tour only lasted a few days, we were treated to a dazzling display of Japanese technology. Our guide is president of Global Link, headquartered in Venice, California. She runs a consulting business to gather and compare information on the United States and Japanese housing industries. Virtually any comparative statistic concerning housing, energy, or demographics for the two countries was on the tip of her tongue. Her sources are the Department of Energy, the Department of Housing and Urban Development, the *Statistical Handbook of Japan* and her own extensive contacts in government and industry.

We were able to see firsthand the industrial machine that, with half the population of the United States and virtually no native resources, produces twice as many automobiles and an equal number of houses each year as we produce here. When contrasted with China, it was as though we had journeyed 50 years into the past and then, after a brief plane ride, 25 years into the future when we reached Japan. This is, of course, using the United States of today as base zero; with the current state of affairs, we may never make it to the Japanese point of development.

Solar Water Heating

The contrast between our two countries was most pronounced when we examined the solar water heating industry. Figures provided by the Solar System Development Association are astonishing. Approximately 3 million Japanese homes and businesses have solar water heaters; this contrasts with about 300,000 units in the United States. The inventory of the heaters in stock exceeds the entire number of heaters sold to date in the United States. Production capacity of each of the six largest Japanese producers exceeds the combined capacity of all of the United States producers. The heaters are made of corrosion-resistant stainless steel and plastic. They have a 20-year life expectancy, and the Japanese government requires that the manufacturer warrant the entire installation for a minimum of 10 years.

Obviously, there are good reasons for this 20:1 ratio of solar acceptance. Japan is isolated and must import most fuel; energy savings are regarded as a patriotic duty, and fuel prices are quite high. The heaters themselves, like other Japanese products, are less expensive and more durable than their American counterparts. The heaters are drastically cheaper than American models because they are much smaller (the Japanese consume less hot water); also, they are of a much simpler design than those sold here. The typical Japanese solar water heater is a self-contained batch or thermosiphon heater that combines collector with storage tank. It is installed on the roof, costs from $600 to $1000 installed, and contains 50 to 60 gallons of water. The typical American system has a collector system on the roof with a remote-mounted heat exchanger, pump, control box, and storage tank. It costs $3000 to $4000 installed and has a capacity of 90 to 120 gallons of water.

If these heaters are so good and so cheap, why haven't the Japanese flooded the American market with them? The Solar System Development Association answers that they don't feel that the heaters are large enough to satisfy American demands. They also worry (with good reason) that the lightweight, clear-span roof trusses in vogue in the United States and Canada would collapse under the weight of one or more of their heaters. A logical way to increase capacity would be to install two heaters in tandem. A rugged post-and-beam house or a conventional house with a center bearing wall would carry these heaters with no trouble, but a trussed roof would certainly have trouble, particularly in snow country.

The least expensive (less than $500 in Japan, not installed) solar water heaters are a batch type, in which the collecting surface and the storage tank are one and the same. Homemade "bread-box" batch heaters of similar but much more primitive design have been popular among owner-builders in the United States and Canada.

Hitachi Chemical Company's Hi-Heater (HE-2000BK) is an excellent example of the state of the art in batch heaters. A polyethylene collector molded in the form of several tangential cylinders comprises the body of the unit. It is encased in a galvanized, insulated steel box and is glazed with clear fiberglass. A small tank with a float, similar to a toilet tank, sits atop the unit and admits water to the collector. The hot water is gravity-fed to the house. The scheme has several advantages; first, an inexpensive plastic collector can be used since it is not under pressure; occasional freezing will not hurt the unit because of the shape and lack of pressure. Finally, by simply shutting off the inlet valve, you can use all the hot water in the unit without diluting it with incoming cold water. The heater is equipped with an air vent to permit using it this way. I think this is one of the cleverest and most cost-effective water heaters ever devised. If you have a sturdily constructed roof and can make do with 200 liters (about 60 gallons) of hot water a day, I highly recommend

World-renowned Hitachi batch-type solar water heater. This unit was being tested for efficiency by the Chinese in a Soochow laboratory.

this heater. Bear in mind that you will have limited pressure unless you have a tall roof. A small in-line, faucet-activated hot water pump could be used if the lack of pressure is bothersome. For further information on these heaters, contact Hitachi Chemical Company (437 Madison Avenue, New York, NY 10022). Because the units are not actively marketed in the United States, it will take some time to receive yours after you've placed an order.

We were taken on a tour of Yazaki's Hammamatsu solar water heater plant to see Japanese manufacturing technology in action. Yazaki claims this to be the largest such plant in the world, with a capacity for producing over 20,000 passive solar thermosiphon systems and 5000 active collectors per month. We watched an incredible array of machinery that automatically welded the stainless steel collectors, pressure-tested them, and even packed the completed units into the usual Styrofoam-lined packages employed by the Japanese.

The Sanyo batch-type solar water heater on display at company headquarters. The storage tank is integral with the collector and has a reflective surface. Noriko is standing at right.

The water heaters, called Solar-Ace, are shipped in two sections: the stainless steel collectors and, separately, an insulated plastic storage tank. The tank has a polished stainless steel front that reflects additional sunlight down onto the collector. When mounted on a sloping roof surface, water circulates through the collector panel from the storage tank due to the tendency of hot water to rise; hence, the thermosiphon designation. Due to the more complicated construction techniques, the Yazaki heater costs about $200 more than the Hitachi batch heater. Unlike the Hitachi, this heater is actively marketed in the United States. For additional information, contact the American Yazaki Corporation (13500 Ashurst Court, Livonia, MI 48150).

In addition to the two companies just mentioned, we also toured the research and development departments of Sanyo and Sharp Corporation. We were treated to a display of futuristic talking appliances, flat-screen color television sets that hang flat on the wall, and every imaginable sort of photovoltaic cell-operated appliance. Sanyo markets a unique cold-weather solar water heater that utilizes heat pipe technology. Unlike the more typical passive Japanese systems, this one operates on full line pressure. In configuration, it looks almost exactly the same as the Yazaki unit, but there the similarities end. This unit has no water in the absorber plate; instead, there is a phase-change transfer medium. As the medium is heated, it evaporates and moves up into a heat exchanger in the storage tank where it heats the

A unique, super-efficient Sanyo hot water heater uses heat pipe technology.

water. The water cools the medium, causing it to recondense and flow back down to the absorber plate. Since the tank is fully insulated and the medium will not freeze, this is an ideal heater for cold climates. Even though this efficient unit uses advanced technology, it is competitively priced with the Yazaki unit; unfortunately, Sanyo has no plans for exporting the unit to North America. When they do, it will be ideal, for it is manufactured in modular sections so that the capacity can be easily varied.

More Innovations

Imaginative technology surrounded us everywhere. A huge Yazaki factory was entirely heated and cooled by solar power; electronic dictionaries translate Japanese into several other languages (notably, they do not work in reverse). A unique typewriter with a dot matrix system reproduces Chinese characters perfectly (IBM had decreed that this was an impossibility). Our local train from Osaka to Tokyo moved at lightning speed compared to trains in the United States; the Bullet train passed us as though we were standing still.

Upon my return home, I ordered a small version of the dot matrix typewriter, and it has been a major factor in preparing the manuscript for this book. The typewriter operates either on batteries or AC current and weighs less than 5 pounds. Despite its light weight and 2-inch thickness, it sports a full-size keyboard with calculator functions. There is also an extra keyboard with a separate shift key that adds 45 extra characters to the standard keyboard. The machine also has a liquid crystal correctable display that allows corrections to be made before the words are actually typed on the final page. This wondrous machine enables me to compose in the woods, on a mountaintop, on a train, or whenever I am traveling. It also works with no noise, no vibration, and only a few moving parts; the whole device is electronic. Surely, such sophistication costs several thousand dollars; indeed, correctable electronic typewriters (large office machines) made in the United States do cost this much. My lightweight wonder set me back less than $150. Of course, it has its limitations; it can't make carbon copies and the dot matrix type is crude and a bit light; I also question its durability. But for the price nothing else comes close.

I have been singing the praises of the Japanese economy for several paragraphs, and there are those who argue that it is unpatriotic to deal with the Japanese, citing huge trade deficits in the Japanese favor. Those who scream the loudest are union members who are trying to put up a smoke screen for their excessive wages, and automobile executives who are trying to excuse their mediocre products.

Michael Curtin of the Pacific News Service has written a very persuasive article, "The Myths That Keep U.S. Business Out of Japan." In it he points out that the $18 billion trade deficit so widely quoted is actually quite deceptive. The U.S. market is much bigger than the Japanese market, so he quotes percentages of gross national product for a more accurate comparison. Japanese goods only represent 1.3% of the U.S. gross national product, but U.S. goods imported into Japan represent .9% of their gross national product. U.S. companies operating inside Japan made $20 billion in sales in 1982, although Japanese companies in the United States made only $5 billion. In addition, the Japanese paid us over $2 billion in patent and licensing fees. Finally, $21 billion in oil sales from U.S. companies bought in other parts of the world and sold to Japan are excluded from the figures. The Japanese gained a reputation as a closed market back when they excluded 490 product categories from importation. Now, they only exclude 27 categories, 22 of which are agricultural. (That might explain why a steak dinner costs over $100 in Tokyo.)

We saw ample evidence of the American presence in Japan; McDonald's and other fast-food chains from the United States were everywhere; American-brand label clothes are obviously a status item. Ironically, the Harley-Davidson motorcycle is adored by the Japanese. Much of the criticism of their presence in the United States stems from their great success with a limited number of highly visible and desirable products. Before we cross off Japan as a trading partner, we should stop to consider that they are the largest single market in the free world outside the United States.

Japanese Houses

In Tokyo, we architects were finally able to get our teeth into some contemporary Japanese architecture. The ABC Housing Corporation took us on a tour of a housing demonstration village. Land is so expensive in Japan ($250 per square foot versus $10 in the United States) that contractors get together and lease a large tract upon which to erect demonstration homes. ABC specializes in solar houses, so their Shukugawa dem-

ABC Housing Corporation's model solar house features a south-facing courtyard with a solar greenhouse.

onstration house not surprisingly bristles with Trombe walls, greenhouses, sunspaces, and solar mass. Not a scrap of the traditional Japanese post-and-beam framing was visible, though. Construction costs in Japan run about $38 per square foot for a well-made, traditional post-and-beam framed house. This compares with about $35 per square foot for a cheap attached townhouse in the United States. Unfortunately, the life of the post-and-beam frame in Japan seems limited. The Japanese consumer is rapidly becoming Americanized and wants plaster ceilings with no exposed beams. We saw a demonstration house under construction in which virtually all the intricate framing was slated as an underlayment for other finishes. A single "token" beam supported by a row of posts was all that was to remain visible.

Of course, there is still a large market for traditional Japanese architecture and even the luxury models we saw had the traditional Japanese entry and tatami room with movable partitions. One of the great benefits of the traditional frames is that they allow complete flexibility of arrangement of interior and exterior walls. This flexibility frequently results in smaller, more efficient floor plans with more usable space than larger houses with fixed walls.

Traditional Japanese houses are very carefully planned structures based upon standard modular sizes of the tatami mats and the sliding shoji screens. The mats are approximately 3 by 6 feet, and the rooms are made up of various numbers
(continued on page 53)

The interior of this greenhouse shows how to make double use of a space. The stairs are enclosed within the greenhouse.

DIA System Housing has constructed a dramatic solar house with skylighted courtyard, inset roof decks, and solar collector all in one smooth shape.

Suburban sprawl in Tokyo. A typical mix of single-family houses with apartments is in the background. A playground is in the foreground.

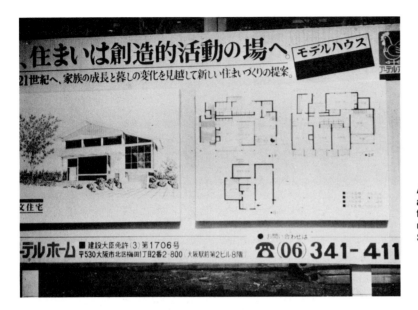

An aggressive billboard advertises a new house design. Displaying the floor plan and dimensions would be unusual for advertising in the United States.

This model house shows the use of fire-resistant tile roof and stucco walls. Flammable materials are prohibited on the exterior of buildings within the city of Tokyo.

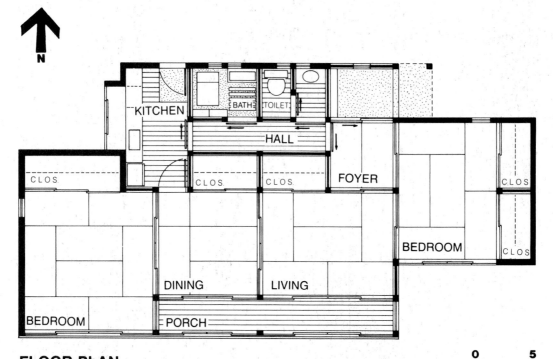

FLOOR PLAN

0 ——— 5

Traditional post-and-beam Japanese house is designed around 3- by 6-foot floor mats. Great flexibility of use is obtained by the sliding screens between rooms. Even in a small house of less than 1000 square feet, a 40-foot-long space can be achieved by sliding or removing screens. With the addition of one or two "permanent" walls, this house would be well-suited to our country; some will like it just as it is.

The traditional Japanese interior features 3- by 6-foot floor mats and minimal furnishings.

Deep-blue tile roofs are everywhere.
A cul-de-sac of older houses shows
off traditional roof forms.

of full and half mats. A small 6 by 9 bedroom may consist of three mats, a 9-foot square would contain 4½ mats, and so forth. The plan shown here is a composite of various traditional plans somewhat altered for American tastes.

For those with lots of time and money, who are really serious about the study of Japanese house architecture, I recommend the 500-page tome, *The Japanese House, A Tradition for Contemporary Architecture* by Heinrich Engel (Charles E. Tuttle Company, 1964). This book is very expensive and a bit rambling, but covers its subject extremely well. The only shortcoming is a lack of detail on just how the tricky joinery is actually executed. For those who want to learn more about this intricate joinery, I recommend *The Art of Japanese Joinery* by Kiyosi Seike (John Weatherhill, 1977). Brightly lighted, high-contrast photos of actual joints set against a black background show these techniques more clearly than any possible drawings. The only improvement would be to have the actual joint in front of you to examine.

Unfortunately, Japan has become so Westernized that these contemporary books cannot do full justice to the traditions of the country because so many of them have vanished or are in the process thereof. There exists a truly fine reprint of a wonderful book by an American scientist written just 100 years ago. Edward Morse was professor of zoology at the University of Tokyo from 1877 to 1883. A friend suggested that he was "frittering away his valuable time on the lower forms of animal life" and should make a record of

Japanese life as it existed at that time. The result was *Japanese Homes and Their Surroundings,* reprinted in 1961 by Dover Press. The book is superbly illustrated by Morse's pen-and-ink drawings, which capture the scene in far greater detail than any camera could ever hope for.

Sadly, much of this beautiful workmanship is being forgotten as the world of electronics, computers, and prefabrication takes over Japan. We were able to view a "model subdivision" of prefabricated houses that had been set up on a parking lot in downtown Tokyo. Unlike the United States, where prefabrication frequently means cheap materials and obvious construction joints, these were solid, two-story houses of the highest quality. By using the same techniques they use in automobile manufacturing, the Japanese are able to lower the cost of a typical, prefabricated, 1200-square-foot house to around $30,000. According to Noriko, the average Japanese family has that much money in the bank. But those savings don't help with the $100,000-plus cost of a lot unless the family already owns property. The Japanese government and employers typically make construction loans at 5.5%. Commercial banks in Japan currently charge 8.7%. These latest figures were given by Noriko in a February 16, 1983, interview with the *Wall Street Journal.*

The future looks even brighter for manufactured housing in Japan. Misawa Homes of Nagoya, Japan, has devised a new construction technique using a new ceramiclike construction material with superior insulating qualities that can be cast into fully finished wall panels. The entire house

An exhibit of prefabricated houses in downtown Tokyo. A typical two-story house costs $35,000 (U.S. currency) on the owner's lot.

can be erected at the site in only four hours. These houses, like those of many other Japanese builders, are guaranteed for 20 years; contrast that to the typical U.S. builder's guarantee of 1 year. Urbanimage Corporation of Boston is in the process of producing an educational film showing a Misawa house from start to finish. The film is being partially funded by the National Endowment for the Arts and will be made available to both Japanese and American television stations.

For those who want to take advantage of the design possibilities of traditional Japanese post-and-beam framing with modern prefabricated panels, Bob Dakin has designed a 900-square-foot, 1½-story beauty. Plans are shown for it in Chapter 25.

6 New Zealand

Of the dozens of countries that I have visited in my travels, New Zealand is my favorite; a place where I think I would be happy for the rest of my life. Possibly, this is tempered by the memory of my grandfather who planned to migrate there at the turn of the century until he saw his savings wiped out by serious illness and stayed here instead. New Zealand is sparsely populated—it is just over two-thirds the size of Japan, yet it has a population density of only 30 people per square mile. That's about half the density of the United States and only 4% of the density of Japan.

Most people in New Zealand live in detached single-family dwellings; many date from the Victorian era. Construction materials other than lumber are usually imported from England or Australia. Since this increases costs considerably, houses are well maintained and seldom abandoned. The 1890s bungalow shown on the next page is quite typical of detached houses throughout the countryside. Corrugated metal roofing is popular and is frequently bent into curved shapes as on the porch and bay window roofs of this house. Houses in towns and cities are frequently two stories in older neighborhoods. In the suburbs, small ranch houses of less than 1000 square feet predominate; they are reminiscent of American housing of the 1950s.

As an island-nation highly vulnerable to escalating fuel prices and import costs, New Zealand has worked hard to achieve energy efficiency. Wood stoves and solar water heaters are more common there than in the United States. As a relatively poor nation (about one-half the per capita income of the United States), houses are of modest size, and considerable attention is given to cost-saving building methods.

A unique prefabricated house system is gaining popularity with cost-conscious owner-builders. This system involves post-and-beam frames with exterior panels somewhat similar to those featured in this book. In the New Zealand system, a grid of post-and-beam framing is precut in a factory, to be bolted together at the site by the owner. Wall and roof panels are then installed over the post-and-beam frame. The typical model is a 1000-square-foot ranch house with exposed cathedral ceilings. The overall designs are quite pleasant from the exterior, but the inside has a busy "panelized" look that I find unattractive. The 4-foot post-and-roof beam spacing is efficient and logical, but the resulting exposed members are too numerous for good looks, especially in a small house. The house is designed for a post-type foundation that is very popular in New Zealand due to its low cost and adaptability to a wide variety of terrain. For more information on this unique building system, contact Portal-Lock Owner-Built Homes (Box 798, Rotorua, New Zealand).

Since houses in New Zealand are more modest than those here, they usually have only one

Here's a simple, L-shaped, 1890s Victorian bungalow.

bathroom. For more convenient use, the plumbing fixtures are separated into compartments with the toilet separate from the rest of the fixtures. A unique plumbing fixture is the Pacific Handbasin, which replaces the normal tank toilet lid with a fiberglass washbasin. The unit requires no plumbing and allows the water that is used for hand washing to empty into the toilet tank below so that it can be used for flushing. The unit is manufactured by P. S. Johnson & Associates (Box 13–171, Onehunga, Auckland, New Zealand).

Bathtubs in New Zealand are smaller but deeper than their American counterparts. Similar deep tubs are marketed in the United States, but as "soaking tubs" at prohibitive prices. Many of my clients have looked in vain for such tubs at reasonable prices in the United States. A wide variety of sensible, well-designed fixtures is available from Clearlite Plastics (54–58 Hillside Road, Takapuna, Auckland, New Zealand). Since foreign exchange is lopsided in favor of imports, New Zealand is eager for exports. The prices of the fixtures mentioned above are so reasonable that they would still be a bargain, even with shipping costs and duty.

Pole Houses

Pole-type structures have been used all over the world for centuries, but they have only started to become popular as permanent homes fairly recently, since the development of pressure-treated wood. Pole houses are very popular in New Zealand because they are adaptable to rough terrain. Since New Zealand's economy is dependent upon farmland, there are strong incentives to use rugged, less-valuable terrain for homesites. Our country would be better off if it had the same priorities. Unfortunately, our priorities are just the opposite; good farmland has been, and continues to be, encroached upon by housing development.

I have designed several pole houses for North America, and I've found that they are popular in two very different climatic regions. People in the Deep South like them because these houses are elevated to take advantage of natural breezes. And clients in Canada and Alaska like them because they don't have to dig extensive foundations in frozen earth; in these cold climates snow is packed around the foundations as insulation.

It is awkward to design a pole house because the poles must be carefully laid out and may not coincide with a good layout for the rooms. Since it is cheapest to use round poles for the structural supports, they are usually left exposed, either inside or outside the house. The round poles do not lend themselves to embedment in the walls because of irregularities in the poles themselves. Because of the difficult details involved and weathering problems, I usually place the poles inside the house.

In the United States, good information and plans for pole houses are hard to find. The only detailed reference book in North America is *The Owner-Built Pole Frame House* by Barbara and Ken Kern (Charles Scribner's Sons, 1981). They give a lot of very good background on pole building and continue with excellent descriptions of enclosing the house using the 1-inch framing system developed by Homer Hurst. (See Chapter 12 for Family Homes Cooperative factory-built houses that use this technique.) Unfortunately, the book is entirely aimed at owner-builders, and it is assumed that they will develop their own plans

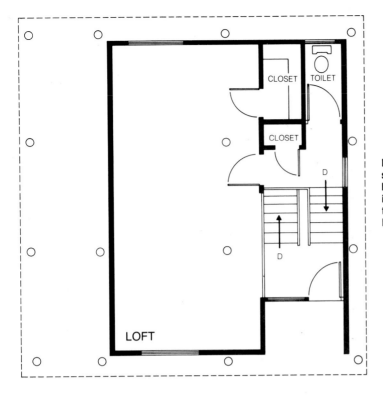

SECOND FLOOR PLAN

Pole houses are ideal for remote areas with sloping terrain. This version (floor plans shown here and perspective drawing on next page) with its large sleeping loft, is used as a ski house, but the design would be serviceable as a full-time house with a few added partitions.

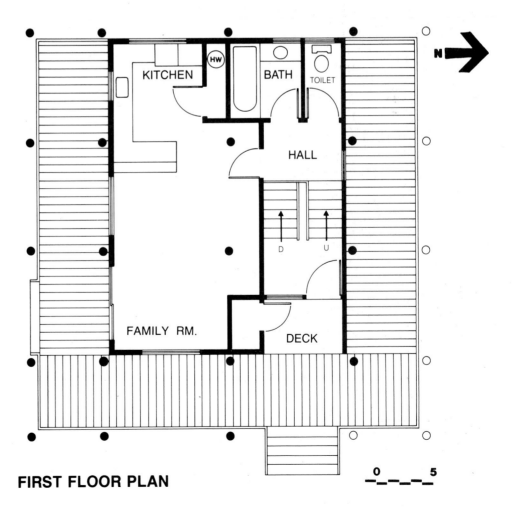

FIRST FLOOR PLAN

0 _ _ _ 5

for their houses. The only complete design shown in the book has an excellent plan, but it has an awkward exterior appearance.

In New Zealand, poles are usually set outside the building walls, making a strong aesthetic statement for the building; everyone knows a pole house when they pass one. The plan shown here came from the book, *Poles Apart, A Book on the Pole House* (Business Publications, Box 68–222, Newton, Auckland, New Zealand). The book contains plans for a dozen well-designed pole houses of quite varied size and shape. Working drawings are available for all the houses from Residential Management (Bowndown Building Centre, Box 271, Auckland, New Zealand). I show one pole house design in Part IV, but I hope the wide variety of designs from New Zealand will inspire more Americans to use this technique to build on sloping land, rather than wasting valuable farmland for housing developments.

Hundertwasser's Waste Disposal Systems

Several years ago, my friend Fredrick Hundertwasser invited me to visit his farm in New Zealand to see firsthand some of his novel construction and waste disposal methods. Fredrick is a dedicated conservationist. Although painting is his first love, building and conservation are close seconds. He has spent several years searching for the ideal method of disposing of human and house-

hold wastes. After examining the commercial composting toilets, he bought two Swedish models for testing. He was considerably disillusioned:

Many parts broke and I had to order new parts and pay lots of import duty. I did not like the electricity involved; the humming noise of the vent (why go to nature and hear constant technological noise like at the dentist?). Then, too, I did not like the design (more like a refrigerator). I am an artist and suffer ugliness. Ugly things never work. The Clivus is ugly too—the ugliest part is hidden under the floor. Also, I did not like the flue-vent to evacuate air and smells. I wondered what it would be like if 2 million people in a city like Vienna all had compost toilet chimney vents . . . I started to experiment myself with homemade humus toilets.

Fredrick's requirements were simple. The toilet must be simple and easy to build, it must not have a vent to waste precious heat, and it must be attractive. Finally, it must do the job well and be easy to maintain. He carried out his earliest experiments on board his sailing vessel. The first models had a small vent stack with heat supplied by a kerosene lantern. Then came the breakthrough. His research uncovered a technique that predated the water closet and was originally called an earth closet. In this system, rich, humusy soil, such as you find on the forest floor, was used to cover the feces or garbage and eliminate the smell. No vent or external heat source was necessary. As long as liquids are reasonably limited, the toilet works very well. Many of Fredrick's friends and acquaintances in Vienna and New Zealand use his toilets. Several of my clients have tried them with great success.

Fredrick's final design uses a 30-gallon plastic garbage can that has been liberally perforated on the bottom. It is mounted in a simple wooden enclosure with space on the bottom for ventilation. A tray catches any excess liquid. A second unperforated can is filled with earth for covering the waste. The perforated can is arranged so that it can be rotated in relation to the toilet seat; this prevents buildup from occurring in one spot. After each use a small amount of earth is transferred by the user from the second can to the first. Virtually a perfect ecological system. The only

drawback is that urine input must be limited, and so Hundertwasser has a separate urinal that is hooked up to his water purification system (see later). Much to my surprise, there is no odor whatsoever. The cost is much less than $50. An ideal solution—for some people.

It is obvious that most health departments as well as conservative guests would not be pleased by such an arrangement. It would be an excellent solution for a temporary toilet facility while you are building your house or saving money for a more conventional water system. For one or two people living in a remote area, it would be a fine disposal system. Unlike the expensive commercial models, you are only making a very small investment—if it's not your cup of tea, there is nothing lost but a bit of your time and a garbage can. A system such as this might enable you to build where construction would otherwise be impossible. Small plots of land near a body of water or areas with solid rock or a very high water table can pose very difficult problems. Even an old-fashioned pit privy can't be used in some such situations.

Disposal of the composted waste could be a problem. Fredrick recommends letting the filled garbage can compost in a warm area for six months before using the contents. Even then, it should only be used as fertilizer for nonedible plants, and care must be taken to wash hands and all tools that come in contact with the compost. He has had the results thoroughly tested, and they were found to be safe. Researchers have gotten similar results from most composting toilets, but caution is still advised. There is just too much possibility for some slipup to take a chance and use the product on edible plants. Perhaps it can be used on fruits and vegetables after several years of decomposition, but not after such a short period.

Water Purification

Hundertwasser has been equally attentive to the problems involved with purifying greywater. Those who have tried to use commercial composting toilets are well aware of the problem. Even though the expensive composting toilets process toilet wastes successfully, what do you do to safely dispose of wash water? Fredrick was acquainted with the work of Dr. Kathe Seidel of Krefeld, Germany. He had already planted rows of black alder trees to purify the water and improve the soil along his tidewater canals. Dr. Seidel put containers of water plants in a stepped formation next to each other and transformed

This simple composting toilet uses a box container. The container at right holds humus that is layered into the box after each use.

extremely dirty water into crystal-clear drinking water at the last outlet. She used various varieties of reeds and rushes, particularly *Schoeoplexus lacustris.* Fredrick has used cypress, papyrus, and *Equisetum hiemacis* (winter shade grass). For warm climates he also uses water hyacinths, swamp grasses, and even floating water lilies. There are endless varieties of water plants that can purify water.

In North Island's semitropical climate, Fredrick has an outdoor water purification system constructed of precast concrete sheep-watering tanks. It is amazing to watch the plants at work—the purification process is virtually instantaneous. The flow from the outlet end is constant and almost matches the inlet flow, but the outlet is clear and the inlet is dirty. Of course, this is an outdoor water purification system and it wouldn't work in northern climates where water freezes. It would work in a greenhouse, though, and that is the arrangement that Fredrick uses in Vienna. Gregg Allen, a Canadian architect friend, has successfully used a similar purification system in

greenhouses in very cold northern climates. One of his houses has had such a system in operation for almost 10 years, and it continues to function well. On the occasions when the water was tested, no pathogens were found.

Such a system is not without its special problems, though. Grease is an enemy of the digestion process and can clog the gravel beds. It is best to install a small commercial grease trap under the kitchen sink and be careful not to pour any quantities of grease down the drains. Obviously, any chemical poisons will also wreak havoc with your natural disposal system. If they are strong enough, they will kill all the plants and necessitate a fresh start.

Fredrick has been experimenting with his alternate waste-disposal systems for almost 10 years; long enough for a thorough testing. Both the systems are labor intensive and require constant attention—like a garden. Unless you have the time and interest, I would not try these techniques. If you are someone to whom the environment

Concrete tanks filled with rushes step down the slope of the yard to purify waste water to drinking purity. Note the glasses in the foreground.

Bottles are cast into the walls on a flat plane rather than showing the usual circular ends. This allows a wide variety of patterns.

matters deeply and have the time to devote, I heartily endorse these methods.

Bottle Walls

Glass manufacture is an energy-intensive process. Except for a few progressive areas, bottles are discarded with trash and crushed or dumped into landfills. For many years people have constructed crude walls with bottles embedded into them. Usually, the bottles are stacked on their sides with the tapered necks pointing into the living space. The result is not very handsome and is difficult to clean. For his studio in New Zealand, Fredrick has devised a new technique for recycling bottles. He designs prefabricated panels carefully composed of bottles turned 90 degrees so that the profile of the bottles shows through the walls. He builds the panels in horizontal position so that the bottles can be selected for size, design, and color before fabrication. The finished panels have intricate designs and are equally handsome from either side.

Fredrick starts the panels by constructing a wooden frame of 1 × 6s to the size of the finished panel. Next, he places the frame flat in a bed of sand. He then selects and arranges the bottles in his desired pattern. After he is satisfied with the arrangement, he anchors the bottles in place with mortar. Nails are driven through the wooden frame into the mortar space to provide a bond. After the mortar has set, the panel is reversed and mortared from the reverse side. If the process is done properly, the reverse side will need very little mortar—just a thin coat between the bottles. The finished panel is then set into place in the

wall. The result is a handsome translucent glass wall for which the only expense is a bit of mortar and a lot of labor. If you have the time and very limited funds, this is a good technique to consider.

Sod Roofs

Fredrick's farm buildings have an assortment of sod roofs, representing his experiments over the years. Sod roofs are used in the United States and Canada, but seem to be limited to underground houses. For some reason, people who build underground think in terms of a sod roof, but others ignore them. Since northern New Zealand has a high water table and very dense clay, the farm buildings are all built well above ground level. The principal requisites for a sod roof are a low pitch (less than 27 degrees) and a heavy roof structure capable of supporting at least 60 pounds per square foot. Fredrick's buildings are constructed with heavy timbers that are supported by relatively closely spaced posts. This is intuitive design and considerably overbuilt, but a lot safer than vice versa.

The sod itself is not waterproof; it only serves as a protective cover for the roofing, which is waterproof. Since the roof itself is fully protected from the ultraviolet rays of the sun, relatively inexpensive waterproofing materials can be used. Fredrick used corrugated asbestos-cement board for his decking and roof surface. Since he is in a warm climate and needs little insulation, this method works very well. He did have to seal the overlapping joints of the corrugated roof material, though. The sod is held in place at the edges of the roof by a simple row of stones—less expen-

Fredrick Hundertwasser stands on the sod roof of his "bottle house."

Fredrick Hundertwasser's studio is constructed of bottle walls and a sod roof.

sive than the usual pressure-treated wood edging and much more attractive.

For most North American climates, insulation is needed under the sod. Although any of the waterproofing materials described in Chapter 10 for underground houses can be used for sod roofs, they are more expensive than is really necessary. There is no actual water pressure under a sod roof, and the thickness of the sod minimizes thermal stress in the roof membrane as well as protecting it completely from the sun's rays. The least expensive roof membrane would be 20-mil polyethylene film. It is available from large plastics houses in 20-foot-wide rolls. It must be used on a very low pitch roof or the sod will slide right off it. It is very slippery and difficult to work over, and it can be damaged easily. If you use polyethylene film, test it for tears and holes by drenching it with a hose before applying the sod. The only way to repair the plastic once the sod is in place is to remove all the sod and start over.

There is another low-cost roof membrane that is labor intensive, but it doesn't damage as easily as polyethylene, and it can be used on much steeper roofs. This superior roof membrane usually goes under the misnomer of "hot tar." Actually, real hot tar roofs are one of the most durable roofs known. Unfortunately, tar gives off poisonous fumes when heated, and the material has been outlawed for some years. The substitute is actually hot asphalt, and although it makes a dandy roof, if not covered by sod or another covering it degrades under sunlight after a few years. The material is sold in 50- or 100-pound cakes that must be heated to the melting point before installation. The "tar" is applied over half-lapped layers of 30-pound building paper that become embedded in tar as you progress up the slope of the roof. Two by two pressure-treated battens should be embedded in the top coat of tar at 18-inch centers. This will give something for the sod to rest on to prevent sliding; it will also hold back the flow of water for a healthier roof. Materials cost is only $12 to $15 per square (100 square feet).

The sod itself is applied in two layers; the first layer is placed roots up, the second with the roots down. Until the sod is firmly rooted, you may have to water your roof in dry weather. This roof is labor intensive, but the overall cost is very low and the final result is beautiful and ecologically satisfying.

The houses of New Zealand are excellent examples of charming, moderately priced structures that are efficient and well constructed. Our building industry can learn a great deal from this remote island nation.

NORTH AMERICAN SOLUTIONS

7 Owner-Built and Self-Help Housing

Self-help or owner-built houses are taking an increasingly important share of the North American housing market. The housing boom of the late 1960s and early 1970s created such a demand for houses that powerful labor unions were able to stiff-arm the construction industry into absurdly high wages. These wages have had a spillover effect on nonunion wage rates for single-family housing. Even before land and material prices skyrocketed, new houses were out of the question for a large portion of our society. With an increase in prices, people became more interested in building their own houses. But money has not been the only factor; the desire for alternative energy and energy efficiency and for hand craftsmanship has played key roles as well. The typical contractor is out to make money and is not about to spend a penny extra for more insulation, proper siting or better-quality design or materials. Of course, there are many exceptions to this rule, but these contractors know that they are offering a superior product and price their houses accordingly, thereby shutting out even more people from the market.

Labor has traditionally accounted for about 50% of the cost of a new house in our part of the world. A contractor's overhead and profit consume 20 to 30% of the cost. These figures add up to an enormous incentive for ambitious people to perform all or part of the construction work themselves. Schools catering to owner-builders have cropped up everywhere. When I first started writing, The Shelter Institute up in Bath, Maine, was the only place that provided courses, but now there are dozens of such schools throughout the United States and Canada.

Contracting It Yourself

The degree of owner participation in construction and the percentage of savings can vary widely. It is rapidly becoming routine for owners to do their own contracting on a custom-built house. A contractor I know remarked that the days of full-contract houses are virtually over: "No cost-conscious homebuilder would consider hiring a general contractor to do everything. Now all we get is a labor contract; the owner buys his or her own materials." Since you will not be likely to operate as efficiently as a general contractor, you cannot expect to save all of the usual overhead and profit figure (around 25%); 10 to 15% is a more likely savings. But if you are building in an area of expensive houses, where contractors ask and get very high markups, your savings can be staggering. Be very careful when operating in such areas, though. Price fixing and favoritism are rampant; the lumberyards get together to rig prices and grant under-the-table discounts to favored contractors. Several times, when confronted with such practices, I have arranged for the materials to be shipped in from an area a little farther away, but from one that I know has more reasonable prices.

A human being should be able to change a diaper, plan an invasion, butcher a hog, conn a ship, design a building, write a sonnet, balance accounts, build a wall, set a bone, comfort the dying, take orders, give orders, cooperate, act alone, solve equations, analyze a new problem, pitch manure, program a computer, cook a tasty meal, fight efficiently, and die gallantly. Specialization is for insects.

Robert Heinlein

It's reasonable for almost everyone contemplating a new house to handle contracting, scheduling, and purchasing materials. If you do a good job, you will save money, maybe lots of money. If you do a bad job, you may spend more money and wind up with a lot of workmen who don't like you. You may also get hurt or unknowingly sabotage your own house.

A word of caution: Do not attempt to do your own contracting unless you are a reasonably forceful person who can be diplomatic and can manage people well. If you're too easygoing, people may take advantage of you. And if you are impatient or unreasonable, you could alienate the workmen and wind up spending more money than if you had hired a contractor in the beginning.

Supplying Your Own Timber
Even if you don't get directly involved with contracting your house, you may be able to save by furnishing the timbers. In most parts of the country, framing lumber is transported many miles and goes through several markups before it is used for construction. In many cases, my clients have taken advantage of unwanted mature trees on their property and have used this natural resource for their new house. Remote stands of trees can be transformed into lumber or timbers for a post-and-beam frame with the Mobile Dimension Saw shown here. If you want to do more of the work yourself, you can use one of the various chain saw lumber mill attachments that are described in Appendix A.

Warning: This is dangerous, time-consuming work; don't start to harvest trees by yourself unless you are prepared to make a major commitment. Those who plan to use their own trees should read the book *Chainsaw Lumbermaking* by Will Malloff (Taunton Press, 1982).

Building It Yourself
The next level of involvement, after handling the general contracting, is actually building the house yourself. The leap between being general contractor and being builder is a very big one. Don't underestimate the job; it requires total commitment and contains many, many pitfalls for the unwary and inexperienced. In this case, a serious mistake might even kill someone, possibly yourself.

Although the owner-builder schools promote themselves as being designed for people who are going to pick up tools and actually build their own houses, I think they are more of a help for

The Mobile Manufacturing Company will furnish, upon request, a list of owners of this saw, so you can hire someone in your area to come to your property and cut logs into lumber.

those who are going to do their own general contracting. By reading some good references and taking a short building course, most people can understand the building process and take on the contractor's job. Actually learning how to do rough and finish carpentry, lay masonry, and do wiring and plumbing in a two-week course is an impossibility. If you are handy with your hands and are a putterer who regularly uses tools, you are a prime candidate for building your own house; but that does not mean you should do it entirely by yourself. Even if you could do every bit of the work on your house unaided, it would take such a long time that you might never finish it. There are numerous abandoned, partly completed houses dotting the countryside to attest to the many people who underestimated the job.

I strongly recommend that you hire professionals to install your foundation and to erect the frame of your house. This is particularly true if you are using traditional foundation methods. A stacked, surface-bonded block foundation or pressure-treated wood foundation is within the realm of a skilled amateur, but only if you are very long on time and short on money. The frames for the houses in this book are available from several sources, listed in Appendix A. Many contractors will travel to erect the frames, but they can be easily erected by any reputable local framing crew. Again, a skilled amateur can manage the operation, but others should hire help. The wall panels described in Chapter 20 are a boon to the owner-builder. They can be either purchased from sources listed in Appendix A or can be easily job-fabricated. Some building code officials may give you a hard time if you build the panels yourself, since they involve a new technique that's unfamiliar to most people. Since the major suppliers have obtained code approval, purchasing the panels will alleviate this problem.

Whether you purchase components for the shell of one of the houses recommended in this book or hire someone to stick-build a shell on your site, you should be able to complete the house without too much difficulty. Once the shell is up, you can select the trades in which you feel most proficient and hire professionals to perform the balance of the work. Your worst problems will probably be scheduling and financing.

Prime candidates for attention from the owner-builder are insulation and plumbing and wiring. Insulation is rarely done properly by contractors, and it is not a skilled trade. It just takes time and care, commodities sadly lacking in today's build-ing market. The mechanical trades are vastly over-priced for the work they usually perform. Even though less skill is required than for finish carpentry, the mechanical trades usually command several dollars an hour in premium pay; again, the ominous union influence.

Group Efforts

Self-help housing implies much more than the involvement of isolated homeowners who perform all or most of the work on their own houses. The basic idea of self-help housing is that of user control of the housing product. This can be a very powerful force if a sizable group or community gets together, because by pooling its talents and energies, a great deal can be accomplished in a short time.

Banks, insurance companies, building inspectors, land speculators, and other forces that can impede the building process can be dealt with much more successfully by a group than by an individual. Rural America (1900 M Street NW, Washington, DC 20036) has done considerable work in group housing efforts. (Read more about them in Chapter 12.) And the American Friends Service Committee (20 South 12th Street, Philadelphia, PA 19107) has helped almost 10,000 families in organized self-help housing projects since it began its program in the 1960s. Other groups instrumental in helping individuals pool their efforts are: CO-OP America (2100 M Street NW, Suite 316, Washington, DC 20063), Institute for Community Economics (151 Montague City Road, Greenfield, MA 01301), and the Federation of Appalachian Housing Enterprises (Drawer B, Berea, KY 40403).

In Canada, architect Charles Haynes has been a major force in furthering the cause of self-help housing. He has worked extensively with groups of students at the Centre for Continuing Education (University of British Columbia, Vancouver, BC V6T 1W5). Three different designs by Haynes have been constructed by students at UBC Solar Village Experiment, each for a materials cost of less than $15,000. For additional information on this program and the houses, contact the Canadian Self-Help Housing Association, Box 4134, Vancouver, BC V6B 3Z6. If you like any of these designs, detailed working drawings are available.

Plans for Haynes's Acadia house, for example, include 33 large drawings containing an almost indescribable wealth of detail. A professional builder would tend to scoff at these plans be-

Shown is one of Charles Haynes's expandable houses. This is the basic house.

The interior of Charles Haynes's expandable house. This view is of the dining and kitchen areas.

cause they contain so much information, but the great detail they contain leaves few questions unanswered for the amateur. The first couple of sheets contain design drawings and cutouts for constructing a scale model of the house. The usual floor plans, cross sections, and elevations are followed by 20 pages of constructing and cutting details that show every single framing member. Virtually every piece and process of the house is detailed, including all the pieces needed to build the kitchen cabinets. The electrical plans not only show the location of the fixtures and outlets, but contain pictorial diagrams showing how to wire each junction box, fixture, and outlet.

If you are in the market for a passive solar house slightly larger than 1000 square feet and plan to do much of the work yourself, I highly recommend this set of plans. They are almost like having a skilled professional guiding your work. See the order blank for ordering plans in Appendix C.

Sources of Information

Beginning builders need all the help they can get. Charles Haynes has written one of the best books ever for the novice. It is titled *Self Help Solar Housing, Design and Construction Manual for Acadia House* (Scrivners Publication Trades, 1980). Although the book is written as a construction manual specifically for the Acadia house, it would be useful to anyone building his or her own house. It gives good, strong instructions for each step, including materials, tools, and safety precautions. The book is worth buying for the 30-page bibliography alone; this is one of the most extensive publications lists I've ever seen, and it is cross-referenced by both title and author. The book is profusely illustrated with excellent ink drawings and murky black-and-white reproductions of color slides. The drawings and photos illustrate good-quality standard frame construction with allowances for superinsulation and cathedral ceilings. The detailing is excellent and should be studied by anyone contemplating a well-insulated house using standard construction methods.

For those interested in superinsulated houses using post-and-beam framing, my own book, *A Design and Construction Handbook for Energy-Saving Houses* (Rodale Press, 1980), gives step-by-step directions for construction of 12 different post-and-beam houses with 6-inch-thick infill walls for maximum insulation value. These earlier designs are a bit larger than those featured in this book. There is a short bibliography featuring books of vital interest to the novice.

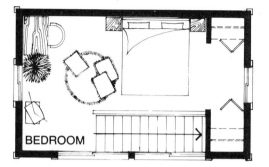

SECOND FLOOR PLAN

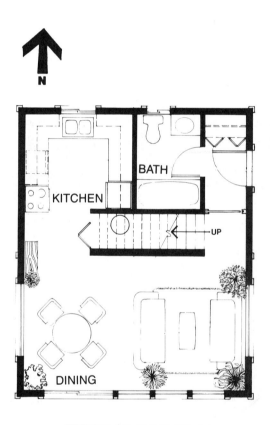

FIRST FLOOR PLAN

Charles Haynes has designed two winners that are easily expandable. Well-detailed plans are available for the inexperienced owner-builder. The basic house plan is expanded in the second set of plans shown here.

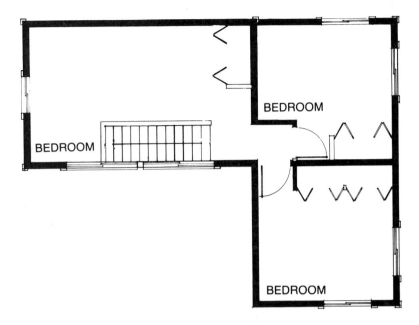

SECOND FLOOR PLAN

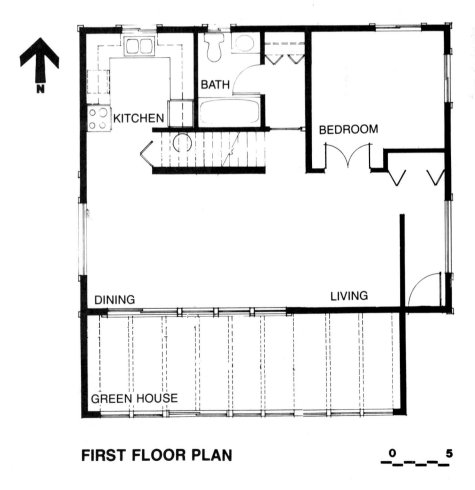

FIRST FLOOR PLAN   0 _ _ _ 5

In *A Design and Construction Handbook* I recommended *Architectural Graphic Standards* by Charles G. Ramsey and Harold R. Sleeper (John Wiley and Sons, 1981) as the standard reference book for construction details. You might want to look it up in a library rather than buy it, since the price has recently doubled to $100. The gap has been nicely filled by a new general reference, *Architectural Draftsman's Reference Handbook* by Jack R. Lewis (Prentice-Hall, 1982). Many of the construction books aimed at the beginner are written by people whose knowledge of their subject is limited. If it is an expensive book, check it out at the library before you buy it.

Many excellent periodicals will be of help to you whether or not you actually do the construction yourself. Absolutely tops in the field is the bimonthly, *Fine Homebuilding,* published by Taunton Press (Newtown, CT 06470). *New Shelter,* published nine times a year by Rodale Press, isn't as well presented, but has been improving consistently. Both are fairly recent entries into the magazine field, and back issues are well worth purchasing.

There are two completely different magazines with the title *The Owner-Builder.* One is published in Australia, the other in California—both are worth reading. The Australian version is devoted to rammed-earth and post-and-beam dwellings of energy-conscious design. There are frequent designs for hot climates, a problem that seems to be overlooked by North American architects and designers. The quarterly is edited by John and Gerry Archer, who wrote some of the books referenced in Chapter 9 for rammed-earth construction. For subscriptions and back issues, write Box 4036, Melbourne, Victoria 3001 Australia. The American quarterly is an expanded newsletter published by the Owner-Builder Center. Its primary purpose is to promote the publisher's building courses, but it is quite valuable as a source book. The plans and books for sale are top quality, and the classified advertisements contain a fine selection of goods and services. It is avail-

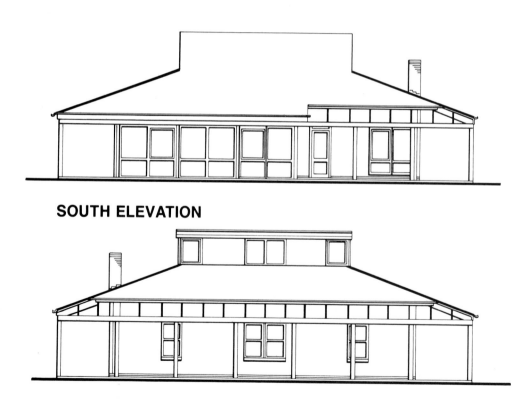

SOUTH ELEVATION

NORTH ELEVATION

A fine design for a house for a warm climate, as featured in the Australian magazine, *The Owner-Builder.* The north-south orientation has been reversed to make it suitable for this hemisphere (the sun is in the north in Australia).

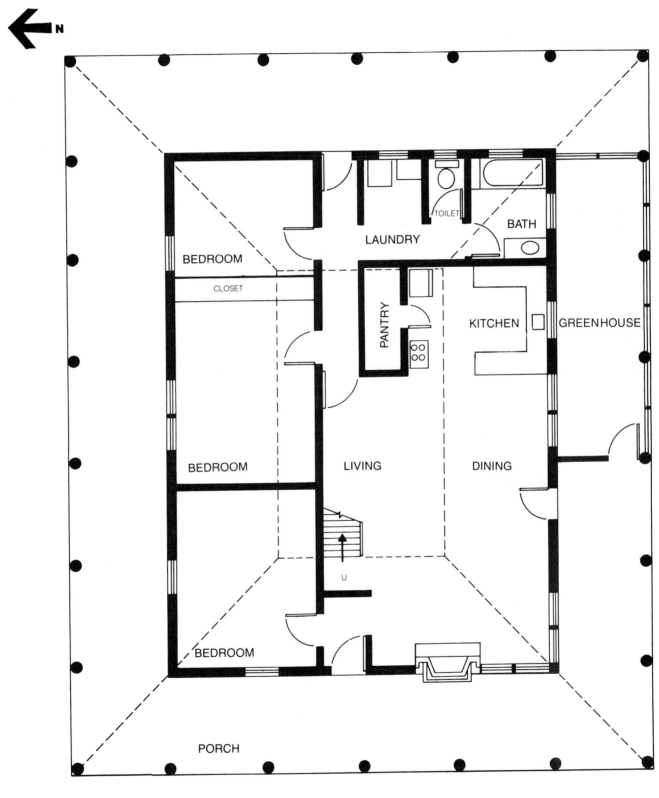

N

BEDROOM

CLOSET

LAUNDRY

TOILET

BATH

PANTRY

KITCHEN

GREENHOUSE

BEDROOM

LIVING

DINING

U

BEDROOM

PORCH

FLOOR PLAN

0 _ _ _ _ 5

able free or for a nominal fee from the Owner-Builder Center, 1516 Fifth Street, Berkeley, CA 94710.

A worthwhile East Coast monthly newsletter, called *New England Builder,* has been recently introduced and appears to be a winner. Its articles are aimed at professional builders, but they are simply written so that the novice can also understand them. Again, many valuable ads make this paper a good source. The cost is $8 for 12 issues and may be ordered from NEB, Box 97, East Haven, VT 05837.

No one knows exactly what percentage of the houses built each year are owner-built. The exact definition is a bit fuzzy, and many owner-builders conceal their participation to mollify banks or building inspectors. Estimates run from 20 to 35%, depending upon how enthusiastic the group quoting the statistics is concerning self-help housing. Whatever the exact number, the movement is growing by leaps and bounds and has conventional contractors alarmed. A backlash by contractors and workers who feel that they are being cut out of their rightful work is likely. This puts an extra burden on you, the owner-builder, to build it right so that the opposition has no grounds for criticism. The going is hard, but it is your money that you are saving. There's nothing quite like the sense of satisfaction that comes from successfully completing a major project like your own house.

8 Structural Polystyrene Foam Houses

As the cost of labor has gobbled up an increasing portion of the housebuilding budget, home buyers have searched in vain for less labor-intensive construction methods. According to the American Productivity Center, a Houston nonprofit consultant, the construction industry is the only one in which production has dropped steadily since 1965. Their figures add up to a staggering 31% decline from 1965 to the present (*Wall Street Journal,* April 21, 1983). While owner-built houses, modulars, and trailers will help many hardworking people to own their own houses, the mass market is still left out in the cold. From a logical standpoint, our current procedure of building a house of thousands of small pieces of lumber and vainly trying to stuff insulation between them is ridiculous. The time is ripe for sweeping changes.

As energy prices sharply escalated, it became standard practice in northerly climates to cover the outside of a conventionally framed house with a layer of foam insulation sheathing. The extensive use of this material has brought the price down and has made it widely available. A few manufacturers have gone one step further by constructing the entire wall of polystyrene and eliminating the conventional framing altogether. Facing materials applied to both sides of the foam become the structure of the house. The resulting houses have an amazing degree of structural rigidity, far in excess of what you can get with conventional construction methods. Since these systems are so radically different from those currently in use, getting approval from building code officials and banks can be difficult. Most of the houses featured in this book make use of foam-core panels that are applied over a post-and-beam frame. In this way, I can get around problems with officialdom. However, the greatest potential for this method is to make the walls themselves load bearing.

At this writing, several manufacturers have distinguished themselves by designing and marketing load-bearing, foam-core housing systems. This building technique reduces air infiltration to a bare minimum, so the energy savings are tremendous. The houses require only 10 to 15% as much energy to heat and cool as conventional houses of similar size. The energy reductions are actual homeowner's in-use tests, not some engineer's estimate. The performance is actually much better than calculations would suggest. The improvement comes from eliminating the vertical air flow or chimney effect that occurs in stud walls with conventional fiberglass insulation. The roof losses are also considerably reduced, since there is no need for a ventilated attic space to wick heat to the outside. Let's examine each of the systems and compare their performance.

J-Deck, Inc.

This Columbus, Ohio, firm has been the leader in the development of foam-core panel houses. They have been using this technique for over 20 years and are now in full swing with mass production of the panels. Production capacity at the main plant is 15 houses per day. Jim Jackson, the president of J-Deck, has worked successfully to obtain code approval to use his panels as load-bearing walls. Do not assume that this means that all such panels are approved. As I understand the situation, each manufacturer has to get his own manufacturing process certified as acceptable. Since the panels are proliferating rapidly throughout the country, I would expect code standards for them to be established shortly. In the meantime, check the code carefully before you build.

Jackson's forte is low cost. He panelizes the entire house, including pressure-treated panels for the foundation. He claims that his 960-square-foot shell can be erected by three inexperienced men in one working day. The materials cost for this shell is less than $5000. The cost does not include doors and windows, which are cut in later. It does include completely finished exterior walls and ceiling. Finish roofing is applied after erection.

J-Deck has applied its system to a wide variety of buildings, including commercial structures and two-story apartment buildings. Except for their radical method of construction, the houses are of relatively ordinary design. Most of the houses in this book could be adapted to use this system since they were designed around 4-foot modules, and J-Deck's panels are each 4 by 8 feet. In case there are still any doubters out there, Jackson can supply photos and backup data from a certified testing laboratory showing three 4 by 8 panels supporting a superimposed load consisting of 10,000 pounds of concrete block.

Jim Jackson has recently announced that he is taking his unique system one step further. Five of his most popular models are offered as complete kits for the owner-builder. High-quality doors and windows are installed in the panels at the factory. All wood members are factory-stained, and every part is numbered for easy identification. Jim has even prepared a videotape of the erection process so that the completely unskilled can see just how it is done.

Delta Industries, Inc.

This second major foam-core panel manufacturer, located in Columbus, Ohio, has also obtained code approval for its panelized system. The trade name for the product is Thermacraft Houses. Delta recently purchased the system from U.S. Systems Corporation. Although the panels are similar to the J-Deck panels, Delta's houses are quite different because Delta's main thrust is energy efficiency, not low cost.

Delta has hired top-flight designers, and the plans show this care. They make extensive use of pressure-treated panels to produce a line of bermed houses. Since the grade is elevated around the house, the foundations can be shallow, saving considerable construction costs. Some of the savings is offset by the cost of backfilling around the house. These houses have been designed with their dramatic south glazing facing the street, but they are still cleverly arranged for privacy. The berming will also reduce noise if the house faces a busy city street. Delta likes to maintain control of erection so that it can ensure weathertight construction. All windows are set into place with foam spray insulation, and all panel joints are sprayed and caulked. The prices are more than those of J-Deck, but the quality designs may be worth it.

I have two favorites among the several houses in the berm series. The Terra Casa is a relatively large, three-bedroom, two-bath house with fine detailing and an excellent plan layout. A garage is beautifully integrated into the house and protects the living area from the north winds. Cathedral ceilings sweep up to a second-floor master bedroom suite. For 2200 square feet of fully erected shell, the price is less than $40,000. That's not rock-bottom budget, but this is a very elegant house.

Back in the lower-budget category, Delta markets a 900-square-foot bermed solar shed with attached greenhouse for about $16,000, fully erected. This is a story-and-a-half basic house that would be great as a starter house, retirement house, or vacation cottage. There is also a nice 960-square-foot house for about $12,000, erected. This price includes a roof and other finish work; therefore, the price cannot be directly compared to J-Deck's.

Integrated Building Systems

This Grand Haven, Michigan, firm uses curved panels with a 5½-inch-thick polystyrene core to make arches for earth-bermed structures. While the panels themselves are quite similar to those of the preceding manufacturers, the houses are quite unique; they can be likened to a large, buried Quonset hut. Floor plans are relatively large due to the minimum curvature of the arches, but they are well laid out. These houses cost about the same as a conventional above-ground house or considerably less than the usual concrete underground houses. They are dependent upon a uniform load condition for their structural stability, and the earthen berms could shift over the life of the house. A liquid synthetic rubber waterproofing material similar to the Gates material, which I recommend in Chapter 21, is used as a waterproofing membrane. This is an excellent material, but it might be difficult to apply uniformly on a nearly vertical curved surface. These houses are quite well-designed and appear well-constructed; I have some reservations about long-term durability, though.

Cubic Structures, Inc.

J-Deck and Delta have refined a system that has been around for several years. Cubic Structures has used the same core material, expanded polystyrene, to create an entirely new construction method. In its method, massive polystyrene blocks are tied together with concrete posts and bond beams, and then the entire structure is sprayed with concrete inside and out. The foam provides the formwork for all the concrete work so labor is reduced to a minimum. The result is a fireproof, virtually bombproof structure that can withstand tremendous loads. To prove its point, the company has a delightful publicity photo of a 7½-

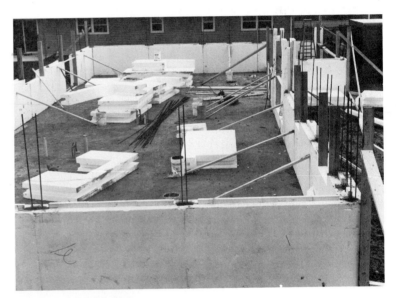

Solid polystyrene walls are reinforced with concrete posts at 4-foot intervals. The wall panel provides both insulation and form for the concrete.

Tapered roof panels are tied to bearing walls and then the entire structure is coated with a cement-based product called Insulcrete.

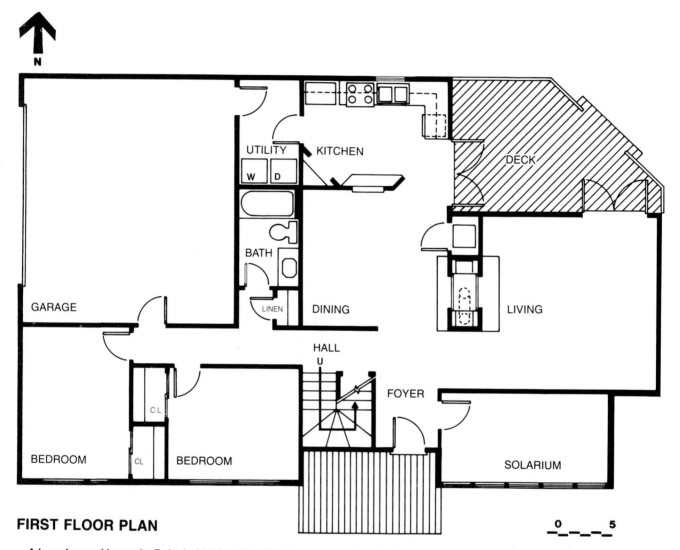

N

FIRST FLOOR PLAN

UTILITY

W   D

KITCHEN

DECK

BATH

GARAGE

LINEN   DINING

LIVING

HALL
U

FOYER

CL

CL

BEDROOM   BEDROOM

SOLARIUM

0 _ _ _ _ 5

A large bermed house by Delta Industries. Note that the garage forms a buffer on the north and west. A cathedral ceiling in the living room sweeps up to encompass a large master bedroom suite on the second floor. The first floor is a bit below original grade.

ton truck perched on top of the roof of one of their houses.

Cubic Structures also manufactures a product called Insulcrete, which is a modified portland cement coating for exterior insulation systems (see Chapter 19). The house design resulted from their involvement with this insulation system. The level of insulation in these houses is awesome. The walls have 12-inch-thick foam cores; the tapered roof averages 24 inches thick. Heating bills should be virtually nonexistent. For the winter of 1982–83, the bill for electric heat was only $118.

Materials costs for the system are quite high, but the labor costs are low, so the system balances

out as a net saver. When you consider that the heat and maintenance on these houses are almost nonexistent, they are quite a bargain. Cubic is aiming the system at the do-it-yourself market to make it competitive. The homeowner erects the foam panels on a prepared foundation and pours the concrete posts and the bond beams. Then Cubic sends in a franchised applicator to spray the Insulcrete coating on both sides of the structure. The remainder of the house is completed in conventional fashion.

Limitations

The major limitation to all four systems is in the mechanical trades. Wires, pipes, and the like are

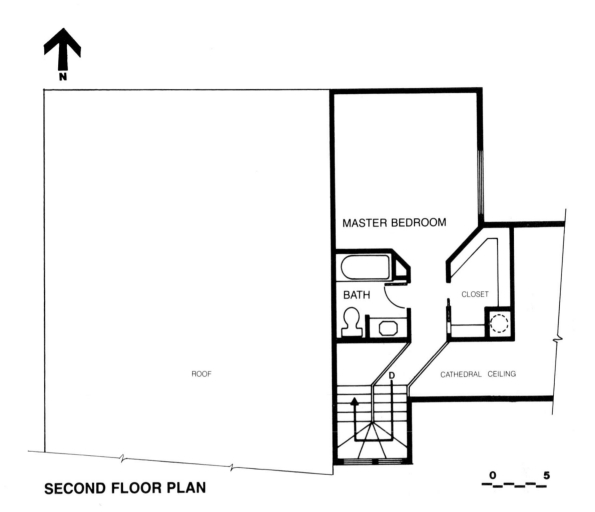

N

MASTER BEDROOM

BATH

CLOSET

ROOF

CATHEDRAL CEILING

D

0 — — — 5

SECOND FLOOR PLAN

almost impossible to install in these panels. J-Deck does provide a small raceway inside its panels, but it is difficult to use. Plumbing can be easily designed so that it doesn't have to run along an exterior wall. Restrictive electric codes demand that electric outlets be placed on *all* walls. The usual solution for electrical wiring is to use a baseboard raceway. These are fairly expensive and will offset some of the savings resulting from the panelized construction. (See Chapter 22 for detailed solutions.)

The other major limitation involves transportation. All four companies are located in the north-central part of the United States, so they are not likely to help someone as far away as Maine or California. And transportation costs are too high to transport a whole house more than 400 miles. The companies are working on franchising the process to suppliers spotted around the country, and you may want to check with the companies to see if they have a franchise in your area.

9 Rammed-Earth Construction

Rammed-earth construction is a centuries-old building technique that the energy crisis and high construction costs have helped revive. Even though it is a virtually unknown technique in our country today, it is probably the most pervasive building technique of all time. The Chinese used this method to build their Great Wall several centuries before the birth of Christ. There are other examples that are hundreds of years old throughout Europe and Asia. For those who wish to explore the history further, there is a comprehensive book, *Down to Earth* by Jean Dethier (Thames and Hudson, England, 1982; available also from Facts on File, New York). Although the text is dotted with historical and factual inaccuracies, it contains a fascinating collection of earthen architecture. Dethier's nationalism shows, since he erroneously credits much of the development of rammed-earth construction to France, and he completely leaves out North America and Australia, continents that both have significant examples of this architecture.

Rammed-earth structures are constructed by hand or machine by compacting a carefully selected sand-clay mixture within restraining formwork until the material reaches a dense, stonelike consistency.

As a small child, I remember being shown a rammed-earth church in Stateburg, South Carolina. (I had announced at the tender age of five that I was going to become an architect.) An elderly architect friend of the family took me under his wing and proceeded to show me the more interesting architectural sites of my native state. Mr. Ellington astounded me by telling me that this elegant church was made of plain dirt, obviously unaware of the fact that it was actually constructed in 1857 and is a strong testimonial to the durability of this building type. Stateburg, South Carolina, has a climate characterized by torrential rains and hurricanes that test the mettle of any building. One of my clients has built a new house very close to a rammed-earth barn that was constructed by a French Canadian around the turn of the century. It, too, is still in excellent condition.

A small development of federally funded rammed-earth houses was built in Gardendale, Alabama, in 1936. The houses are all still occupied and in good shape, which is more than one can say for most other houses built in low-cost developments that long ago. The U.S. Department of Agriculture and the Portland Cement Association have both done extensive research on stabilized soils for paving and building materials. Stabilized soil is a sand-clay mixture to which one adds a small amount (5 to 15%) of asphalt or portland cement. In 1940, the U.S. Bureau of Standards conducted tests of various types of construction materials for four different loading conditions. The bureau compared rammed earth and soil cement (or stabilized soil), both 14 inches thick, with 8-inch-thick brick, block, and tile walls. They also compared a 6-inch-thick wood frame wall with the others. The stabilized rammed-earth wall outperformed all the other masonry materials in all four of the tests. In two of the four tests, the frame wall performed better than any of the masonry materials.

Full details of the testing are described in the out-of-print book, *The Rammed Earth House* by Anthony Merrill (Harper and Brothers, 1947). A good technical library should have a copy. The Portland Cement Association publishes two engineering bulletins on soil cements. The *PCA Soil Primer* EB007.04S and *Soil-Cement Construction Handbook* EB003.09S are available for $2 each from PCA, 5420 Old Orchard Road, Skokie, IL 60077. At the moment, they are the only good technical references on the subject available in this country. The PCA bulletins are intended for use for road and airport construction, but many of the principles are equally applicable to house building. A truly fine Australian book on all aspects of earthen construction is *The Earth Builder's Companion* by John and Gerry Archer (Grass Roots, 1981; available from the Owner-Builder Center, 1516 Fifth Street, Berkeley, CA 94710). All these references will be useful when confronting a dubious building inspector. Rammed earth is not a common building technique, and getting approval from the powers that be may take some doing.

If rammed earth is such a widespread building technique and such a good one, why is it so rare? Because there is simply no one with a vested interest in promoting the material. It employs mostly materials available right on the site and does not use much in the way of expensive equipment. No one stands to make a profit except the individual homebuilder; hence, no one has anything to sell and we have a "forgotten" technique. Also, there is the problem of labor—traditional rammed-earth techniques required laborious hand tamping and frequent repositioning of small forms.

Modern Designs

In the United States, one young California architect, David Easton, deserves most of the credit for the renaissance of rammed-earth building. He has used those architectural skills that are usually employed to design intricate but unbuildable structures to devise methods for building economically with rammed earth. Using his techniques, he can construct all the rammed-earth walls for a medium-size house in just one day. David's techniques are described in consider-able detail in his privately published book, *The Rammed Earth Experience,* available for $12 postpaid from Blue Mountain Press, Blue Mountain Road, Wilseyville, CA 95257.

The secret to David's success with rammed earth lies in his unique form system, which consists of a movable plywood box 6 feet long by 7 feet high by 14 inches wide. The forms are heavily constructed of 1⅛-inch subflooring plywood, braced laterally with 2 × 10s at 16-inch centers. Fourteen pipe clamps (a row of seven at each end) hold the form together as well as provide support for the end boards. The pipes that support the 1⅛-inch end pieces have removable wedges that make for easy form removal. Beveled 2 by 6 keyways are attached to the inside of the end boards to form an interlock for adjacent panels. David makes every other panel with 6-foot gaps between and then goes back and fills in the voids.

In order to be able to use his large formwork panels, David uses a specially designed concrete foundation. The foundation has a 1 × 2 recess at the top on each side, making a tongue exactly 14 inches wide. The large form is set down on the foundation, with the bottom two pipe clamps and the recesses in the concrete providing a solid base for the form. A compressor and a pneumatic tamper are then used to tamp the soil-cement mixture into place in the forms. Since the walls are quite heavy, good footings are important. In areas with a mild climate, David uses a 12-inch-thick reinforced concrete footing; in areas with a deep frost line, he recommends a gravel trench footing such as I describe in Chapter 18.

The walls are only constructed 7 feet tall to provide a natural break point for the heads of the windows and doors. Above the 7-foot point, David constructs a concrete tie beam, which serves as a header for doors and windows and as a structural element to tie the top of the building together and provide anchorage for the roof or second-floor structure. David uses redwood or cedar for his form boards and leaves the form in place as a decorative trim element.

Electrical and plumbing work are carefully planned beforehand, and the pipes and conduits are embedded right into the rammed walls. Electrical conduits are placed vertically in the walls, with lateral runs in the floor, or concealed in the roof or floor beams at the top of the wall. Conduit and piping survive the ramming process without difficulty, but electrical boxes have to be reinforced with wooden wedges to prevent the forces from collapsing them.

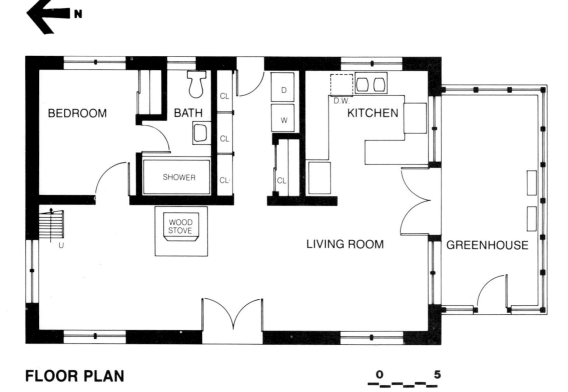

N

FLOOR PLAN

BEDROOM

BATH

CL

CL

CL

SHOWER

WOOD
STOVE

U

D

W

CL

D.W.

KITCHEN

LIVING ROOM

GREENHOUSE

0 _ _ _ _ 5

David Easton's rammed-earth cottage has unusually massive walls. A sleeping loft is tucked under the eaves. This house is designed for a narrow, south-facing site with a greenhouse on one end.

The west view of David Easton's house has massive, rammed-earth walls topped with a sod roof.

The finish of rammed-earth walls is particularly attractive in its natural state. A 50–50 mix of linseed oil and turpentine (the same finish often used for oak frames) makes a good final finish or a base for paint. If the outside is to be left exposed, I recommend two coats of 5% silicone masonry waterproofing compound. Buried portions of the walls can be waterproofed in similar fashion to masonry walls. In cold climates, insulation will be necessary to meet energy codes and to keep heating requirements at a reasonable level. Two or three inches of blue Styrofoam should be used just as on a masonry wall, not forgetting to insulate the bond beam. The exterior finish can be Plekko or Drivit, as described in Chapter 19.

Insulation

David's houses are built in relatively mild climates, so he does not have to confront the problems of insulation. Rammed earth, like its earthen cousin, adobe, faces a continuing controversy with the engineering establishment over the necessity, amount, and proper application of insulation. Various federal and state bureaucracies have decreed that earthen walls, even very thick ones in mild climates, must be insulated before they will meet regulations for government loans or state building codes. Even though such buildings have been built for centuries and have been relatively easily heated and cooled, the engineers say that they must have insulation.

All sorts of subtle factors that can significantly affect the heating and cooling of a building are not factored into the rigid formulas in vogue with the engineering community. Studies reported in *Solar Age* (July 1983) have shown that the traditional, commonly accepted R values for insulation are not at all accurate for heavily insulated houses. It seems that the engineers who originally devised the system didn't conceive of R-40 walls and R-60 roofs, and their formulas, when pushed up to those high values, become quite inaccurate.

Devotees of heavy mass buildings, such as adobe, rammed-earth, and log construction, have similar complaints with the accepted methods for calculating heat losses. Standard heat loss calculations are based upon a relatively thin stud wall in which hollow spaces are filled with a relatively low-mass insulating material, such as fiberglass. There is nothing in these formulas to account for heavy mass walls that absorb and transmit heat slowly. Even though earth and logs are relatively poor insulators, they absorb considerable quantities of heat, and it takes a long time for the heat to penetrate them. There is also something of a flywheel effect that helps to reduce heating and cooling requirements. All this is difficult, if not impossible, to prove using standard engineering formulas. But it can easily be proven by the residents of such buildings. Temperatures stay reasonable and heating and cooling bills are low, despite engineering calculations that indicate the contrary.

I am reminded of a story by David Wright, the noted passive solar architect, who revised a plan for some clients to provide passive solar heating through south-facing solar glass. In the design revision, he eliminated most glass on the other three faces and concentrated it on the south wall. His calculations showed that about 80% of the heat would be supplied by the sun. The engineers for the power company, using standard tables, announced that David had doubled the heating load. Subsequent occupants of the house proved that the "experts" were wrong and that David's calculations actually erred on the conservative side. Similar owner testimonials are available for earthen buildings. Your state code, building inspector, or bank may disagree, but from my own experience with such buildings, I would recommend insulation only for climates with winter heating loads in excess of 4000 degree-days.

Adobe Versus Rammed Earth

While we are on the subject of insulation, we should compare rammed earth with adobe, since they are, in many ways, so similar. To be practical, the rammed-earth wall has to be constructed as a monolithic unit of full thickness. If insulation is used, it must be installed on either the inner or outer face of the wall. This means that another finish material must be added to the surface of the insulating board. Adobe, on the other hand, is made up of individual sun-baked bricks. It is relatively easy to build a cavity adobe wall and place the insulation between the wythes of brick. This avoids any extra materials expense and takes little extra time to install.

Adobe construction is much more common than rammed earth and has been described fully in many books and publications. The best of these is the Archer book I mentioned earlier in reference to rammed earth. Adobe shares many of the advantages of rammed earth, except that making the adobe bricks is a very slow process. Thousands of small units must be made by hand and then laid up in a wall using basically the same skills required for laying normal brick. I feel that the rammed-earth technique is much better suited for the owner-builder. It is certainly a better deal for a contractor; paying labor to produce adobe bricks these days would be prohibitive.

Materials

Adobe and rammed earth share the benefit of using materials readily available on the site and not requiring energy-intensive transportation of materials over long distances. As the energy crunch continues and fuel prices escalate, this factor will make the advantages of these materials even more attractive. You cannot take just any old material and use it for ramming or adobe. All topsoil and organic materials must be excluded. The ratio of sand to clay for rammed earth should be 30% clay to 70% sand. Since this rarely occurs in nature, you will have to alter the mix by adding appropriate materials. Addition of a stabilizing material such as portland cement or asphalt strengthens the mix and makes the exact composition less critical. The methods for analyzing the soil and determining the exact ratio of sand to clay are too lengthy to describe here. The *PCA Soil Primer* gives a good technical description, while the Archer and Easton books give excellent "seat of the pants" methods for determining composition of soils. Easton has a simple and obvious method of mixing the materials. He uses a standard garden tractor with a garden tiller and mixes the dry materials right on the ground.

Floors

Although David Easton usually pours a concrete floor slab, rammed earth is equally at home for a floor. In fact, it makes an excellent slab-on-grade floor for any house, whether the rest of the structure is rammed earth or not. The price of materials is certainly right. A particularly handsome floor can be made by constructing a gridwork of redwood or cedar in a square or rectangular pattern. Two- to three-foot modules will work best, depending upon your floor plan—choose a module that works well with the layout of the building. For my houses with 8-foot bay spacing, 2-foot squares would be ideal; for David's houses, 18 inches or 3 feet should be used. My clients who have used this technique found that using about 15% cement in their soil-cement mixture worked best; they tamped the mixture down with a hydraulic tamper. You can also use a somewhat wetter mixture, leaving out the wooden dividers and substituting score lines to simulate tile. After the floor has thoroughly dried, it can be sealed with the same linseed oil–turpentine mixture I recommended you use to coat the walls. The final finish can be paste wax or polyurethane. If the floor is not thoroughly dry and well-sealed, the urethane will discolor. Be safe and use the wax.

Plans

Finding a plan suitable for a rammed-earth house may take a bit of looking. Many plans designed for masonry houses would be suitable. Any of the Finnish houses shown in Chapter 4 would be ideal for this technique, with the prefabricated masonry houses with a center bearing wall being the best suited. In addition to the house shown in this chapter, David has other plans for sale; he also runs workshops for those who are interested in learning the technique directly. He can be contacted through Blue Mountain Press. This is a fine money- and energy-saving technique, and I hope to see it catch on and become a common building method.

10 Underground Houses of Pressure-Treated Wood

The energy crisis has spawned an amazingly large group of devotees of underground housing. Dozens of books have been written on the subject; some have enjoyed time on best-seller lists. Unfortunately, most of these houses are constructed of concrete, which is heavy and expensive. I get hundreds of letters from would-be builders of underground houses who are on a limited budget. My general advice has been to steer clear of this building type because it requires careful custom structural design and expensive construction detailing to ensure success. I have steered many of these builders to earth-bermed houses rather than completely buried structures because the structural requirements for bermed houses are essentially the same as those for basements; normal construction methods can be used. Recent design innovations permit the use of pressure-treated wood rather than concrete as a structural medium. This technique considerably reduces the cost of materials as well as eliminates much of the special skill required for actual construction. No matter how you go, underground construction is relatively new, and you should carefully weigh the advantages, disadvantages, and special precautions involved before you decide to build this way.

Advantages

The biggest single advantage of an underground house is the drastic reduction in heating and cooling costs. A fully buried house with only the south wall exposed, one that uses state-of-the-art insulation and shuttering techniques, requires little or no supplemental heat in moderate climates.

The house still needs good insulation, but the earth cover acts as a buffer against extremes of air temperature. In many cases, you can achieve almost the same performance levels by berming the walls and superinsulating a conventional roof structure. If the enormous costs of the heavy roof structure and superwaterproofing required in an underground building are channeled into extra roof insulation instead, the total cost will be less and the performance very similar.

Those of us who abhor noise are very fond of underground houses. The mass of earth around you is quite effective at damping out traffic, lawnmowers, and other obnoxious creations of modern society. Going underground may let you take advantage of a low-cost lot that would be objectionably noisy or have unacceptable views if you were to build a conventionally designed house on it.

Underground houses with fully buried roofs also make sense from a land-use standpoint. In densely populated areas, an underground house can occupy most of the usable area on the lot. If you have a flat, buried roof, the top of your house can easily become a garden or other outdoor space. A properly designed house of this sort is virtually

An underground house on which I consulted. Backup heat is rarely needed. Note the level of the earth mound at right.

invisible to the passerby. Many people argue quite logically that it makes sense to use otherwise unsuitable land for underground housing and save valuable flatlands for agricultural purposes. Farmland is being consumed so rapidly by the housing industry that we face shortages in the near future. Several states are enacting laws to preserve farmland and prevent its use for development. In the future we will see increasing use of "difficult" sites for new houses.

Disadvantages

Your greatest stumbling block to building an underground house will probably be acceptance. Banks, building inspectors, and neighbors are all likely to be hostile to the concept. We live in a conformist society, and living beneath ground level is certainly not conforming. The bank will look at the house from a resale standpoint, and they will be likely to tell you that the extra costs incurred in building underground cannot be recouped in the sale of the house. If they take this attitude, they will either limit the amount they will lend or flatly turn you down.

Since this type of construction is more demanding than conventional building types, neither the bank nor the building inspector is likely to look with favor on amateur owner-builders. Many building codes contain clauses prohibiting the use of basements for living space. The typical inspector charged with enforcement of this code may very well determine that your entire house is a basement and is therefore illegal as living space. Neighborhood groups have actually gone to court

and won the right to have offending structures demolished. Although attitudes are rapidly changing and most of these pitfalls are unlikely, it will pay to check very carefully before you commit yourself to a piece of property that is ideal for an underground house, but not for much else.

Underground houses of reinforced concrete construction typically cost double the amount of conventional houses. True, energy costs are drastically reduced and there are no exposed walls nor roof to maintain, but raising the additional money and paying interest may just make such a house out of the question for you. Fortunately, the innovative construction techniques that I describe in this chapter considerably narrow this cost gap. If you are able to do the construction yourself, you may even be able to beat construction costs for an aboveground house.

No matter who does the construction work or what structural system is used, excavation, drainage, waterproofing, and backfilling are much more critical than in a conventional structure. If you build completely underground, you are actually building a pressure vessel, and the tiniest leak will spell disaster. Even experience is no guarantee of success. A very reputable construction firm that has built several underground structures is currently being sued because a new office structure for a nearby town leaks like a sieve. The structure is located beneath a parking lot, and no one wants to foot the bill for digging it up to find out what went wrong. Let this be a lesson. Do it right the first time; repair costs can be astronomical.

Even if you do not have any outright leaks, dampness can be a problem. In dry, arid climates, this can actually be a benefit, but most parts of North America are not arid and will require forced ventilation or even dehumidification to control moisture buildup in underground houses. The resultant electrical consumption will offset some of the energy savings inherent in these structures.

Underground houses also impose planning restraints upon the house designer. Building codes and common sense dictate that bedrooms and all major living spaces have access windows for fire safety. Moreover, due to the extremely heavy roof loads, structural spans are limited; this results in relatively narrow rooms or exposed structural posts. Underground houses built with these constraints tend to have long, narrow plans with the south wall exposed. Although this is an ideal shape for solar gain, the size of your lot can easily limit the size of your house.

Special Precautions

Do not even consider building an underground house in clay soil without advice from a soils engineer. Certain types of clay can increase their dry volume by 22 times when water is added. In fact, clay of this type, called bentonite, is actually used as a waterproofing material. The dry clay is placed in corrugated cardboard sheets that are applied to the surface to be waterproofed. When the clay becomes wet, it expands and forms a watertight membrane. This same expansive property can spell disaster for foundations or underground houses. These clays can exert tons of force on a structure, collapsing walls and sometimes pushing the structure out of the ground. Even excavating large quantities of clay from around the structure will only diminish the expansion, not eliminate it.

Clays that do not expand dramatically can still exert a force of over 100 pounds per cubic foot per foot of depth below the surface. By contrast, sand and gravel exert only about 40 pounds per cubic foot. These are dry weights; saturated materials will increase the pressure by 62 pounds per cubic foot for every foot of depth. A wall designed to withstand 40 pounds per square foot of dry gravel, which is subjected to 160 pounds per square foot of wet clay, will be very likely to fail.

With these conditions in mind, any underground structure except one built against a rock cliff or into a bank of solid sand or gravel requires that you thoroughly excavate around the exterior walls. Starting about 2 feet away from the footing, the earth should be excavated to at least a 60-degree angle sloping away from the wall, and a perforated drain tile should be placed at the bottom of the footing. The resulting excavation should be backfilled with a well-graded gravel tamped in 12-inch layers that slope slightly away from the house. Then the gravel should be topped with a thin layer of dense clay to prevent surface water from penetrating the gravel backfill. On occasion I have used insulation board and polyethylene to divert the unwanted water. If you go this route, a second perforated drain tile should be placed at the edge of this barrier to catch the water. This second drain is particularly vital if you have a fully buried roof or if the grade slopes toward the house. This backfilling method will cost you considerable extra money, but the extra expense should buy you a lifetime of confidence in the integrity of your structure.

If you are in an area of more than 2000 degree-days, insulation is a must for your underground structure. Ground temperatures typically stay in the mid-50s year-round. If you are in an area where summer cooling is of prime importance, you may not want to insulate against this temperature. In very humid climates, the insulation is necessary even in summer to prevent condensation problems. In cold climates, installation of the insulation is vital. Not only must the concrete be insulated against the cool earth, but the edges of slabs, parapets, and the like must be insulated as well. Concrete absorbs heat readily and transmits it easily. This property makes it ideal as a

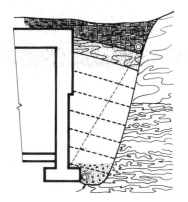

Use care in backfilling underground walls. The original material must be excavated beyond the 60-degree line (dashed in the illustration). Fill should be granular and placed in 18-inch layers sloped slightly away from the house. Cap the granular fill with a layer of clay and provide a second drain tile to catch surface runoff before it penetrates the backfill.

heat-storage medium, but it means that you must insulate all exposed portions or the concrete will wick the heat right out of the house. When insulating concrete underground structures, I usually recommend 2 to 4 inches of blueboard closed-cell extruded polystyrene. The brand usually available is Styrofoam. If the underground structure is detailed in such a way that the insulation is within the wall cavity or otherwise protected, urethane or expanded polystyrene can be used instead; you'll find that both are cheaper than the closed-cell extruded polystyrene in terms of installed R value.

Structural designs for underground houses are much more demanding than those for conventional aboveground structures. Run-of-the mill designers and engineers are not usually competent to design such structures, so if you purchase plans for such a house, you should check that they come from a reputable source. It is also very important to make sure that the design loads are not exceeded. A design for a sod-roofed structure with 1 foot of earth cover will not work for a typical earth-insulated roof with 3 feet of cover. According to research by the Rural Housing Research Unit (RRU) at Clemson University, it costs four times as much to construct such a roof as to build a conventional roof insulated to comparable levels.

The standard solution to these heavy loads is to build the roof of poured or precast concrete. Contrary to general beliefs, concrete is not a magical, superpermanent material. Just because you are using concrete, do not think that you have an infallible structure. Concrete is very strong in compression, which makes it ideal for domes and curved shell structures, for, if properly designed, these are always in compression. There have been some truly delightful underground structures built using free-form concrete, but these tend to be expensive and not suited to most tastes. Flat-slab concrete construction needs expertly designed and placed reinforcing steel to perform properly. You also need to build a very heavy temporary structure to hold the slab while the concrete cures. It will surprise most people to discover that concrete is a plastic, not a rigid, material. Under constant heavy load, even properly designed concrete slabs gradually deflect (sag) over the years. Interior partitions can be cracked or crushed by this deflection. Water can puddle in the center of your roof rather than drain off. So if you're planning on building a concrete roof, precautions must be taken, such as crowning the slab for drainage and installing a compressive material over the top plate of interior partitions.

If you do decide to use concrete for your structure, I would strongly recommend that you use prestressed concrete planks for your roof. Although these are expensive and require heavy machinery to install, you have much better control of quality, and you have the resources of the precast company to fall back on for the proper design of your roof. The supporting exterior walls can be either poured reinforced concrete or heavily reinforced block, either conventional or surface bonded. The precast planks must be securely anchored to these walls. This can be accomplished by weld plates cast into the bottoms of the ends of the planks and welded to a steel angle atop the wall. The alternate method is to fasten the planks with anchor bolts set in the wall; however, these can be difficult to align properly. The weld plates are easier, but more expensive, and they require hiring an additional trade.

Sources of Information

The material in this chapter is of necessity a brief overview with emphasis upon techniques that I find lower the cost and make construction easier. For those who are serious about underground construction and wish to read further, I have compiled a list of little-known, but very worthwhile sources. For a thorough study of minimum-cost underground construction, I recommend the publication, *Alternatives in Energy Conservation; The Use of Earth-Covered Buildings* (Stock No. 038-000-002864, Superintendent of Documents, U.S. Government Printing Office, Washington, DC 20402). It's quite a bargain at $3.25.

The second book is an elementary textbook for concrete design. If you do go ahead with a concrete structure and want to design and build it yourself, this book is a must: *Simplified Design of Building Foundations* by James Ambrose (John Wiley & Sons, 1981). It is also an excellent reference even for those beginning builders who are only pouring a floor slab or a few footings. And it's invaluable for people who are building retaining walls or anything tricky; check your local library for a copy.

For the absolutely best book on details for underground structures, I recommend *Builders Manual and Design Guide for Earth-Sheltered Construction* by Brent Anderson and Charles A. Lane (Concrete Construction Publications, 1983). The magazine, *Concrete Construction,* by the same publisher, contains a wealth of valuable information on this subject. A collection of reprints on earth-sheltered construction is available for $4 from Concrete Construction Publications, 426

South Westgate, Addison, IL 60101. Back issues of their magazine are also available; the June 1982 issue has several important articles on earth-sheltered housing.

For those who anticipate problems, I recommend *Earth Sheltered Housing: Code, Zoning and Financing Issues,* prepared for the U.S. Department of Housing and Urban Development (HUD) by the Underground Space Center, University of Minnesota. Copies are available for $4 from HUD User, Box 280, Germantown, MD 20767.

Designs of Pressure-Treated Wood

There is no question that there are considerable advantages to building underground. Unfortunately, the bottom line is that the high costs of conventional concrete construction put these houses out of reach for most of us. Again, we are indebted to RRU and the U.S. Department of Agriculture (USDA) for a breakthrough in the cost of earth-sheltered houses. The RRU/USDA group has been doing solid research on low-cost housing for many years. Their Solar Attic house, which is described more fully in Chapter 12, is famous for reducing the cost and complexity of solar heated and cooled structures to make them affordable for the average homeowner. Now, they have worked their magic upon earth-sheltered structures. Their system of pressure-treated walls for below-grade structures is the outgrowth of decades of hard work to reduce housing costs.

Jerry O. Newman, one of the prime movers in this venture, has written a fine evaluation paper on a low-cost panelized house that utilized pressure-treated prefabricated wood panels for the foundation. Even though this research took place almost 10 years ago, the designs and techniques they developed are still viable today. A 960-square-foot house was completely finished in 1976 for less than $10,000. Of course, construction costs have more than doubled since then, but the savings are still impressive. Newman's evaluation, Bulletin #1544, is still available (Stock No. 001-000-03609-2, Superintendent of Documents, U.S. Government Printing Office, Washington, DC 20402).

The results of this early study were applied to the development of a panelized system for constructing the walls of the earth-sheltered house shown on the next page with pressure-treated lumber. The walls are assembled from 4 × 10-foot panels that can be either shop- or job-fabricated. Framing for the panels is 2 × 6s set at 1 foot on-center. A double plate is used at the top and bottom of the panels and is offset to tie the panels together. These panels are 10 feet tall because of the inclusion of a 2-foot-deep crawl space for rock storage and heat distribution for the solar heating system. Two-inch-thick extruded polystyrene is used to insulate the crawl space, and the upper-floor walls are insulated with fiberglass. RRU performed a careful analysis of the costs of this wall versus a site-built reinforced concrete block wall. The pressure-treated wood wall cost almost exactly a third as much as the block wall. In addition, the inevitable delays due to weather and unpredictable masons were also eliminated. As you can see, this puts the cost of an underground house back in league with a conventional aboveground structure.

High-quality materials are a must. The framing lumber and plywood must be free from knots and damaging defects; fasteners should be of stainless steel. Do not use galvanized or aluminum nails. They disintegrate rapidly under certain soil conditions.

The wall panels I just described are only one part of the carefully designed system for the entire house. The roof and floor structures are designed as massive beams to support the earth-sheltered walls. Lateral partitions provide additional bracing at approximately 12-foot intervals. Obviously, the same system could be used without a crawl space, with a concrete slab providing bracing for the bottom of the panels (the panels would then be shortened to 8 feet long). I would not increase the spacing of the lateral partitions unless I also thickened the panels; this is a job for a professional, not an amateur. If you use the system, use it as it is or get outside help with the design.

RRU has gone to great lengths to detail their house thoroughly. There are 23 sheets to the set of working drawings. This is the most completely detailed set of drawings I have ever seen, except for the extraordinary set for Charles Haynes's house, which I talk about in Chapter 7. Since much of the construction is unusual and critical, this attention to detail is very welcome. For ordering information, see Chapter 12.

The energy statistics for this house are amazing. RRU calculates that the earth berming reduces the heating requirements by 50% over an aboveground house. Reclaimed heat from the house, which is transferred to rock storage, reduces heating requirements by another 10%. The solar heating system, which combines domestic hot water and space heating, provides 35% of the space heating and 70% of the domestic hot water

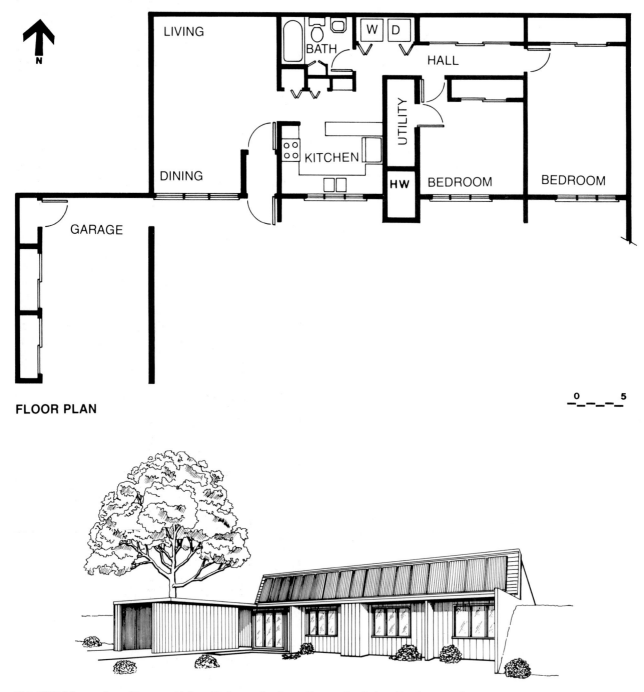

FLOOR PLAN

This USDA house from Clemson University has a simple, well-organized plan. Roof trusses incorporate solar collectors on the south face that preheat domestic hot water and provide space heating.

supply. With careful water conservation and a bit more insulation, any additional backup heating could probably be eliminated. As designed, the system has a 6-gallon, high-recovery, backup electric water heater and resistance coils in the furnace. The house contains 1080 square feet of floor area and is very efficiently laid out for such a small house. The novel solar heating system consumes only a tiny fraction of the floor space; most of the mechanism is in the attic and the crawl space.

The solar system has two storage mediums. In the first, the hot air from the collectors is passed over three water storage tanks, where it gives up much of its heat. And then this same air, no longer hot but still warm, is passed over rock storage. This two-medium system works because the collector channels are horizontal rather than vertical, enabling the collector air to get much hotter than it would in conventional designs. By passing the air over the tanks first, heat is stored for both domestic hot water and space heating. The furnace is designed to pass air over these same tanks to provide space heating for the house. The rock storage also releases heat to the living area. Since the system uses inexpensive site-built collectors and combines water heating with space heating, the overall cost is quite reasonable. I find this to be an elegant small house and think it is well worth your consideration. The plan even makes great sense for an aboveground house if underground doesn't appeal to you.

Buried Wooden Roofs

If you are a purist and want a fully underground house, you may want to consider building your roof structure of heavy timbers rather than of poured or precast concrete. If you go this route, I strongly recommend that you use the timbers for the roof only, and build masonry or concrete walls to support the earth pressure. It is of course possible to make both walls and roof of wood, but the roof must support thrust from the top of the wall as well as vertical loading from the soil above. I prefer to use a wooden roof structure and bolt it to the top of a masonry wall. If you do a thorough job of waterproofing and build your roof with a positive slope, I see no need for using pressure-treated timbers. If you employ all pressure-treated wood in the sizes necessary to support earth cover, your cost will approach that of concrete construction.

I recommend native, roughsawn, support timbers spaced 3 feet apart, covered with 3 × 6 tongue-and-groove planking. The maximum safe span for this system is 10 to 12 feet. The illustration shows a safe design for a structure similar in size to that of the RRU house. It is designed for 3 feet of earth cover and a 50-pound snow load (425 pounds per square foot total). Note that the loads in the center of the house are supported by

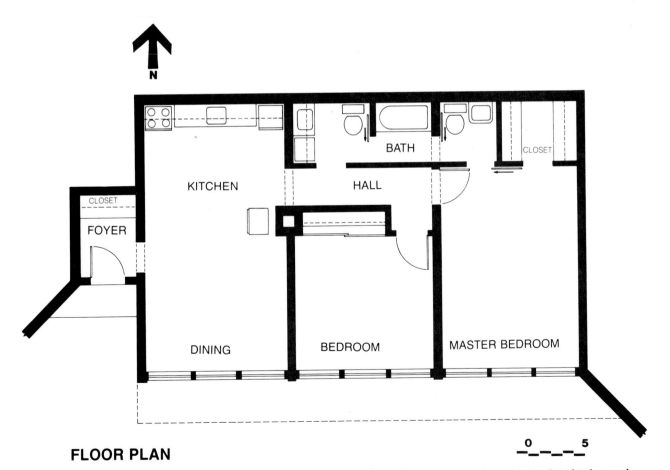

FLOOR PLAN

This small, masonry-walled underground house has lateral bearing walls to allow a short-span, wood-framed roof to be used to support an earth-covered roof deck.

the lateral walls. The load on each of these walls is over 50,000 pounds. Needless to say, they require very sturdy footings to prevent differential settlement. The exterior walls carry only one-half as much roof load; again, the services of a soils engineer are required.

To insulate your roof, I recommend rigid urethane board, such as Thermax, or High-R. It is readily available in 2-inch-thick, 4 × 8 sheets. I would use 2, 4, or 6 inches, depending upon the severity of your climate. A 6-mil polyethylene vapor barrier should be applied over the wood decking before the insulation board is nailed in place. For a roofing and/or waterproofing membrane, I recommend EPDM synthetic rubber, such as in the Carlisle system, or Bituthene as described in Chapter 21. I would enclose the entire building in an envelope of this rubber. If you economize and use small sheets from scrap, you will have more work to do sealing the joints. Even just one improperly sealed spot will produce a nasty leak, and the extra joints do increase the possibilities

for error. Weigh this carefully against the considerable cost savings of using leftover materials.

By following these recommendations, you can achieve a high-quality, buried roof for less than half the cost of a concrete structure. If you have a good supply of native timbers, access to EPDM rubber, and do all your own work, your roof could even cost less than a conventional one. And you will have the added bonus of a handsome, finished, beamed ceiling, much better-looking than raw concrete.

A final postscript: As I finish the final draft for this chapter, the local radio station has just announced that the outside temperature is 98°F. The thermometer on the wall above my desk registers just 73°F. Of course, I have moved my typewriter down to the bottom level of my hillside house where three of the four walls are completely buried. This gives you an idea just how dramatic the benefits of earth sheltering can be.

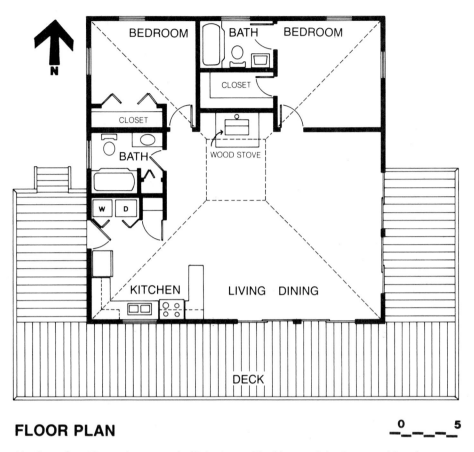

N

BEDROOM   BATH   BEDROOM

CLOSET

CLOSET

BATH

WOOD STOVE

W   D

KITCHEN   LIVING   DINING

DECK

FLOOR PLAN

0 _ _ _ _ 5

Northern Counties makes several efficient, good-looking models at reasonable prices.
The Rotunda shown here is space-efficient and cost-effective.

from a 576-square-foot, one-bedroom efficiency up to a 1936-square-foot monster. The 1024-square-foot model can be purchased with either two or three bedrooms and is the most sensible size. The larger houses are expensive and waste a great deal of space in the center.

The Blue Ridge and Mont Blanc series are steep-roofed chalets with a glass gable and deck on the south. They range from a 700-square-foot cabin with one bedroom and a large loft, to a 1600-square-foot, five-bedroom model. There are at least a dozen variations on this theme. These houses are priced at the low end of the scale and are quite a bargain. They are designed with pressure-treated post foundations so that they can be adapted to a wide variety of terrains.

The Sierra is a well-designed passive solar house with a steeply pitched roof and a center chimney. The 1600-square-foot plan contains a two-story sunspace next to the chimney, as well as three bedrooms. The square floor plan and steep roof expose a minimum of area to the weather. The shell package costs $26,000 and is quite a bargain

for such a house. High-quality materials are used throughout, and the company will make any reasonable changes or substitutions.

Northern Counties welcomes custom designs and will build to your design. Unfortunately, this is only one company, and shipping costs are such that their market is limited to the southeastern states. If you are a long way from this region, you might try to encourage one of your local companies to build something along the lines of one of Northern Counties' houses.

The old standby of high-quality manufactured houses, Acorn Structures, has bowed to economic pressures and produced a lower-priced series called the Cottage Houses. These range from $25,000 to $40,000 for the unerected shell. These houses are a bit smaller, but of somewhat higher quality than the houses of Northern Counties. Since Northern Counties is in Virginia and Acorn is in Massachusetts, you will probably be dealing with one or the other rather than having the option of comparing their merits. Acorn certainly has one of the finest reputations of any company any-

Manufactured Houses

There are hundreds of manufacturers scattered around the country making what the industry calls manufactured houses. Unlike modulars or trailers, these houses are made in large, flat sections that are put together at the site by a crane and a crew of workmen. As a general rule, these manufactured houses come in two varieties: poorly designed and cheap, or well-designed and expensive. The firms that do manufacture well-insulated houses of good design, typified by Acorn Structures, usually market large, expensive houses for the well-to-do on a low-volume basis. For some reason, manufacturers in the United States always equate good taste and value with exorbitant price tags. Nowhere is this more evident than in the manufactured house industry.

A distant cousin of the manufactured house is the precut or kit house where the owner or contractor is furnished with a truckload of unassembled parts that accomplish the same end. This type of house can produce major savings for the owner-builder; much smaller ones for a professional contractor. Some good examples of this type are covered in detail in the next chapter.

My research has uncovered exactly one manufacturer that bridges the gap between the two varieties of manufactured houses. Not only does this manufacturer bridge the gap, it bridges it with an awesome variety of well-designed houses in all sizes and price classes. These elegant houses are manufactured by a company called Northern Counties (Box 97, Upperville, VA 22176). Prices for the smaller houses range from $7000 to $15,000 unerected, to $10,000 to $20,000 for the same houses erected. All of their houses come in a wide range of sizes. These prices are for 700- to 1200-square-foot shells, including foundation, full exterior shell, and interior partitions. Interior partitions are finished on one side only. No mechanical trades are furnished. At the high end of the scale, erected prices range from $40,000 to $60,000 for houses 800 to 2000 square feet.

I find 3 of the 50 or so models offered by Northern Counties of particular merit. My favorite is a 28-foot-square, one-story house called the Rotunda. It has a clear-span, hipped cedar roof topped by a large skylight in the center of the house. Five sizes of this house are manufactured. They range

Northern Counties' Rotunda model house has an efficient square shape and dramatic center skylight.

This precast concrete apartment building in Rochester, New York, was constructed rapidly, but at a very high construction cost.

Since price competition is very keen on the low end of the market, the incentives are to use the cheapest, ugliest materials possible. These units are usually built in rather primitive warehouse-type factories with unskilled labor. But the potential for high quality is great, and these units are taking an ever-increasing share of the housing market.

Modular houses have two significant drawbacks. The major one involves the energy costs in shipping lots of air lots of miles. Before energy costs escalated so much, it was quite reasonable to ship an "empty" module several hundred miles to its final destination. All the advantages of completely finishing the house in a factory begin to be offset by the shipping and erection costs. This makes us stop to reexamine the advantages of panelized construction. The ideal combination is a "wet" core, which contains baths and kitchen, and all the mechanical trades in one small unit, with a panelized shell designed to be erected around the core.

The second drawback is in the inherent size that can be reasonably shipped over the highway. The modules can only be one story high and 12 or 14 feet wide. This results in some very predictable and not too attractive modules.

During my several years of association with modular manufacturers, I tried unsuccessfully to show them the advantages of combining modular and panelized construction. The manufacturers felt that anything that wasn't fully modular somehow wasn't "pure."

Prefabricated panels used in conjunction with a mechanical core give the designer an infinite range of possibilities in the overall size and shape of the house. No longer are we restricted to a "double-wide trailer" look.

The panels discussed in this book require little capital investment and can be manufactured almost anywhere. The resulting cost per square foot is less than conventional construction but a bit more than budget-level modulars. If a very efficient plan that reduces building square footage is used along with load-bearing panels, the cost per square foot can be reduced to the bare minimum. Recent breakthroughs in adhesives and foam insulating materials have made these panels possible. Previous attempts at panelized building were stymied by the difficulties involved in properly joining and sealing the panels together. Now that these problems have been solved, the stage is set for a virtual explosion in panel usage.

day. It was designed to produce one complete house every 14 minutes. . . ." In an attempt to stimulate the transition from a war economy to a civilian economy, the U.S. government poured $50 million into this project before it pulled the plug. It's too bad the project didn't last, because this was a very advanced house for its day. Fifty million dollars is nothing in the development of an airplane, yet the government was unwilling to subsidize the development of advanced housing. Even today, the Lustron houses are still almost like new, with their porcelainized finish and steel frames. As with other such schemes, the Lustron Corporation relied upon overly sophisticated details, expensive union labor, and capital-intensive manufacturing facilities to produce their housing.

The high-volume survivors of American attempts at manufactured housing are house trailers and the closely related "modulars." These have a generally well-deserved image of shoddiness and are usually regarded as second-rate housing.

11 Prefabricated and Factory-Built Houses

Prefabrication of building components is an ancient art. It was used by the Greeks and Egyptians. The Chinese and Japanese have taken advantage of the techniques for centuries. Early settlers of the Americas had whole houses cut up in Europe and shipped across the ocean. Even huge stone mansions were carefully fabricated, numbered, and shipped to the New World for erection.

In other major countries of the world, house prefabrication is the rule. The favorite method is to use large, precast concrete panels to build big apartment complexes. The concrete panels are used for both the exterior skin and the interior partitions. By using steam-cured, high-strength concrete, these wall-bearing structures can be constructed 20 stories high. The system is so thoroughly worked out that the panel and connection designs are standardized throughout most European countries.

Since I have had considerable experience with various types of prefabricated systems, I was selected as supervisor for an experimental trial of such a system in the United States. A New York State agency erected several apartment buildings for the elderly using this technique.

Building the building was an adventure of a lifetime. Since the factory labor to produce the panels was prohibitively expensive, the panels were imported from Canada. American cranes were not sufficiently beefy for the job, so a crane was imported from Denmark. Instructions for the crane were in Danish with French subtitles. The American architect had to show off and design

the most complicated one of these buildings that had ever been built.

After a normal teething period, the system did work. The details of the system had been planned very well. The panels were too complicated for the Canadian plant to make economically, and the transportation costs were ridiculous. The net result was a building built in half the time at twice the cost of conventional American construction methods. The inefficiencies of importing the panels plus the absurdly high union wages killed the project. The complex design of the building was the last straw. I firmly believe that a modern plant, closely located to the project, paying reasonable nonunion wages, would have produced far different results. The old folks did get a very beautiful building in a hurry, and I learned a great deal about prefabrication methods. This was only one of the most recent of American fiascoes resulting from half-hearted flirtations with large-scale manufactured housing techniques.

The most ambitious manufactured housing project ever undertaken was devised here in the United States. It was to do for housing what Henry Ford had done for the automobile, and it almost succeeded. As Gyrla Sebestyen described in *Large Panel Buildings* (Budapest: Publishing House of the Hungarian Academy of Sciences, 1956): "The Lustron Corporation had established the world's largest 'house factory' in a former Curtiss-Wright military aircraft factory. In this factory, fitted with 600-ton and 1800-ton presses, a steel sheet processing machine 180 feet long, and the world's largest enameling furnaces, production was to proceed continuously, 23 hours a

the lateral walls. The load on each of these walls is over 50,000 pounds. Needless to say, they require very sturdy footings to prevent differential settlement. The exterior walls carry only one-half as much roof load; again, the services of a soils engineer are required.

To insulate your roof, I recommend rigid urethane board, such as Thermax, or High-R. It is readily available in 2-inch-thick, 4 × 8 sheets. I would use 2, 4, or 6 inches, depending upon the severity of your climate. A 6-mil polyethylene vapor barrier should be applied over the wood decking before the insulation board is nailed in place. For a roofing and/or waterproofing membrane, I recommend EPDM synthetic rubber, such as in the Carlisle system, or Bituthene as described in Chapter 21. I would enclose the entire building in an envelope of this rubber. If you economize and use small sheets from scrap, you will have more work to do sealing the joints. Even just one improperly sealed spot will produce a nasty leak, and the extra joints do increase the possibilities

for error. Weigh this carefully against the considerable cost savings of using leftover materials.

By following these recommendations, you can achieve a high-quality, buried roof for less than half the cost of a concrete structure. If you have a good supply of native timbers, access to EPDM rubber, and do all your own work, your roof could even cost less than a conventional one. And you will have the added bonus of a handsome, finished, beamed ceiling, much better-looking than raw concrete.

A final postscript: As I finish the final draft for this chapter, the local radio station has just announced that the outside temperature is 98°F. The thermometer on the wall above my desk registers just 73°F. Of course, I have moved my typewriter down to the bottom level of my hillside house where three of the four walls are completely buried. This gives you an idea just how dramatic the benefits of earth sheltering can be.

longer hot but still warm, is passed over rock storage. This two-medium system works because the collector channels are horizontal rather than vertical, enabling the collector air to get much hotter than it would in conventional designs. By passing the air over the tanks first, heat is stored for both domestic hot water and space heating. The furnace is designed to pass air over these same tanks to provide space heating for the house. The rock storage also releases heat to the living area. Since the system uses inexpensive site-built collectors and combines water heating with space heating, the overall cost is quite reasonable. I find this to be an elegant small house and think it is well worth your consideration. The plan even makes great sense for an aboveground house if underground doesn't appeal to you.

Buried Wooden Roofs

If you are a purist and want a fully underground house, you may want to consider building your roof structure of heavy timbers rather than of poured or precast concrete. If you go this route, I strongly recommend that you use the timbers for the roof only, and build masonry or concrete walls to support the earth pressure. It is of course possible to make both walls and roof of wood, but the roof must support thrust from the top of the wall as well as vertical loading from the soil above. I prefer to use a wooden roof structure and bolt it to the top of a masonry wall. If you do a thorough job of waterproofing and build your roof with a positive slope, I see no need for using pressure-treated timbers. If you employ all pressure-treated wood in the sizes necessary to support earth cover, your cost will approach that of concrete construction.

I recommend native, roughsawn, support timbers spaced 3 feet apart, covered with 3 × 6 tongue-and-groove planking. The maximum safe span for this system is 10 to 12 feet. The illustration shows a safe design for a structure similar in size to that of the RRU house. It is designed for 3 feet of earth cover and a 50-pound snow load (425 pounds per square foot total). Note that the loads in the center of the house are supported by

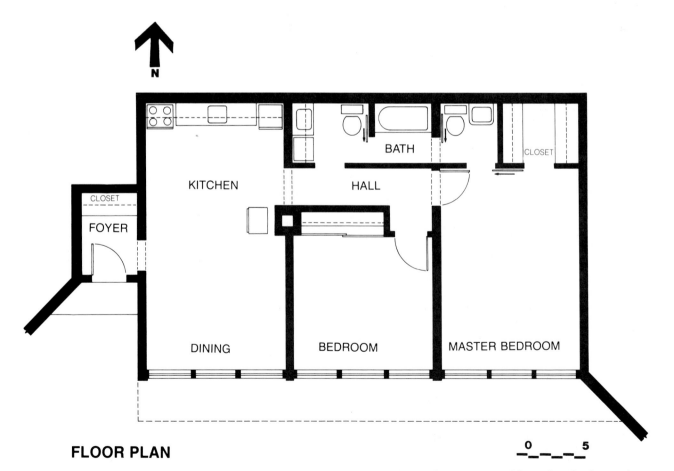

FLOOR PLAN

0 ____ 5

This small, masonry-walled underground house has lateral bearing walls to allow a short-span, wood-framed roof to be used to support an earth-covered roof deck.

where. It will not give you the lowest price, but it will give you a hassle-free, quality house in a hurry.

TVA Houses

The Tennessee Valley Authority (TVA) commissioned a series of designs for manufactured passive solar houses. They accepted bids from interested companies for producing such housing and then worked with the companies to develop efficient designs. Three modular companies and two panelized firms were selected as finalists. Unfortunately, one of the panelized firms was a recent victim of Reaganomics, and the other has not received approval from TVA for its designs.

However, two of the three modular manufacturers that were selected by TVA are actively pursuing sales of their solar homes. They give priority to very low cost; the designs are quite ordinary. They are simple, one-story boxes with good, straightforward plan layouts. The only distinguishing features are the passive solar glazing and added thermal mass. The Sunliner, by Monroe Modular Homes (Route 5, Industrial Park, Madison, TN 37354), is a practical plan because of its center-hall, air-lock entry. For mild climates, the Sunburst, by Dixie Royal Homes, Inc. (460 East 15th Street, Cookeville, TN 38501), has larger rooms but no entry hall.

As is all too often the case, the hands-down winner in the TVA houses competition isn't in

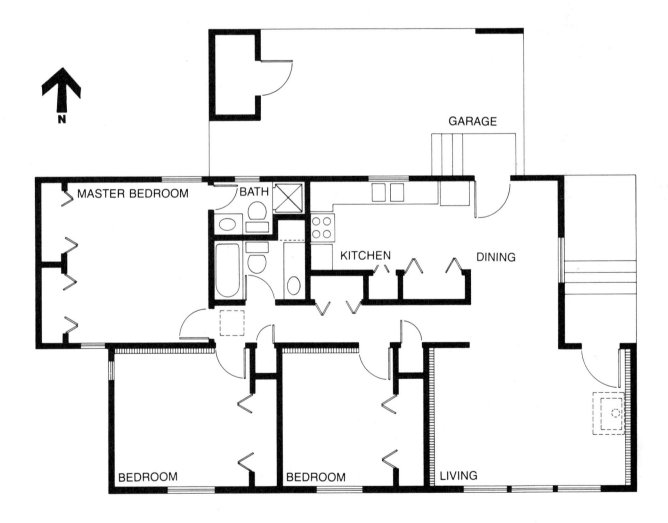

FLOOR PLAN

0 _ _ _ _ 5

The Guerdon Suncrest shown here has never been put into production. Although designed for modular production, this would be an excellent choice for those designing a conventional house. The shaded areas in the living room and two bedrooms represent masonry added to increase thermal mass to make heating easier.

production. Guerdon Industries (Box 6020-A, Denver, CO 80206) has won a National Passive Solar Design Award (1980) for its Solarwood modular home. This is a 1400-square-foot, four-bedroom house that manages to create a good passive solar design without large windows at ground level. It is an excellent design for situations that require privacy and security.

Another Guerdon design is a favorite of mine. The Suncrest is just a little larger than the basic houses of the other modular home companies, but it has a much more sophisticated plan. The carport and overhanging roof serve to completely hide the modular origins of this house. It remains to be seen whether Guerdon will eventually market these houses. They are well worth the wait. The contract with TVA specifies that the house designs are the exclusive property of the developers for a period of three years. After that time they are free for anyone to use.

Since modulars have a rather limited sales territory due to shipping costs, the TVA houses will have a limited geographic market. This is too bad because the very nature of modular housing makes these designs attractive for other parts of the country. Since modulars are not truly mass-produced, they lend themselves readily to changes of floor layout, fenestration, insulation levels, and the like. Many companies boast that they can virtually build a custom-designed house on an assembly line. The TVA houses could be produced by almost any modular manufacturer anywhere. By the time you read this book, the three-year exclusive rights will have expired. If you like one of these designs, see if you can get a local modular manufacturer to make one for you. Several other plans have been devised for efficient houses built by the modular process. (See Chapter 12 for additional sources of plans for modular-style houses.)

Hexacell Panel Houses

Panelfab International Corporation (Box 2777, AMF, Miami, FL 33159), the panelized company that didn't receive TVA approval for its designs, brings back some old memories. Some years ago I helped develop a portable house-manufacturing plant that was supposed to revolutionize the housing industry. The project was a complete fizzle. To my great amazement, Panelfab is manufacturing the very panels that we developed but couldn't market. They've gotten around the mar-

keting problems we had by selling them in foreign countries that do not have the restrictive building codes nor the prohibitive union labor costs that we have here.

The secret to these panels is the core material, Hexacell, which is a specially treated kraft paper expanded to form numerous six-sided cells. To make a panel, the Hexacell core is expanded, roller-coated with glue, and then bonded to the two outer skins with heat and pressure. The cellular structure can be made any thickness. In our system, the cores were 3½ or 5½ inches thick so the panels could be joined with standard framing members. Even with plasterboard faces, the panels are enormously strong. The framing members are only used to tie the panels together. Building code officials want nothing to do with this system, though the core is fire retardant and the panels are much stronger than conventional walls.

Unlike the foam-core panels, this method does require a fair amount of machinery, and the bonding process uses quite a bit of energy. The panels are usually supplied uninsulated because of the difficulties of pouring insulation into the cells. Because of their airtight construction and the thousands of tiny cells, the panels have about the same R value as a conventional stud wall insulated with fiberglass. If you should use this system, I would add insulation by using a layer of Thermax or R-Max on the outside of the wall under the finish siding. This would enable you to use the standard panels without disrupting the fabrication process.

In our early version of this process, we packaged the whole fabrication system so that it fitted onto the back of a standard tractor-trailer. We even included a generator so that it could be completely self-contained; we basically designed a portable factory. With today's spiraling energy costs, a system of this type makes great sense. In virtually every system of manufactured housing components, the stumbling block is transportation. It makes much more sense to take the factory to the house rather than vice versa.

Panelfab has done a great business exporting the system to underdeveloped countries throughout the world. I think it is high time to try it here at home. Even if they never get their TVA approval, I would recommend their panels for a home.

12 Kit Houses and Plan Sources

For those who plan to do most or all of their work themselves, a good set of plans or an actual package of materials is vital. Obviously, you can buy all of your own materials and fabricate everything yourself, but it will speed construction immensely if you can buy everything you need in one place. House kits are very different from precut houses. Many precut companies throughout the country offer variations on the dreary tract-type ranch house. Usually, these are large, inefficient houses that are not very economical to build. A typical package includes only materials for the exterior shell and possibly framing for interior partitions. The companies I recommend offer truly unique houses, and the kits are very complete.

Shelter-Kit, Inc.

This southern New Hampshire firm has long been a favorite of mine. They have been busy fabricating small, efficient houses since 1970. Their houses come in modules, encouraging people to build houses in stages; start with a basic living unit and then add on, a module at a time. As demand has increased for small houses, they have supplemented their original houses, designed to be built in stages, with a Lofthouse series. The Lofthouse is available in either 16- or 20-foot-square models. These are chalet-style houses with limited headroom on the second floor. The configuration is quite efficient and costs are low. The structure is a lightweight post-and-beam frame for quick, easy erection by the homeowner. The post-and-beam frame allows clear-spans that permit complete flexibility of partition placement.

Costs for the basic shell without plumbing, electrical, or finish kits are low. The 256-square-foot Lofthouse is $7600, the 400-square-foot version $12,000. These include all materials for a weather-tight shell, including nails, fasteners, roofing, windows, doors, and the like. Mechanical trades and interior finish are not included.

A big advantage of the Shelter-Kit system is that the house packages are small enough to fit into a U-Haul trailer. The company arranges for a one-way truck rental, and you drive or fly to their plant and drive your own house home. Shelter-Kits have been distributed all over the eastern United States and Canada using the drive-it-yourself method. If you are importing a house to Canada, make sure that you register the shipment as building materials, not prefabricated housing components. The difference in duty is enormous. Shelter-Kit has recently joined a trucking association that will transport house packages at reasonable rates if you don't want to drive a huge truck yourself. Shipping a client's Lofthouse 20 from New Hampshire to North Carolina costs less than $500. Shelter-Kit's address is Franklin Hills, Franklin, NH 03235.

Family Homes Cooperative (FHC)

FHC is an innovative housing group that has been working for the last seven years to develop a low-cost housing system for rural areas. They are located near Beckley, West Virginia. Criteria for the project included conservation of materials and energy and the use of native materials wherever possible. The houses are complete from concrete for the footings, up to the last coat of paint. Theoretically, if you were isolated in the woods somewhere with only this kit and the necessary tools, you could finish the house completely. No other manufacturer offers anything more complete. Even the modular houses I talked about in Chapter 11, which are advertised as entirely complete, are not this well-appointed. The kit even comes with an air-to-air heat exchanger to purify the air without wasting heat (see Chapter 17).

The structure of these houses is completely unique to the building industry. It is a refinement of a system of building with 1-inch lumber, origi-nated by Homer Hurst of the Virginia Polytechnic Institute. The walls in the FHC houses are framed with native oak 1 × 18s set 4 inches on-center. Those dimensions will seem odd to anyone familiar with construction, but they work because FHC has all the details worked out. The houses are precut in the 14,000-square-foot factory; the oak studs and plates are notched together for accurate assembly and predrilled for fastening. Bracing is by means of steel corner braces, also predrilled. Exterior sheathing is Du Pont Tyvek, a novel material that breathes moisture, but not air. There is no conventional rigid sheathing board; Tyvek is a flexible plastic sheet. Exterior siding is native poplar, also predrilled for installation. The foundation consists of pressure-treated posts set on concrete footings. The roof system is composed of lightweight trusses fabricated from 1-inch lumber set to align with the wall studs.

Superinsulation is an important feature of the FHC houses. The walls have 9-inch fiberglass

SOUTH ELEVATION

The two-story FHC house shown here squeezes four bedrooms and a study into a two-story house with ground dimensions of only 24 by 32 feet. A similar design has three large bedrooms in place of the four.

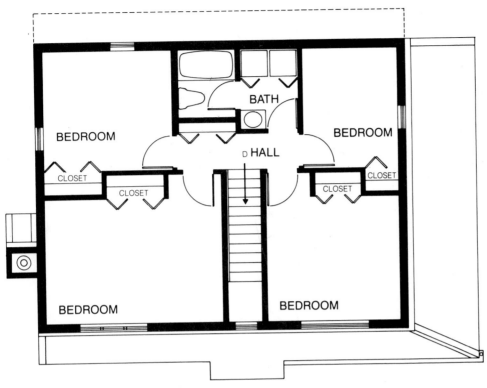

SECOND FLOOR PLAN

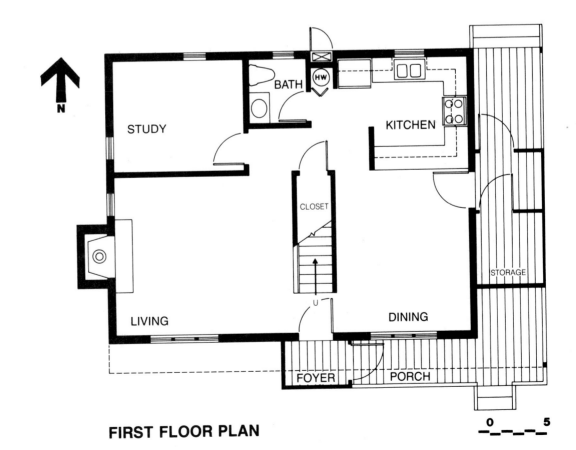

FIRST FLOOR PLAN

0 _ _ _ _ 5

FHC provides low-cost, superinsulated houses. The Hillside model is shown here.

insulation compressed to 8 inches to fit between the studs, giving an R value of R-28. (This is a tested value, not an estimate.) The ceiling is insulated with 12 inches of fiberglass; windows are double glazed, and all caulking and sealants are included. The unique framing system has the framing members penetrating the exterior wall only 40% as often as in standard framing systems. The entire structure uses about 50% as much lumber as 2 × 4 stud-framed houses.

FHC offers five different house sizes using this unique system. They range from a one-bedroom retirement house of 600 square feet up to a four-bedroom house of 1400 square feet. The complete package for a three-bedroom, 960-square-foot house is less than $15,000, and that includes almost everything imaginable. FHC will erect this house for an additional $7000. Plans for all of the houses are also available if you should want to build one of them with your own materials.

Your tax dollars helped finance this housing system, so take advantage of it if you can. The FHC factory and basic research were developed with a U.S. Department of Housing and Urban Development (HUD) grant. Unfortunately, this does not mean that other federal agencies look favorably upon these designs. Building code officials and banks are other formidable hurdles. Of course, if you build in a noncode area and need no bank financing, you will not need to worry. In dealing with officialdom, I would stress the government involvement, since this may be perceived as an endorsement. The houses are limited to ranch styles and are very conventional looking, but they represent one of the best

values around. As an added bonus, they conserve resources at all levels—materials, fabrication, and transportation.

Bow House, Inc.

Bow House of Bolton, Massachusetts, takes an unusual approach to kit houses in that they supply everything *except* normal lumberyard items. As the name indicates, they specialize in authentic "bow-roofed" houses. The rafters of the original Cape Cod houses with this roof style were formed by shipwrights. Bow House supplies a modern version, which is laminated to form the curve. This curved roof not only gives the houses a striking architectural character, but also provides nearly full use of the second floor without expensive dormers, gables, or gambrel roofs. Without these kits, cutting the rafters and trim materials to such a curve would be prohibitively expensive.

Bow House goes on to supply completely authentic materials for exterior and interior finish and trim items. The exterior finishes are all first class: 16-inch white cedar roof shingles, red cedar clapboard siding, authentic corner moldings, authentic reproduction-grade doors and windows, and even handmade glass in authentic sizes. Interior finish materials include 1 × 12 pine flooring; stairs; authentic window and door trim and baseboard moldings; and authentic hardware and stains.

Strictly speaking, these are not affordable houses unless you are willing to do a great deal of work yourself. Kits for all materials except stock lumberyard materials for the smaller two-bedroom and bath quarter capes and half capes (1182 and

This Bow-House half-cape is a traditional gem.

The close-up of the Bow House shows how curved, laminated roof beams allow a low eave line with a generous second-floor area.

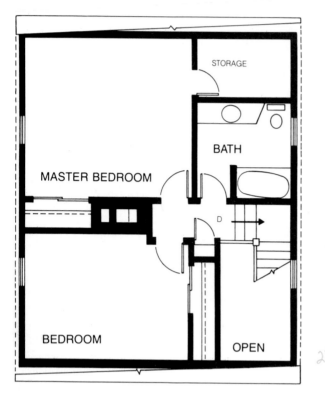

SECOND FLOOR PLAN

1340 square feet, respectively) run less than $20,000. You should expect to spend a little over $40,000 more for materials and labor to complete one of these kits. Shipping costs are much less than for most kits since you are only shipping lighter finish and trim items. The package fits easily on a medium-size truck. A detailed materials list for standard lumberyard items is also furnished. Detailed plans for the houses are available for a $50 deposit that is refundable, should you decide not to order the house.

Bow House also has an extensive list of options, including custom storm windows, antique ballast brick, water-struck common brick, wainscoting, custom mantels, and custom light fixtures. They also provide design services to aid with interior layouts. All of the basic houses are designed to accommodate a one-story addition on the first floor if you need more space. Aesthetically, I like the elegant bow-roofed structure standing alone. If you are willing to devote a great deal of labor, one of these house kits will enable you to have an heirloom-quality house at a bargain price.

The Bow House plan allows a generous second floor due to the curved design of the rafters. For those who want an authentic traditional house, this one is the ticket.

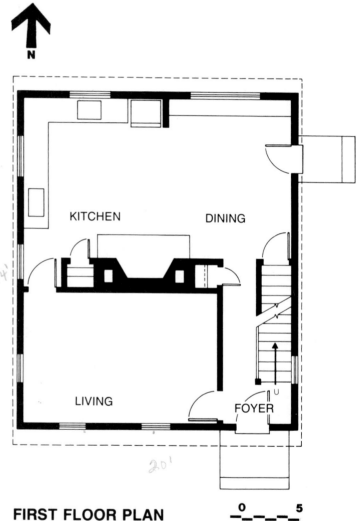

FIRST FLOOR PLAN

House Plans

Everyone is familiar with the dreary books of house plans sold on the newsstands. People who are desperate for a set of plans buy all of them that they can find and pore over the sketches, trying to find something suitable. You will notice that these plans books never show any photographs of their houses, just perspective drawings. There are good reasons for this presentation. Most of these houses have never been built and few of them ever will be. The plans are often so inadequate that the builder only uses them as rough guides, if at all. The general idea is to get the prospective homeowner to part with a good deal of money for a large package of five or eight plans that they don't really want. From my experience with many people who buy plans, all they usually want are two or three sets of plans, not a huge package. It's not unusual for the pricing of these plans to be set up in such a way that it costs more to order three sets than it does to order five. A few of the plans I am about to describe are sold through such plans books, but they are sold by a company I know and respect, and they do have a money-back guarantee.

Plans can vary widely in the amount of detail provided. The very best I have ever seen are provided by Charles Haynes (see Chapter 7). The NCAT plans (later in this chapter) and FHC plans (earlier in this chapter) are distant seconds. All of the rest are relatively equal. Most plans show electrical layouts, but few show details of mechanical trades. Usually, structural details are purposely vague, as requirements vary from region to region.

Plans by Government Agencies

By far the cheapest source of plans is the U.S. government. Of course, the plans aren't really free—your tax dollars pay for them. They are available for a token charge, and several of them are very, very good. For many years, the U.S. Department of Agriculture (USDA) has been preoccupied with developing prototypes for low-cost homes. Unfortunately, this is a well-kept secret and very few of the houses ever get built on the open market. The houses tend to be small and lack visual appeal. Lately, they have concentrated on passive solar techniques, and the quality of design has improved. Regardless of aesthetics, the floor plans work well, and the houses are designed to be built for as little as possible. Two commercially available books contain selections of plans from the USDA houses. You might check these out if you are interested, since ordering the plans can take months. *Vacation Homes and Cabins* (Dover Publications, 1978) contains plans for 16 houses. *Low-Cost, Energy-Efficient Shelter,* edited by Eugene Eccli (Rodale Press, 1976), shows several additional houses. The USDA plans are available from your local Agricultural Extension Service whose offices are usually located at land-grant universities and colleges; check your phone book under U.S. Government Agencies for the one closest to you.

The most famous of the USDA houses is the Solar Attic house, developed by the Rural Housing Research Unit (RRU) of Clemson University. This group later went on to develop the pressure-treated underground house I discussed in Chapter 10. The Solar Attic house is USDA Plan #7220 if you wish to order it. The solar attic is a semiactive solar system that adds about $6000 to the construction costs of the house, but it has been thoroughly tested and works very well.

The Clemson group has also done considerable research on low-cost, panelized post-and-beam framed houses. The USDA Miscellaneous Publication #1020 describes the development of an 800-square-foot, very low-budget house. Plans for the house are #5997, again from the Extension Service. It is also shown as house #15 in Dover's *Vacation Home and Cabins.* If you are willing to do some of the work yourself, you can still build a basic house of this type for less than $10,000.

A tiny post-and-beam saltbox cabin of 776 square feet is another rock-bottom budget unit from the USDA. It has one bedroom on the first floor and a low-headroom sleeping loft on the second floor. One of my clients built this house last year for less than $5000. He did make extensive use of salvaged materials, and all of the labor was his own. The plans are in the same bargain-basement category as the cost of this house. The USDA only charges the direct printing costs for its plans, usually under $5.

The National Center for Appropriate Technology (NCAT) has developed plans for superinsulated, two- and three-bedroom basic living units. These are very simple, one-story ranch house structures; they do not use any novel technology. They just beef up standard construction methods to provide very high levels of insulation. The plans are so detailed that almost anyone could build the house himself or herself, or hire a relatively inexperienced contractor to do the work. Alternate plans for the two-bedroom unit allow it to be modularized. Since it is so small, you could literally build it in your backyard and then truck it to the site. It might also be possible to talk a local modular housing contractor into building the house in his factory and delivering it to your site.

The highly detailed plans are moderately priced. For $50 you get either the modularized or the conventional version of the two-bedroom, 896-square-foot house; for $75, the three-bedroom, 1288-square-foot unit. Materials for the smaller house are estimated at $16,000; the larger one, $26,000. Plans are available from NCAT, Box 3838, Butte, MT 59702.

In addition to its modular houses, the Tennessee Valley Authority (TVA) has undertaken an ambi-

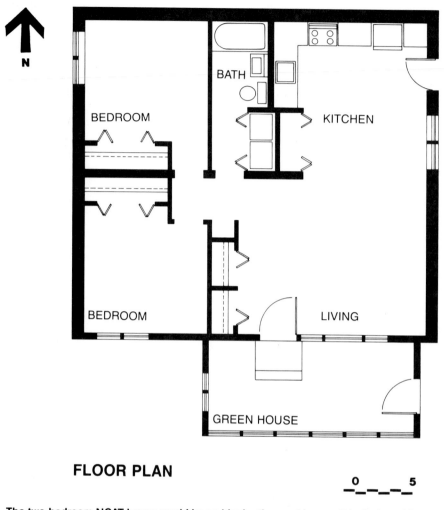

FLOOR PLAN

0 _ _ _ _ 5

The two-bedroom NCAT house would be an ideal retirement house. It is designed for superinsulated, double-wall construction and can be either shop- or site-built. For shop building, the house is built in two sections and assembled at the site.

tious program to design and build a wide variety of site-built passive solar houses. Eleven different designs have been developed, ranging from 1000 to 2000 square feet. The emphasis has been placed on solar, not low cost, but the houses are well designed. It would be possible to adapt many of the cost-saving ideas described in this book to these houses. A portfolio describing all 11 houses, *Solar Homes for the Valley—1979 Design Portfolio,* is available from TVA, 310 TVA Credit Union Building, Chattanooga, TN 37401. The actual working drawings are only $9 per set. They are available from TVA Mapping Service Branch, 200 Haney Building, Chattanooga, TN 37401.

Rural America, working with HUD, has developed a series of very small, extremely low-budget houses. The houses are so small that they won't meet restrictions in some building codes. In fact, HUD had to waive some of their own regulations

to allow construction at all. The prototype house was built with donated labor for a materials cost of $10,500. Working drawings for five different designs are available for $20 per set. Order them from Rural America, 1346 Connecticut Avenue, NW #519, Washington, DC 20036. A small donation for a brochure would be appreciated.

Middle America Solar Energy Complex (MASEC) is a now defunct organization that was set up by the government to develop passive solar designs specifically for the midwestern region of the country. Although the organization has been axed by the federal government, the plans that were developed live on. They are now available from *Better Homes and Gardens* home plans (see below).

Magazine Plans

Better Homes and Gardens has one of the most extensive building departments of any of the popular magazines. They have attracted good architects, and they actually build and evaluate their houses. The houses tend to be large and expensive, but I have selected a few of my favorites, all smaller than the magazine's usual fare.

The first houses are the MASEC houses mentioned above. One design is for a modular-type house of 1296 square feet. It obtains its passive solar gain by a large south glass wall backed up by water-filled cylinders. It is Plan #19930. The second house is relatively similar, but is designed for standard construction with very thick walls for superinsulation. Plan #19926 contains 1200 square feet. These are ordinary-looking ranch houses with well-designed floor plans.

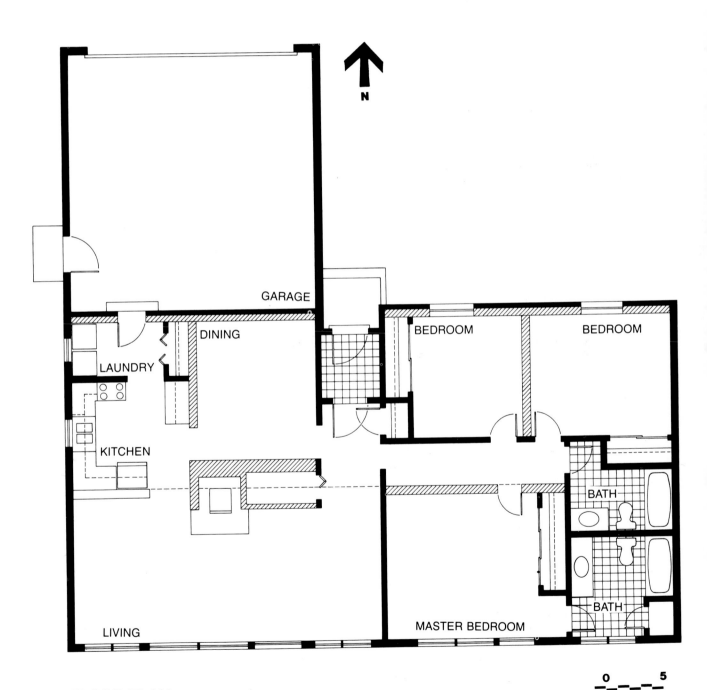

FLOOR PLAN

The MASEC house gains heat storage by interior masonry walls, shown shaded on this plan.

Better Homes and Gardens (Box 374, Des Moines, IA 50336) has done a great deal with passive solar houses. I have selected two fine examples. Architect Daryl Hanson has designed a traditionally shaped house that is bermed on the north and has a sunken greenhouse on the south. It has 1850 square feet and can be set up with three or four bedrooms (one bedroom can be a study). I would eliminate the ugly fake chimney on the front and substitute two Velux skylights. Aside from that one flaw, I find it a real winner. The other solar house won first place in a contest sponsored by the magazine, the American Institute of Architects, and the U.S. Plywood Association. It has three bedrooms in its 1872 square feet. The Hanson house is Plan #19863; the award winner is Plan #19915. In the truly affordable range, I could only find one winner. It is called the Meadowlark. The efficient saltbox shape contains 1299 square feet. It is quite similar to my Jones house, but much smaller. Order Plan #19859. These plans are rather expensive: $95 for the first set, $25 for each additional set, and $135 for a set of five drawings. There is a money-back guarantee if you are not satisfied.

Garden Way Compact House Competition

In 1982, Garden Way Publishing Company and the National Association of Home Builders sponsored a contest for compact houses. The 33 winning designs were published in *The Compact House Book,* edited by Don Metz. Winners are required to make working drawings of their houses available to the public. From the houses in the book, I have selected five that are not only compact, but also affordable (see table). Bear in mind that this is a design competition, so most of these houses have not been built and tested in use. Unless otherwise noted, all of these houses are less than 1000 square feet and have two bedrooms and one bath. All of the houses feature conventional, but well-insulated construction.

Solar House Plans

There are two extraordinary passive solar houses that I must mention. The first is a small saltbox design aimed at the owner-builder. It contains two bedrooms and a sunspace in its 1140 square feet. A remarkably complete set of plans is obtainable for only $20 per set. Order from Homestead Design, Box 430N, Langley, WA 98260.

The other impressive design, at the opposite end of the cost spectrum, is the Saunders Shrewsbury house, which made waves in the solar field when it was first introduced. Although much more

Selected Garden Way Compact House Competition Winners

Linda Brock Box 915 Bozeman, MT 59715	A simple, rectangular, gable-roofed house built on a slab-on-grade. One bedroom and one bath are located on each of two levels. The second floor can be expanded to add a bedroom. In my opinion, this house offers the most living space for the least money of any in the competition.
Thomas M. Haskill 234 Ellsworth Avenue, #10 New Haven, CT 06511	A south-facing hillside house with the entrance on the second level. Bedrooms are on the lowest level opening out to a terrace. A third-level loft is a bonus. Profile is traditional garrison-style saltbox. Space layout is handled skillfully.
Neil Husher Kathyann Cowles 11 Sheridan Street Cambridge, MA 02140	A 24-foot-square pole house with delightful roof lines. Three stories soar above a pole platform to catch the view. Unusual roof lines add to this house's charm. Extras are a greenhouse and a sleeping loft. This is my favorite as the handsomest house of this collection.
Keith Krolak 941 E. Polk Street Morton, IL 61550	A simple rectangular passive solar design. Conventional two-story layout with gracefully angled interior partitions, which make the space seem larger. Louvered south portico covers greenhouse and shelters south glazing. House is super-insulated with double stud wall construction.
Michael Underhill 2538 Times Boulevard Houston, TX 77005	An elegant solution for hot-weather housing, or a vacation house. Living room and bedroom units flank an open porch with sliding shutters at each end. This is known as a "dog-trot" house. I lived in one once and it was delightful.

expensive than the Homestead design, it can be appropriately categorized as affordable solar. The very same shortsighted engineers who used to say that flights to the moon were impossible and that front-wheel-drive vehicles were impractical have said for years that it is impossible to heat a house 100% from the sun. If you did try to completely heat a house from the sun's rays, it would take an impossibly big and complicated system and you'd have to have some backup heating system anyway. Norman Saunders has shown such engineers just how wrong they were.

In Shrewsbury, Massachusetts, Saunders designed and built a low-cost, 100% passive solar house. It has been through two seasons, and it works perfectly. It not only heats in winter, but it cools in summer. All room temperatures are uniform year-round, and there is no backup system whatsoever. And he has done this without expensive, complicated plumbing or fancy electronic controls. Not only this, but he achieved such perfection in a house that cost no more than a conventional structure.

Plans for the house itself are available from Norman B. Saunders, 15 Ellis Road, Weston, MA 02193. They are $75 per set. In addition, you must pay a royalty fee for any patented items you use. The fee for the use of all of them for any one house is $275. The royalty is steep but will be quickly offset by those nonexistent heating bills.

If you want to read more about Saunders's detailed solar system and just how it works in this house, get yourself a copy of *Saunders Shrewsbury House: 100% Solar Heating, Fully Automatic, Truly Low Cost* by William A. Shurcliff, 19 Appleton Street, Cambridge, MA 02138. Order directly from the author: $9 postpaid.

Smallplan

This is a company that I have put together to handle distribution of the plans from my various books. All of the houses of my design that are shown in Part IV of this book have working drawings that are available through Smallplan. Several additional interesting designs, without working drawings, are shown in Part II. If there is sufficient interest, working drawings will be prepared for the most popular of these houses. Requests for modifications and custom designs are welcome and are referred to me by Smallplan. All plans are $30 for the first set and $15 for each additional set included in the initial order. An order blank for plans of houses shown in this book is found in Appendix C.

Part III

Applying New Techniques

REDUCING COSTS

13 Finding Low-Cost Property

Building costs are drastically influenced by the geographic location of the city in which you choose to live. Costs in some major cities are far more than double those of other, sometimes more desirable cities. Since the affordability of a house is directly related to one's income level, we can't simply compare house prices or annual mortgage costs without also considering the average income in the area. This is done by stating the mortgage payment as a percentage of household income.

For instance, in St. Louis, the annual mortgage payment of $8100 (on an average $64,100 house) requires only 24% of the average household income. In contrast, San Diego, with an annual mortgage payment of $14,900 (on an average $116,000 house) requires a staggering 47% of the average income for housing payments. Other reasonably priced cities (mortgage payment less than 30% of annual income) include Philadelphia, Houston, Boston, Kansas City, Cleveland, Indianapolis, and Milwaukee. The high rent district, in which the average house price soars above $100,000 and the mortgage payment exceeds 40% of the average income, includes New York, Los Angeles, San Francisco, and Portland, Oregon.

Thus, over a 20-year mortgage you could save $165,000 by living in St. Louis rather than San Francisco. And that's an "average" house, not a sensibly designed, cost-saving one. Typical major cities not listed above have house prices in the mid-$80s that require 35 to 40% of the average income for mortgage payments.

Of course, most people don't want to live in large cities, and certainly not very many will want to live in the select list of "bargain" cities. But this list will also give you a good idea of the costs in the areas surrounding the cities. Trendy cities and states tend to be overpriced and overpopulated. There is a distinct population movement away from the North and East to the South and West. If you are looking for a reasonably priced area in which to build a house, you should avoid the growth areas. In addition, several states have restrictive, expensive building codes that considerably increase the cost of a house. For these reasons I would avoid the following states: Arizona, California, Colorado, Connecticut, Florida, Hawaii, Massachusetts, New Mexico, Oregon, Washington, and Wyoming. Unregulated areas which are comparatively inexpensive may be found in the following states: Alaska, Arkansas, Indiana, Kansas, Kentucky, Maine, Missouri, New Hampshire, North Carolina, Ohio, Oklahoma, Pennsylvania, Tennessee, Texas, Vermont, and West Virginia. You may have other, overriding considerations, but these suggestions will give you a good idea of where to look if you have a free choice.

Small Lots

Your best buys in property are located in small- to medium-size towns and cities of the Northeast and the Heartland. There has been a great trend in recent years to raze old, unoccupied houses. Older houses tended to build up, not out, to have several stories, like the efficient houses in this book. Hence, the lots these houses were on are relatively small. Since the typical "ranch" house most builders offer today won't readily fit these smaller, older lots, they go begging, often at astoundingly low prices. You can realize enormous cost savings by buying a lot on which an old house once stood because you will not have to drill a well, put in a septic system, set electric poles, build a road, and the like. These savings can run from $5000 to $20,000 or more, and that's on top of the savings in the cost of the lot. Of course, you won't have much room to move about and you do have to pay taxes for those services you didn't need to install but were there anyway. In the balance, though, a small city lot could mean the difference between owning your own home and not owning one.

A small rural lot is also a good bet. Zoning regulations prohibit small rural lots in many areas, but there are ways around the regulations. Rather than buy property outright, try to arrange a 99-year lease. Farmers are in dire straits all over the country. By leasing an unused parcel from a farmer, you not only get a bargain, but you help out the farmer. You will not find such a deal at your friendly local realtor; you have to get out and make it happen. Advertise in a local farm paper, put a notice on the bulletin board at your local farm co-op, or just drive around and ask questions when you see a likely piece of property. Since you are only leasing the property, it will be easy to insert a clause that protects you if you don't hit water, can't get a building permit, or just don't build. Sometimes the lease can be arranged with a small down payment plus a yearly rental payment. In this case the rental payments don't start until you are living in your house.

Problem Lots

Tract builders only build on level lots that are large enough to hold a sprawling house. When they have a steep, rocky area that they have to buy as part of a housing tract, they frequently just write it off as unusable. Sometimes a lot is too small to contain a builder's standard model and fit behind the building setback lines. One of my clients was actually given such a lot—no charge. If you can get permission to build on it, good luck! He had to drill a new well for his neighbor so he had legal clearance for his septic system. And he had to file a variance and build a three-story house to fit behind the setback lines. The hard work was well spent; the lot has a 270-degree view of the ocean and is now worth a small fortune.

Buyers are also scarce for steep or marshy lots. These can be ideal sites for hillside or pole houses that are too much trouble for the average builder.

Both sites can pose problems for waste disposal and may require special systems and/or a variance (see Chapter 15 for alternate waste disposal systems). All the basic houses in this book are designed around post-and-beam frames that are readily adaptable to pole-type construction. In sandy, marshy, or wet clay soils, pressure-treated pilings may be driven into the soft material to support the house. This is an accepted, sturdy foundation that is rarely used except in waterfront locations. Never try to use a standard foundation or basement in soft clay unless the foundation has been specifically designed for your site by a competent civil engineer. Even then, you can have trouble. Wet clay can expand and collapse foundation walls no matter how well designed they are. Use pilings if you can.

Communal Access Roads and Property

Many of my clients have saved substantially by jointly owning their access roads or property. Unimproved building lots (i.e., without roads or services) can cost four or five times as much per acre as a larger tract. If several families buy jointly, they can slash the initial cost of the property. You may also be able to get a much nicer, more private piece of property for your money. If you are the first to build in the area, you can choose your neighbors and set the tone for the neighborhood. If several of you build at one time, you can trade labor and share contractors. There are also substantial savings in jointly running power lines. Wells and septic systems can be jointly owned, but there can be problems unless you have some very well thought-out legal agreements covering maintenance, repairs, and the like.

Kevin Berry is building four houses at once for some of my clients. He estimates that each homeowner is saving over 10% just because he can build all four houses at the same site, all at the same time. This is in addition to the substantial savings realized from panelized post-and-beam construction. In this instance, small building lots were deeded to the individual homeowners to satisfy the bank. The previous owner of the property sold them the building lots outright in return for the down payment on the property. Payments on the balance of the property will be spread out over a number of years. The access road is jointly owned by the homeowners, and an escrow account has been established for road maintenance.

Other clients of mine have bought into an existing land corporation and now own an undivided interest in a large tract of land. This arrangement can be very economical, but will usually severely limit your borrowing power with the bank. The clients who have taken this route had cash from a prior home sale or built slowly and paid for the project as they went.

In case you have no desire to own property jointly with anyone, you still may want to look into joint ownership of a road. Since readily accessible building sites are used up first, many fine sites go unsold because of the expense of building a long road to them. If you can get several families together and subdivide a piece of off-the-road property, the cost of a road can be shared by several people. Sometimes you can even persuade the town or county to take over maintenance of the new road. In order to do this, you will have to build the road to their specifications, which will cost more money, but you will usually save money in the long run.

Precautions

In your quest for bargain property, be very careful not to get taken. Have a title search done to make sure that the seller really owns the property and that there are no liens against it (in other words, credit taken out with the property as collateral). Make absolutely sure that you are zoned properly for a single-family or duplex house. It is quite possible for someone to sell you a lot on which you can't legally build. Water supply and septic system approvals should be carefully checked before you buy. You may want to make final acceptance of the property contingent upon receipt of a septic system permit. Sometimes, in areas where water access is a problem, sale is contingent upon drilling a well that provides a stated minimum rate of water.

Finally, get yourself a U.S. Geological Survey detailed map of the area and explore all of the roads. You might find an even better site than the one you've picked out. You might also find a chemical factory, power plant or another hazardous source of pollution that you'll want to steer clear of.

14 Configuration and Orientation

The configuration of your house does a great deal to make it more affordable. By going up instead of out, you can begin to make substantial savings in costs. As we have seen, the cost of a building lot can be significantly reduced if your house's perimeter is compact. If you build two stories rather than one, you will have roughly half as much roof and half as much foundation to build. You also save on heating and cooling costs, since there is less exposed exterior surface area to lose heat in winter and gain it in summer.

The physical shape of your house is directly related to how much material is used in its construction. A circle encloses the most amount of space for a given area of wall. Since a circle is expensive to construct, we settle for a square or very close to one. Even if you build a one-story house, it will be more efficient if it is a square rather than a rectangle. Again, there is less exposed area, and you will save on heating and cooling costs.

It is important to consider interior privacy when building a small house. If you build two stories plus lofts, there are distinctly different areas to which people can retreat if they want to be by themselves. Even though you may be just as far removed in a one-story house, you are psychologically more alone on another floor.

Multifamily Dwellings

We are the only major civilized country in the world where people live predominately in detached, single-family houses. This is a luxury that has been afforded us by our wide-open spaces and relatively low building and energy costs. Since low costs are a thing of the past, we must rethink our addiction to single-family houses. I do not see any possibility of getting Americans to prefer apartment dwelling over houses, but I do think that if the price is right, many people will find duplex houses attractive. I have designed my basic Civic house in such a fashion that it can be built as two attached units to form a duplex. Both floors are designed so that they can be efficiency apartments. It would be possible to construct the house with a two-story family living unit on one side and two efficiency apartments on the opposite side. In this way, you could use the income from two apartments to pay off the mortgage on the house. You could even construct the duplex unit with four apartments as an income-producing investment. The layout of the two floors is such that it would be simple to convert the units from two efficiencies to one family unit, or vice versa.

Multiple dwelling units are the only economical possibility for preserving our stock of fine large houses. Many communities have shortsighted ordinances that prohibit more than one dwelling unit per building lot. These ordinances are now being ignored in many places. Taxes and heating costs have become so high that the choice for many is abandonment or subdivision.

Spatial Efficiency

We can no longer afford to build houses that waste space. Let's compare my very popular Jones saltbox from my second book, *A Design*

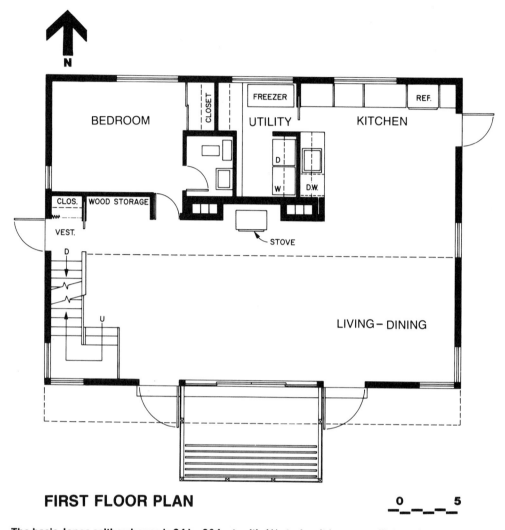

N

BEDROOM

CLOSET

FREEZER

UTILITY

KITCHEN

REF.

D

W

D.W.

CLOS.

WOOD STORAGE

VEST.

D

U

STOVE

LIVING – DINING

FIRST FLOOR PLAN

0 ___ 5

The basic Jones saltbox house is 24 by 36 feet, with 1½ stories. It is a very efficient design that has since been updated to use the panelized system featured in this book. See the order blank in Appendix C for plans.

and *Construction Handbook for Energy-Saving Houses* (Rodale Press, 1980), with the space- and cost-efficient Civic house (see illustrations here and on page 116). Both are designed as basic, three-bedroom family houses. The Jones house has 1540 square feet of floor space; the Civic has 1280. I was able to reduce the ground area of the house by a whopping 40% while reducing the interior square footage by only 18%. Not only that, but the room sizes remain generous. Waste space is what has been eliminated. In fact, the main living space is exactly the same size in both houses. Advances in building and mechanical technology allow us to build a much more energy-efficient building and eliminate space-wasting central furnaces and tank-type water heaters.

Although the bedrooms in the Civic house are smaller than the Jones bedrooms, there are actually two additional lofts that can be used as sleeping spaces, study areas, or for additional storage. The net result is actually 6% more area.

How did I work this magic? Where did I find the extra space? I have slashed circulation space, which contributes nothing to usable living space, to the bare minimum. The Jones house had a rear entrance through the kitchen, and the kitchen area was greatly enlarged to accommodate the traffic flow. Although the kitchen itself in the Civic occupies much less floor area, the work space is of similar size. Luxuries such as a sauna and a masonry heat storage column were eliminated.

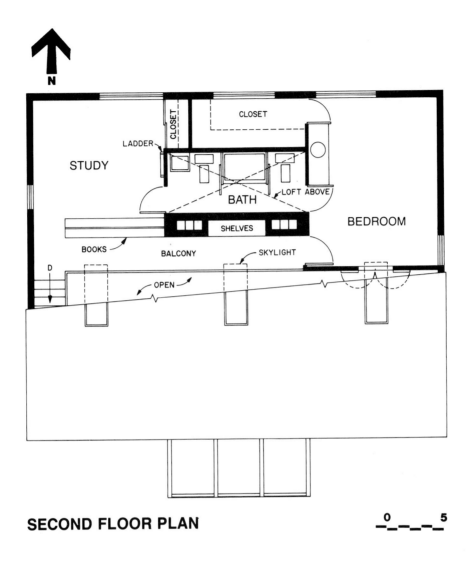

SECOND FLOOR PLAN

0 _ _ _ _ 5

More advanced construction techniques make the heat storage column unnecessary. Bathroom, closet, and laundry spaces are arranged in more space-efficient fashion, and the mechanical space is eliminated entirely. The Jones house had a cathedral ceiling opening to the second floor. The Civic has two full floors that utilize the space more completely. The monopitch roof on the Civic is economical to build and also allows a cathedral ceiling. So as not to waste space, the sloping area is occupied by two sleeping lofts. The lofts and living-dining area are open to each other, making the whole area quite spacious.

The final reason for the increase of efficiency lies in the contemporary shape of the Civic. The relatively shallow slope of the roof keeps the volume low yet still allows space for lofts. These lofts, by the way, are the most popular place in

these houses for young and old alike. I had stuck to the more traditional shape of the Jones house in the mistaken belief that the public wasn't ready for a change. My mail tells me otherwise. Two of my most popular houses from *Design and Construction* are the Volkswagen and Tompkins houses, both of which have this general shape.

Avoid Duplication and Unnecessary Spaces

Many people build houses that contain spaces they never use. Several years ago the "family room" became popular. It was added as an adjunct to the kitchen. Families with such a room soon found that they spent little, if any, time in the formal living room on the opposite end of the house. The separate, formal dining room has become almost as obsolete as the formal living

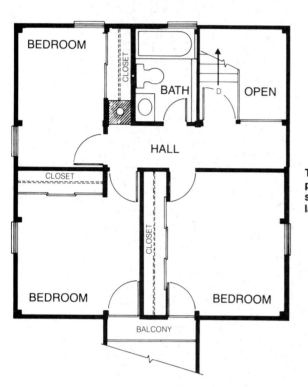

SECOND FLOOR PLAN

The Civic house is 24 feet square and encloses two full floors plus lofts. By eliminating wasted mechanical and circulation spaces, it has almost as much usable living space as the larger Jones house.

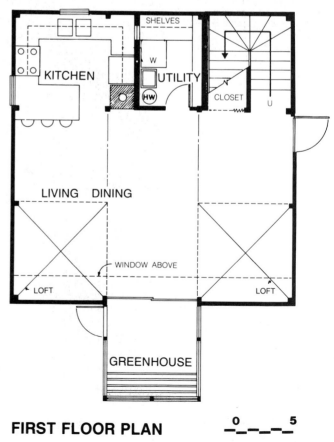

FIRST FLOOR PLAN

0 _ _ _ _ 5

room. It is used rarely, if ever, and serves mostly as a storage space for furniture. Why not take some of the area usually allotted to the living and dining rooms and incorporate it into one truly useful combination living space? The master bedroom might be enlarged for use as a private sitting room in place of the formal living room. People in other countries get by with much less living space per person, yet their houses are comfortable and livable.

Do you really need a garage? A modern, high-quality automobile gains nothing by having its own expensive house. Garages are really carry-overs from the days when cars didn't start well in the cold, and inferior paints had to be protected from the weather. Actually, most people use their garages as storage spaces for various, assorted junk. It's much cheaper to build a small storage shed instead. If you do insist upon a garage, you may want to consider building it yourself at a later date. In this way, you won't be making expensive mortgage payments on a space of secondary importance. The Civic house is designed so that a garage can be attached to the north wall if the site permits. The second version of the Civic house shows such a garage. In this case it is a workshop. It does have a garage door for occasional use if the car needs repairs.

A basement is a prime candidate for elimination as a cost-saving move. The laundry makes much more sense upstairs, and construction efficiencies have eliminated the furnace. If you are going to use the basement as a work area, get ready to transport materials and tools up and down stairs. If you really need the space of a basement, you would be much better to build it above grade. If you have a steeply sloping site and do want a basement, by all means build your house into the hillside. It is possible to build the first floor of the Civic house right into the slope. If you do need more space, you can easily add another level below the first floor of the Civic. Stairs to the lower level can be right under the stairs to the second floor.

Orientation

Since the basic Civic house is a square, it can be adapted to almost any conceivable site. But it is critical that the high wall face south. Windows on the other three sides have been reduced to a bare

minimum. Try to face the high wall within 45 degrees of true south. If you have a choice between southeast and southwest, southeast is much preferable. Since the walls are panelized, you can add windows almost anywhere. But try to avoid unnecessary windows on the north and west. Also, remember that windows lose considerable amounts of heat. If you add many windows, you will either have to increase the heating system or add thermal shutters for nighttime use.

Privacy can be a problem on small lots, particularly if you are trying to orient your house for maximum solar gain. South-facing windows may look out over a busy street or into a neighbor's yard. Remember that the sloping glass of the greenhouse creates a daytime privacy barrier by reflecting the sky rather than permitting a direct view inside. Windows that open into the greenhouse are shielded by this phenomenon. Nighttime thermal shutters provide complete privacy. For ground-level rooms, a fenced courtyard solves the problem nicely. For two of my clients, I have designed triangular courtyards. Their house is set at a 45-degree angle to the lot lines. The courts enable the house to be set close to the street, with private courtyards, so there is little space wasted in a front yard. The extensive rear yard is a garden and play space for the kids. Actually, the southern exposure suggested the 45-degree lot placement. In practice, the scheme works so well that you might want to cheat a bit on your orientation to duplicate it.

Whatever you do, don't rush the siting of your house. Once a mistake, always a mistake. Try putting stakes in the ground exactly where you think you want your house. Then mark where the windows and individual rooms will be located; garden lime or colored chalk is good for this purpose. Don't forget about the automobile. Plan your driveway and turnaround area so that you can get in and out with ease. If you plan to add a garage, barn, or workshop, now is the time to consider their proper locations. Try to visit the site several times with all members of the family before you break ground. Take along some folding chairs so you can sit in each room and get a sense of room relationships, outside views, and the like. Consider all the possibilities. You may change your mind and select another house design that is more suited to your lot.

15 Water Supply and Waste Disposal; Water-Saving Fixtures

People frequently underestimate the utility costs when they are drawing up budgets for low-cost houses. The cost of water and sewage disposal can easily overwhelm the finances for a small house. For large, expensive houses, these items are only a small fraction of the overall cost. But for small houses these items can easily consume 30 to 40% of the budget, and they are not costs that can be significantly reduced by cost-saving measures you can use elsewhere. This is particularly true in rural areas where you must drill your own well and install a septic system. Estimates for these items are at best educated guesses because of the variable nature of the systems. Municipal sewer and water systems can save you a great deal on first costs, but this advantage is offset by higher land costs and smaller lot sizes. Typical city connections cost between $400 and $1000. But in addition to this first cost, you also have to pay for your city services in taxes or sewer or water bills, and these costs are going to escalate over the years. A drilled well and septic system can range from $4500 to $10,000, or even more in difficult circumstances. Weigh these cost differences carefully before you commit yourself to a piece of property.

Water Sources

Assuming that you opt for country property without city mains, let's examine your possible sources of water. The usual water supply in this country is a drilled well. Wells can vary widely in depth, and your cost is directly related to this depth. You can get an idea of probable depth and cost by checking with close neighbors.

You are usually required to have the water tested for harmful bacteria before putting the well in service. Even if your bank or health department doesn't require testing, it's a good safety precaution. Much more important than a bacteria test is a test for trace chemical and metal contamination; deep underground water veins can carry such contaminants for miles. Local laboratories are usually not equipped to test for these contaminants. For proper professional testing, contact Water Test Corporation, Scytheville Row, Box 186, New London, NH 03257.

If your water should have an incurable bacterial contamination, don't despair. There are newly developed, effective means of controlling the problem. Ultraviolet sterilizing systems have been adapted for pool purification for people who are sensitive to chlorine. These units are available from pool suppliers and are acceptable to most health departments. Chlorinators are cheaper and also readily available. Health departments are not fond of them for private houses because they require frequent maintenance to operate properly. If you have chemical contaminants that are harmful to humans, you should arrange for another source of drinking water.

Pump Types

Submersible Impeller Type—the usual pump for quality installations. The pump is installed below water level inside the well casing, where it is protected from freezing. The usual depth of the unit is about 250 feet, maximum, although large, multistage units can pump up to 1000 feet. The unit must be removed from the well for servicing; an extremely difficult task for deep wells. *Do not use this type of pump in sandy conditions.*

Jet Type—the most common type for less expensive installations. Depth is limited to about 85 feet. The pump is installed aboveground where it is easy to service. The mechanism is durable and has few moving parts. The pump must be protected from freezing, and it is moderately noisy. Sand will also damage this pump.

Shallow-Well Piston Type—the old standby for shallow wells. Depth is limited to 22 feet. This pump can be used with slightly sandy water. The pump can be offset from the well and must be protected from freezing. A handle can be attached for hand operation if necessary. These pumps are quite noisy and need periodic maintenance.

Deep-Well Piston Type—must be positioned directly over the well and will pump to depths of 600 feet. This is the pump usually used with farm windmills. It can also be used with a hand-force pump. It is simple and easy to maintain. This type is no longer in common use.

Submersible Helical Rotor Type—similar to a standard submersible pump, except that the water is pumped by a helical rotor rather than an impeller. An expensive, top-of-the-line, but hard-to-find pump that is used for deep wells with heavy concentrations of sand. Will pump up to 1000 feet. The pump must be removed from well for servicing.

Springs and dug or driven shallow wells are possible alternatives to deep-drilled wells. These are usually much cheaper than deep wells and are fed by different aquifers so that they may be free of chemicals. In some cases, they will be subject to contamination from surface water and will need a purification system. Shallow sources of water are much more likely to run dry during the summer and fall months, so try to check the source during a dry period before you become dependent upon it.

In areas with extremely deep water tables or chronic water shortages, a cistern designed to collect roof water may be used as a source of water. If you use a cistern, you will probably have to ration your water usage. Luckily, in areas of the country where cisterns are common, water is usually available from bulk trucks to replenish the cistern during dry months of the year. If you live in an industrial area, the rainwater may become contaminated with chemicals and thus not be suitable for drinking. A good cistern design includes a diverter device so that dirt washed off the roof by the initial rainfall doesn't contaminate the cistern. My basic Civic house has a monopitch roof that is ideal for use with a cistern, since the water can easily be collected in one spot. My earlier book *A Design and Construction Handbook for Energy-Saving Houses* (Rodale Press, 1980), gives details for construction of a 4000-gallon cistern. Even if you have another water source, a cistern can be a handy, extra supply for watering the garden or as an emergency water supply during power outages or drought periods.

Water Conservation

Both water supply systems and sewage disposal systems are related in size and cost to how much water you actually use. It is therefore imperative to eliminate unnecessary water use. Most plumbing supply manufacturers now market 3½-gallon flush toilets as their standard fixtures, although some still stick to the old 5-gallon flush toilets, so make your selection with care. If you have a really serious water supply problem, you may want to use one of the minimum-water toilets described later in this chapter, or possibly a completely waterless toilet, such as Hundertwasser's, described in Chapter 6.

Typical consumption of water in the United States varies from 60 to 80 gallons per person per day, depending upon which authority you consult and how careful the consumers are in their use of water. Many state codes enforce these quantities as the minimum allowable for an approved dwelling unit. By using waterless or minimum-water-use toilets and practicing stringent conservation measures, it is quite possible to cut these consumption figures to 10 to 15 gallons per day and still live quite comfortably. Recent water shortages have shown that people respond enthusiastically to water conservation when faced with the likelihood of having no water at all.

Water Savings

Other countries have lived with water shortages and waste disposal problems far longer than we have. Sweden, in particular, has areas of country-side with rocky soil where using conventional toilets just isn't possible. To solve their problems, they have developed most of the better brands of composting toilets, many of which are now available in this country. The Swedes have also done research on low-flush toilets. IFÖ Sanitar AB of Bromolla, Sweden, has developed a line of water-saving toilets that are probably the finest toilets made anywhere in the world. Except for their streamlined shape and tall, narrow flush tank, they look just like conventional toilets.

They work by a siphon process instead of the gravity feed system that our toilets use. A small knob in the center of the tank lid is pulled up to start the siphon action, which sucks water up a concentric tube to the top of the overflow tube, where it is discharged into the toilet. Thus, the effective distance for the water to fall is measured from the top of a tall tank rather than from the bottom of a squat one. The extra force of the

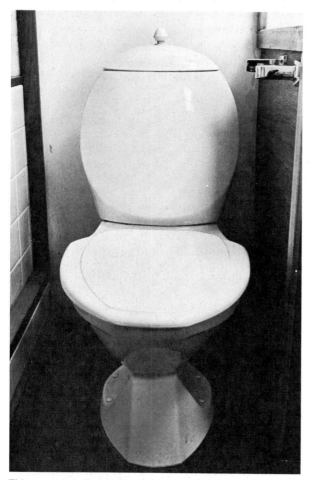

This super low-flush toilet uses about 2 quarts of water per flush.

water along with a more efficient bowl shape allows the volume of the tank to be greatly reduced. The elegant-looking toilets are complemented by a full line of matching fixtures. The toilets are about $300, and the other fixtures are at comparable prices. They are available in this country from: Western Builders Co-Op, 2150 Pine Drive, Prescott, AZ 86301.

Even though this toilet is a bit expensive, it can save you money because it requires a smaller septic tank and disposal system than 5-gallon toilets. A final word of caution: The outlet for this efficient toilet is only 6 inches from the wall rather than the usual 12 inches. If you do plan to use one, make sure that you put the drain in the correct place.

If the $300 IFÖ toilet is more than the budget allows, there is a Canadian alternative. It is the Royal Flush-o-matic manufactured by Sanitation Equipment Limited, 1081 Alness Street, Downs-view, ON M3J 2J1. Cost and roughing-in dimensions are the same as for a conventional toilet, but this model uses only 1 quart per flush. There are a couple of drawbacks: It's funny looking, and it's made of plastic. The action of the toilet is very simple; it has a mechanically activated flap rather than a trap for a water seal. When the flap is in the closed position, there is water in the bowl, but there isn't a large trap that needs filling nor evacuating by water. The toilet meets all national codes in Canada and the United States. It is used as standard equipment in the Family Homes Cooperative houses and can be purchased from FHC in the United States (see Chapter 12). I would caution you to make sure that the sewer line has plenty of drop and that the septic tank is close to the house if you use this toilet. Otherwise, you may have trouble with the sewer clogging because of the low volume of water.

To save all water possible, use flow restrictors at all water faucets and shower heads in your house. Low-flow shower heads can more than cut water flow in half; low-flow faucet aerators are about twice as good at saving water as standard faucet aerators. These restrictors not only save water, they also save fuel for heating hot water. If you are using a small, instantaneous water heater, you may have to use flow restrictors in order to have hot enough water.

Even though the past several years have been unusually wet in many areas of the country, potential water shortages are a ticking time bomb, no less serious than energy shortages. Wasteful industrial and residential water consumption is

This owner-built Japanese soaking tub provides warm comfort at modest cost. The shower stall is to the left. The natural cedar trim sets off the white tile of the tub and surround.

steadily lowering the permanent level of underground water sources. Certain areas of the Northeast and Southwest are already experiencing chronic water shortages that will get worse as populations continue to grow. Even if water conservation does not directly affect the cost of your new house, it is a very worthwhile endeavor.

Wastewater Disposal

Wastewater disposal is another big-ticket item for the budget-conscious homebuilder. Even though city sewage hookups are relatively inexpensive, you pay for them through taxes and user fees. If you are within municipal limits and have access to a sewer, you will undoubtedly be required to connect to the system and pay the appropriate charges. If you don't now have a sewer system but your city decides to build a system, you will be obligated to hook up to it and pay for the hookup—at a cost that can exceed $1500. Some of the options that follow may be useful to you, but

you will still have to make the official connection if the health officials are on their toes and it is physically possible to hook your house up to the system.

Septic Systems

A septic tank with a perforated tile drain field is the accepted method of sewage disposal in rural and suburban areas of North America. These systems work well if the soil and slope are right. Unfortunately, the same conditions necessary for a properly working septic system are also ideal for farmland (i.e. good topsoil cover, level land, good drainage, porous, well-drained soil, and so on). Since we are rapidly losing our valuable farmland to housing developments, you might want to consider building on some not-so-ideal property and using another type of disposal system (see later in this chapter for a discussion of alternate systems).

Since you are most likely to use a septic tank as your disposal method, it will pay to examine costs carefully. If you are on level land with good drainage and at least 2 feet of soil cover over rock, you will be allowed to install an "in-ground" septic system. These are simple and easy to install; the cost will vary from about $1200 to $3000, depending upon the size of the system and the region of the country. The tank itself can be steel, fiberglass, precast concrete or site-built concrete and concrete block. The capacity will vary from 500 to 1000 gallons, depending upon the regulations and the number of bedrooms. Typical health departments require a 750-gallon tank for a three-bedroom house. The steel and fiberglass tanks are relatively inexpensive, light, and easy to install. However, they are easily damaged by trucks and heavy equipment, and the steel tanks have a very short life span. I do not recommend either of these. The usual standard of the industry is a precast concrete tank, which is very heavy and has to be delivered by a special truck to facilitate installation. These can be expensive in remote or inaccessible areas.

It is quite possible to construct a septic tank yourself at the site. In some cases, you may have to do this or use a lightweight, easily transported tank. A good, seviceable, site-built tank can be constructed of concrete and concrete block. The walls of the tank and the baffle are constructed of stacked-bond, 8-inch concrete block set on a poured concrete slab. The tank is covered with a site-cast concrete slab, which is then slid into place. Excellent details for installing a septic system are available in a pamphlet, *Onsite Domestic*

Disposal Field Alternatives

The traditional septic tank is an excellent means of waste disposal. It causes few problems of its own; the difficulties always arise with the disposal field, which must have a relatively large area of level ground with good drainage and absorption. When these conditions are difficult or impossible to meet, other means of effluent disposal should be considered.

Lagoons—may replace the conventional underground absorption field in areas with impervious soils. A properly sized lagoon can serve several septic tanks, but the design is critical and must be made by a professional. Lagoons must be relatively shallow to allow for proper evaporation, and the inlet piping must be at the bottom to prevent freeze-ups. A fence is usually required around a lagoon.

Evapo-Transpiration Systems—use closely spaced piping close to the ground surface to grow plants. They are good for rocky soils in warm climates. Do not use such a system where the temperature regularly drops below freezing. Plants must be selected carefully or the roots will clog the piping. Hundertwasser's stepped tank system is a variation of this type (see Chapter 6).

Sand Filters—an alternative system to the one usually proposed by health officials. Sand filters can either be a trench type similar to a standard disposal field, or a cleanable bulk filter with a recirculation tank. In the first type, sand is merely used to replace impervious material in what is otherwise a conventional disposal field. The second type uses a tank similar to a septic tank with a pump to circulate the effluent through a sand filter. The second type takes up much less space, but it does require power for the pump and periodic maintenance of the filter.

Aerobic System—basically a small version of a commercial system like those used by small communities. A conventional septic tank breaks down wastes by treating them with anaerobic bacteria (bacteria that grow only in an airless environment). In an aerobic system, on the other hand, a pump is used to aerate the effluent so that airborne bacteria can purify the effluent. For residential use, these units work best if they are attached to the outlet of a conventional septic tank. These systems are expensive and require careful monitoring and maintenance. For cramped, steep sites or those close to water, this may be the only solution that will be approved by health authorities.

Most aerobic plants are giant affairs intended for municipal use. Two companies that market high-quality systems suitable for residential use are:

Cromaglass Wastewater Treatment
  Systems
Box 3125
Williamsport, PA 17701

Hitachi Chemical Company of America
437 Madison Avenue
New York, NY 10022

(Both are approved for individual house use in the United States under National Sanitation Foundation standard No. 40.)

Sewage Disposal Handbook. The order number is MWPS-24 and it is available from Midwest Plan Service, 122 Davidson Hall, Iowa State University, Ames, IA 50011. I also recommend a companion publication, *Private Water Systems Handbook* (MWPS-14). These fine references are available for $4 each. The same source has excellent plans for a wide variety of farm structures if you need this information.

If you do install your own septic system, you will probably encounter stiff opposition from your local health authorities. There are virtually no laws prohibiting owners from doing their own work, but the inspectors will worry (with some justification) that the job won't be performed properly. A few areas of the country require that the installation be performed by a licensed contractor, and other areas will require inspection by one. The most important single factor to consider is proper grade for drainage. All piping must slope gradually and uniformly to the end of the system. In addition, it must be firmly supported so that it maintains the proper slope. If any fill is necessary, it must be thoroughly compacted before installing drainage piping. If an area of piping does settle, sludge will collect there and clog your system. Materials for a simple, basic system in an area with good drainage will cost $500 to $700, as opposed to $1500 to $3000 to have one installed, so you have the potential to save a good deal of money. *Warning:* This is very hard work and quite exacting. Unless you are really hard up, hire a professional.

With any on-site disposal system, you should do what you can to limit the load on the system. Garbage disposals are a particular enemy of the septic system. Many codes require doubling the system size if you use one; others outlaw disposals altogether. Septic systems must have sludge pumped out every 3 to 5 years; installing a garbage disposal will increase the frequency to about once a year. Failure to remove sludge from the system results in clogging the perforated tile and will cost you a new drain field; an expensive oversight.

Other Disposal Systems

There are many other systems for sewage disposal, but they are usually difficult to get approved by health authorities. In many areas, steep slopes, bedrock, waterways, and the like will preclude a conventional septic system. In fact, in many cases, you can purchase property for very little money because it has problems with sewage disposal. If you think you want an alternate waste disposal system and have the perseverance to fight it through with the authorities, there are many bargains awaiting you in properties with the problems mentioned above.

Alternate systems can vary in size and cost from something simple and primitive, such as a pit privy or Hundertwasser's composting system, to elaborate commercial units, such as a Clivus Multrum or Ecology One Microsanitizer. Costs can vary from a few hundred dollars to several thousand dollars.

All the alternate systems, except the pit privy and the Ecology One unit, use some variation of a natural composting process. The pit privy simply collects the wastes and they gradually decompose over the years; Ecology One sanitizes the wastes (see the discussion that follows this section). All the various composting toilets have similar virtues and vices. On the positive side, they do not consume any water, and they produce as an end product a high-grade fertilizer that may be used on ornamental plants. Almost all the composting toilets require fans, electrical heating, and mechanical or manual mixing of the waste. The units require careful attention, just as do garden compost piles. Kitchen wastes and other matter rich in carbon must be added periodically to balance out the high nitrogen content of bathroom wastes, and liquid buildup and fruit flies can cause problems. For a society trained to "flush and forget," these units can pose insurmountable problems. But for those who care about the environment and waste and are intrigued by the composting process, these toilets are a fine solution.

Composting toilets pose special problems when dealing with building inspectors and health departments. Most codes do not recognize this type of disposal system, and in order to get it approved,

A well-designed pit privy is still an ideal low-cost alternative for some people. The Victorian version shown here is quite elegant.

the governing official will have to stick his neck out and give you a special permit. If you can assure the official that you are a responsible individual who will properly maintain the system and give the authorities permission to monitor the results, you may be able to get such approval. Our local village of Woodstock has received federal funds to install an experimental waste disposal system that incorporates a large number of composting toilets. In this case, permission was granted because the houses are packed so closely together that there is no available area for proper septic systems. (The usual system requires 600 to 1000 square feet of ground area.) The definitive text on these systems is *Goodbye to the Flush Toilet* by Carol Hupping Stoner (Rodale Press, 1977). This excellent book gives detailed pros and cons on composting toilets as well as sources for plans for building your own.

Microsanitizer

For those who are concerned about the environment or want to build in an area where conventional systems just won't work but do not have the time or conviction to deal with compost systems, modern science has devised a fine alternative. Ecology One (3675 East 11 Avenue, Hialeah, FL 33013) markets a system that completely sanitizes sewage, filters out the solids, and either reuses or discharges the treated effluent. The system is marketed in three different configurations depending upon the intended use, but the basic mechanism is the same for all three systems. The systems consist of a low-flush toilet, a macerator or sewage grinder, a holding tank with a pump, a sanitizing device called a microsanitizer, and a filter cartridge with a replaceable filter. Except for the microsanitizer, this system is similar to those used on airplanes, trains, boats, and other public transportation. The big difference lies in the small microsanitizer box, which contains a sealed microwave unit that allegedly completely sanitizes the wastes. The manufacturer has received U.S. Coast Guard approval for overboard discharge of effluent and has laboratory tests to prove the effectiveness of their unit.

The marine unit just mentioned simply disposes the effluent overboard; the same system may be used with a holding tank for irrigation water. One client has used an underfloor distribution system to water flowers in a commercial solar greenhouse. A second variation of the disposal system is intended for mobile homes and adds a filter that allows continual recirculation of the flush water. This would be an ideal variation for areas of extreme water shortages. Although it is primarily intended for mobile homes, it could be used in a permanent house if one were willing to spend extra time and money in frequent filter replacement. Two filters must be replaced once a month (normal use for a family of four).

The residential and commercial version of the microsanitizer system the company promotes most highly also filters household greywater and discharges the effluent into a small disposal field similar to that which is usually connected to a septic tank. The field can be very small (usually about 300 square feet), and since it is disposing of sanitized effluent, the pipes can be installed adjacent to waterways, bedrock, or on slopes—areas that would prohibit a conventional distribution system.

There are some limitations to this disposal scheme, however. It requires a dependable source of electrical power, which might preclude its use in remote areas. The sewage from the primary tank is treated in batches, and while there is enough reserve capacity for a couple of days of use, extended blackouts would knock out the system. The 55-gallon primary tank, pump, and filter would be best installed in a basement or crawl space; special allowances would have to be made for a slab-on-grade house. The microsanitizer unit itself is quite small and can be installed above the floor. The unit consumes 1400 watts of power, but only for a few minutes when actually processing sewage. Maintenance for the household system consists of changing a filter once a month and flushing out a greywater screen. The system appears to be very well constructed and should require a minimum of attention, but as with all things electrical and mechanical, there is always the possibility of breakdown. You are also dealing with a new technique that would not be familiar to a local plumber. All in all, though, this looks like a fine solution to difficult situations. The manufacturer quotes an installed cost of $2500 for the residential system with disposal field. This price would be considerably cheaper than an aboveground septic system, such as would be required in areas that can't support a conventional septic system.

Holding Tanks

The conventional standby for difficult sewage disposal situations is to install a holding tank that is frequently pumped out (at considerable expense) by a septic system cleaning company. The clever Japanese have developed a toilet especially for this purpose which uses an astounding *1 cupful* of water per flush. There is a catch—it uses a chemical foam and a tiny air compressor that mixes with a small amount of water to flush the toilet. The electrical consumption is minuscule, and the toilet is available either as a 12- or 120-volt model. Unlike most low-volume toilets of reasonable price, this one is constructed of china and looks similar to a conventional toilet. The toilet model is called Pearl and is manufactured by Nepon of Tokyo. It is distributed throughout the United States and Canada by John Averill (Box 33, Sandstone, WV 25985).

I did not include this toilet with the other low-flush models because the water volume would be insufficient to transport the waste to a conventional tank. Also, the chemicals would interfere with the action of the bacteria in a septic tank. Although not specifically recommended, this toilet would be ideal for use with the microsanitizer system I just described. With normal use for a family of four, a 250-gallon holding tank would only need to be emptied once or twice a year. For comparison, a normal, low-flush toilet holding tank system uses a 1000-gallon tank and is emptied every two weeks. The Pearl toilet and 250-gallon holding tank can be installed for $500 to $700; quite a bargain compared to some alternatives.

16 Energy-Saving Equipment

The permanent and movable energy-related equipment that is used in your house can have an enormous impact upon your energy bills. The dollar value of the energy savings can be staggering, as Ecotope, a Seattle-based group of engineers specializing in energy use consultation, has discovered. Ecotope has calculated that, over a 20-year period, the energy savings in the 968-square-foot Family Homes Cooperative (FHC) house can result in a $48,000 cost saving when compared to a conventional builder's house with minimal insulation. This cost figure does not include potential savings from cooking, refrigeration, or small appliances, so the total savings over a 40-year assumed life of a house could easily exceed $100,000. The Ecotope figures are based upon electric heating with very conservative inflation factors. In reality, no such savings would actually occur because extremely high electric rates would force the use of heavy insulation or a switch to other sources of fuel for the houses that are being used for comparison.

My definition of energy-saving equipment includes any manufactured item associated with the house that impacts upon the consumption of energy. Heating and cooling devices are so complex that I've devoted an entire chapter to them, Chapter 17. In this chapter here I speak of all the other energy-related items: windows and doors, along with traditional energy devices, such as hot water heaters, heat exchangers, and small appliances. Cost savings cited for various appliances are based upon manufacturers' published energy consumption and fuel cost data as required by the U.S. Department of Energy. Energy costs are based upon the national average for 1982. Obviously, there are considerable fluctuations in energy rates and appliance usage patterns, but the relative savings should be accurate.

Windows and Doors

In the new breed of superinsulated houses, windows and doors become the primary source of heat leakage to the outside. They should be selected just as carefully as any appliance, since they are permanently built into the structure and cannot readily be changed. Regardless of what make of window you use, concentrate them on the south side for maximum heat gain. Even using triple-glazed, double–weather-stripped windows throughout, $5000 of the $48,000 savings in the Ecotope calculations resulted from solar gain in south-facing windows.

Peachtree Door Company makes a line of magnetically weather-stripped, foam-core steel doors. FHC markets a dandy, foam-insulated, red oak entrance door if you prefer wood as I do. If you must place an entrance door on a windy side of the house, make sure to use an air-lock entry. Do not use sliding glass doors except in an interior location, such as between the house proper and a greenhouse. Marvin, Pella, and other quality manufacturers now market what they call "patio replacement doors." These units have one fixed glass and a hinged door. They are a vast improvement over sliders in both cutting down on air infiltration and assuring better security.

Operating windows should be strictly limited to areas where they are needed for safety or ventilation. They should be of either casement or awning-hopper type. Windows that slide in any direction (including double-hung windows) should be avoided, since they cannot be well sealed. If your design calls for large areas of south-facing glass, the panes should be stationary and should be equipped with insulating shutters. Arrange your ventilation above or below the windows.

Bedrooms must have at least one fully operating window of 5 to 6 feet in area not more than 3 feet from floor to the sill. All the window manufacturers that I recommend make special windows designed for easy egress. Check your code carefully, since the exact size requirements vary.

Small, progressive window manufacturers have responded to the energy crisis with high-quality, weathertight windows. All the better companies make triple-glazed windows; many are also double weather-stripped. For instance, a double–weatherstripped Weathershield casement window has one-seventh the air infiltration of highly advertised lumberyard brands.

I have singled out four brands of windows, each with unique features, for my personal recommendation. In my opinion, Weathershield represents the best value for the dollar on the market if you are concerned primarily with energy savings. Their windows are available triple glazed with double weatherstripping at very reasonable prices. Weathershield windows are standard equipment in the FHC house packages (see Chapter 12). Marvin is still my favorite because they are custom-made and can be obtained in any size or style without paint. They are available with triple glazing and double weatherstripping, but at a hefty premium price. Even though these windows are custom-made, they are frequently delivered more quickly than competitively priced, ready-made windows, which have to be ordered from a warehouse.

Two window companies make fine premium-priced windows. Hurd makes a super, energy-saving window that employs a product called Heat-Mirror. Heat-Mirror is a plastic film with a special coating that reflects heat. The Hurd windows are triple glazed with a layer of this clear plastic between two layers of glass. The exterior surface of the window frame is clad in aluminum for durability. Heat-Mirror works well for reducing

cooling loads in summer as well as trapping heat in winter. Hurd windows have a perfectly uniform frame profile, which makes them desirable for use in our panelized walls. At the moment these windows are extremely expensive, and I hope that mass production will bring the cost down.

Pella Company makes another premium-priced window with unique features. Again, the exterior frame is aluminum clad and the windows are triple glazed, but with ordinary glass. The unique feature of these windows is a thin venetian blind set between two of the layers of the glass. The result is not quite as good as the Hurd unit, but you have the advantage of a built-in window shade. This helps a great deal in summer, and of course provides privacy without additional external curtains. Again, a steep price, but very high quality.

Heat Exchangers

If you build a really tight house, what do you do about moisture buildup and stale air? These are very real problems in well-sealed houses. Of course, you could open a window, but that defeats the purpose. Air-to-air heat exchangers transfer the heat from exhaust air into cool, fresh air drawn from outside the house. A more detailed description of the operation of these exchangers, as well as sources of supply, is given in Chapter 17. Heat exchangers do not directly save energy—in fact they consume it. But they are virtually a necessity for tight houses in a cold climate. If you have less than 3000 degree-days in your heating season or have only a moderately insulated house, you do not need to worry about getting one.

Water Heaters

Water heaters consume almost one-third of the energy used by private houses in this country. This is completely unnecessary and easy to rectify. The "worst-case" American house has a large, poorly insulated tank that is heated with an electric resistance element to an absurdly high temperature 24 hours per day. These monstrosities are unheard of in the rest of the world. Virtually everyone else uses demand-type water heaters that only heat water when you are actually using it. Progressive countries such as Japan and Israel use inexpensive, batch-type solar water heaters for a major portion of their water-heating needs. Unlike space-heating systems, which are linked to insulation levels and the size of your house, water heaters are independent units and you have no one to blame but yourself if yours uses too much energy.

Whatever heat source you use for hot water, it makes no sense to use expensive energy to heat the water to a high temperature, only to mix it with cold water to bring it to a comfortably warm temperature to make it usable. Start your energy savings by reducing the water temperature to between 105 and 110°F. The only possible reason for hotter water is for proper operation of a dishwasher; these do need much hotter water. All major brands of dishwashers are available with a booster heater to raise the water temperature. Make sure that your dishwasher is equipped with a booster—better still, wash the dishes by hand.

Instantaneous hot water heaters are now stocked by most reputable plumbing supply houses. They are usually referred to in the trade as "demand-type" heaters. Fuel sources can be electricity, natural gas, or propane. The electrical units are cheapest to buy, but the savings are quickly eaten up by the cost of heating water with electricity instead of gas. The beauty of these units is that they only consume fuel when you are using hot water. For a small family, or as a backup unit for a solar water heater, the electrical instantaneous units are the most sensible choice. If you use sizable quantities of hot water, electricity will be expensive regardless of the type of heater. In this case, I strongly recommend one of the gas instantaneous units. In addition to the extra cost of the gas heater, you will have to provide a vent for it. Although small, unvented instantaneous heaters are common in other countries and they are marketed here, the American Gas Association does not approve their use in this country. For a tightly constructed house without a heat exchanger, they could be dangerous, particularly if they run for long periods of time. However, several of my clients have used these small units with no problems. Water flow is limited and flow restrictors must be used to ensure adequate pressure. Costs for the electric and small unvented gas models are around $200. The larger gas/propane models are about double the price.

For those who must reduce first cost to an absolute minimum, the standard tank-type heater, new or used, is the obvious choice. If you must use electricity, add a timer and heavy insulation to the basic tank. If it is a used tank, install a new, high-efficiency heating element. The commercially hyped, insulated water tank jackets are thin and overpriced. For an electric heater, I recommend building an enclosure of 2-inch Thermax. The enclosure should seal all sides and the bottom and have a hinged panel on the front for access to the electrical connections. Build the enclosure before making the final piping connec-

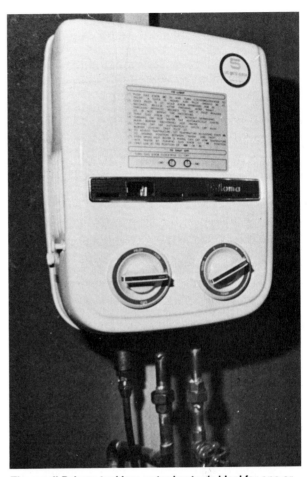

The small Paloma tankless water heater is ideal for one or two people, provided that flow restrictors are used to cut down on hot water consumption.

tions. You can buy commercial units with this level of insulation, but they charge several hundred dollars extra. You should also use a plastic thermal break connector on the hot water line to help keep the hot water in the tank. Finally, insulate all hot water lines from the tank to fixtures. If you do all this, you can reduce the electric heating cost to about one-third.

A gas tank-type heater is a much better buy than the electrical units. Again, be wary of the very expensive, superinsulated commercial units. For instance, Sears sells a high-priced, superinsulated gas water heater that costs over twice as much as another unit of the same size. After reading the fine print on the required energy use table, you discover that the expensive unit saves an amazing $4 per year in fuel costs. Recovery rates are virtually identical. The gas heater should also have a thermal coupling and insulated piping. Do not try to insulate with Thermax since the burner needs air for combustion and the vent pipe gets very hot. A commercial insulating jacket can be used, but make absolutely sure that you maintain proper clearances for combustion air at the bottom and the exhaust stack at the top. The Sears Model No. 415.33036 30-gallon, gas hot water heater costs about $130 and is the best buy for the cost conscious. Fuel costs should be between $100 and $200 per year.

Solar water heaters are widely touted because they theoretically eliminate all or most of the fuel costs. Unfortunately, many of the active solar models sold in this country are engineering monstrosities that cost around $4000 installed. They also have a rather limited life span and tend to break down a lot. If you are out of your mind enough to use an electric water heater that costs $1000 per year to operate, these heaters are a great alternative. Typical active solar units have a copper or aluminum collector mounted on the roof through which an antifreeze solution is circulated. These collectors are connected to a remote tank with a heat exchanger through which the heated antifreeze solution flows to actually heat the water. In the more extravagant systems electric resistance backup elements are provided in the tank for cloudy days or periods of excessive consumption. All this is watched over by a control system that costs several times as much as a conventional water heater. As long as there are federal and state solar tax credits, energy-conscious, gadget-loving homeowners will continue to install these units.

Fortunately, for those of us who care about saving natural resources, there are practical solar devices at reasonable cost. These are called passive solar, or batch-type solar, water heaters. They are usually rooftop mounted and simply collect the sun's heat directly in a black tank housed in an insulated box. Steve Baer popularized these "breadbox"-type solar water heaters in this country in the early 1970s. Until recently, they weren't available commercially but were only homemade units that were highly subject to variations in the skills of those doing the fabrication. In order to work really well and to prevent nighttime freeze-ups, the heaters usually have a manual shutter system that insulates them when the sun isn't shining.

As we have seen in Chapter 5, it is now possible to make very sophisticated heaters of this type for a reasonable cost. The Japanese are just starting to export them in quantity. Fortunately, U.S. companies have not been entirely asleep, and there are some good American-made units to choose from. The American units are larger,

An award-winning solar water heater of the batch type graces my kitchen roof. Its 35-gallon capacity is skimpy.

heavier, and more expensive than their competition; shipping costs and excessive roof loads could pose problems.

Commercially available passive solar water heaters are typically an insulated box containing a 30- to-50-gallon tank. Freeze control is provided by triple glazing, electric heaters, or insulated manual flaps or shutters. Shutters give maximum efficiency, but are a nuisance to open and close. One commercial unit has solved the shutter problem nicely. The Sunrunner by TEF Manufacturing of Fresno, California, is a water heater with an internal, motorized automatic flap. They are so confident of the dependability of this shutter arrangement that they guarantee the unit from freezing anywhere within the continental United States for a period of five years. The shutter motor is activated by a nonelectrical furnace limit thermostat. The motor itself is run on 24 volts. It is normally connected to a 110-volt relay inside the house, but could be used with photovoltaic cells or a wind generation system.

Refrigeration

Right behind water heating in residential energy consumption is the refrigeration of food. Operating costs of typical refrigerators and freezers are high because they are poorly insulated and have excessive frost buildup. To correct their initial mistakes, the manufacturers install automatic electric resistance heating systems to eliminate the frost. If a refrigerator is very well insulated and designed so that moist air from the refrigerator box itself does not come into direct contact with the coils, no frost will form and foods will not have their usual tendency to dry out as in a conventional refrigerator.

Let's examine three possibilities for refrigerating and freezing food. First, we have the "normal," 15-cubic-foot, side-by-side refrigerator-freezer that costs from $900 to $1200 to purchase. It is equipped with "extra-heavy" insulation and has a 6-cubic-foot freezer and a 9-cubic-foot refrigerator, both with automatic defrosting mechanisms. This contraption costs from $300 to $400 per year to operate at 15¢ per kilowatt-hour electric rates (which is what I am paying now in 1984).

An alternative—a manual 11-cubic-foot refrigerator—has 10 cubic feet of refrigerator space and 1 cubic foot of freezer, all behind one door. As a companion, we add a 6-cubic-foot, chest-type freezer, also with manual defrost. The purchase price of the two units together is between $500 and $600, and the energy consumption is between $100 and $200 per year. Not only do you get more capacity, you get it at considerably lower cost. Without figuring inflation, you save over $5000 in a 20-year period. You do have to do some work to earn that $5000 though; these are both manual defrost units and will have to be defrosted periodically. But the $5000 savings is going to be worth this effort to most people.

Want to save even more money and have greater capacity with no defrosting? A top refrigeration designer has gone into business custom-making refrigerator-freezers. If you design the unit properly, it does make sense to have the two units combined. Larry Schlussler of Sun Frost in Arcata, California, has a very special 17-cubic-foot refrigerator-freezer that reduces the electrical consumption to an amazingly low cost of less than $30 per year. This magic was worked by using superinsulation and devising a three-compartment refrigerator-freezer with the freezer in the center compartment.

All the mechanical equipment is located on top of the unit where it can get maximum air circulation. Since the freezer is in the middle, it is surrounded by cold and doesn't require much extra energy for cooling. The two refrigerator sections are so well insulated that they can be cooled without condensing frost. Not only do you save energy normally spent with automatic or manual defrosting, but the foods are not dehydrated as in a conventional refrigerator. The refrigerator can be made to run on 12 or 24 volts DC or 110 volts AC. It is primarily designed to be used for alternate energy applications such as wind power or photovoltaic systems, but I think it makes great sense for almost anyone. The initial cost is quite high, over $2000, but the 20-year cost saves another $1000 over the manual defrost refrigerator and freezer package. As an added bonus, you get an elegant, custom-made cabinet in your choice of woods or Formica.

For about the same price as a side-by-side refrigerator-freezer, Larry markets a 4-cubic-foot, chest-type refrigerator-freezer. It's practically all refrigerator with just a small section for ice-cube trays. It could be just the ticket for those on a budget with no commercial source of electricity. Consumption is 17.5 ampere-hours per day.

Ranges

As in other energy-related appliances, considerable progress has been made in cooking ranges. Again, the Japanese are leading the way. Sanyo markets an inexpensive, single-burner, induction-type table range that has a great many advantages. The primary advantage is very low energy consumption—less than gas cooking. Those who like to cook and loathe electric ranges, as I do, will be delighted by the instant response to the heat control. You must use iron pots to cook on this range since it cooks by heating the pot, not by heating a burner. American manufacturers have mastered this same technology, but, as usual, they've taken the usual approach—that of marketing anything new as a superluxury item. Chambers and Sears both market full-size ranges with induction-type heating, but their prices are too high to justify the energy savings. In the meantime, buy the Sanyo or wait for prices to come down.

Convection-type ovens are another energy saver. The convection oven saves energy by using fan-forced circulation to cook the food. The result is shorter cooking times with a lower oven temperature. They can be either gas or electric fired. Because of potential poisonous fume buildup, I prefer the electric models. Jenn-Air makes a dandy one, but it is expensive. Sears imports a line of expensive combination microwave-convection ovens that are similar to the Sanyo. The cheapest model costs about $600, and it cannot be built-in. Several companies market very small, portable convection ovens that work very well; as a matter of fact, I have used one of the small portables for several years and recommend it highly.

Washing and Drying Clothes

The typical automatic washing machine not only wastes energy, it wastes precious water. If you use hot water for washing, it wastes even more energy. An *electric* dryer is just as absurd as an electric water heater. My nudist clients in Florida have solved the problem nicely, but the rest of us should select laundry equipment carefully.

Many years ago, American appliance manufacturers marketed dandy two-tub washing machines. The clothes were washed in one tub and rinsed and damp-dried in a separate spin tub. The big advantage to this system is in water savings. You can reuse the wash water, starting with lightly soiled light colors and progressing to darker, heavily soiled clothes. If you are using hot water, you don't have to use so much of it. The sole surviving American manufacturer of this superior energy- and water-saving machine is the Hoover Corporation. But their unit is on the small side and you must load up the washer several times to do a regular-size load; the two-tub configuration means that you keep busy all of the time. The washing action, however, is very efficient and much faster than "modern" automatics. If you live in an area of water shortages, this is the machine to use. It also eliminates the necessity of a separate dryer; clothes are damp-dried and dry very quickly, indoors or out. The Hoover is manufactured in Canada, but is available throughout the United States and Canada. It costs less than $150, which makes it quite a bargain when compared to the typical $900 price tag for a washer and dryer pair. If you must have a full-size

washer and dryer, choose them carefully. The washer should have a suds-saver feature, which permits reuse of wash water, and it should have controls that automatically adjust the amount of water used to the size of the wash load. Unfortunately, machines with these features tend to be a bit higher priced, but the water savings is worth the extra expense.

The very best, lowest-cost clothes dryer is called a clothes line. If you must have a dryer, get a gas-fired one. Even though they are a bit more expensive, the energy savings will pay the extra cost in a matter of months. Do not dump the exhaust directly into the house, though. This can cause ruinous moisture buildup, especially in tight, new houses. And gas exhaust fumes are deadly. In winter months, you will want to use a heat exchanger to capture the waste heat. Brookstone (127 Vose Farm Road, Peterborough, NH 03458) markets a dandy unit for about $50 that can be used with gas or electric dryers (most such units can be used with electric dryers only).

Small Appliances and Gadgets

Let me finish up this chapter with assorted bits of advice: Check the electrical labels carefully before purchasing appliances. A television set can use 12 watts or it can use 250 watts. If you use it a lot, the inefficient one could cost you a great deal of money. Similarly, radios, hi-fi sets, and kitchen appliances vary greatly in energy consumption. Try to avoid anything with a resistance heating element in it. If you want an electric blanket, get an electric sheet instead. It uses a third of the electricity because it goes under you and the covers, rather than on top. Norelco has devised a tidy little fluorescent lamp bulb that screws into a conventional incandescent socket. The manufacturer claims that an 18-watt fluorescent bulb gives off just as much light as a 75-watt incandescent bulb. For more information contact: Philips Corporation, 1 Westinghouse Plaza, Bloomfield, NJ 07003.

17 Heating Systems

We have spent some extra money and effort to make our building shell well insulated and airtight. Now we can reap the benefits. Just as there has been a revolution in building construction, there has been a corresponding one in the design of heating systems. Inefficient furnaces used to discharge much of their heat up the chimney. They needed a heavy, expensive masonry chimney or an equally expensive insulated, stainless steel prefabricated chimney to withstand this heat for fire safety. In contrast, modern heating devices are designed to discharge virtually all of the heat they produce into the living area rather than up a chimney. So little heat is exhausted that many of these heaters and furnaces use only a plastic pipe for their exhaust vent. Since these units are more sophisticated than their predecessors, they do cost more. But as with so many other energy-efficient systems, when you deduct the cost of an expensive, space-consuming chimney and factor in the fuel savings, you are still way ahead with the latest technology.

Heating Requirements

Technology has advanced to the point that it is technically possible to build a house that would require no additional heat source whatsoever. Just the body heat from the occupants and from normal at-home activities would warm the house. The designs in this book aren't quite that sophisticated, but they are very good. The superinsulated, Canadian self-help houses are so well constructed that they require only 20,000 Btu of heating in an area of 12,000 degree-days, about 10 to 15% of the heating energy required by a conventional house in that climate. The plans in the back of this book give suggested heating system sizes for my basic house in a variety of climatic regions. For those who want to design heating systems for other houses or for significant variations on my designs, I highly recommend the book, *Passive Solar Design Calculations* by Charles Haynes, available from Architecture Shop, 210–2182 W. 12th Avenue, Vancouver, BC V6K 2N4. He is the architect for the widely acclaimed Acadia and Canadian conserver houses (see Chapter 7). Haynes gives the clearest instructions for calculating heat losses that I've ever seen. Not only are his calculations suitable for houses with solar orientation, but they also work well for any house. In addition to the book, he sells computer programs that are available for *any* computer.

Solar Heating

All the houses shown in this book are designed with thermal mass and a major side facing the sun. This is now standard procedure for any reputable house designer. These are what are called passive solar houses, which are in distinct contrast to active solar houses. Active solar systems require elaborate, expensive collectors and mechanical storage and distribution systems. Passive solar systems work simply by letting the sun penetrate a glassy south facade and warm the contents of the house. Thermal mass stores solar heat for nighttime use, and on the better-equipped passive houses, night insulation closes over glass areas. J. D. Nisson, president of Energy Design Associates in New York City, says in a letter responding to a *New York Times* article (October 3, 1982) on solar heating problems:

Active solar space heating is already obsolete—no matter how competent the design or installation. It was an early attempt to replace fossil fuels as a heating source for energy inefficient houses. It was like solving the problem of a leaky bucket by finding a cheaper source of water rather than plugging up the leaks. . . . It has been sobering for us in the energy-design community to realize that we had overlooked the holes in the bucket. . . .

The proper procedure for finishing off a passive solar house is to insulate and weatherseal so effectively that the relatively small quantity of heat you receive from the sun will keep your house warm. For nights and cloudy days you will only need a very small "backup" heating system. Most of these backup units vent right through the wall and do not need a chimney. Let's examine the various kinds that are available.

Kerosene Minifurnaces

Before the word kerosene sets you off, please note that I'm speaking about permanently mounted, fully vented, sophisticated heating units quite unlike portable kerosene heaters. They do use the same fuel, though, and they use it extremely efficiently. At the moment, Kero-Sun is the principal marketer of these units. They are available in two sizes: 20,000 and 30,000 Btu per hour. This is about one-fourth to one-third of the output of a conventional residential furnace. Provided that you have a reasonably open plan or a means of circulating the heat, one of these units will be suitable for a well-insulated, modestly sized house almost anywhere in North America.

This is the system installed in my moderately insulated, 1200-square-foot house. In a 7000-degree-day winter, it consumed 160 gallons of kerosene; that's $200 worth. I have recommended it to numerous clients and, at this writing, 11 that I know of have been installed. All are working perfectly.

The unit itself is a rectangular box approximately 2 feet high by 2½ feet long. It must be mounted on or near an outside wall and will project into the room 1½ feet. It has a direct venting system that consists of concentric intake and exhaust tubes that go through the wall. Combustion air is drawn from outside and prewarmed by the exhaust from the heating unit. In this fashion, no room air is consumed by combustion, yet all exhaust gases are vented outdoors. Waste heat from the exhaust is reclaimed by the incoming airstream.

The combustion system itself is a rather simple, easy-to-maintain pot burner hooked up to a sophis-

Several Japanese manufacturers are now marketing vented kerosene minifurnaces such as this Kero-Sun Monitor 20 made by Hitachi.

ticated electronic fuel delivery system and a superefficient heat exchanger. The unit is controlled by a wall-mounted heat sensor that selects one of three burning levels to satisfy the thermostat setting. A variable-speed fan runs at the optimum speed to extract the maximum amount of heat from the heat exchanger.

The unit comes in two models, the Model 20 and the Model 30, corresponding to the rated output of the furnaces. The units are essentially identical. The differences lie in the output, control systems, and fuel delivery options. Although both units have a clock-operated timing system to turn on and off automatically, the Model 30 can be cycled twice a day and the Model 20 only once. You might want to set the timer to shut the heater off at night and in the middle of the day as well. In this case, you should get the Model 30. Both heaters have connections for an external fuel tank. In addition, the Model 20 has an internal capsule tank. If you are only planning to use the heater as an occasional backup, you should consider the Model 20 since you won't need to install a separate tank and fuel line.

The separate tanks are a bit of a problem. A standard 250-gallon oil storage tank can be used, but they are expensive and really much too large. The fuel companies list 150-gallon tanks in their catalogs, but no one can ever get them. Two 50-gallon drums are the usual compromise. They are not very attractive and will have to be replaced after a few years. Kero-Sun makes a 5-gallon, wall-hung, portable feed tank that I use for my heater. Normal installation for any of the tanks requires that they be above the heater so that the fuel will feed by gravity. If you can't arrange the tank above the heater, a small pump is available to lift the fuel from a basement or buried tank.

These small furnaces are relatively expensive for their size, around $700. They obviously have to have electricity to operate, but they are very, very stingy in their fuel usage. If you compare the cost with that of a conventional furnace and chimney, you will see that these new furnaces are indeed a bargain. Of the units available on the market today, they are my first choice.

Direct-Vent Gas Furnaces

Numerous types of small gas furnaces with efficient venting systems similar to the kerosene units are available. These heaters have a much wider range of sizes than the kerosene furnaces. For similar size units, the cost of the furnace is only about half as much, but because the gas units have less sophisticated burner controls and

fans, the kerosene units use one-third to one-half less fuel and maintain a more uniform room temperature. The gas units are available in sizes from 12,000 Btu up to 50,000 Btu per hour.

Sears has by far the best prices on the gas units and markets two that are directly comparable to the Kero-Sun models. The 20,000-Btu model does not require electricity to operate. This unit is well worth considering if you are in a remote area where there are frequent power outages. It does have an optional blower, which I recommend, but you don't have to use the blower for the unit to function. At less than $300 including the blower, this heating system is a bargain. Remember, though, that the cost difference between this unit and the Kero-Sun will be eaten up by greater gas fuel costs in three to six years, depending upon the amount of use and the rate of fuel cost escalation.

Catalytic Gas Heaters

Catalytic devices are used in many fields to save energy. A catalyst allows a fuel to burn more efficiently at a lower temperature than would otherwise be possible. Catalytic gas heaters have long been popular for industrial uses because of their high radiant heat component. That is, they heat the objects in a room, not the air itself. The major drawback to their use for residences has been the lack of a practical venting method. Thermal Systems of Tumwater, Washington, has devised a vented, thermostatically controlled catalytic heater that meets or exceeds the efficiencies of the Kero-Sun Monitor series.

The trade name for this series of catalytic heaters is Cat. They are AGA approved for both propane and natural gas. Although the heaters only consume 6000 Btu per hour, the output is comparable to a 10,000-Btu conventional heater, due to the radiant heat component. This heater would be suitable as the main heat source for the Civic house in moderate climates (under 5000 degree-days), but an additional heat source would have to be provided for the bedrooms. Thermal Systems has thought out the problem of power failures or remote usage. As an option, the heaters come with a 12-volt electrical system that could easily be hooked up to a backup power supply. For mild climates or remote areas or to use in add-on rooms, this is an ideal heating unit.

Electric Heat

When you have a thoroughly insulated small house, there is an enormous temptation to use electric heat as the primary heat source for your house. Electric heaters are very cheap to install, and if they are located in an area that is only occasionally used, then they would be a logical choice. For instance, you might want to heat the main floor of the Civic house with the Cat heater and use electric heaters in the bedrooms and bath.

But do not fool yourself. Electric heat is wasteful and *very* expensive. It may be 100% efficient in the house, but generating and then transmission losses reduce that efficiency to about 33%. Remember that some type of fuel has to be consumed to generate the electricity, with hydro-electric power as the only exception. Manufacturers of electric heating devices are fond of citing costs based upon 4 or 5 cents per kilowatt-hour. Since several companies are now charging 15 cents per kilowatt-hour, these manufacturers' claims are absurdly understated. Experts are widely predicting a tripling of electric rates by the end of the decade. That "all-electric house," which had a utility budget rate of $50 per month when it was built, could be costing $500 per month in a few years. Think about this, and use electric heat sparingly, if at all.

If you do use electricity as a heat source, you should choose a radiant type rather than the more common resistance baseboard heaters. Aztech makes the most commonly distributed radiant heat panels, and these are now readily available from most electrical distributors. Sears also markets these radiant panels. Since radiant heat warms your body and the objects in the room rather than the room air directly, it is possible to be comfortable at lower room temperatures. Continental Glassheat (70 Remington Boulevard, Ronkonkoma, NY 11779), radiant panel manufacturers, can produce test results of identical structures showing up to a third reduction in heating costs by using radiant rather than resistance heating.

For those who don't want radiant heating panels hung on their walls, there is a fine Norwegian imported radiant ceiling. This system consists of heating elements that come in a flexible roll form and that are attached to the supporting members before the finish ceiling material is applied. The ceiling can be plasterboard, plywood, or wood board. Some years ago, there was an American version of this system in which the elements were embedded directly in the plasterboard. The system worked very well, but it was prone to damage in installation. Also, the special sheets of plasterboard were expensive to ship and difficult to store. For obvious reasons, this system never made it in the competitive marketplace.

Another radiant electric heating system has been making inroads because of its high-quality construction and superior performance. It is called Softheat and is marketed by Intertherm in the United States and Canada. This heater is basically a water-filled radiator with an electric heating element. Since there is a significant radiant component to the heat produced, you can be comfortable at lower temperatures and thereby use less electricity. And because the water stores heat, the element cycles less frequently, also saving a bit.

Thermal Mass
Buildings that have large quantities of materials that absorb heat readily are easier to heat and cool in the long run. Ideal materials are stone, brick, water, and even heavy wood timbers. The basic Civic house has a masonry floor, which is insulated around the perimeter, for its thermal mass. The Tennessee Valley Authority modular solar houses have brick-lined exterior walls to beef up their thermal mass.

My basic saltbox (Jones) house (in my book, *A Design and Construction Handbook for Energy-Saving Houses*, Rodale Press, 1980, and reprinted in this book's Chapter 14) has a massive chimney/heat storage wall in the center of the house. This wall is quite effective, but it takes up valuable floor space and is expensive to build. Since the Civic house, presented in Chapter 25, is smaller and more thermally efficient, it doesn't need as much mass. For those who want to improve its efficiency, I have shown optional interior masonry partitions.

Heat Exchangers
Older houses used to experience severe problems with dry air in winter, which was due to the heating system's sucking large quantities of dry outside air into the house to replace heated air. With the new generation of well-insulated houses, we have the opposite problem; now the air has too much moisture. Well-sealed, new houses are so tight that the moisture generated by cooking, bathing, and breathing has nowhere to go. In extreme cases, water will actually condense and run down the walls. The problem can be easily remedied by exhausting moist air from the house and introducing drier cold air from outdoors to replace it. Unfortunately, this wastes valuable heat and the drafts created are not at all pleasant for the occupants.

In countries where energy has been in short supply for many years, air-to-air heat exchangers have been developed that work in a similar fashion to the direct-vented furnaces I spoke of earlier in this chapter. That is, the warm airstream is passed around a cold-air intake, thereby prewarming the replacement air brought into the house. Commercial units that do the job well cost around a $1000. Competition will undoubtedly bring the price down rapidly. Mitsubishi imports a full line of heat exchangers, and I have been using two of the smallest ones in each of my houses with good results. I put one in the kitchen area and the other one in the bath. This small commercial unit costs less than $150. I question durability, though, because the core is only a paper-treated material.

Plans for building your own heat exchangers are readily available from several sources. I like the Canadian ones best. Family Homes Cooperative (FHC) in Beckley, West Virginia, has put together a really fine kit for an air-to-air heat exchanger. It is furnished with their complete house, but is also available separately. Until the commercial market responds with reasonably priced units, the FHC kit is the best solution. For their address and other sources, see the listing of heating devices in Appendix A.

Fans

Low-velocity fans can play an important part in heating an energy-efficient house. A fan and a small ductwork system leading to the bedrooms and bath can take the place of the large distribution system that is attached to the furnace in conventional heating systems. In this fashion, you can distribute the heat from the superefficient, direct-vent furnaces, which I discussed earlier, to the bedrooms and eliminate the need for any other heating devices. Since the bedrooms are not occupied much of the time, you can operate the fan only when needed. If you want individual control in each of the bedrooms, you would be better off using one of the electric systems I discussed earlier.

In addition to the heating circulation fan, the Civic plans also show two hot air exhaust fans for summertime use. They should have variable speed controls so they can be turned on high speed to cool the house rapidly after the sun is down. After the house begins to cool, the fans can be turned to low speed to maintain the air circulation without producing annoying noise.

Cooling

The most economical method of cooling is to use fans. If your area is too hot or humid for that to be

sufficient, you will have to resort to air conditioning. Since we are discussing well-insulated small houses, one or two window-type air conditioners will be quite sufficient. The same low-velocity fan/duct system that I spoke about to circulate warm air will work equally well for the cool air. Make sure that you follow the instructions on the Civic plans exactly. It is very important to have ¾ inch of clearance underneath the bedroom doors for the air to circulate correctly.

Small heat pumps would be ideal for cooling these houses, but none are manufactured at the moment. Since manufacturers are now promoting small heating units, small heat pumps cannot be far behind. Fedders has the best reputation of the major heat pump manufacturers.

Wood Heat

Long-term readers of mine may be surprised to find wood heat relegated to the end of this chapter. There are several reasons. First, wood heat is not well-suited for a small, well-insulated house. You need an expensive chimney and a relatively expensive wood stove to start with. You will find that even the smallest available wood stove will produce more heat than a well-insulated house needs. The only way to control this is to turn the draft down, but modern wood stoves that are burned with the draft nearly closed produce large quantities of dangerous creosote. Stoves and chimneys require careful attention and maintenance, and most people don't have this kind of commitment; they have become accustomed to just plugging in a maintenance-free appliance and forgetting it. Insurance companies, fire departments, and code officials are becoming increasingly alarmed by the rising numbers of deaths associated with wood-stove fires. Some areas have gone so far as to ban wood heating completely. The days of cheap barrel stoves with a single-wall stovepipe run up the side of a house are dwindling fast, and rightly so.

If you are building a large house in a cold climate or in an area where fuels other than wood are scarce, you will probably use wood as your primary heat source. If you renovate an old house that already has a good chimney, wood is the fuel to consider. Even with an expert insulation job, an old house will lose more heat than one of the panelized houses in this book, so you'll need a good, inexpensive source of heat. There are many old standbys and several new wood heating systems that are worth looking into.

Cast iron is the material to look for in a wood stove. The imported brands have dwindled in popularity due to inflation and currency exchange rate price escalation. Keep your money at home and buy Yankee ingenuity. The line of stoves produced by Vermont Castings in Randolph, Vermont, is superior, in my opinion, to almost anything else on the market. Their stoves all open up so that you can use them in fireplace mode and view the fire. They also have accessory units that allow them to burn coal and, finally, they have provisions for heating domestic hot water.

Catalytic Converters

Corning Glass Works has recently developed a catalytic converter that can be incorporated into a wood stove near the outlet pipe to improve combustion efficiency. Several companies have developed stoves that incorporate this device, and retrofit units are available that bolt directly to the stove outlet. It is significant to me that the major domestic and imported cast-iron stove makers have shunned this device. Their contention is that it adds little to the efficiency of a well-designed stove that is burning well-seasoned wood, and that it has to be replaced periodically. It undisputedly does increase the efficiency of simple box or barrel stoves. Proponents of the converter argue that many people are not that careful to burn dry, seasoned wood and that superefficient stoves that are damped down for a maximum burn period produce large quantities of creosote.

Both sides of the argument have their merits, but I will withhold my personal, unqualified approval until these units have been adapted by major manufacturers such as Vermont Castings or Jøtul. Also, if you do buy a converter, I would recommend the Corning brand rather than one of the imitations that have invaded the market.

Masonry heating stoves, which include Russian fireplaces and Finnish contraflow stoves, are enjoying a flurry of well-deserved popularity in this country. Again, they provide too much heat for a small house, but they are a dandy solution for a big one. The major benefit to these stoves is that they burn the wood very hot, thereby consuming most creosote-producing volatiles. If properly constructed, they release their heat slowly for many hours after the fire has died out. The Finnish stoves have the added charm of fireplace doors, somewhat similar to the Vermont Castings' stoves, so that the heater can be used either as a fireplace or as a superefficient heating unit.

As efficient as they are, these stoves have their drawbacks. Clients who have built the Russian fireplace have complained that they produce

The Snorkel stove is constructed of welded aluminum plate. The stove is submersed in water to just below the feed door. The tubes are for heat exchange.

so much heat that they are unsuitable for anything but mid-January weather. Cracking is not unusual in stoves built by masons inexperienced with these particular heaters. It is vital that high-temperature refractory mortar and castable refractory cement be employed in the construction of these units. Do not cut corners with common brick or flue tile liners, because they will not hold up under the intense heat. See the Grant house in Chapter 24 for a well-done, Finnish stove installation.

My personal wood-stove favorite is constructed of aluminum. Of course, this is impossible—aluminum melts under wood-stove temperatures. The Physics Department at the University of Alaska has devised a superefficient, pollution-free submersible aluminum stove that is marketed as the Snorkel Stove (Box 20068, Seattle, WA 98102). Its primary purpose is to provide an economical source of heat for a wooden hot tub, but I have found it to have application as a heating unit as well. The stove is a rectangular aluminum box that is bolted to the side of a hot tub so that the

An induced-draft wood-burning boiler produces virtually no creosote and little smoke.

body of the stove is submerged. The feed door and the sleeve for the flue are the only parts above water. Since the stove is designed to heat water rapidly, air circulation is ample, and the fuel burns briskly and with little or no smoke. I have been using this stove for two years, and I have seen no appreciable creosote buildup. My hot tub is fitted with an insulated cover, and the sidewalls and floor are also insulated. I did this assuming I would be using a propane heater, but now that I have a Snorkel instead, I find that the tub stays quite hot for days on just one good charge of wood.

This past winter, I experimented with the hot tub/stove combination as an auxiliary heat source. I connected a fan-coil heating unit to the tub with insulated pipes, and I have found that it produces enough heat to keep the bottom floor of my house toasty, provided, of course, that I keep the stove supplied with wood about once a day in below-zero weather. For far less than the cost of a cast-iron wood stove and a chimney, I have a nonpolluting, wood-fired hot-tub stove that also can serve as an auxiliary heating system.

There are other wood heating devices that burn cleanly and safely. The University of Maine has developed and licensed a wood boiler that burns wood with a forced downdraft. Like my hot-tub stove, it burns cleanly and efficiently, but unlike my stove, it requires electricity to operate, and it is very expensive. It is designed to heat a reservoir of water, which in turn heats the house. By storing heat in the reservoir, the furnace can be allowed to go for intervals of several days between firings. For a detailed description of the operation of this system in one of my houses, see the Knopf house in Chapter 24.

For those on a rock-bottom budget who have an existing chimney, a simple, pot-type, oil-burning heater may be the answer. A 50,000-Btu heater of this type costs less than $150 at Sears. They are not the latest in fuel efficiency, but they will get you through until that ideal heating system comes along.

Other Options

Major furnace manufacturers have recently introduced state-of-the-art, full-size furnaces that are so efficient they don't require conventional venting methods. These early units are quite expensive, and we can expect some growing pains. You'll find a listing of them in Appendix A. If you are purchasing a larger furnace for an old house, make sure that it is sized correctly. A furnace that is too large wastes a great deal of fuel.

Sales of photovoltaic systems in 1983 will be about $250 million, totaling 18 megawatts of capacity. This represents a quadrupling of the market since 1981 and a thousandfold increase since 1973. By 1990, production will increase further by a factor of more than 25, to 500 megawatts a year, constituting a market worth more than $1 billion. A new type of cell is being introduced commercially by several American and Japanese companies, and this may drive the price per watt to below $2.50 by 1990 and seriously challenge conventional methods of generating electricity. Photovoltaics will be cost-competitive before you can build the next nuclear power plant.

Paul Maycock,
President, Photovoltaic Energy Systems, Alexandria, Virginia—from a December 22, 1983, interview with the *New York Times*

BUILDING THE HOUSE

18 Foundations

Aside from the basic configuration of the house, the foundation offers the greatest opportunity for implementing cost-saving techniques. Tradition dictates that we build our houses on a heavy, expensive concrete footing topped by either a basement or crawl space constructed of energy-wasting, expensive concrete or concrete block. Both these techniques waste space, time, and money. The wise owner or contractor will pass them up in favor of solutions that will do the same job for a fraction of the cost.

My primary consideration in saving foundation costs is to eliminate masonry and masons. Both the materials and labor are unduly expensive. Masons comprise one more difficult-to-schedule outside trade for the already complex building process. Weather plays an important role here; the masons can't work in very wet or cold weather and hence are subject to huge backlogs of work. This can cost the small homebuilder many thousands of dollars if he only builds a few houses at a time and is stymied by the lack of foundations. Since the foundation is the first operation, the carpenters must be paid to do nothing or be laid off completely.

Also, in order to make optimum use of cost-saving modular components, the foundations must be constructed exactly to planned dimensions. It's been my experience that masons are inherently immune to working in exact dimensions. The re-

sultant mistakes are difficult or prohibitively expensive to correct. Concrete and concrete block are energy intensive, both to manufacture and to transport. Fortunately, there are several superior techniques that allow us to avoid these materials entirely.

Foundation Configurations

Quite simply, we have three possible ways to attach a building to its site. We can elevate the house on piers or poles that are embedded into the earth. This technique is ideal for wet areas, hot climates, or very uneven terrain. It is also used extensively in extremely cold climates where a very deep frost line makes conventional foundations impossible or extremely expensive.

The second configuration is a slab-on-grade with no basement or crawl space. Over 50% of the houses in the United States were constructed this way in 1982. This does not mean that the slab is a prevalent construction technique; it simply means that most houses were built in the South in 1982, where this technique is common. Slab-on-grade foundations require flat land and a well-drained site. It offers the greatest potential for cost savings, and most of the foundation types that follow are variations upon this basic configuration.

The third foundation method involves a more conventional buried first floor. In this case, how-

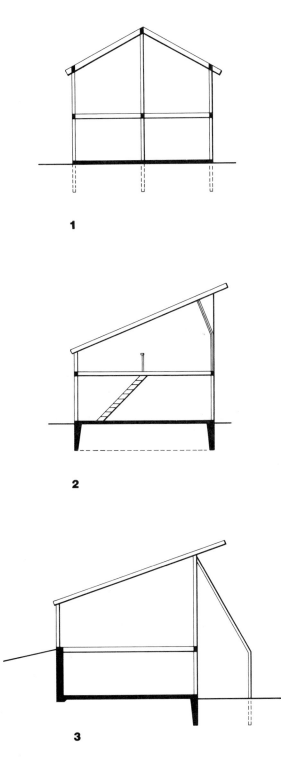

1

2

3

Here are three types of foundations: (1) An embedded, pressure-treated pole-type foundation like this one is economical. (2) A slab-on-grade foundation is widely used in the South, but provides valuable thermal mass for northern houses. (3) If possible, use a basement for living space by opening it out to grade on the south. If the grade doesn't slope properly, a sunken courtyard will work as an alternative.

ever, we make full use of the space rather than relegating it to basement status. A partially buried first floor makes great sense for sloping sites. It costs a bit more than the other two schemes but is quite cost-effective if the space is efficiently used. This scheme is frequently used in builders' so-called raised-ranch houses. Unfortunately, in such ranch houses the lower level is usually occupied by a garage and utility-storage space rather than a usable living area. My basic panelized houses are all designed to take advantage of this foundation type where the terrain is suitable.

Termite Protection

Insulated foundations can make warm, snug homes for termites. Insulation placed on the outside of coventional masonry foundation walls can hide entrance tunnels for the pests. Banks and building codes in warm areas of the country usually require that the ground around foundations be treated with a poison before backfilling. A sheet metal termite cap and the use of pressure-treated lumber will give you added protection.

Embedded Post

The embedded, pressure-treated, post-type foundation is equally applicable to either an elevated or a slab-on-grade foundation. This method is commonly used for the raised type but it's quite unusual to find it used for slab-on-grade applications. I have used this technique for my slab houses for many years with great success, and the price is certainly right. A local contractor who has constructed many of my houses estimates that the foundation cost for a 24-foot-square basic house is less than $100. This foundation does have to be used with a post-and-beam frame, and as a matter of fact, is widely used in pole-type farm buildings. If it had wider applicability, I am sure that it would be very extensively used.

If you want to see this type of foundation, just visit your local farm co-op and ask to watch a pole building going up. The foundation is simplicity itself. Post holes are dug at 8-, 10-, or 12-foot intervals, depending upon the structural design of the building. Pressure-treated 6 × 6 or 4 × 4 posts are set in place and capped with a pressure-treated sill, and you have a fine foundation. In southern climates, you can simply backfill the posts and you have a completed foundation. In northern areas, we trench between the posts and install a footing drain and rigid insulation board. See the construction details, with the working drawings, in Appendix B for exact construction procedures.

Pressure-treated wood forms a sill member between embedded posts. Two layers of 2-inch insulation board provide insulation.

Even though this is a very unusual construction technique, we have had very little problem getting it approved by building departments throughout the country. There are two reasons: First, it is structurally sound and easily defended and understood by structural engineers. Second, and probably more important, building inspectors in all parts of the country are familiar with pole-frame farm buildings and know that they work well. Contractors are another story. In many cases, they simply refuse to try the new technique. We are at a crossroad in the construction industry. Those contractors who persist in stubbornly sticking to the old ways will soon perish. Most people can no longer afford the status quo.

Pressure-Treated Panels

Pressure-treated wood foundations have attracted wide attention as an alternative to conventional masonry below-grade construction. They comply with virtually all the codes. A major drawback is that it is difficult to construct the wood foundation below grade unless an excessive amount of earth is removed. And it is not well-suited to very soft wet clays, but indeed, any foundation may have trouble in such a situation. These foundations are usually used in the construction of houses with a full basement, most of which is below grade. The walls are constructed in sections, or panels, and dropped into the excavation; insulation and finishing take place within the basement area. The foundation itself rests on a gravel bed topped by pressure-treated timbers. Anyone who knows a lot about foundations knows that it is a very fine, cost-saving system.

Take a look at the panelized wall system described in Chapter 20; it has recently been adapted for foundations. The major advantage to panelization is that both surfaces are fully finished so that assembly work does not have to be performed down in a trench. This makes the system ideal for a house without a basement. The laminated panels are several times stronger than site-assembled materials, which makes them more suitable for difficult soil conditions. They are ideal for a 4-foot-deep foundation; they are set upon a pressure-treated plate just as in the basement version, and the sill plate at floor level ties them together. The in-place cost is less than half that of masonry, and the thermal performance is much better.

Dry Stone

A Welsh drain or dry stone foundation is an excellent way to support heavy loads, such as a masonry wall, without resorting to expensive, poured concrete foundations. This is an ancient foundation technique that has been used for centuries. More recently, it was popularized by Frank Lloyd Wright. Execution of the foundation is simplicity itself. An 18-inch-wide trench is dug to below frost line and filled to grade with a medium-size, 2-inch stone. A conventional mortared stone wall is then built directly on top of the stone bed. In my versions, I have added a thermal break of Styrofoam blueboard in the middle of the foundation to prevent migration of cold or moisture into the house.

This system is well-suited to sandy, rocky soils that drain well. Do not attempt to use this with soft clay soils, since the stone bed can actually migrate into the clay and disappear.

Reaction from code officials to this foundation type has been mixed. None have rejected it outright, but one official did require us to pour a 4-inch-thick bond beam on top of the stone before proceeding with the above-grade walls.

Surface-Bonded Block

Surface bonding, which does not use typical masonry skills, is a superior method of building masonry walls. In this system, concrete block are simply stacked up to the desired configuration and then both sides of the wall are plastered with a fiberglass-reinforced, surface-bonding cement. This method of construction has been in wide use for over 10 years and has proved to be a thoroughly durable system. Since the block are first stacked up dry, critical dimensions can be checked and any necessary corrections made before the surface bonding is applied. This is also a technique that doesn't require professional masons. In fact, one problem with the technique is that masons don't like it and have refused to follow proper procedures. If you do want a masonry foundation, this is the strongest and cheapest way to build it. For our post-and-beam houses, we reinforce the walls at 8-foot intervals to correspond to the spacing of our structural posts.

The actual construction of a surface-bonded wall is very easy. A conventional mortar joint is used only once, at the base of the wall, to set the first course of block on the footing. The block are then simply stacked up to the desired height. Three-core block should be used so that the cores will line up, since it is important to reinforce the wall at bearing points (two-core block do not permit this). The wall should then be checked for dimensional accuracy and any corrections made. Once all is aligned and level, both surfaces of the wall are coated with a special fiberglass-reinforced, surface-bonding cement. Reinforcing rods are inserted into the cores at the points to be reinforced, and the cores are filled with concrete. The resultant wall is strong and waterproof. This system is not limited to foundation walls. It can be used equally well for retaining walls, partitions, or exterior building walls. See Chapter 19 for uses and limitations of this method for walls for the main structure of your house.

Slab-on-Grade

This last construction method I'll describe will be familiar to contractors all over the South. In this method, the house is supported on a reinforced concrete slab that is turned down at the edges to form integral footings. It has long been a favorite cost-saving technique for my houses. In order to be useful in cold climates, edges of the slab must be carefully insulated or the slab must be below the frost line. One drawback to the system is that if you're installing underfloor plumbing and wiring, it must be accurately placed before the slab is poured. If there are any delays in the mechanical trades' work, foundation work—and all else that follows—will be delayed.

This problem can be eliminated entirely by avoiding underfloor mechanical trades altogether. See Chapter 22 for abovefloor plumbing installations. Integral coloring and surface patterns can be used at the time the floor is poured to avoid the expense of additional floor coverings.

Selecting Foundation Type

Most savings are interconnected. The type of foundation you use can save you a substantial sum of money; combining cost-saving foundation construction methods with an efficient configuration for your house can reduce the foundation costs to a tiny fraction of those incurred in building a conventionally designed house. For instance, cutting the ground-level perimeter in half by building a two-story house rather than a one-story one can save as much as 50% in foundation costs, regardless of the type of foundation used. A panelized, pressure-treated wood foundation or directly embedded post foundation can reduce costs another 60 to 80%.

The amount of time required to build your foundation and the amount of hand labor required are two factors to be considered carefully. If you are a contractor or are hiring one to build your house, the quickest, least labor-intensive methods will be preferred. The fastest possible foundation is the pressure-treated panelized type, closely followed by a monolithic slab and footing foundation. Contractors may prefer the latter type since they will have a finished slab to use as a work space. Embedded-post and stacked-bond masonry foundations are likely to be preferred by the owner-builder who has more time at his disposal. No matter which of these systems you go with, you will save considerably over the cost of conventional masonry foundations.

19 Masonry: Stacked Bond, Exterior Insulation, and Thermal Mass

The term masonry usually refers to the materials and construction of a brick, concrete block, or stone wall. Conventional walls are constructed by setting individual masonry units into beds of mortar and then cutting the mortar joint flush, or tooling it in a variety of styles, a process that requires a great deal of practice and skill. Even some so-called professional masons often lack the skills to accurately build a wall. Consequently, I do not recommend conventionally built masonry walls except for unusual cases. There are new, simpler methods of building that eliminate this expensive skilled masonry from the picture.

I used to not recommend masonry at all because of the problems in insulating it. Masonry walls, if uninsulated (and most are uninsulated) wick house heat to the outside. Those that are insulated are usually insulated on the interior so that all the potential thermal mass of the masonry is lost. Other countries that felt the energy crunch long before we did have devised low-cost, efficient systems for insulating the outside of masonry walls of either old or new buildings, upgrading them and making them much more energy efficient. These systems are of great value in rehabilitating an old brick building. Although masonry construction isn't for everyone, the new building and insulating techniques drastically reduce the costs and make its use now possible for low-cost houses.

Stacked-Bond Walls

The stacked-bond technique was developed by the U.S. Department of Agriculture (USDA) at the Georgia Experiment Station in 1966. It has been thoroughly tested in the intervening years and has proven to be a superior, cost-saving technique. The system cuts the construction time by 50%; furthermore, the construction can be done by unskilled labor, which means that owner-builders can save up to 50% of the cost of hiring a contractor to build a conventional wall. Professional masons tend to scoff at this technique and belittle its strength, but actual tests show the flexural strength to be twice that of conventional mortared walls. This technique does for masons what latex paints did for high-priced union painters —instant obsolescence.

One of the largest companies now selling surface bonding cement (which, by the way, was originally manufactured by Owens-Corning) is the W. R. Bonsal Company. They have done a great deal to promote the system, including preparation of an excellent instruction manual, *Building with Surewall Surface Bonding Cement,* available free from W. R. Bonsal Co., Illesville, NC 28091. For more detailed reading, the USDA has prepared two bulletins on the subject: *Surface Bonding of Concrete Blocks,* Agricultural Information Bulletin No. 343, 1970; and *Construction with Surface Bonding,* Agricultural Information

This unique and attractive Chinese masonry wall uses brick laid flat and on edge in alternating courses.

Bulletin No. 374, 1972. Both are available from the U.S. Government Printing Office, Washington, DC 20402, for 60 cents apiece.

Surface bonding cement can be made from scratch by the contractor or owner-builder, since there is nothing proprietary in the mix. Cement is mixed with lime, calcium chloride, calcium stearate, chopped glass fiber, and water to produce the bonding mix. Pigments can be added to the mix so that the surface will never require painting. A full listing of materials suppliers and directions for mixing your own bonding cement are supplied in the above agricultural bulletins.

A brief description of the application of surface bonding cement is given in Chapter 18. Basement and foundation walls are particularly well-suited for this material because it is highly waterproof. If you have ready access to concrete block at reasonable prices, you might want to consider building an entire house using this process. Block walls can readily be substituted for the panelized

walls for the Civic house; the Siporex houses shown in Chapter 4 would be ideal for this application. As I noted in Chapter 10, the high strength makes surface bonding a natural for underground houses. If you are planning to use this technique for a whole house, you will be far ahead if you purchase the raw materials and mix your own. The materials must be purchased in large quantities anyway, so it wouldn't pay to buy them for a small foundation. And since the materials cost only about one-third as much as the finished product, the savings would be substantial for a large job like an entire house.

Surface bonding complies with all major building codes, so it can be used almost anywhere. However, since it cannot be exposed to temperatures over 150°F., chimneys and Trombe walls (glazed masonry storage walls) are out. Any wall that you are using to hold back earth should be properly engineered, and this is particularly true of a surface-bonded wall. Reinforcing must be added to the cores and fully tied to the foundation.

Usually a bond beam is required at the top of the wall. The size and spacing of the reinforcements are critical and should be verified by a professional engineer.

Exterior Insulation

Most masons don't have much time for surface bonding, but they are wildly enthusiastic about exterior insulation systems. This is because the rapid growth of exterior insulation installations throughout the country has spawned franchised dealers who distribute the materials and hire high-priced union masons to perform the work. The potential for energy savings in existing buildings by using this system is so great that owners are willing to spend freely to have their buildings insulated, even when money is tight.

Exterior insulation systems were originally developed in Europe where stucco exterior finishes are popular. The key to their use was the development of various additives to make cement-based stucco flexible and adhesive. An adhesive layer of stucco is applied to a masonry wall surface and used to bond a layer of expanded polystyrene board to the face of the building. This insulation board is usually 2 or 3 inches thick, but you can get it in other thicknesses as well. (Doctors who renovated an old school building in my town into a clinic actually applied two 4-inch layers of foam to the outside walls.) The exterior surface of the insulation board is coated with another layer of adhesive into which a layer of fiberglass mesh is pressed. Another layer of adhesive and a colored finish coat complete the process.

The resulting finish is handsome and durable. The additives make the stucco so flexible that you can actually break the insulation board underneath without damaging the surface coating. The coating is completely waterproof, so it protects the masonry from weather. Since the insulation is on the outside of the wall, the thermal mass of the masonry becomes useful as heat storage for the interior of the building, rather than wicking away the heat as in an uninsulated masonry building. I make extensive use of this exterior insulation for insulating masonry foundations and underground walls of my houses. The buried portions of the walls do not require the expensive colored finish coating, and this reduces the cost significantly.

The most widely distributed brand of exterior wall insulation and finish system is Drivit. This is the original European import, and the company maintains strict quality control by distributing only through franchised dealer-installers. Usually, Drivit installers are not interested in small residential jobs and certainly not in merely a small foundation, but if you are planning to insulate a large building, you may be able to get a reasonable bid from these people. The smaller competitors of Drivit are usually willing to sell to individuals, particularly if you use a contractor's mailing address. Write for detailed literature first so that you have a thorough knowledge of the products and coverages before you order. It is imperative that the fiberglass mesh used in the system be treated for alkali resistance—otherwise, the cement will eat the mesh. If the firm offers two price ranges of mesh, you should order the better one.

Exterior insulation board should be installed so that it exactly lines up with the wall sheathing to avoid awkward flashings.

Two smaller firms that have served me well are El Rey Stucco Company, distributors of Insul-Flex Exterior Insulation, and Kern-Tac, distributors of Plekko-Therm. El Rey distributes from New Mexico and Kern-Tac from Tacoma, Washington, and New York City. The materials are packaged in 5-gallon pails and are quite heavy; therefore, you should try to locate a distributor in your region to avoid high delivery charges. Since this is a very widely used technique, I expect sources of supply to proliferate rapidly.

STO Energy Conservation, Inc., of Rutland, Vermont, markets another line of exterior wall insulation products that come in a much wider variety than their competitors. Although STO markets a similar additive, which is mixed 50% with cement, they also market extremely versatile, ready-mixed products called STO Dispersion Adhesive and STO RFP. These products are acrylic copolymers, which are waterproof and very flexible and can be applied to almost any type of construction material as a bonding agent. The flexibility makes these products ideal for prefabrication and complicated details such as windowsills and curved surfaces. STO also markets a black, waterproof adhesive mastic that is ideal for bonding insulation to underground masonry walls. Conventional petroleum-based waterproofing compounds will rapidly eat polystyrene insulation boards. *Do not use them.* Finally, STO markets a heavy-duty, fiberglass armor mat for areas subject to extreme abuse. STO products are sold by regional distributors throughout the United States and Canada. A complete listing for all major distributors of exterior insulation products is provided in Appendix A.

Stone Walls

Stone is the only masonry material that nature provides free and ready for use. If you are lucky and have an ample supply of stone on or near your property, you may want to consider building all or part of your house of stone. Building with stone is a highly labor-intensive venture, so be prepared for a lot of hard work or a huge bill from a professional mason. If you hire a professional, look at several of his jobs. Stone laying is highly personal, and you may not like the appearance of the finished product. You can considerably reduce the cost of hiring a professional by finding and transporting the stone to the building site yourself. Just make sure you confer with your mason as to the exact type and size of stone he wants to use.

The house that I designed for Linda Weido is a good example of how to use stone economically. The house is a story-and-a-half, 24- by 30-foot rectangle with the long side facing south. A continuous greenhouse abuts the south wall. A gravel foundation as described in Chapter 18 is used to support the heavy walls. Since the south wall of the house proper is protected by the greenhouse, it is built of solid stone with no insulation. The east and west walls are of cavity-type construction; a 2-inch layer of urethane insulation board was built into the cavity as the wall went up. The north wall of the house is again of solid stone, this time with the insulation on the inside. The interior insulation sacrifices the thermal mass of this wall, but the white interior surface that results breaks the monotony of all stone walls and provides a reflective surface for the sunlight shining on the north wall. To minimize the labor required, the stone walls terminate at the second-floor deck, and the upper portion of the house is entirely constructed of wood. By designing the house this way I have avoided the need to lift heavy stone to the second floor and also have avoided the complexities of building a stone wall to a slope. Because the 6-inch-thick wood walls are flush with the outside of the 18-inch-thick stone walls, the second-floor loft gains about 50 extra square feet.

As you can see from the photographs on the next page, Linda's walls are highly unusual works of art, hardly the usual plain stone walls. Linda did most of the work herself over the course of two summers. Because the walls are so unusual, they soon attracted the attention of some of the more artistic of the local masons. Linda was able to reenact Tom Sawyer's famous whitewashed fence caper. The masons liked what they saw enough to want to try their hand so that they could say that they had worked on the job. Just as Linda was beginning to tire of the project, an infusion of new blood arrived to push her over the top.

Thermal Mass

You will notice that many of the houses in the book show masonry walls in the middle of the house. These walls were placed there to increase the volume of heat-absorbing material inside the house and create a flywheel effect to smooth out heating and cooling fluctuations. The cheapest way to build these walls is to use the surface-bonded concrete block method that I just described. To get the maximum effect from your wall, fill the block cores with sand.

Linda Weido's free-form stone walls are reminiscent of Gaudi.

A close-up detail shows Linda's "bird nest" corner.

In the Civic house, the wall is a focal point of the living room, and for such a wall you might want a more decorative effect. I highly recommend the alternating bond Chinese wall, which I showed at the beginning of this chapter. If native stone is available, you might want to try your hand at a creative mosaic wall such as those in Linda's house.

There are many fine books on the subject of stone-work. The subject is so extensive that I will not attempt to cover any of the methods here. A listing of the books that I recommend is in Appendix A.

Masonry floors are an excellent way to add thermal mass to a house economically (so long as you don't cover them with rugs, thereby insulating them from the living space). Brick, slate, flagstone, and quarry tile are the most commonly used materials. Quarry tile has to be installed over a rigid surface; all the other materials can be set over a sand or fine gravel bed, which will save you money over installing them on a suspended floor or over a concrete slab. I have used this sand/fine gravel bed technique widely for many years with good success. The floor is prepared by leveling and compacting with a mechanical tamper. Then a 6-mil polyethylene vapor barrier and 3 inches of sand or fine gravel is laid down. The masonry units are then hand placed and leveled. A dry grouting mix is placed in the joints after dampening the whole floor, and the floor is then flushed with water and the joints are brushed to compact the mortar. After the mortar has set thoroughly, the floor is cleaned and sealed. This method costs less than a typical raised wooden floor and is completely fireproof and rotproof. If you install the floor yourself, you can realize even greater savings. Detailed step-by-step instructions and photographs for this technique are provided in my book, *A Design and Construction Handbook for Energy-Saving Houses* (Rodale Press, 1980).

A 44-foot-tall masonry chimney absorbs heat from the greenhouse. A Russian fireplace provides heat at the base of the chimney.

20 Prefabricated Shells; Post-and-Beam Frames with Insulated Panels

For many years I have used post-and-beam framing techniques for clients who want to build truly economical houses. These frames are ideal for small, simple houses; they go up quickly and make an attractive energy-efficient structure. The structures employ plank-and-beam floor structures and open cathedral ceilings with loft and storage areas. The resultant shell is considerably more efficient in the use of space than conventional construction.

The major drawbacks to this fine system occur in the exterior skin, both roof and walls. Although the basic structure is quite economical, traditional framing methods for the walls and roof require redundant framing members and excessive amounts of labor for fabrication. But now these limitations have been erased by the recent widespread availability of wall and roof panels. Since these panels are quite strong, they make it possible to greatly reduce the size of the framing members for the post-and-beam frame. Depending upon the individual design, the savings in lumber usage over conventional construction range from 42 to 56%. Furthermore, much of the wood savings is translated into an increase in the thermal efficiency of the walls, because rigid insulation replaces the wood framing members with their lower R value.

Many post-and-beam framers throughout the country are adapting their frames to use panelized walls, and some have modified their roof

> Almost every design is unnecessarily overburdened with weight—due to a system of interlocking directorates; manufacturers have been only *selling* materials instead of also *studying* their best use.
>
> *Henry Ford*

structures to accept roof panels. But virtually none has reengineered his system to take maximum advantage of the savings possible by combining the strengths of both materials. The frames I have used for the panelized houses in this book have been slimmed down to take advantage of the strength of the wall panels. Whereas most framing members in my older designs are 6 inches thick, the new houses use 4-inch-thick members, except in a few areas of heavy stress. My frames are designed around 8-foot-square panels rather than the usual 4 × 8 units. The posts are spaced at 8-foot centers around the exterior wall of the building. Since the panels overlap framing members on all four sides, they make an extremely strong wall and provide virtually airtight construction.

The reduction of the member sizes and lengths enables the frame to be quickly and easily fabricated by carpenters who are completely unfamiliar with post-and-beam framing. Even an unskilled worker can cut out one of these frames with a bit of practice. The smaller size of the members extends the availability of the frames to relatively treeless areas of the country and also makes it possible to ship a frame a considerable distance.

For those who wish to fabricate their own frames, detailed cutting diagrams are provided in Appendix B. Completely fabricated frames, as well as sets of scale sticks that are used as cutting guides, are available from several sources; these are listed in Appendix A.

The panelized houses are shown in detail in Chapter 25. The obvious combinations of 8-foot modules are 24 × 24 feet and 24 × 32 feet. Both sizes can be erected in 1-, 1½-, and 2-story versions, with or without basements. If the basements are included and they are designed into a south-facing slope, the designs in this book can provide an incredible range of living area in just two basic house sizes. The smallest 1-story unit has 700 square feet (including two sleeping lofts); the largest 2-story unit with basement has 2300 square feet. A duplex unit 24 feet deep by 48 feet wide contains two 1300-square-foot apartments to round out the range.

The panelized post-and-beam system is by no means limited to 8-foot modules, but it has proven to be the most economical layout of the many that I have tried. Any multiple of 4 feet can be readily used. The system worked very well for the Octagon house, which has sides of 12 feet. The Octagon can be found in Chapter 25, and virtually any of the custom houses shown in Chapter 24 could be constructed using this system as well.

ROOF STRUCTURES

I provide two roof designs for the houses shown on the working drawings in Appendix B. The most popular scheme has roof trusses that slope down to the north with a monopitch. This opens up the south wall for a solar greenhouse and provides space for sleeping or living lofts at either end on the south wall. Since I specialize in passive solar designs, I have found this to be the more popular scheme among my clients. The latest version has been modified to permit the greenhouse to be added at a later date.

The second design is a conventional gable roof, which Kevin Berry offers on his low-cost version of the house. Kevin is the contractor who has built most of the panelized houses shown in this book. Both schemes have structural members at 8 feet on-center, and both offer sleeping lofts.

In Kevin's version, the loft area is in the center of the house. Both this and the monopitch roof sheme utilize 4 × 8 prefab roof panels of 6 × 8-inch thickness, and both have dramatic cathedral ceilings.

Ironically, the only area in which American contractors have employed standardized, shop-built components is in roof construction. Unfortunately, the roof trusses that are so popular waste both space and materials. Standard roof trusses are designed to be installed at 2-foot intervals, and in this configuration, they occupy all the available space under the roof slope. This is space that you have paid for, and it should be made available as living area. The major benefit gained from trusses is that they provide a clear-span, wide-open space with no interior supports. Since most houses are cut up into rooms, this approach makes little sense except as a means of putting a roof on quickly.

Standard roof trusses are constructed of 2 × 6s that come together at the eaves to form the point of a triangle. In olden days when 6-inch attic insulation was considered adequate, this worked out fine. Now, you must skimp around the edges if you use the widely recommended 10 or 12 inches of insulation to make it fit. Also, fiberglass insulation must have a ventilation space above it to allow moisture to escape. Normal attics are designed so that air enters the attic at the eaves and exits at the gable ends. With standard truss construction and heavy insulation, the entrance passages for the air are blocked by the insulation, which can cause it to waterlog with moisture.

By contrast, our heavy timber trusses have rigid structural panels or decking placed over them, and the trusses are exposed, decorative elements in the house. Since they are spaced at 8 feet on-center, the sloping area under the roof can be incorporated into the house. The panelized roof deck provides superior insulation and a fully enclosed, insulated, and finished roof and ceiling in a fraction of the time required for conventional roof trusses filled with fiberglass insulation and covered with a Sheetrock ceiling.

An alternate scheme that we have used quite successfully with both roof designs eliminates the panels in favor of 2 × 6 tongue-and-groove decking with 4 inches of rigid insulation boards applied over the decking. This is an ideal system for an owner-builder working alone with plenty of time. The materials costs are about the same as the panelized system, but there is about 50% more field labor required. Since the 2 × 6 decking

Eight-foot-square panels are applied to walls and roof of a post-and-beam frame. The walls have exposed foam for stucco.

Rigid insulation board is applied over wood roof decking. Wood strapping provides support for sheet roofing as well as permitting overhangs in both directions.

rather than the insulated panel is the structural element, this method does permit more flexibility in the amount of insulation used. In very mild climates, 2-inch Thermax would be more than adequate over the decking. The insulation is slightly more effective since it can be butted, eliminating any framing members between the insulation boards that would otherwise break the seal.

Ribbed metal roofing or Onduline are ideal finish materials for this system; they have structural value and can be installed over spaced nailers rather than over expensive plywood. I use 1 × 6 rough-sawn pine nailers spaced at 2 feet on-center which are anchored into the trusses and decking with serrated barn spikes. The sheet roofing is then nailed to the pine nailers. Not only is this an economical system, but it also prevents any possibility of condensation between the insulation and the roofing material by providing a completely positive means of ventilation.

PREFABRICATED PANELS

These panels come in a variety of materials and thicknesses. They can be purchased ready-made or constructed in the field. Even if they had no other advantages, they would be worth using for their superior insulation and weathersealing value. It is no secret that traditional fiberglass insulation isn't all that it's cracked up to be. Numerous studies show disastrously low installed R values for fiberglass insulation; its performance is greatly dependent upon the adequacy of the vapor barrier and the absence of penetrations for wiring, plumbing, and the like. In contrast to a typical stud wall, a panel wall is virtually all insulation. Furthermore, the foam cores are not affected by moisture. Mechanical trades are relegated to raceways, and the panel adhesives seal the whole unit almost air- and moisture-tight.

Panel Materials

The panel system is made up of four or five components. They consist of a core material, an adhesive, one or two facing materials (the two sides of the panel are usually faced with different materials), and perimeter framing, or splines.

The foam cores are either polyurethane (UR) or expanded polystyrene (EPS). The core thickness is usually 3½, 4, 5½ or 7½ inches. The polyurethane is much more expensive than EPS, but a much better insulator. Therefore, the EPS panels are usually thicker than the polyurethane panels. Either core material can be ordered in almost any conceivable thickness up to 48 inches. There are 150 suppliers of EPS board stock in the United States and approximately 30 polyurethane suppliers. Sources are listed in Appendix A. The table shows my recommendations for panel thicknesses for wall and roof panels in various climatic conditions.

Insulation Requirements

Degree-Days	Foundation	Wall	Roof
7000+	4" BB	5½" UR	6" UR
5–7000	3" BB	5½" EPS; 4" UR	4–6" UR; 5½" EPS
3–5000	2" BB	3½" EPS	3" UR; 3½" EPS
3000–	—	3½" EPS	2" UR; 3½" EPS

EPS = Expanded polystyrene foam
UR = Polyurethane foam
BB = Blueboard (extruded polystyrene foam)

Several different adhesives have been used by the manufacturers and contractors in constructing the panels. The most thoroughly tested of the adhesives is Mor-Ad 336, by Morton Chemical Company, Chicago, Illinois, a structural urethane laminating adhesive that has been used for several years by J-Deck (see Chapter 8) for their EPS core panels. According to the manufacturer,

it is equally suitable for polyurethane-cored panels. This adhesive complies with all major codes for structural panels. If you are constructing load-bearing panels, this is your adhesive. For my Shingleton house, as well as the second version of the Civic house (see my first book, *30 Energy-Efficient Houses,* Rodale Press, 1977). I used a low-grade epoxy adhesive. This works well and is very strong. It is also expensive and messy. Several commercial panel manufacturers use 3M contact cement (Fastbond 30) for laminating panels and my clients and contractors have used it with varying success. Hot weather is required, and there is a delay in the fabrication sequence because the contact cement has to set up for 30 minutes before assembly. A jig is required to ensure exact alignment, since the pieces can't be adjusted after assembly. This adhesive is expensive but readily available everywhere, and you can always sell any excess to a cabinet shop.

After experimenting carefully with all of the available adhesives, I have settled upon 3M 4289 Mastic Adhesive as the best all-around adhesive for the small contractor and owner-builder. It was developed by 3M especially for this purpose. It comes in 1-quart caulking cartridges as well as 5-gallon cans for easy installation. It is readily available throughout the country wherever 3M products are sold. It is ideal for the skin-type panels described in this chapter. If you are using structural, wall-bearing panels such as those described in Chapter 8, see Appendix A for a listing of structural adhesives.

Facing materials can be almost anything that comes in a 4 × 8-foot panel. Foundation panels are faced on both sides with ½ inch of pressure-treated plywood. Exterior wall nonstructural panels have Sheetrock on the inside face with CDX or a finish plywood on the exterior. Structural wall panels have Texture 1-11 or other such plywood on both faces. Roof panels have Texture 1-11 plywood on the inside face with CDX on the exterior. I would strongly recommend using a roughsawn plywood without the grooves, since the resulting holes, where the grooves meet the beam at outside walls, are very difficult to seal. Also, the grooves that create the pattern expose the glue lines of the plywood, which is not desirable. Woodpeckers, looking for insects in voids in the inner plies, have been known to destroy houses with Texture 1-11.

The edges of the panels can be joined with splines if factory-built panels are used, or they can have a simple flush frame if my system of 8-foot-square panels attached to a post-and-beam frame is employed. If splines are used, the panels are usually made in standard framing thicknesses. In my design, I custom-cut roughsawn lumber for the framing. The center member of the panel is a full 2 × 4 inches. This member joins the 4 × 8 panels at the center of the unit. All four edges of the panel are framed by full 1 × 4 framing members. I chose the 4-inch thickness for rigidity and the extra insulating capacity and because with them I am able to use stock window jambs (see Window and Door Installation, later in this chapter). With the normal manufactured panels, one uses 2 × 4s, 2 × 6s, or 2 × 8s as splines to join the units.

Factory-Built Panels

Foam panels are available from several sources across the country for $1.70 to $3.50 per square foot, depending upon core and facing materials and thicknesses. Some manufacturers ship free within a 200-mile radius, but most charge extra for shipping. Most factory-built panels have the foam recessed on the edges to accept splines. Usually the recess is 1½ inches on the top and bottom and ¾ inch on the sides so that standard 1½-inch-thick framing members can be used as splines. Since the panels are made to order, any spline width can be accommodated. If the inside face of the panels is Sheetrocked, the cantilevered edge is unsupported and can be damaged in shipping and handling.

Some codes will require Sheetrock or even fire-rated Sheetrock for the inside face of wall panels. Usually single-family houses are exempt from these requirements. Make sure that you let code officials know what the panels' core material is since the material does make a difference in some codes. For instance, New York requires fire-rated Sheetrock over urethane foam, but has no requirements for polystyrene (EPS).

Panel sizes are usually 4 × 8 feet, but 4 × 9 can be special-ordered. Panels are also available with a 9-foot outer skin that projects from the bottom edge of the panel for attachment to a wooden floor framing system. Panel manufacturers usually do not cut standard-size pieces of plywood to make special-size units. Normally, odd-size units are cut in the field. Edges of the panels can be readily backcut with a router to accommodate the necessary splines. If you have large window or door openings to cut, keep these in mind when ordering the panels. The panels are installed first, and the openings are cut after installation. The scrap pieces that result may be used to make up odd-size pieces. In my designs, I group the

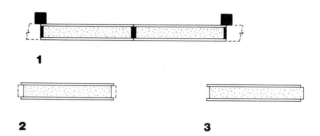

1

2   **3**

There are several types of wall panels: (1) An 8-foot-square panel of my design that has a 2X6-foot center strut and a 1X6-foot perimeter frame. It is designed for attachment to structural posts spaced 8 feet on-center. No joinery is required. (2) A 4X8-foot panel with recessed edges to accept a 2X6-foot spline. This is the typical commercial panel marketed by J-Deck and others. It can be used in a wall-bearing system. (3) A 6-inch tongue-and-groove panel in which the core is offset to form the panel joint. No spline is required. This panel is used with a traditional, braced post-and-beam frame. It has the best thermal qualities of the three types, since no wood members penetrate the skin. It is marketed commercially by Vermont Laminates; see Appendix A for the address.

This mockup of a section of panel shows how the anchor spike is driven next to the spline rather than through it.

windows into a large area on the south face of the house and use minimal windows on the other three sides. Special site conditions will dictate window sizes and placement.

Installation over a post-and-beam frame is quick and easy. Jim Jackson of J-Deck says that three men can put up the panels to enclose a 968-square-foot house in just one day. One of my 1200-square-foot saltboxes was enclosed by two inexperienced workmen in just one weekend. Installation begins by nailing the panels directly to the members of the structural frame with serrated barn spikes. A bead of construction adhesive or Mono caulking is applied to the frame surfaces before the panels are set in place. A spray foam insulator such as Instafoam is sprayed into the recesses on the panel edges before the spline is set in place, and the spline is then

anchored with nails through the exterior plywood skin. It is not necessary to use any nails through the Sheetrock face, since the insulating foam is an excellent adhesive for the Sheetrock. On the jobs where a roughsawn plywood is the exterior finish, batten strips are applied at 16-inch intervals to create a board and batten effect. Any normal wood or composition siding can also be applied as the exterior finish.

Site-Built Panels

In my experience, site-building has slashed costs $1 to $2 per square foot from the factory prices. Such a savings was realized with $12-per-hour skilled carpenters, but since the panels are very easy to build, the price could be cut still further by using unskilled labor at or near minimum wage. If you are an owner-builder building the panels in

This photo and the next four show construction of a garrison-style, braced-frame saltbox with oak frame by Bob Dakin and Kevin Berry. Here the frame is ready for panel installation.

The panels are job-fabricated on the floor deck and carried outside for installation.

The panels are tipped into place against the frame. A bead of sealant has been placed around the perimeter of the panels.

The panels are anchored with barn spikes. The gap at the bottom of the panel is left for wiring. It is later filled with scrap from windows.

your spare time, you can discount the cost of labor altogether.

Site-built panels can be made in an infinite variety of sizes and shapes. You certainly have much greater flexibility than you can get with purchased panels. If you are a great distance from a manu-

facturer, this may be the only way to take advantage of this superior building system. You can either build your panels in 4-foot widths as the factory builders do, or you can build my 8 × 8 units and eliminate most field joinery. You can even combine the systems and build a 4 × 8-foot panel that is framed on three sides with a recess on one side for a spline. This enables you to take advantage of my system without having to maneuver heavy, large panels into place.

Building my fully framed 8-foot-square panel is easy if you organize the work. The crew and I set up a nailing jig on two sheets of plywood to ensure that the panels are square and the center divider properly spaced. We then fasten two sheets of plywood to the exterior face of the frame with 6d galvanized common nails. We flip over the panel, apply adhesive, and insert the foam core. At this point, the panel is light enough to be moved easily by two people. Panels can be finished to this point at a work place remote from the house site. Even if they are constructed right in the house, they should be moved to their approximate final location before installing Sheetrock or other interior finish. With Sheetrock installed, the panel can be tipped easily into place by two people. If it has to be carried, four husky sets of hands or machinery are required.

The inside face of the foam core and wooden frame members are now coated with adhesive and the Sheetrock set in place and nailed around the perimeter. Nails should be eliminated or kept to a bare minimum at the butt joint in the center of the panel. We have used open-mesh fiberglass joint tape rather than the usual paper tape. The tape is self-adhesive, but we wrap it over the sides of the panel and tack it so that it can't be dislodged during panel erection. If the erection schedule allows drying time, the joint can even be finished and the panel prime-painted before

The north wall has been completed. The wall surface is completely finished on the inside with no cutting around the structural members.

A panel frame of precut members is assembled on the deck. The center member is a 2X6. All others are 1X6s.

Chipboard or plywood exterior skin is applied to the panel frame.

The panel is flipped over, and adhesive is applied to the exterior skin.

Precut slabs of foam insulation are installed in the cavities of the panel.

Foam slabs are pressed into place and another coat of adhesive is installed for the inside layer of Sheetrock.

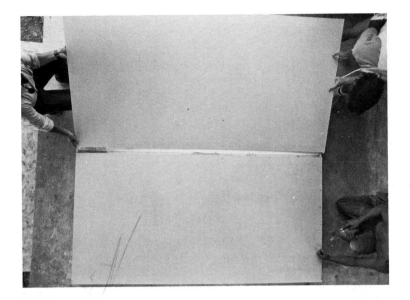

The Sheetrock is set into place and nailed around the edges. The center joint is taped with self-adhesive fiberglass tape.

erection. Make absolutely sure that the framing members have been sprayed with stain before installing the panels; this operation will require very time-consuming masking if done later.

There are several tricks that we have learned in setting the panels. First, always use a nail or similar spacer between the panels, both vertically and horizontally. This will allow room for proper caulking between the panels and also allow the plywood skin some room for expansion. This is very important. Do not attempt to drive the barn spikes through the 1-inch-thick edge members because the nail might split them. Instead, drive the nail alongside the member through the foam core. In this fashion, the wood member still transmits the nail's holding power, but there is no chance of damaging the wood. If the posts are slightly out of alignment, it may be necessary to angle the nail so that it passes through the 1-inch edge member near the post. It is a good idea to have a helper inside the house to watch that adhesive is not smeared on finished, inside panel faces and to make sure that the anchor nails are being driven correctly and are not missing any of the frame members.

With my supervision and direction, wall panels for an 1100-square-foot, story-and-a-half house were job fabricated and erected in 3½ days. Two workmen worked full time with occasional help from two others to set the completed panels in place.

Window and Door Installation
Since the post-and-beam frame supports all roof and floor loads, windows and doors can be cut through the panels anywhere except through a structural post. The panels are rigid, structural

units and do not require additional framing for normal-size windows. The windows are simply set into holes cut into the panels and anchored to the outside plywood skin. The perimeter of the opening is sprayed with Instafoam just before inserting the window. Panel cores are usually 3½ or 5½ inches thick so that they accept standard-size window casings. I have devised a method of installing a vinyl trim on the edges of the Sheetrock before the windows are set in place. Since the window casing is installed behind the Sheetrock rather than flush with the finish surface, the core thickness should be increased by ½ inch. This technique has several advantages. First, it adds about R-4 to the insulation value of the walls; it provides an instant, fully trimmed window installation; and finally, it makes the large panels more rigid. Doors or very large window openings should have full-height framing members built into the panel at the sides of the opening. No special tools are required except that a large Makita saw (13 or 16 inches) will make cutting the openings quicker and easier. The opening can be marked with long nails and cut from both sides if a Makita isn't available.

Toxicity of Materials
Speaking as someone who was recently poisoned by a factory's toxic chemical emissions, I am highly concerned about building with any materials that could pose health problems. Many people who call me to talk about construction with the foam panels have expressed their concerns about possible toxic reactions to the foam. Such concerns are usually prompted by remembrances of the federal ban on the use of urea-formaldehyde foam as an insulating material. The foams we are using come as a fully cured board stock and are sealed within a panel. By contrast,

The window is installed simply by cutting an opening in the panel. Sheetrock is allowed to project into the opening and is trimmed with molding to avoid trim.

the urea-formaldehyde was a field-installed material that used a small amount of a dangerous chemical, formaldehyde, as a solvent. If the foam was properly mixed and properly installed, the solvent evaporated, leaving harmless foam. But enough of the foam was improperly installed to cause national alarm, and many unhappy home-owners had nasty physical reactions to the fumes. Unlike in European countries where the process originated and is still in widespread use, there was no licensing or supervision required of installers in this country.

A few people are sensitive to even minute traces of formaldehyde, and these people would be bothered by even a properly installed insulation job. Since the process is now illegal, it's a moot point. But other sources of formaldehyde must still be reckoned with. For instance, it is used in the glues that are bonding agents for many building materials, and it is extensively used in pressed chipboard, plywood, plywood finish paneling, or underlayment board, Formica and other plastic laminates, and in furnishings and

carpets. If you are one of the few people affected by formaldehyde, you should avoid using any of these materials inside your house. If you use the panelized system, I recommend using Sheetrock for the inside panel face rather than plywood or paneling. To be absolutely safe, I would use 3M Fastbond contact cement as the adhesive for the Sheetrock. This is a water-based adhesive and has no nasty chemicals to leach out into the wall. Use solid wood interior doors as I describe in Chapter 23 and avoid chipboard and plywood where possible. If either of these is used, seal thoroughly with paint or varnish. Avoid all laminated furniture and carpets. If your house is weathertight and therefore doesn't have as many air exchanges per hour as "leaky houses," see Chapter 17 for information on air-to-air heat exchangers, which will help to dispel any unhealthy buildup of irritating chemical emissions in your house.

Erecting the Panels

A major drawback of most panelized systems has been overcome in my version. Since, in most of the systems, we are dealing with inflexible factory-made or site-built panels, most methods of installation will allow little or no tolerance in the frame. I have devised a method of installing the panels in pinwheel fashion and custom-fitting the corner gaps after the panels are erected so that a dimensional variation of plus or minus 2 inches per wall can be tolerated. In actual practice, the variation is usually ½ to 1 inch, but even this small variation can be fatal if there is no means to accommodate it. Even if an amateur owner-builder or sloppy union carpenter erects a corner post an inch out-of-plumb, this system will conceal the error; you won't have to dismantle the structure and correct it.

I have devised two different sequences for erecting the shell of my houses. In the first sequence, the entire post-and-beam frame, including floor decks and finished roof, is installed first and then the wall panels are fabricated and attached to the completed frame. The major advantage of this

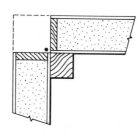

This open corner detail provides leeway for frame irregularities and a raceway for vertical wiring. Scrap material from window cutouts is used to fill the gap after wiring is completed. By using this detail, a 4-foot construction module can be maintained in both directions. It also gains 200 to 300 square feet of usable space, at little cost in most houses.

This photo and the next two show the Civic house under construction. The prefabricated post-and-beam frame has posts spaced 8 feet on-center. Panels provide bracing for the frame. The bracing shown here is dangerously inadequate.

Eight-foot-square panels are attached to the outside of the frame with 8-inch barn spikes. Windows are cut into the wall after panels have been installed.

The finished wall after installation of windows and siding.

scheme is that because the roof and floor decks go up first, you have a weatherproof work space in which to construct your wall panels. Second, floor panels can be constructed right on the second-floor deck so that no lifting is involved. This scheme is particularly important if Sheet-

rock is used for the interior panel skin, since you must be completely protected from the weather so that there is little chance for water damage to the panels. If you use plywood-skinned panels or purchase factory-made 4 × 8 units with a plywood skin, you should consider my second scheme.

159

Post-and-beam framing saves over 2000 cubic feet in this two-story house—enough for two extra bedrooms. It also results in better proportions.

This shows a prototype panelized house of my design constructed in the early 1970s.

The second erection scheme is accomplished by erecting one floor at a time. This is easier and safer for the owner-builder, but the panels will have to be protected from the weather. Awkward temporary braces are eliminated, since the panels provide bracing for the frame as you progress. Because the second-floor walls are erected before the roof, it is easy to trim out the top of the panels. If you elect to use this easier system, I strongly recommend that you get a coat of waterproof sealer on your Sheetrock before delivering it to the job site. Glidden Insulpaint is the product of choice for this purpose. In addition to protecting the panels during construction, the paint is a fine vapor barrier, protecting the wall insulation from moisture inside the house, once it is complete.

The plank-and-beam floor system used in my houses has many bonuses in addition to its strikingly good looks. Since the bottom of the decking is the ceiling plane, the floor-to-floor height of the structure can be reduced from 9 feet to 8 feet. This reduces heat loss, since there is less exterior wall to lose heat. It also enables me to use 8-foot-high wall panels. If I were to use conventional floor-framing methods, the first-floor panels would have to be 9 feet high. Finally, since all Sheetrock ceilings and corners are eliminated, taping and finishing costs are drastically slashed. On a recent panel job, the entire taping bill was $160. This compares to $1500 or more for a typical fully Sheetrocked house of similar size.

Unlike other "new" building systems, this one has stood the test of time. Post-and-beam frames have been around for centuries, but the panels are a comparatively new technique. Jackson of J-Deck built his first panelized house in 1960, and his firm has furnished laminated panels for hundreds of buildings since then. I designed the Shingleton house 10 years later. At this writing, 11 of my recent panelized designs are either completed or under construction, and this is in addition to three versions of the original Shingleton house that have been built.

21 Roofing

A compact, multilevel house slashes roofing costs just as it does the cost of a foundation. If you only construct half as much roof, it will usually only cost half as much to install. In addition, my basic houses have a simple, single-pitch roof with no ridge, no valleys, no complexities whatsoever. If you forego a chimney or skylights, there is only one vent stack to interrupt the entire roof process.

Since my roofs are small and simple, they are ideal for do-it-yourself projects. Just have the contractor cover the roof with 30-pound felt rather than the usual 15 pound. The cost difference is slight. Since the felt is always used under shingles, you are only paying for the extra thickness. In an emergency, the 30-pound felt will last up to a year as a temporary roof. Also, securely anchor the edges with batten strips to prevent your temporary covering from blowing away. If you are using a roof system that eliminates the plywood deck, the 30-pound felt can be installed right over the insulation board. The nailer strips for wood shingles or ribbed roofing will hold it in place.

There are a number of good roofing materials to choose from, and I'll run down those that I've had experience with here. They break down into two basic categories. The first category contains flexible or liquid materials that require plywood or other solid structural decking material for their application. If you use plywood as your decking, be sure to install metal or wood edging around the perimeter of it because plywood is notorious for delaminating at the edges of roofs. The second category of materials has inherent structural strength and doesn't require a solid substrate. The materials in this category are excellent for use over a rigid insulation board, such as Thermax or R-Max.

The following materials should be used over CDX or better plywood decking:

Asphalt Roll Roofing

This is the old standby—relatively cheap and very easy to apply. This material makes a long-lasting, economical roof, but it's not very attractive. Since our houses are two stories high and have a mono-pitch roof, appearance usually isn't a factor. But if you approach the house from above, or the roof is prominent, you may wish to consider another material. Roll roofing comes in 36-inch-wide rolls and is installed half-lapped so that 18 inches of the material is exposed. The concealed portion of the material is nailed to the roof deck, and the exposed area is anchored to the preceding course with roof cement. Detailed instructions for application are packed with the roofing and should be followed exactly. Pay careful attention to the instructions for unrolling the material and letting it flatten out before installation. The roofing project can be held up if you forget this step; omitting it can also result in a ruined roof. Life expectancy: 20 years plus.

Two layers of 2-inch-thick polyure-thane insulation board are laid over a continuous vapor barrier. One by six strapping supports Onduline or metal roofing.

Asphalt Shingles

This is the usual roofing material in the United States. It is a bit more expensive and a bit less durable than the roll roofing above, but it is also a lot more attractive. Spend the extra money and get fiberglass-reinforced shingles. Even though many contractors don't like these shingles because they are more difficult to cut, don't let them talk you out of them. Life expectancy: 15 years plus for unreinforced shingles; 20 years for reinforced.

EPDM Sheet Roofing

This is a synthetic rubber sheet material of approximately the same thickness and composition as an automobile inner tube. It is manufactured in rolls 40 feet wide and is usually used to reroof large commercial buildings. It is expensive (about $1 per square foot) and permanent. It is primarily marketed by Carlisle Rubber Company (Carlisle, PA 17013), to large roofing contractors. Since it is manufactured in huge rolls and sold in minimum quantities, roofers frequently have odd-size scraps left that are just about useless to them. These scraps make excellent flashing, as well as excellent whole roofs for small houses. Many of my clients have used the material as waterproofing for underground houses or as a base for sod roofs.

The joint cement used with the system is virtually flawless, so smaller pieces can be spliced to make up a roof. We have paid 10 to 50 cents per square foot for the remnant material and have used it for roof decks, a Japanese soaking tub, a hot tub, and for numerous flashings for difficult roofing conditions. Application is very easy. The surface to be covered is coated with a latex cement, and

the roofing is rolled out on top of the cement. Joints or flashings are sealed with lap cement. Carlisle has very detailed directions for installing the material. Life expectancy: 50 years plus.

Since the Carlisle roofing has such a fine reputation, it is in great demand. They only sell through roofers and there is a waiting list for the material. If you have trouble locating it, there is a competitor with a very similar product. W. R. Grace & Company (Cambridge, MA 02140) markets a product called Bituthene, which is a good substitute for the Carlisle product. Bituthene has a factory-applied adhesive backing that makes it easier to apply than the Carlisle product. The adhesive not only sticks to the roof or wall substrate, but also sticks to the roofing material itself; to make a seam, you merely overlap the roofing 4 inches and press into place. The manufacturer claims that the material is also ideal for vertical applications for waterproofing walls. Bituthene is distributed by lumberyards and is easier to obtain than the Carlisle roofing, but it has not been on the market as long, so durability, particularly of the adhesive, could be a problem.

Urethane and Neoprene Liquid Roofing

These are liquid roofing systems that require considerable labor or special equipment for application. They can be applied by roller, but the process is tedious and time-consuming. Commercially, they are applied with an airless sprayer. Both materials can be applied directly to plywood, and both bond tenaciously. If you are using prefab plywood roof panels with a plywood top skin, you may want to prime the panels before installation, thereby assuring an immediate, watertight roof.

Since the panels have been prime-coated before installation, all that has to be done to waterproof the roof is to caulk the panel joints with either neoprene or urethane caulking. These materials are applied in three coats, with the top coat containing an integral color. A wide variety of colors is available, but the panel joints will show. I do not recommend these materials if the roof is highly visible.

ERA Corporation of Minneapolis markets the urethane system, and Gates Engineering Company of Wilmington, Delaware, markets both systems. The urethane system is about 65 cents per square foot for materials, while the neoprene system is pushing $1 per square foot. The urethane system can be sprayed directly over urethane foam insulation as a roofing material. The insulation should be spray-applied over an existing deck. The insulation and roof coating could both be applied by the same contractor. I have had one of these roofs in place for over 10 years, and it is doing beautifully. Life expectancy: urethane roofing, 10 years uncoated; indefinite if top coat is renewed every 10 years. Neoprene roofing, 20 years uncoated; indefinite if top coat is renewed every 20 years.

The following materials don't require any decking under them; they may be placed over nailers spaced 18 to 24 inches on-center. The nailers are placed over the insulation board and spiked to the structure below. They may also be used over a plywood deck, but economies may be achieved by eliminating the plywood.

Onduline

Onduline is a corrugated, rigid asphalt roofing material that is new to the United States but that has been used throughout the world for about 20 years. I have seen it in as faraway places as Japan and New Zealand. Most people are attracted to the material because of its extremely good looks; it has deep textured corrugations and comes in a variety of attractive colors (my clients and I favor the deep brown). The material comes with a lifetime guarantee. That is, it's guaranteed for the lifetime of the building on which it is installed. There are numerous restrictions to the guarantee, including damage from hail, so read carefully. The material is slightly porous and will allow moisture to evaporate from within the building. This is a bonus provided there isn't an excessive amount of moisture. If there is too much moisture, ice dams can build up at the overlapping joints and water can back up under the sheets in the spring thaw. On low-pitched roofs, I recommend sealing the horizontal joints with butyl.

Provided that the roof is square and of simple geometry, Onduline is a breeze to install. But flashing at valleys, chimneys, dormers, hips, and the like is a nightmare. I finally got around this drawback by using the Carlisle Rubber material as a flashing; it fits nicely into the Onduline corrugations. If you apply a second layer of the Onduline to cover the exposed flashing material, the flashing doesn't show at all. You will notice that a great many of the houses in this book have these roofs. I have never had a product become so widely used so quickly. Every client who sees it wants it for his or her new house, and I can

Onduline sheet roofing is used on many of my houses. This is a nine-level hillside house that has my first roof of this material.

understand why. It's simple to install, and the material cost is about 40 cents per square foot; if you can eliminate the plywood decking, it costs less than asphalt shingles. And it's remarkably durable. Life expectancy: the life of the building?

Ribbed Metal Roofing

Ribbed steel roofing is available in a variety of finishes and corrugations. Most commonly, it is V-ribbed with a baked enamel finish. It is also available galvanized or with V or rounded corrugations. It is manufactured in 32-inch-wide sheets in 8- to 14-foot lengths in 2-foot increments. It is attached to the roof with special neoprene-gasketed nails. Unlike the Onduline, it comes with a wide variety of accessory flashings to manage almost any roofing condition. Cost is 40 to 50 cents per square foot for full-length sheets, but mill ends are available in the Midwest for 18 cents per square foot. This makes it the best bargain around next to a do-it-yourself thatched roof. You have to pay shipping costs for mill ends, and putting on the roof will take more work because of the many small pieces you'll be working with. You may also wind up with an "interesting" color variety and have to repaint the roof to have it all match, but if you are on a tight budget, this is the way to go. Life expectancy: 50 years.

Homemade Wooden Shakes

Hardwood shakes were the traditional method of roofing until standing-seam terne roofs displaced them. Because of their beauty and durability, there has been something of a revival of the art of shake splitting in recent years. This is one of those labor-of-love affairs, but if you have a small roof area and lots of time, shakes can give you a virtually free roof. Shakes are usually hand-split with an axlike device called a froe. Logs are cut into lengths corresponding to the desired length of the finished shingle. A mallet and the froe are then used to split the chunk of log into shingles. Froes, which require a great deal of practice before the final product is acceptable for use, are available from the Brookstone Company. Clever folk have even devised a homemade machine for splitting these shakes. Full details are given in the April 1977 issue of *Popular Science* in the article "Shakemaker Lets You Split Your Own," by M. Robinson.

Red oak is the wood of choice for hardwood shakes. If you are in a heavily forested, remote area, this roofing material is not recommended, because it is a fire hazard. Even in suburban areas you may have to treat your shakes with fire-retardant chemicals to get fire insurance coverage. You may have to count on that 30-pound felt for temporary roofing for a long time, but when your shake roof is finished, you'll be proud of the results. Life expectancy: 40 years plus.

Standing-Seam Terne

As my longtime readers know, terne is my very favorite roofing material. Until recently this roofing technique was virtually a lost art. Terne is a lead-coated steel that is usually installed in a pattern with upturned vertical seams at 18- to 24-inch intervals. The material is manufactured in 50-foot-long rolls that are cut into sheets and bent into roofing "pans" in a sheet-metal shop or preformed at the factory. The pans are fastened to the roof with anchor clips, and the roofing seams are crimped together to form a weather-tight seal.

Terne is lightweight and fireproof, permanent, and, for the knowledgeable, easy to install. I give detailed instructions for fabricating and installing the roofing in my book, *A Design and Construction Handbook for Energy-Saving Houses* (Rodale Press, 1980). This is an expensive roof; material costs about $1 per square foot. Depending upon their skill, roofers will charge anywhere from 50 cents to $3 per square foot for installation. The original terne roof on Thomas Jefferson's Monticello is still in good condition, more than 200 years after it was placed there. Many of my readers have followed the directions in my book and installed their own roofs. For materials sources, contact the Follansbee Steel Company, Follansbee, WV 26037.

Cedar Shingles and Shakes, Slate, and Tile

All of these are materials that must be installed on steeply pitched roofs (over 6/12). They are all expensive and heavy; in the case of slate and tile, extremely so. Cedar, although very beautiful, is a fire hazard; slate and tile are fireproof and may reduce your insurance rates. All of these materials are discussed in detail in *A Design and Construction Handbook*.

Future Possibilities

There are several durable, weatherproof chemical coatings that can readily be applied to plywood in a factory, such as Du Pont's Tedlar and General Electric's Silicone. As the use of panelized housing grows, we can expect to see factory-applied coatings for roof panels becoming more common. At this writing, they are available, but only as a special-order item. I expect them to be more readily available at a reasonable price within the next two to three years.

22 Installing Wiring and Plumbing Systems

Mechanical trades such as wiring, plumbing, and heating make up almost 40% of the budget for a typical house, even more for a small house since you usually have to have basic mechanical services no matter how small the dwelling. Since these systems cost so much money, it is worth the trouble to study them carefully. In Japan and Europe, prefabricated housing systems are constructed so that pipes and wires can be snapped together in the field quickly and economically. But trade unions and restrictive codes have prevented these advances from being implemented in this country. Even though we cannot take advantage of the latest technology, there are still many ways to save on these trades if you plan ahead.

ELECTRIC WIRING

Wiring for electricity poses major problems for designers of affordable houses. Although most building codes allow some flexibility, or at least have an established appeal process, electrical installations are rigidly controlled by the inflexible National Electric Code (NEC). It would make good sense in prefabricated housing systems to concentrate the electrical wiring in interior partitions so that you can avoid piercing the exterior envelope of the house or using expensive raceways. The NEC allows you no such options. The exact spacing is specified, and a minimum of one outlet per wall is required. A factory-made wiring harness such as those used in automobiles and airliners would be an ideal solution. Plug-type connectors such as those used in these industries would speed construction and slash costs. Unfortunately, anything of this nature is taboo. The only legal way around the NEC is to build in a remote site and not connect to the power lines—hardly an option for most of us. Since we are stuck with an inflexible code that is not at all likely to be modified anytime soon, let's see how we can comply without breaking the budget. Lights, switches, and other devices can be concentrated, quite legally, on interior partitions. The working drawings in Appendix B have been drawn to minimize all electrical work involving the exterior shell. Several different strategies are available so that you can avoid disturbing the integrity of the exterior walls.

Floor Outlets

One easy, but expensive, way to supply the required outlets for the exterior walls is to install them in the floor adjacent to the walls in question. Floor outlets consist of a heavy cast box that has a round plate with a flush screw-type cover. The box itself costs $30 to $40. For all of this money, you only get one receptacle rather than the usual two. Also, you have to remove the cover in order to use the outlet. Even though there are drawbacks, floor outlets may be cheaper and more satisfactory than an expensive raceway installed around the perimeter of the house. If you are building a small house on one floor with only a few required outlets, this is the solution. If you are using a concrete slab-on-grade or a masonry floor, you will have to install the outlet boxes and conduit and have the installation inspected before the floor is put in place; however, if you have a crawl space or basement, the outlets can be installed at any time.

Internal Raceways

A second solution to the wiring problem is to build a conduit or raceway into the wall panel or masonry wall for later installation of wiring. Amos Winter, a manufacturer of prefabricated panels, embeds a 1-inch plastic conduit inside his wall panels at 18 inches above the floor, providing a continuous raceway at outlet height around the entire perimeter of the house. The electrician can tap into the conduit anywhere and install an outlet; additional outlets can be installed at any time. J-Deck, another panel manufacturer, provides a 1-inch-square recess around the perimeter of the foam core of their panels for wiring.

A simple square cutout, at bottom center, provides an electrical raceway in prefab wall panels by Vermont Laminates.

Theoretically, this gives you full flexibility to install electrical devices at 4-foot intervals almost anywhere in the wall.

Both of these approaches have drawbacks. The primary one is that the electrician needs to be on the job while the panels are being erected in order to snake a conduit into the spaces provided for him. If you have a cooperative electrician, he can review the wiring with you, and you or the contractor can feed the necessary conduits into place as the panels go up. A second drawback is that the splines or panel edge members need to be drilled to accommodate the conduits and the holes need to be lined up exactly with these internal raceways.

If you are building masonry walls, you will need to have the electrician install conduits at appropriate points in the construction, and this will require interrupting your work and waiting for the electrician. Any technique that requires such close scheduling of trades should be avoided if possible. I've found the electricians I've worked with to be much more dependable and flexible than other building trades and if you have a good one who is willing to work with you, the internal raceways will provide a low-cost wiring solution. This may be especially true if you are using the surface-bonding technique I describe in Chapter 19, because any damage to the block is covered by the bonding cement.

External Raceways

The mechanical engineer's favorite solution to efficient wiring is to use an external raceway. A hollow wiring channel with a snap-on cover is substituted for the usual wooden baseboard. Wiring is easy, and the electrician can come to the job after the shell is fully erected and perform his work all at one time, relatively quickly. There are virtually no penetrations of the insulating envelope of the house. Commercial raceways are available in plastic and metal—expensive and very expensive. In theory, the time saved by the electrician will offset some of the additional cost of the raceways, but in actual practice, the electrician will quote a labor cost per outlet and then add the cost of materials. By this standard formula, you have the worst of both worlds—high material costs with no labor-saving benefit. If you are a contractor employing an electrician by the hour or a homeowner doing your own work, these raceways are a good bet.

The Carlon Company of Cleveland, Ohio, manufactures and distributes a noncombustible, code-approved vinyl raceway throughout the United States and Canada. The baseboard system costs about $1.50 per foot and is made of what I think is an ugly beige plastic. It can be painted, but sand it first; if you don't the paint may chip. Canadians get clipped an extra $2.50 per outlet for a special anchor that would appear to be worth a few cents extra. The system is easy to use and is code approved. If you don't mind its poor looks, it's a reasonable solution.

Wiremold Corporation makes a similar baseboard raceway in steel with a baked enamel finish, a stock item available at most electrical supply houses. It costs about twice as much as the plastic baseboard and must be cut to fit with a hacksaw. The Wiremold baseboard is handsome, but the installed cost is prohibitive. Engineers at the Brockhaven Laboratory have devised a cost-saving raceway for their passive solar house. In this version, a standard 1 × 4 wooden baseboard is used everywhere. On the outside walls, a smaller Wiremold "Plugmold" raceway is installed at the top of the baseboard. Plugmold must still be fabricated with a hacksaw, but the cost is comparable to the plastic raceway. Also, there is a uniform baseboard on all sides, making the room look neater. I make frequent use of Plugmold in my kitchen designs. I run a continuous strip of raceway along the top of the backsplash in the main work area. It is better looking and easier to clean and provides more outlet space than conventional duplex receptacles. I recommend the black, baked enamel finish over the brown primer.

For several years, I have used a site-built wooden raceway for my post-and-beam houses. It is installed as either a baseboard or a chair rail. To be legal, armored (BX) cable must be used inside the raceway. This is a splendid method if you do your own carpentry work, but not cost-effective if the labor is hired. It is very attractive, and the materials are inexpensive.

Corner Raceways

A major criterion in the design of my post-and-beam panelized houses was a low-cost method of installing the wiring without interrupting the construction sequence to thread them through concealed raceways. The same open-corner detail that provides for dimensional adjustment allows the electrician to run the wiring vertically after the wall panels have been installed. A hole is then drilled in the corner framing member of the wall panel, and a hole is made for the electric cable with a pointed rod. By using this method, electrical devices can be installed in any of the

exterior walls within 4 feet of the corners of the house. Since the rooms are of modest size, this spacing meets both the requirements for one outlet per wall and the minimum spacing requirement. If additional flexibility is required, a notch can be cut into the top corner of the perimeter beam. By using this notch, a wire can be threaded to any point on the exterior wall where an electrical device is required.

Access to the corner raceways can be handled in several ways, depending upon the configuration of the building. If there is a basement or crawl space, the wiring can be run through the floor joists to the corners of the house. The wires can also be fed around the perimeter of the house at the base of the wall panels. This technique uses more wire, but frees the electrician from entanglement with other construction trades. A third method is to use floor outlets for the first floor and use these outlets as feed points for the corners. The working drawings in Appendix B show the latter arrangement.

Cost Savings

Although the NEC requires more outlets than most people want or need, it does not require many other lighting devices usually installed by consumers, like ceiling lights. You can take advantage of this because it is much less expensive to install switched outlets in bedrooms and living rooms for plugging in lamps than to put in fixed ceiling lights. And the light from such indirect lighting is softer and more pleasing. In a post-and-beam house, overhead lighting can be very expensive. Where permanent lights are needed, I usually use 40-watt strip fluorescents concealed behind a valance board. These work well under kitchen shelves or wall cabinets and in hallways and bathrooms. The working drawings for the Civic house (see Appendix B) show these fixtures, as well as switched outlets for plugging in lamps. I have provided the very minimum that will pass code and still do a good job.

For more decorative lights in my houses, I use wall- or floor-mounted, can-type fixtures. These can be easily homemade using Underwriters-Approved components. The electrical parts are readily available from larger electrical supply houses. The shade can be fabricated from either a large steel can or white Plexiglas tubing. The commercial version of a two-light wall fixture costs just under $60. Compare this to the nicer-looking, homemade job that costs about $15 for materials, plus your labor. The commercial floor-mounted can costs $25—the homemade version

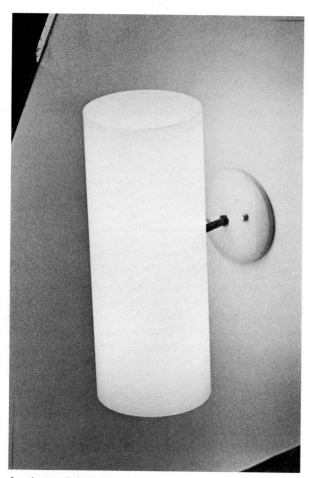

An elegant light fixture can be made with a length of a white Plexiglas cylinder. A double-ended socket provides the interior works.

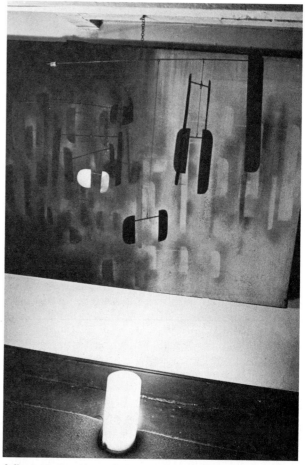

A floor can-type lamp lights a mobile in my dining room. It was homemade with a plastic cylinder and a socket. A tin can also makes a dandy floor can fixture.

less than $5. You might get some static from either the electrician or the electrical inspector about these fixtures, and for this reason I would suggest that you have the electrician install a wall-mounted porcelain socket to satisfy the powers that be. The floor can would usually be wired as a portable lamp, so there is no reason for anyone to complain about them.

The ultimate cost-saving technique for electrical installations is to buy a bit of an electrician's time rather than to hire him for the complete job. I suggest this to all of my clients who are on a tight budget doing much of their own work. You are usually better off to hire the professional to set the main panel and run the heavy feeds. At the same time, you can discuss your detailed electric plans with him and verify the exact location and method of wiring the devices. On his second visit, after you've done the basic wiring, the electrician can tie in your circuits and check your

connections. If you have trouble or questions, you can always pay for another visit. Those who are not that handy can hire on as an electrician's helper and work with him.

Above all, remember that electricity is no bargain and is getting more expensive by the minute. Do not waste money by providing extra capacity that you will never be able to afford to use.

PLUMBING

There are three vital factors to any affordable plumbing fixture installation: low cost, low water consumption, and safety. The first two factors are usually thought to be inversely related because most people have heard that systems that save water also cost a lot of money. Those who have inquired about the world-famous Clivus Multrum composting toilet, which doesn't use any water at all, have found it costs around $2000, plus the cost of installing another system to dispose of the greywater. Of course, there are other, much cheaper types of waterless toilets, and Chapters 6 and 15 give you some useful alternatives. But what do you do if you still want a flush toilet, but are concerned about unnecessarily wasting water? You've got a couple of fine alternatives to the conventional, 5-gallon flush toilet to choose from.

Plumbing Layouts

Unlike electricity, there is no code that requires you to string plumbing pipes all over the house. The less piping and the fewer fixtures you have, the lower your costs will be. Try very hard to put all plumbing fixtures back to back along one wall. In two-story houses, the upstairs bath or baths should be aligned with the plumbing wall of the kitchen below. Most of the houses in this book have very well worked out plumbing systems; study them carefully before you decide on your fixture locations.

If you use a compact, back-to-back plumbing layout, you can take advantage of an efficient arrangement for plumbing your fixtures, called a plumbing tree.

In a plumbing tree, all the supply and waste pipes for the bathroom and kitchen are laid out in a shop, fastened together, and attached permanently to one another with steel angle iron. This prefabricated unit is then brought to the building and set into place, floor by floor. This technique has been used on large commercial projects with repetitive floor plans for years. Major advantages are that the work can be performed on an assembly line basis rather than crawling around on a floor; also, the wall is built around the tree rather than laboriously cut out to receive the piping.

In commercial installations, plumbing trees are required to hold heavy cast-iron piping and are usually fabricated from very heavy steel sections. Even with this expense, contractors save money due to the many identical floors in the usual apartment or commercial building. Now there is a system for the small contractor and the homeowner that is made up of inexpensive plastic brackets that attach to the PVC waste line to hold the hot and cold water supply lines in place next to it. Its advantage is not only that the entire supply and waste system can be fabricated off the job site, but also that it has shockproof mountings that serve as sound deadeners.

If the job is carefully laid out and a 2 × 6 stud wall is used to house the plumbing tree, you can get

by with only minor cutting on the lateral branches of the tree. A second option is to construct two 2-inch-thick walls and sandwich the tree between them; this eliminates cutting altogether.

The various components that are used to fabricate the plumbing tree go under the trade name Water-Fab, and they are marketed throughout the United States by Tech Specialties (Box 186, Stanton, CA 90680). The fittings are made of ABS plastic and are available in either clamped or cemented versions. The clamped model can be used with copper, galvanized, cast-iron, or plastic drain lines. The cemented model is used with either ABS or PVC drain lines.

Materials

After the plumbing fixtures themselves, the biggest single item in your plumbing system is the drainage piping. Many years ago, these lines were made of cast iron, lead, or copper. Except for a few major cities with strong unions opposed to such piping, plastic is now universal for drainage lines within the house. Two types of plastic are in common use: black, plastic ABS piping and ivory, plastic PVC piping. The PVC piping is a bit stronger and a bit more expensive. Some codes will require the stronger piping, so check carefully before purchasing materials. Connections are normally made with a solvent cement, except where the piping connects to metal traps; threaded plastic pipe connections are made at these points. If you are fabricating your own waste system, make absolutely sure everything fits perfectly before you cement any connections. Once a fitting has been cemented to pipe, it is permanent, and the only way to get rid of it is to cut it out and throw it away.

Supply piping is still traditionally ½-inch copper in most parts of the country. If the codes allow, plastic piping does a better job at less cost. Polybutylene flexible piping is the high-quality choice for the budget-conscious. It is relatively new, however, and may have to be special-ordered. Because this piping is flexible, you can do away with many of the traditional fittings. It is connected with a simple metal, crimp-type fitting, so no soldering or solvents are needed to join the parts of the system. Any mistakes can be easily corrected without discarding ruined fittings. A special type of PVC piping is also used for supply piping; however, I don't recommend it as highly because it is brittle and will crack from the slightest freezing condition. This rigid supply piping is known in the trade as CPVC and is readily available in most parts of the country. Either of these plastic piping systems results in an approximate labor and materials saving of 50% over copper, so they are both well worth considering.

Plumbing fixtures themselves should be white. Not only is the cost 10 to 20% less than colored fixtures, but you can mix different brands and still have a color match. One-piece tub and shower units are expensive, but they save you money in the long run. When you add up all the labor and materials required to install a conventional tub and tile or plastic surround, plus the potential leakage problems, these units are an excellent buy. Owens-Corning originated the product and it is my favorite brand. Unless you plan a really large useful cabinet, a small wall-hung sink is a much better deal than a vanity top with a little wooden cabinet below. Stainless steel kitchen sinks are a reasonable choice. Avoid porcelain enamel steel sinks and tubs, because they tend to chip easily. Cast-iron tubs and kitchen sinks are very expensive and heavy, but of top quality.

Simplify

Most plumbing systems are a maze of unnecessary pipes, valves, and fittings. Plumbing codes regularly call for extraneous valves and vent pipes, which are routinely used by plumbers in all areas, whether specifically required or not. If you have a compact plumbing layout with an easily accessible main valve, there is no reason for extra, cheap shutoff valves under every fixture. Similarly, the main vent stack works quite well as a vent for all of the fixtures in a compact system; you don't need to run extra vent lines from each fixture. If a remote fixture is a must, a vacuum-breaker type in-line vent can be used instead of an expensive pipe buried in the wall. If you have an island-mounted sink, you may have to use an in-line vent. Carefully study the plumbing tree layout in the working drawings in Appendix B. The minimum required piping is shown in solid lines with the extra vent lines shown as dotted. Check your local codes before you begin so that you know how much venting is required.

Safety

Safety involves both supply and waste piping in your plumbing system. All waste outlets must be equipped with traps that provide a water seal against dangerous gases. Proper means of venting must also be provided so that water is not sucked out of the traps by water passing through other parts of the system. Supply and waste systems must be entirely separate so that back pressure cannot force wastewater into the supply system. This is the major reason for the overflow fittings on sinks and bathtubs. Portable water-using appliances such as dishwashers and washing machines must be equipped with a backflow prevention device if they connect to a faucet with a quick-connect fitting.

Traditional rigid copper supply pipes are still joined by soldering. The solder is lead-based and can be dangerous if excess solder is routinely used on the pipe joints. This would be much more likely to happen with an amateur, since a professional wouldn't waste the solder. If you are using copper and doing the job yourself, you may want to switch to ⅜-inch-diameter flexible copper tubing and use flared or compression fittings. The fittings are more expensive, but the smaller pipe size will offset the extra cost. Do not decrease the size of the inlet line or the feed to the hot water heater. In some areas with acidic water supplies, copper pipes can be rapidly corroded by the water itself. In these cases, it can be dangerous to use copper supply lines even if the code demands it. Polybutylene piping is clearly your first choice in such cases.

If you are using an open flame for connecting your water lines, keep a fire extinguisher handy. The paper or foil backing on fiberglass insulation will support combustion, so use a heat shield if you are working next to exposed insulation. The hotter the flame, the better the job, with much less chance of leaks. Mapp gas, which is packaged in bright yellow cylinders, burns hotter than propane, which is packaged in blue ones. Even though Mapp requires a special torch for use which might cost you $10 extra, it's well worth it.

23 Interior Finishes, Doors, Trim, and Cabinetwork

Interior finish work is usually the slowest and costliest of all the phases of building a house. No one wants to take the trouble to do all the little things that have to be done to complete a house properly. This is where factory-built housing tends to shine. Units of housing roll down an assembly line and all or most finish work is completed before the units leave the factory.

The panelized housing system I describe in this book has many of the same advantages as assembly line housing. Once the post-and-beam frame has been erected, the ceilings are finished and the second floor and lofts are complete. Installing the exterior wall panels and the doors and windows finishes off the inside of all exterior walls. Almost 70% of the surfaces that would need a finish material using standard construction procedures have been finished off with the erection of the house shell. On one commercial version of this house, the Sheetrocker charged only $160 for taping the entire house (1200 square feet of floor area).

Since we have made giant strides toward saving money and energy thus far, let's turn our attention to lowering the cost of the remainder of the interior work.

Partitions

The layout of these houses tends to minimize the number of interior partitions. And because they are usually attached to the structural posts at the exterior wall, there is no need to make a finished joint between interior and exterior walls—another small saving. For years, I have used framing lumber as the finish casing for doors, windows, and other openings in the wall. This requires just a bit of extra care in selecting the material that will show and the use of a plastic or metal casing bead to finish the edge of the Sheetrock. The expensive finish casing that is normally used is eliminated, and so is the extra time for hanging the casing and its associated trim. It is possible to buy very cheap "prehung" door units that might be a shade less expensive to install, but unfortunately, the door and its hardware may be so poorly made that they will be no bargain at all in the long run. If you make your own cross-buck doors and hang them with simple surface-type hardware, you will have a lifetime job for much less money.

Doors

Various types of board and batten doors are a cinch for the moderately skilled homeowner. I checked them out with a skilled carpenter and have found that they can be built quickly at the site for about the same cost as commercial doors. I use regular, standard-pattern, beaded pine ceiling boards. The tongue-and-groove joint is important for the strength of your door; don't use a shiplap pattern. A simple ¾-inch pine Z-brace is attached to the back with glue and Sheetrock screws. These screws have a high-quality black finish and can be quickly installed with a screw gun. Since these doors are thinner than the hollow cardboard variety available at lumberyards, they must be hung with surface-type hardware. I think this hardware is more attractive and much quicker to install than the standard types, which are mortised into the door. Finally, the doors are stronger because the structural wooden stiles were not cut away to install the hardware. Some large hardware stores stock surface-mounted locksets and hinges. A variety of nice designs of both latches and surface hinges are available from Renovator's Supply, Millers Falls, MA 01349. For heirloom-quality hardware reproductions at reasonable prices, contact the Baldwin Hardware Manufacturing Corporation, 841 Wyomissing Boulevard, Reading, PA 19063. My favorites are their keyhole and square plate latches that are made in black iron with brass oval knobs and trim. The elegant mechanism in these latches is fully exposed to view. For an excellent

A custom insulated door made by Harry Rustad to a design furnished by my clients.

A 3½-inch-thick insulated door is custom-made to fit an odd-size opening. The core is 1½-inch polystyrene.

article on making such doors, see *Fine Homebuilding* magazine, Issue No. 7, or my earlier books. For those who want to build an exterior door, see Issue No. 10 of *Fine Homebuilding.*

Trim

Interior wooden trim serves two purposes. First, it covers unsightly gaps in the construction process where hasty carpenters didn't take the trouble to fit materials properly because "the trim will cover it." Second, the trim provides relief from an otherwise bland interior. My panelized system eliminates both reasons for trim. Since there are fully exposed wooden posts, beams, and ceilings, there is certainly no need for more wood for decorative reasons. Joints in the panels, decking and other places are all covered by the structural members of the post-and-beam frame. The only possible place for trim is at the base of the wall, and there it is needed to protect the wall from damage.

For baseboards, I recommend a relatively narrow (2½ inch) piece of ¾-inch-thick pine or a pre-molded vinyl baseboard of the same dimension. These narrower than normal baseboards are cheaper because they use less material, and they actually make the room look larger because they cover less of the wall surface. I use what is called resawn pine for baseboards in my houses. It is made by sawing a kiln-dried piece of lumber in two lengthwise. The resulting board has one roughsawn face and one smooth face. It is about half the cost of the usual ugly clamshell moldings and is easy to install. In some cases, I have also used it to trim windows and doors. For all windows, doors, and edges of Sheetrock, I use a slip-on plastic edging as described for the windows in Chapter 20. This edging comes in white or brown and is very difficult to damage. It makes a perfect transition from the natural wood of a window or door frame to the painted Sheetrock surface. I also use the same edging wherever Sheetrock abuts a roughsawn post or beam. The edging is quite inexpensive and eliminates most of the spackling associated with Sheetrock.

One major problem with roughsawn wood frames is that they tend to pick up paint and spackle and are quite difficult to clean. Some of my clients have had to apply an additional coat of stain to cover such splatter. This can be an endless process, since the stain can leach onto the white paint, necessitating paint retouching. Wherever possible, all materials should be prefinished. It takes a few minutes to spray stain on the frame before the floor decking or walls are installed, but the same operation might take days after other

finish materials are installed. One of my clients even painted the Sheetrock on the inside face of the wall panels before installation; this not only waterproofed them, but eliminated any need to trim carefully around the post-and-beam structure.

Cabinetwork and Shelving

The kitchen and bathroom are the two most expensive areas in your house. This is largely due to plumbing costs, but built-in cabinetwork also plays a large part. If you are on a tight budget, the cabinetwork can be your safety valve. If necessary, you can just put in some plywood countertops until such time as you can afford to complete the final cabinetwork. The bank might balk at this tactic, but a bit of money put in an escrow account will usually hold them at bay.

The trick to installing or building your own cabinets is to stay away from Formica. Not that it's particularly undesirable, it just takes practice and special tools to install properly. My clients who have done their own cabinetwork have all used ceramic tile or quarry tile for their countertops. The tile top is edged with a hardwood strip, eliminating difficult fitting along the edge. The same tile can also be used as a backsplash to protect the wall behind the cabinets.

The cabinets themselves can be purchased knocked down or built on the job site. If you have reservations about your carpentry abilities, Sears has a wide variety of price ranges for prefinished and unfinished cabinets that are shipped disassembled. These cabinets just slip together and

These oak cabinets were constructed from closets salvaged from a turn-of-the-century resort that was demolished. Interior doors, plumbing fixtures, and lighting came from the same source. This kitchen is in the Knopf house, found in Chapter 24.

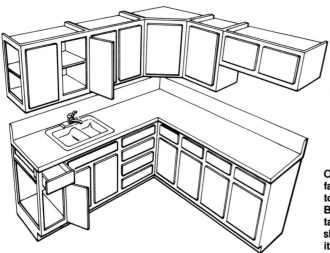

On the left is a section of a kitchen made up of old-fashioned "box" cabinets. No effort has been made to design any of these units for a special purpose. Below is the same section of cabinets specifically tailored for each use. Note the use of shallow open shelving and a recess for sit-down work. Along with its other advantages, the kitchen below is cheaper to build.

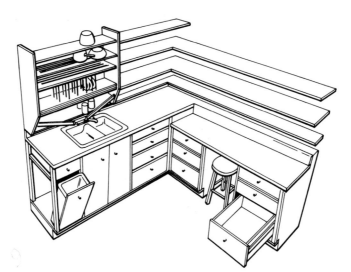

are screwed into place. The only trouble you might have is if something is out of square or level—in an old house, for example. Shimming and leveling a set of cabinets to an out-of-true floor and wall can be a big problem. If this is the case, hire a good carpenter to install the cabinets for you.

Job-built cabinets can save you money, no matter who builds them. You have just bought and paid for solid, well-insulated exterior walls. Now you are going to hire a cabinetmaker to make a set of boxes in his shop that duplicate the work you already have in place. Moreover, since each cabinet usually has an end, you are not only getting two backs, you are getting two sides. In a world short of natural resources, this makes absolutely no sense. The only reason for the duplication is that the easiest way to build a set of

cabinets is in a shop. In earlier days, cabinets were constructed right in place by skilled craftsmen. Over the years, the process has moved to specialty shops where a variety of different size and type units are put together like building blocks to make up a set of cabinets.

You can sidestep this wasteful procedure by either hiring a cabinet shop to make just the fronts, or by building the cabinets right at the job. Again, I took the same skilled carpenter who built the board and batten doors and twisted his arm to build a set of in situ cabinets. Much to his surprise, they were every bit as good as he could have made in his shop, and cheaper, too. They cost just a bit more than the cheapest ready-made cabinets, but quite a lot less than the usual, custom-made box cabinets.

I made several simplifications to reduce the cost without sacrificing quality. Base cabinets are usually constructed with a drawer at the top and a door below, with occasional units that contain all drawers. In order to simplify the process, my cabinets are constructed either with a full door or all drawers. The drawer units are further simplified by using a manufactured drawer unit with a side-mounted slide. The drawer units are one-piece molded plastic in a dark brown color. They are frequently used for hospital construction because they are so easy to clean. The drawer unit with slides, which is designed to be attached to a wooden front, costs less than just the metal hardware for a wooden drawer. These drawers are available from Alma Plastics, 6910 N. Shadeland Avenue, Indianapolis, IN 46220. The catch is that Alma Plastics is primarily a commercial supplier to furniture makers. The drawers are made in about 20 different sizes with 24 packed to a case. The company makes a $15 broken lot charge for each size ordered in less than a case lot, so it will pay to try to standardize your sizes or order a few extra drawers; in the smaller sizes you can buy three extra drawers for the broken lot charge.

The kitchen plans for the Civic house show two full stacks of drawers, all in one size. They also show full construction details for the cabinets described here. The plans show uses for one full case of 24 M-2298-06A drawers, which are 18 inches wide, 20 inches front to back and 4½ inches deep. The drawers are also available in 3½- and 6-inch depths, as well as widths ranging from 11½ inches to 32½ inches. I recommend the side guide kit, M-7212-22. For less than $150 you can have a whole houseful of instant drawers—certainly one of the best bargains I know of in the construction field.

I am constantly besieged with requests for a good reference on cabinetmaking for the beginning builder. Alas, most of the books available are aimed at would-be professionals with a whole shop full of custom tools. For those who want to do it themselves without getting into furniture building, there is finally an excellent text. *The Motion-Minded Kitchen* by Sam Clark (Houghton Mifflin Company, 1983) is the best book available for building simply and economically.

Stairs

Most carpenters are terrified of building stairs, and consequently, stairs are usually ordered from commercial stair shops. The shops usually do good work, but you pay a great deal of money for something that can be easily fabricated right on the job. Open riser stairs are very quick and easy to build from standard framing lumber. A straight run stair, such as the one in the Weiss house, costs less than $100 for labor and materials. Selected 2 × 10s are perfect for both treads and stringers for most sets of stairs. The stringers are temporarily fastened to the treads with finish nails; final assembly is made with 3-inch-long, ¾-inch-diameter dowels. I use two dowels for each end of the tread except for the top and bottom tread where I use one dowel in the center, flanked by countersunk wood screws on each side. The heads of the screws are covered with dowels. These screws are necessary to avoid cumbersome clamps to hold the stringers in

This kitchen, which is the third version of the Civic house in Chapter 24, features easy-access open shelves and butcher block countertops.

alignment while the glue sets. For stairs such as those in the Civic house, where the outside of the stringer is hidden, I use wood screws for the entire assembly. Where open risers are not desired, the backs of the treads are beveled to the angle of the stringer, and the bottom of the stair is covered with plywood or wood paneling. Either version can have the treads covered with carpeting for noise control or aesthetic preference.

Shelving

Shelving is a particularly expensive small item in the modern house. Normally, shelf boards are made from either 1 × 12 pine boards or cut from plywood or chipboard. With the former you have expensive materials; with the latter, you have urea-formaldehyde glue and considerable waste from cutting large sheets down to size. If you use new material, I recommend using 1 × 6 tongue-and-groove sheathing boards. These cost considerably less than the standard shelving boards but require a bit more labor to install. Another option is to use salvaged lumber for such items as shelving. It will be thoroughly dried and much more dimensionally stable than new lumber. In any case, this is an ideal do-it-yourself project. Closets can be made much more useful if you design shelving specifically for the items to be stored.

Rodale's *New Shelter* magazine has detailed plans for a master pantry storage unit that is one of the best uses of space I've seen. This is the type of storage unit that could easily cost $500 or $600 if built by a contractor. The handy homeowner could build it for a fraction of that amount. Detailed plans can be ordered from Rodale Plans, 33 E. Minor Street, Emmaus, PA 18049.

Painting and Natural Finishes

Painting and finishing should always be done by the owner on a low-budget house. In many cases, the homeowner will take his time and do a better job than a professional. A major technique for getting professional results is to finish materials before assembly. This gives crisp demarcation lines that no amount of professional masking can duplicate. Use major brands of paint and varnish, such as Glidden, Benjamin Moore, PPG, McClosky, or Minwax. On my houses, I use Glidden Insulaid as a vaporproof primer, followed by two coats of Benjamin Moore Spanish white semigloss enamel. For floor finishes, I use two coats of Minwax gloss polyurethane, followed by one coat of Minwax satin. McClosky makes a similar high-quality, expensive floor finish. Stay away from cheap, off-brand materials. They do not last and are a waste of material and labor.

Many paints and varnishes are now available using a water-based emulsion so that no volatile fumes or highly flammable vapors are released. *Warning:* Observe all precautions for flammable materials to the letter and then go one better. I just had a client burn down a house with a fresh coat of polyurethane on his floors. Even with all windows open, the house literally exploded into flame. I recommend shutting off the main gas valve and the main electrical breaker so that there is no chance of a spark. All cigarette smokers should be banned from the property until the finish has dried. Similar precautions should be taken when using glues or other coatings with volatile solvents. Better still, use materials without these dangerous chemicals.

Part IV

Detailed Examples of Houses

24 Custom Houses

Each year I design a few custom houses to accommodate clients with special requirements and to test new ideas of my own. Usually, my clients have read all my books and their ideas are compatible with my own principles. Unlike most architects who design exclusive houses for big fees, I keep my fees modest with the understanding that I can share the designs of my custom houses with other clients. Although the designs are rarely reproduced exactly because of the special nature of the houses, I take the successful features and incorporate them into other houses that I feel have broader market appeal. Several of the panelized houses in the next chapter are derivations of my earlier custom designs. I've selected the houses that follow for their wide variation in size and design as well as for their many unusual design features.

KNOPF HOUSE

David and Irma Knopf are college professors. When they first came to me they already had carefully drawn sketches of the house they wanted to build—a contemporary reincarnation of their existing 1920s-style, two-story house near the college campus. It was planned as a retirement house for a several-acre site far out in the countryside. It contains many features usually foreign to my houses; for instance, there is a basement with a two-car garage, and the main living quarters are all located on one floor. This is a rather large house to accommodate the accumulations of a

lifetime of worldwide travel as well as the special features the Knopfs wanted.

The entire south wall of the house at basement level is occupied by a greenhouse and swimming lane. The swimming lane is designed for exercise; it is 50 feet long and 8 feet wide. A solar collector for domestic hot water is integrated into the sloping glass wall on the front of the swimming lane. In order to accommodate the length of the greenhouse and swimming facility, a screened porch and entrance vestibule were integrated with the main living area on either end. The 75-foot expanse of varied glazing makes a striking vista across the farm fields.

The most unique feature of the Knopf house is the heating system. While there is solar heat gain through south-facing windows and a Rumford fireplace, the heart of this system is a wood boiler designed by Professor John Hill of the University of Maine. The boiler burns wood at high temperatures with a forced draft, and the resulting hot water is stored in a large concrete tank located behind the swimming lane. The heat is distributed to the house by means of a radiant concrete floor slab that occupies a 10-foot-wide strip along the south face of the house.

A plastic mat of tubing called Solaroll is embedded into the concrete. Solaroll was designed to solar heat and distribute water, but in the Knopf setup it serves to distribute the water from the

The Knopf house is entered from the west. The garage floor at the left is at original grade. The site has been extensively regraded to provide a 4-foot-high berm except at the garage doors and south facade.

The southeast view shows the greenhouse in foreground. Summer shading is provided by lush morning glory vines. The Exolite roof is coated with a washable white greenhouse paint, as recommended by the manufacturer.

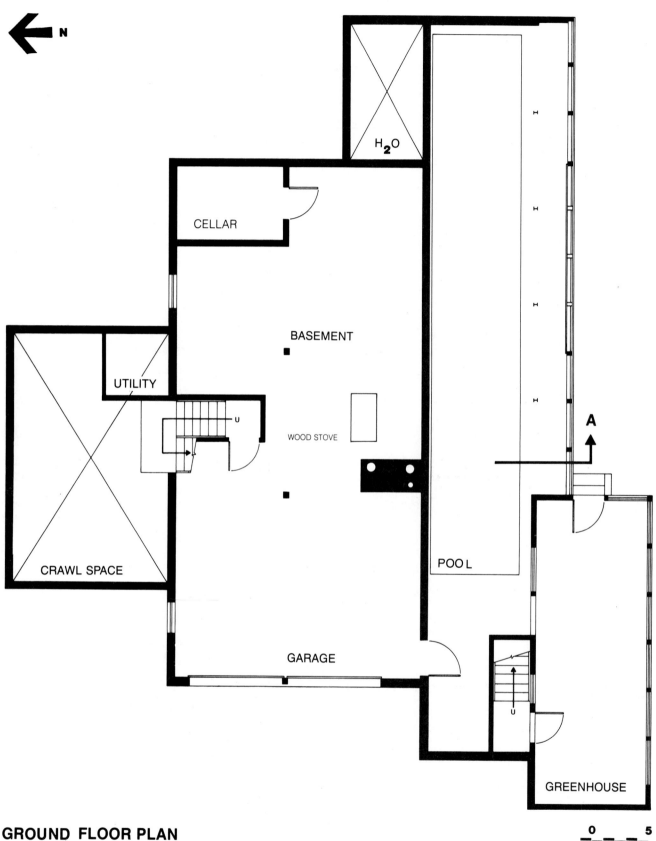

N

H₂O → H_2O

CELLAR

UTILITY

BASEMENT

WOOD STOVE

U

CRAWL SPACE

POOL

A

GARAGE

U

GREENHOUSE

GROUND FLOOR PLAN

0 — — — 5

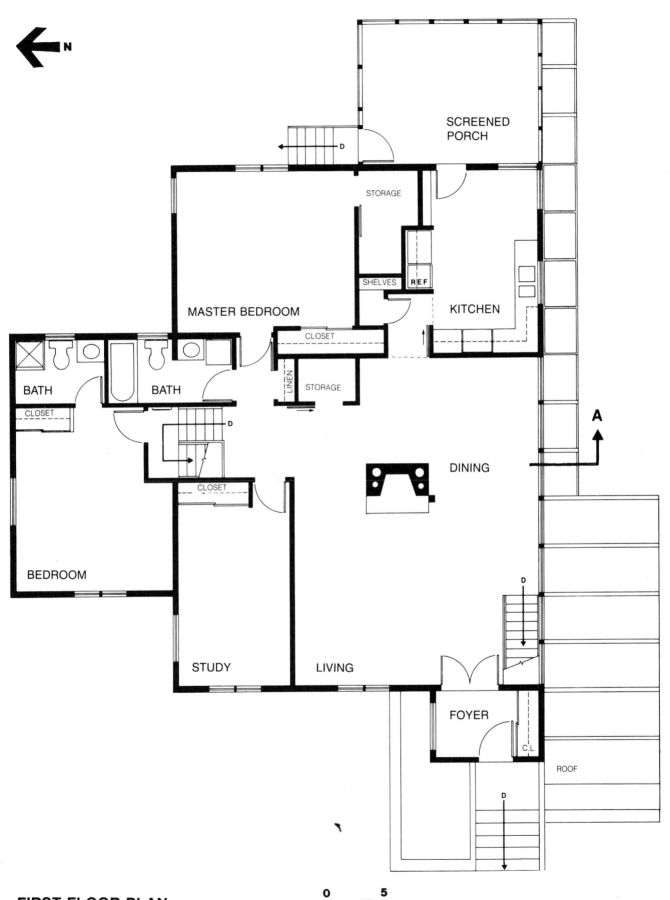

N

SCREENED
PORCH

STORAGE

SHELVES

REF

KITCHEN

MASTER BEDROOM

CLOSET

BATH

CLOSET

BATH

LINEN

STORAGE

A

DINING

CLOSET

BEDROOM

CLOSET

D

D

STUDY

LIVING

FOYER

C.L.

ROOF

D

FIRST FLOOR PLAN

0 — — 5

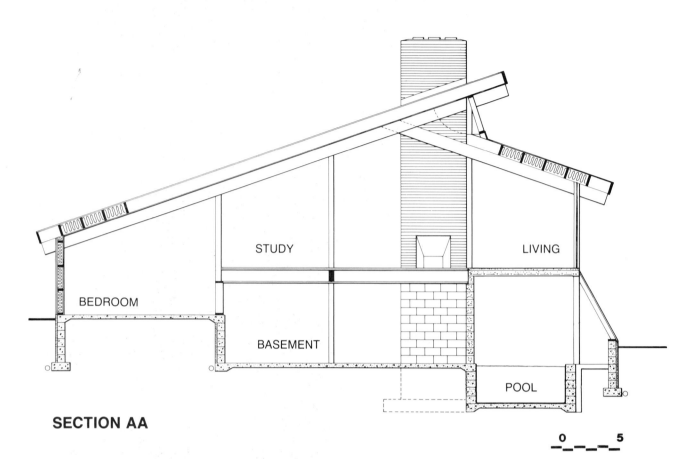

STUDY

LIVING

BEDROOM

BASEMENT

POOL

SECTION AA

0 ____ 5

A Solaroll mat is installed over the structural slab before 1½-inch concrete topping is poured on.

more stable supply situation. In practice, the propane unit has only been tested briefly because David has since retired, and the wood supply and time for cutting and loading it are both ample.

So much heat is stored in the water tank that the boiler only has to be fired for a few hours every other day in severe weather. My original intent was to circulate stratified warm air from the ceiling clerestory area to the back bedrooms, but we found that the radiant floor did not produce the stratification one would expect in such a structure. Instead, a second heating circuit with fan-coil heating units was installed for the master bedroom and study. This is quite an expensive system, but the fuel (wood) is free from the property and other heating systems would have used excessive amounts of fuel. A less expensive, conventional wood-fired boiler was first considered but then rejected because of concerns about creosote buildup and chimney maintenance.

The guest room, which is located at an intermediate level on the north side of the house, is designed for conversion to an apartment if live-in help is ever needed. Special care was given to materials selection to avoid as much upkeep labor as possible. The siding is channel rustic cedar; the roof of lifetime Onduline sheets. Operating sash is aluminum clad on the exterior, a premium unit made by Pella. All exterior trim is also cedar, for durability.

(continued on page 188)

The master bedroom as viewed from the sleeping loft over the closets. The south-facing clerestory provides abundant light as well as natural cross ventilation.

The swimming lane is 48 feet long, just right for swimming laps. Irma does 50 each day. Note the solar collector on the sloping wall at right.

These insulated, custom-made garage doors were designed to blend with the cedar siding. Good American hardware is no longer manufactured for this type of door. They have been something of a disaster because of this. Good hardware can be imported from New Zealand.

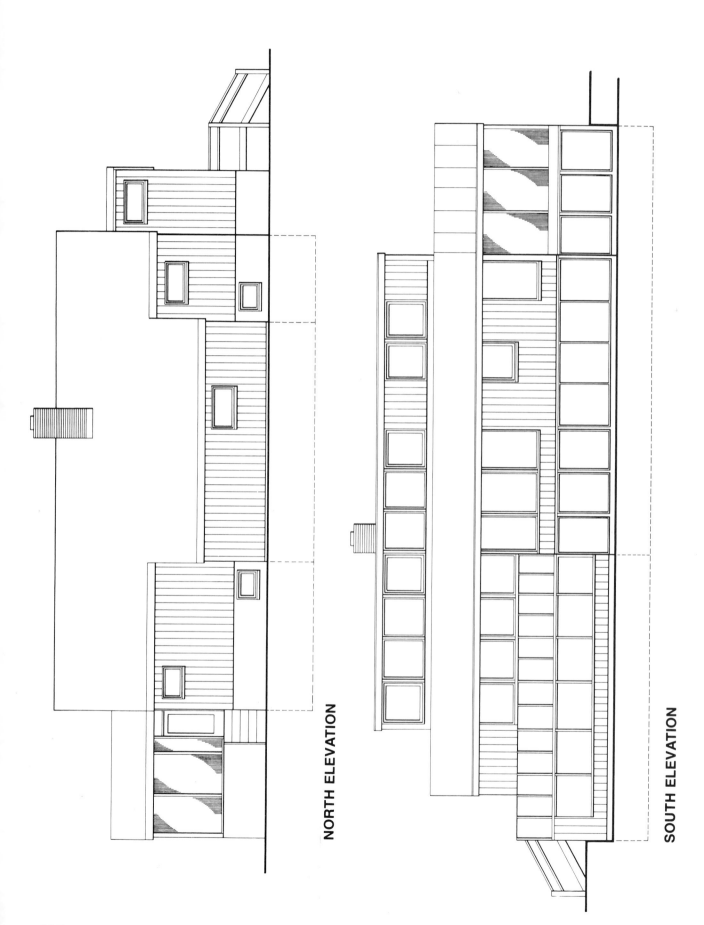

NORTH ELEVATION

SOUTH ELEVATION

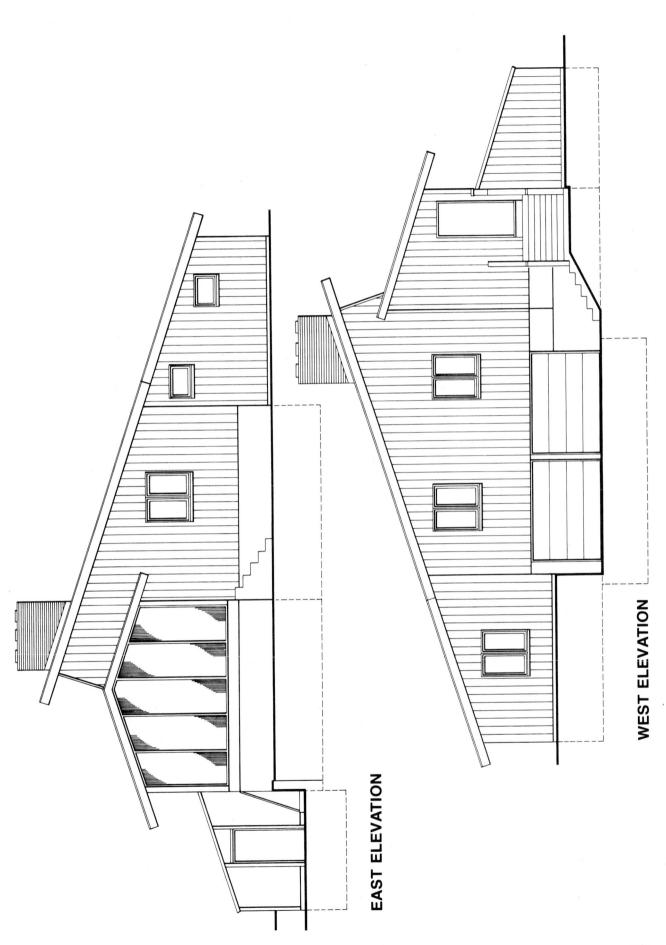

EAST ELEVATION

WEST ELEVATION

The dining room has a spectacular view through the glass wall. The tile floor covers a concrete slab that contains radiant heat system piping.

From the Knopfs' first sketches, careful attention has been given to insulation and siting. The house is bermed to the 4-foot level on the east, west, and north sides, with an opening on the west for a garage entrance. The exterior of the basement walls is insulated with a heavy layer of extruded polystyrene covered with a cement stucco called Plekko. All exterior walls and roofs are heavily insulated with fiberglass and 1 inch of Thermax insulation board. The house was sited so that a grove of trees shelters it from the winter winds and a man-made pond on the south moderates both summer and winter temperatures.

Although I made a few minor changes in the original plan, and the exterior elevations are entirely my doing, the floor plan conforms almost exactly to the Knopfs' original drawings. The only major change was in the design of the front entrance. Irma had originally wanted to enter through the greenhouse at an intermediate level, but one now enters the vestibule. Plans for a three-quarter-scale version of this house with Irma's original entrance are available from Smallplan. See Appendix C. This smaller version resulted from a miscommunication between David and me over the scale of his original graph paper drawing. Since I usually design smaller houses, I immediately assumed that the smaller scale was correct. Although the Knopfs went with their original size house, the smaller plan would be considerably less expensive to build and would work very well with the panelized building system featured in this book.

In order to keep the house within their budget, the Knopfs did all their own subcontracting and much of the finish work. For many of the finishing stages, they hired laborers by the hour and worked with them as helpers. Irma did all the tilework, painting, and finishing herself. David did shelving, thermal shutters, and the like. Both of them worked very hard to perform miracles in transforming a barren corner of a field into a lush garden spot.

Although the house was expensive, the actual cost per square foot was less than $40; considerably less than any contractor would charge to build a similar house.

Performance of the house has generally been good. Strangely, all the unusual systems worked very well; such problems as there were were confined to standard construction items. The plumbing system didn't work properly due to faulty installation of a vent line. The roof leaked because a careless laborer installed the roofing sheets incorrectly without enough overlap; the heavy winter snows melted and backed up between them. The contractor who built the shell of the house provided a new roofing job on the north side where the difficulties occurred, and the roof has been fine since.

Due to the heavy insulation, the Rumford fireplace in the living room provides plenty of heat for mild fall and spring weather. The heavy insulation and extensive mass, coupled with the extensive south glazing, provide ample solar heating in sunny winter weather without any overheating. The clerestories and transoms are arranged in such a fashion that every room in the house (even the north bedroom) receives sunlight in the middle of winter. The radiant floor takes several hours to heat up so the thermostat must be turned up long before sunset to bring up the temperature of the floor in anticipation of cold nighttime temperatures. The mass of warm water in the pool and the concrete structure surrounding it store heat well, creating a flywheel effect so that the house cools slowly.

Domestic hot water is heated by the sun, with an electric hot water heater as a booster. Because the solar collectors are within the pool enclosure and are equipped with vents from the pool to prevent freezing, the domestic solar water system can be operated directly on water pressure without the usual antifreeze and inefficient and expensive heat exchangers that provide freeze protection for a system exposed to the outdoors.

It is an ironic design for a collaboration between clients and an architect who all love traditional architecture. It is one of the most strikingly contemporary designs in this book. It is the result of very extensive planning and discussions in which solar performance and durability were the foremost objectives of everyone involved.

GRANT HOUSE

Robin and Jerry Grant's house site was blasted out of a rock cliff near the top of a mountain. It is an incredibly beautiful, but very difficult building site. Despite this problem, I think this is the most successful house design I have ever executed. In strict contrast to the preceding house, whose design was dictated by the owners' own floor plans, this design is much more my design, my interpretation of the Grants' verbal description of their needs for a house.

Due to initial budget limitations, the house was designed to be constructed in stages—the main house first, with the master bedroom wing, greenhouse, and entry to be added as funds allowed. But it turned out that the Grants were so enthralled with the house that they went ahead and completed the entire structure at one time.

The site for the Grant house was blasted out of solid rock near the top of a mountain. You catch a brief glimpse of the southwest corner as you wind up the steep mountain road to the house.

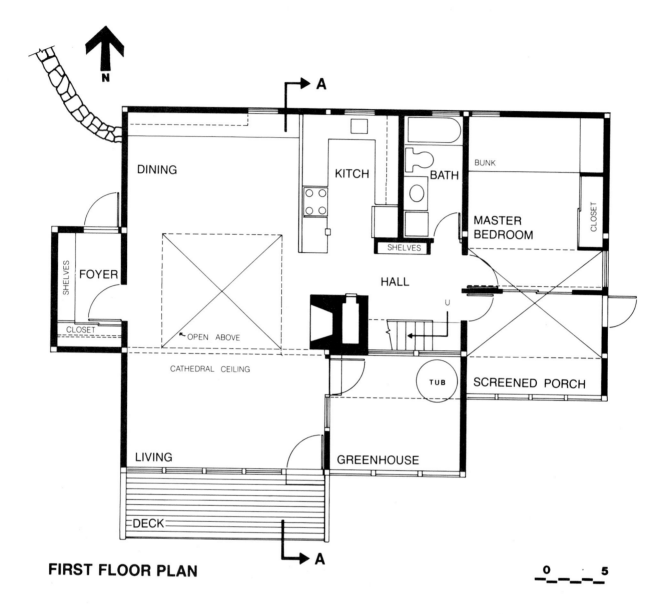

FIRST FLOOR PLAN

0 ___ 5

The Grant house is basically one very large, tall space surrounded by smaller spaces on each of three levels. The scale of the spaces is very unusual for a house. The central living area stretches out in all directions and borrows space from the smaller rooms that surround it. If we include the outside deck, there are a total of 12 different spaces in the house, yet the overall square footage is quite modest. The house has instant appeal for artists, loft dwellers, and others who are used to living in large open spaces. Even though the central space is quite large, it is broken by balconies, the greenhouse, and the freestanding fireplace, so that the space is intimate, not overwhelming.

The massive, Finnish contraflow wood fireplace-heater is the focal point for the living room, and the focal point of a very unusual heating system.

Like Professor Hill's commercial boiler used in the Knopf house, this heater is designed to burn wood rapidly at extremely high temperatures, thereby burning the wood completely and efficiently with little creosote and smoke. Unlike the Hill unit, the Finnish heater has convoluted passages in the masonry to store the heat for hours or even days after the fire has burned out. The heater is somewhat similar to a Russian fireplace except that it has fireplace doors and dampers so that it can be used as a conventional, albeit very efficient, fireplace. (See Chapter 17 for more on these heaters.)

As effective as this heater is, Jerry was not content just to have it responsible for all the heat distribution; he commissioned solar contractor Robert Starr to design a radiant floor system to

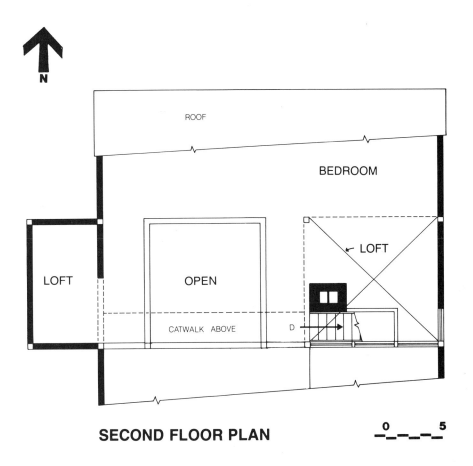

N

SECOND FLOOR PLAN

ROOF

BEDROOM

LOFT

LOFT

OPEN

CATWALK ABOVE

D

0 _ _ _ _ 5

be attached to a heat exchanger within the fire-box. The floor system consists of about 1600 feet of high-molecular-weight polyethylene piping, which is distributed beneath the living room floor. The piping is arranged in four different circuits; a perimeter loop and a central loop on each of two levels. The piping is embedded in 12 inches of sand, with two circuits near the bottom and two near the top. For long-term heating, the bottom circuits are used; for mild weather and quick heat transfer, the top coils are activated. For severe weather, all circuits are used. The sand bed is heavily insulated on the sides and bottom so that little stored heat is lost to the ground. Except for the hard, time-consuming labor of installing the sand bed, the radiant floor was easy and eco-nomical to install. The system can even be used with solar collectors at a future date (as Robert Starr has done in his own house) if the Grants find they need extra heat input or wish to have a completely automatic system that doesn't require stoking with wood.

Jerry went to extraordinary lengths to insulate and weatherseal their house. Walls are a sand-wich, with 1 inch of Thermax on the outside, 6 inches of fiberglass in the core, and another 2 inches of Thermax on the inside, for a total R value of 42. Similarly, the roof has 12 inches of fiberglass with 2 inches of Thermax, for a total R value of 56. Recent studies have shown that the traditional engineering methods of calculating insulating values tend to underestimate the ther-mal effect of unusually thick layers of insulation such as this, but we have proof that it works very well indeed.

The building code in the area where the house is located requires an automatic backup heating system—no exceptions. The Grants' backup unit is a Kero-Sun Monitor 30 wall-mounted minifur-nace. The open nature of the plan and the minimal heating requirements made this unit an obvious choice. The heating calculations, which are also required by code, showed that the 30,000-Btu output of the heater was just right for this struc-ture. During construction, I spent a night in the house when the outside temperature dipped to 14° below zero, accompanied by howling winds.

(continued on page 196)

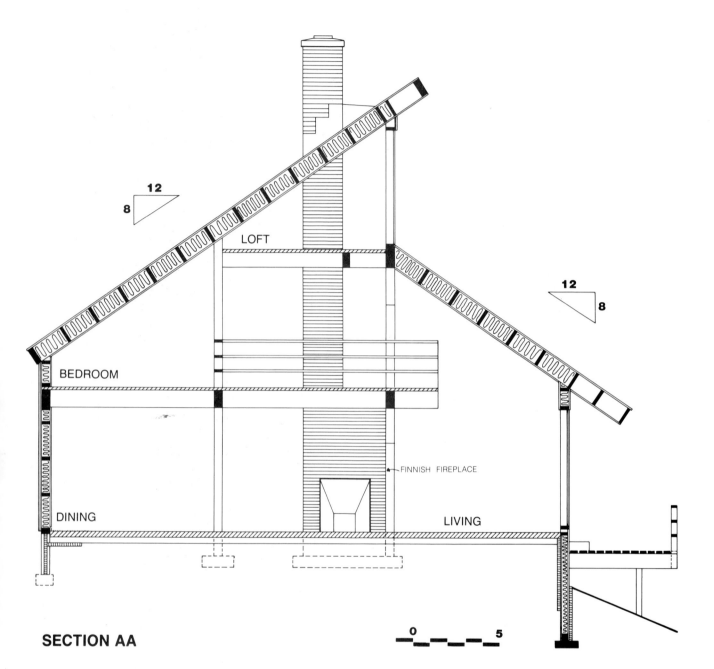

12
8

12
8

LOFT

BEDROOM

FINNISH FIREPLACE

DINING

LIVING

0   5

SECTION AA

The finished contraflow chimney provides the focal point for the living room. The sunspace is behind the chimney.

The south elevation wraps around a dramatic sloped solar greenhouse. Vents at the top of the greenhouse provide excellent summer ventilation. A generous deck at the left extends the living room outdoors. The master bedroom wing is at the right.

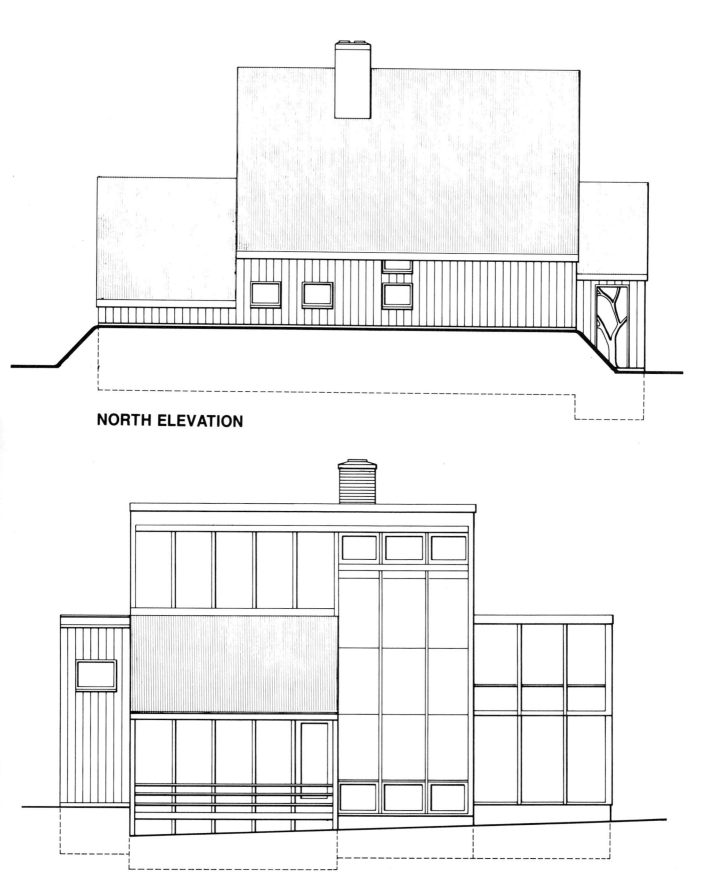

NORTH ELEVATION

SOUTH ELEVATION

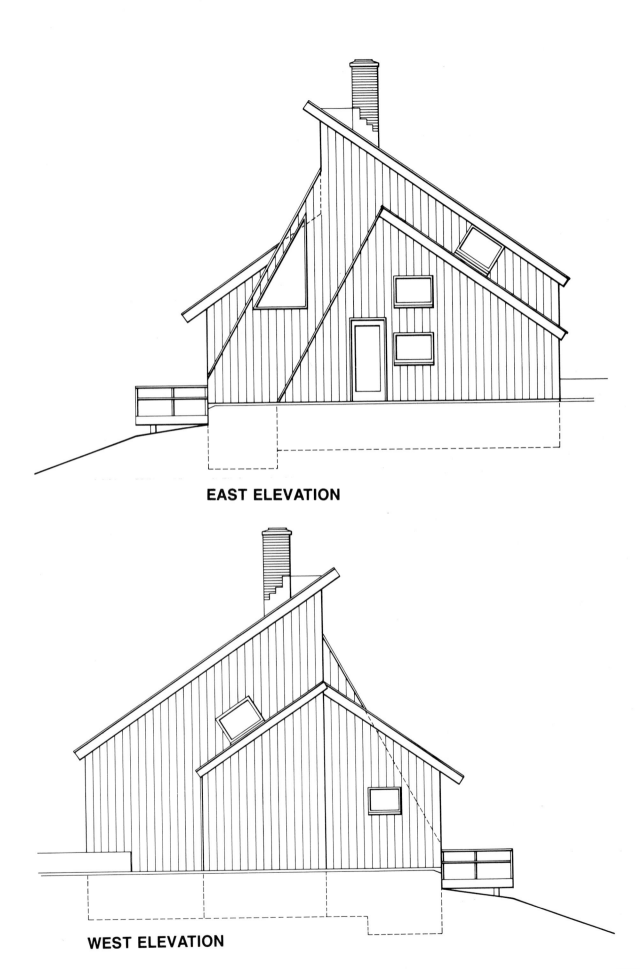

EAST ELEVATION

WEST ELEVATION

The simple post-and-beam frame is embedded directly into the hillside. A workman holding a sheet of roofing stands on the loft floor above the greenhouse. Corrugated Onduline roofing is applied directly over lateral roof rafters. The corrugations provide natural ventilation of the roof cavity.

A view of the completed house from the same angle as the framing shot. The greenhouse and master bedroom wing have been added. The ground level of the master bedroom wing has a double-duty room at the front. Sliding glass panels conceal a screened porch. In the winter, the room serves as a wood storage area; in the summer, the glass is raised and it becomes a screened porch.

Even though the house was not quite completely weather-stripped, the Monitor was able to keep the house very comfortable, in fact, it was too warm for me in my sleeping bag.

In order to deal with the difficult rocky site, pressure-treated poles were set directly on the bedrock. A small amount of hand-mixed concrete was used to level under the posts where necessary. The post-and-beam frame with its point loading allowed us to use this money-saving foundation. Pouring a traditional concrete foundation over the rugged, uneven rock base would have been prohibitively expensive. But by using post-and-beam framing techniques, the frame, including floors, decks, and roof for the initial stage, was erected in a week for less than $10,000.

Robin and Jerry were ecstatic; the building inspector was not. Even though he had reluctantly approved the building system, he had not been called in to inspect the post bearings before the frame was erected. Furthermore, the rock on the north face of the house was but a few inches below grade. He was seriously concerned about the possibility of frost heaving on the north wall; a secondary concern involved drainage from the hillside above the house. We reached a compromise and waterproofed the north wall 4 feet above grade and built an earthen berm that sloped away from the house.

Shortly after completing the shell for the initial stage, the Grants built the additions that they had originally planned to build on later: the green-

The north wall is sheltered by a 4-foot berm. Site-built cedar gutters divert the roof runoff.

house, master bedroom wing, and entrance vestibule. In order to reduce costs, Robin and Jerry and many friends, including their architect, have done much of the finish work on the house. Work has proceeded slowly as funds have permitted.

The central living space is extraordinary. The 6-foot-tall clerestory at the top allows daylight to stream into every corner of the house; the large opening in the second-floor deck permits the light to get to the north wall everywhere in the house. Vent windows in the third-floor loft, as well as in the greenhouse, provide for rapid exhaustion of hot air with no need for fans. A small heat-recovery system captures hot air from the peak in winter and transfers it to the master bedroom and bath. When standing or sitting in the center of the living room, both lighting and acoustics are spell-binding. Due to the reflective roof shapes, light and sound seem to surround you without any discernible source. Even a small portable radio on the balcony produces concert hall sound. Small sleeping lofts above the master bedroom and vestibule open onto the wide-open second-floor balcony; the third-floor loft has a bird's-eye view of the entire house. A catwalk is planned for the near future to permit access to the clerestory for cleaning and for opening and closing the nighttime insulation.

Even though the Grants didn't follow the original idea of building their house in stages to save money, their house still cost less than the average tract house for sale in the United States. And it's a lot more house.

The front door has a hand-carved, tulipwood-tree applique by Harry Rustad, who stands next to his creation.

(continued on page 200)

The open well in the
living room sweeps
up three stories to a
sleeping loft.

The almost windowless north wall is brightly lit by high clerestory windows on the south.

Unique offset treads provide the comfort of a stair in the space normally taken by a ladder.

GUMMERE HOUSE

This house, as my regular readers will know, was first shown in my book, *30 Energy-Efficient Houses . . . You Can Build* (Rodale Press, 1977). It was also published in another book on energy-saving houses, as well as in several magazines. Unfortunately, in each case the presentation was flawed. Either poor photographs, badly drawn plans, or both were used. Due to the extremely narrow site, the original house was a bit small and cramped, except for the living room, which shares some of the excitement of the Grant house. Because of all the publicity, I was besieged with requests for plans for this house. No meaningful plans existed, however; the house had been changed so many times during construction that the skimpy original drawings bore little resemblance to the final product. So, I sat down and redrew the plans, making some minor improvements but still sticking to the original size and layout. Several versions of the house have since been constructed; many of the builders made their own improvements. Most of the houses have

been constructed in the Pacific Northwest where this design is a big hit.

Since there has been so much interest in this house, I show here a version that was built in Washington State by Dick Kellum. By making the house a bit wider and making small internal changes, Dick corrected most of the shortcomings of the original house. The bath is now compartmentalized for more efficient use; the kitchen layout is improved, the awkward partition between the kitchen and study was eliminated, and the study was transformed into a sunspace-dining room. I heartily endorse all the changes. For severe climates, I would go one step further and add a vestibule to shut out the north winds.

The Gummere house shares much of its design philosophy with the Grant house, but it is much smaller and simpler and therefore much more affordable for the average family. Its simple, steep-pitched saltbox roof shape and traditional lines appeal to many people who would not like more

(continued on page 204)

Nestled into the forest, the Gummere house has a cutout on the south corner to provide a sheltered deck on each level.

The dining room has a dramatic glass roof that is sheltered by a leafy canopy.

A close-up shot of the glass roof shows sleek glass-to-glass detailing. The east gable contained a bow window on the original Gummere version, which would be a nice addition.

The north facade presents one tiny window to the elements. A wood storage area flanks the covered front door.

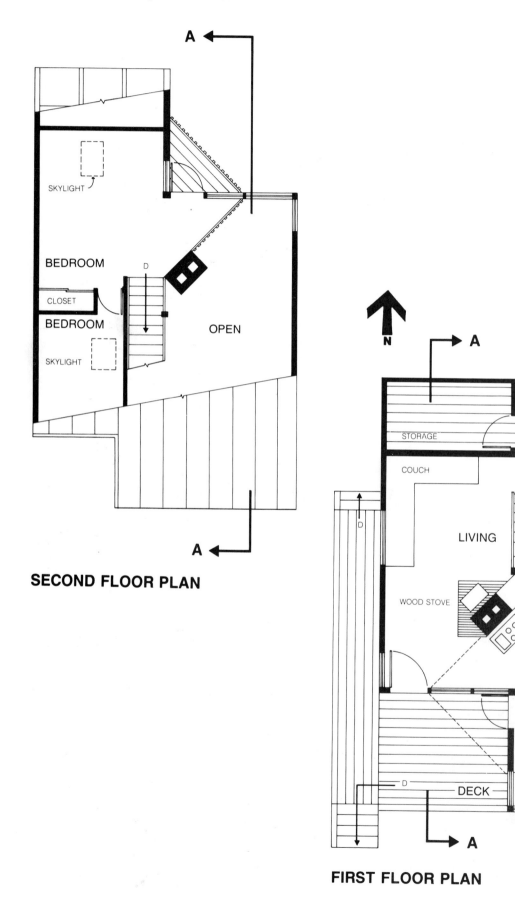

SECOND FLOOR PLAN

FIRST FLOOR PLAN

A close-up of the deck shows an elegant railing design by Dick Kellum that would be nice on any house.

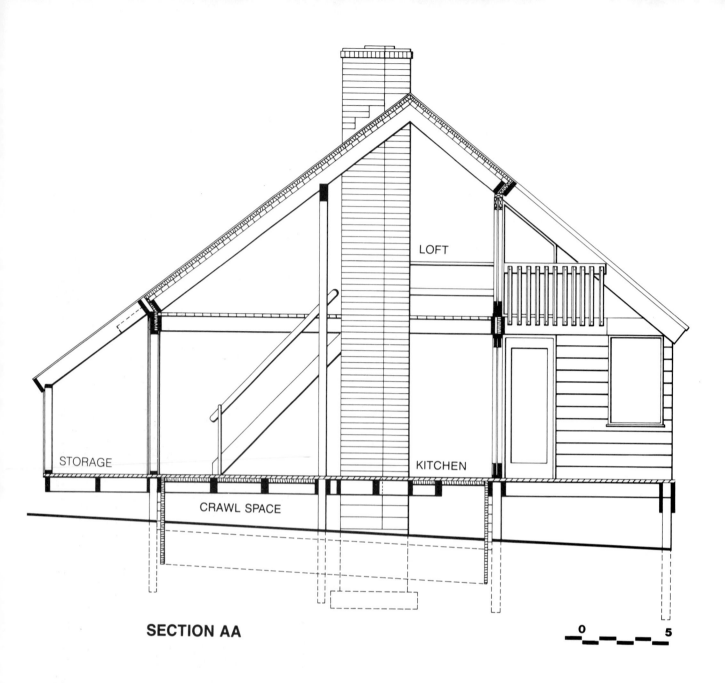

SECTION AA

0 ____ ____ 5

exotic shapes such as the Grant house employs. The design concept is simplicity itself; it is a square, gable-roofed, 1½-story house with ¼ of the house removed on the south face. A sundeck fills in the missing portion of the house, and a 2-story glass wall overlooks the deck and admits sunlight to all parts of the interior. Due to the small size of the house, the interior can be readily illuminated by this one wall. The original house had about 700 square feet; Dick's larger version is up to about 900 square feet. Since many building codes have an 850-square-foot minimum, the larger size means that the house can be built in many more locations.

Construction details were also upgraded by Kellum to make the house more efficient. Weathersealing and insulation were problems in the original house that have been overcome in the improved version. Frame walls 6 inches thick have replaced the elegant diagonal decking that formed the walls of the original house.

One change Dick regrets is the elimination of the masonry chimney. He felt that it would take up too much space and cut up the interior. Now that he is finished, he wishes that he had built the chimney. (I show a chimney on the revised plans because I agree.) The original house cost $18,000 using many recycled materials and minimal insulation and weathersealing. Even after 10 years of raging inflation, Dick was able to build a larger, much superior version for less than $30,000.

Dick's house shows the benefits of sharing a house design with many clients. Each successive builder draws upon the original plans and makes

(continued on page 208)

A wood stove provides the main heat source with electric baseboard backup. I emphatically do not recommend either the baseboard electric heat or the stovepipe installation shown here. The original version had a masonry chimney, which I strongly recommend.

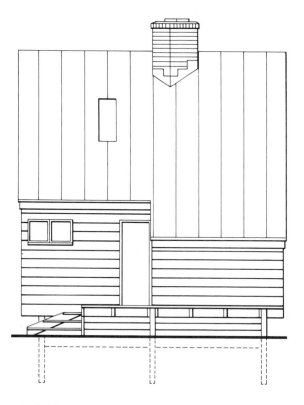

NORTH ELEVATION

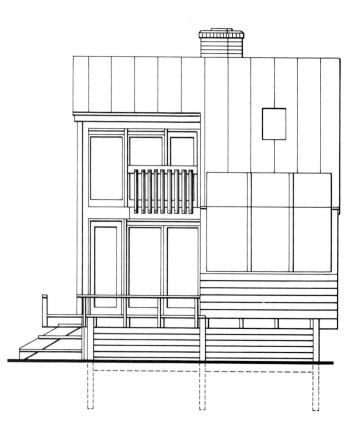

SOUTH ELEVATION

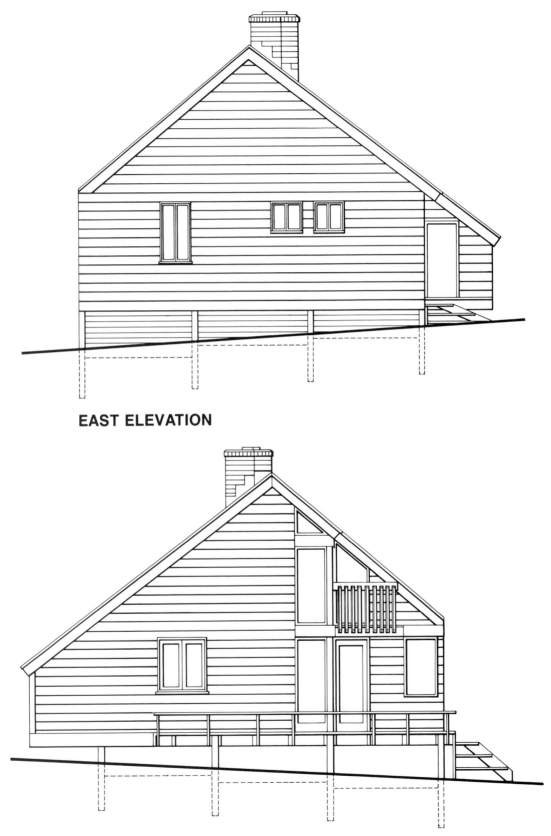

EAST ELEVATION

WEST ELEVATION

changes and improvements to the original. Of course, this is assuming that each builder is intelligent and discriminating. Obviously, disasters can occur by tinkering with an original design. Usually people building one of my house plans consult with me before making changes, and I guide them in their decisions. In Dick's case, he made all the changes and then invited me to the housewarming party when all was complete.

The Gummere house is particularly suited to remote and sloping sites because of its small size and pole construction. (The advantages of pole construction are fully described in Chapter 6.) There are very few good designs for small pole houses, but with Dick Kellum's modifications, I think this one is a winner.

The aforementioned dangerous stovepipe travels upward past an elegant second-floor loft.

This simple kitchen has open shelving and homemade cabinets.

LOWE HOUSE

Michael and Mona Lowe both work for a large research organization and live near an area of showy resort houses designed by trendy architects in the Gwathney/Seigal/Mayer vein. Michael arrived for our first meeting with a pile of cardboard models that looked as though they had come straight from the Sunday *New York Times Magazine.* Then Michael announced that he had come to me because I had a reputation for designing economical houses and he had a budget of only $50,000. I explained that he would have to add at least one more zero to his budget figure to build one of the fancy sculptural houses with curved balconies and stairwells for which he had constructed models. After kindling my wood stove with the cardboard models, we sat down to do some hard work and see what, if anything, was possible within his meager budget.

Aside from the budget, the site posed severe constraints upon the design. The Lowes had picked up the property for very little money because it was considered an unbuildable waterfront site suitable only for recreational use. Several years of hard work and many variances later, the site was approved for construction. Even though Michael had enlarged the site by adding a breakwater, the actual building area, after deducting the required setbacks, was minuscule. The solution was to design a multilevel house with extensive cantilevers to take advantage of the setback areas. One final design problem I had to solve was to create a house that absorbed heat on the south face while still maintaining enough glazing to enjoy the stunning north view.

The Lowes presented me with probably the most difficult design challenge I have ever been given. Fortunately, Michael has considerable design talents of his own, and our ideas meshed together nicely, at least for the floor plans. The original designs called for a rather Spartan affair with a flat rooftop observation deck—very functional, but not very inspiring. I had worked out an efficient

The south face of the oceanfront Lowe house faces the road. The carport is in front of the motorcycle at right.

The solar greenhouse contains stairs and provides excellent summer ventilation for the whole house due to the "chimney effect."

This view from the southeast shows a nice pattern of small and large windows and cutouts for decks.

scheme for setting the house on nine poles; the basic plan worked fine, but had none of the design character Michael wanted. Then Michael had an inspiration: Why not add a south-facing sunspace which also provided the circulation space for the house? Such double use of the space would make the sunspace more economical. This change would certainly give the design the lift it needed, but the economies gained by making one space do double-duty weren't great enough to keep us to our budget. We compromised by shrinking the size of the original plan to make up for the additional sunspace, and we increased the budget by $5000.

At this point, the design process was complicated by my sudden hospitalization for a simple, but elusive ailment. I hired a young architect to work with Michael to finish off the elevations and to do the working drawings. After a couple of weeks, this architect appeared with plans for a huge house bearing no resemblance whatsoever to the original design. Moreover, his design wouldn't possibly fit on the site. Michael and I went back to trading sketches. More changes were made to the plan that, in turn, enabled the elevations to be more in keeping with Michael's aesthetic preferences. Even though the waters got muddied by the intrusion of another architect, this design is an excellent example of what can happen when a client and architect really listen to each other. Although the house is overly complicated for my tastes, I do feel that it is a very successful response to some tricky site and design requirements. The clients were also pleased with the design.

Unfortunately, construction of the house was anything but successful. The Lowes were a couple of hundred miles away and I had not included supervision of the construction in our agreement. Michael is a skilled boat builder with many skilled craftsmen as friends and work associates. Our idea was to have an experienced post-and-beam contractor put up the shell of the house, and then Michael and Mona would do the finish work. We got off to a disastrous start when the building inspector refused to even consider the plans. They didn't look like a ranch house, so they obviously weren't plans for a house. The inspector proposed sending them off to a state review board, which would have delayed approval by six months to a year. He was hostile to the entire design on which we had labored so long and hard. The stairway in the sunspace was dangerous because someone might fall and roast to death. The outswinging front door was equally unacceptable because someone might park a car next to it so that it couldn't be opened. Michael lost his

The west view shows a profile of the solar stair/greenhouse. The large windows at left enjoy the ocean view and are shielded by large vertical and horizontal overhangs.

temper over these unreasonable responses by the inspector, and that didn't further the approval process. I called in an architect who had had experience in these matters, and he got an informal ruling from the state that our plans were OK.

Due to the excessive construction costs in the area, we decided to import both the contractor and the building materials for the house. Unfortunately, the extensive delays by the building inspector caused the start of construction to conflict with my trip to Japan and China. Job relations got off to a very poor start when the next-door neighbor showed up with a shotgun. It seems that his lawyer had assured him that the lot next door was not a legal building lot and he would never have to worry about anyone building there. Problems continued aplenty.

(continued on page 214)

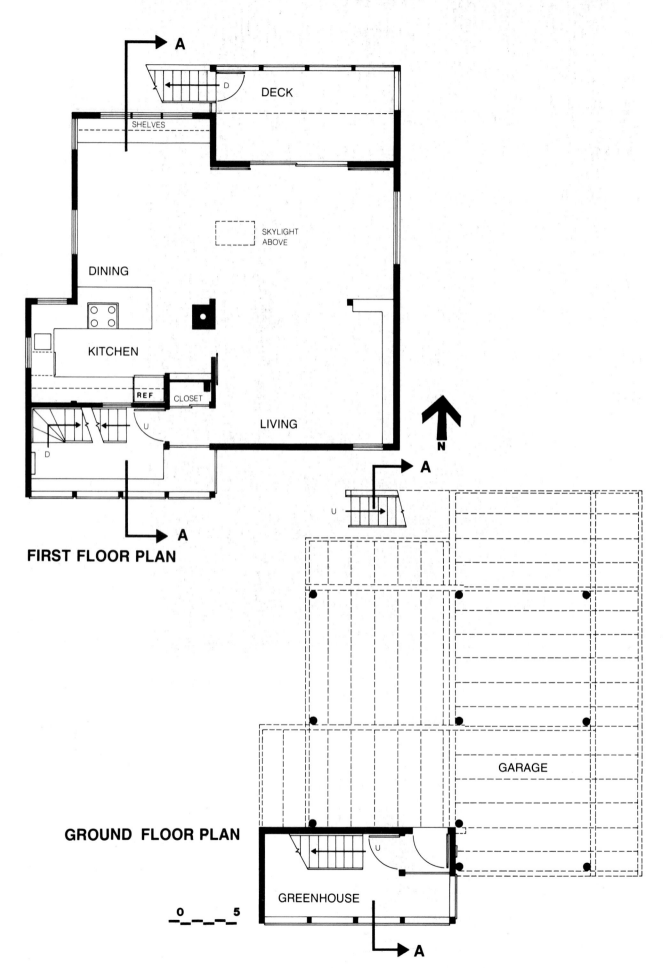

A

DECK

SHELVES

SKYLIGHT
ABOVE

DINING

KITCHEN

REF CLOSET

U

D

LIVING

N

A

FIRST FLOOR PLAN

A

U

GARAGE

GROUND FLOOR PLAN

GREENHOUSE

0   5

U

A

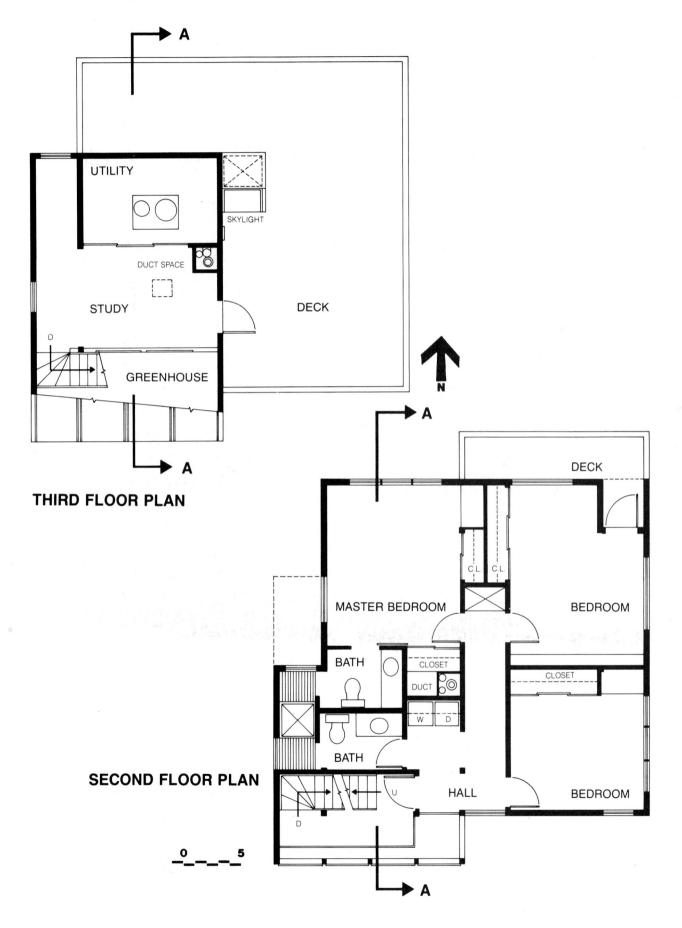

A

UTILITY

SKYLIGHT

DUCT SPACE

STUDY

DECK

N

D

GREENHOUSE

A

THIRD FLOOR PLAN

A

DECK

C.L. C.L.

MASTER BEDROOM

BEDROOM

BATH

CLOSET

CLOSET

DUCT

W   D

BATH

SECOND FLOOR PLAN

HALL

BEDROOM

D

U

0   5

A

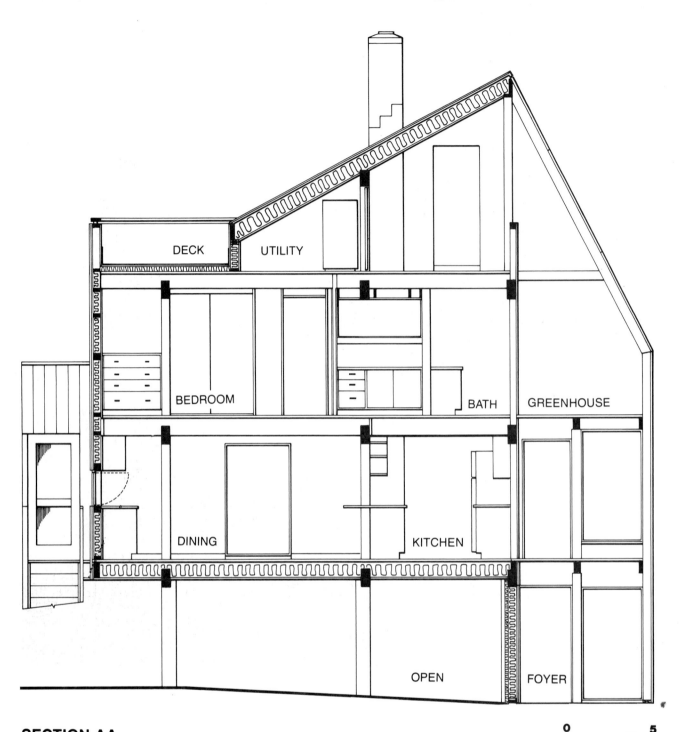

SECTION AA

0 _ _ _ _ 5

Michael had done a superb job of getting the site ready for construction. Water, septic system, electricity, and the piles to support the house were all in place. The timber pilings that support the house are a good economical choice for such a structure. They are cheap, permanent, and quick to install. The only drawback is that in driving them into the ground they don't always drive perfectly plumb. We only had one pole which was noticeably off, but of course it's the one that shows the most. It has since been boxed out with finish wood to give the illusion of straightness. The house is anchored to the pile foundation by

means of Teco split-ring connectors. These are steel connectors that look like short sections of 4-inch-diameter pipe. They are installed in a groove cut in two members to be joined and then bolted into place. The resulting joint is extremely strong, and the fastener is completely protected from the elements (an important factor in ocean-front construction).

To create all the interesting setbacks in the elevations, Michael and I devised a double-cantilevered structural system with the structure cantilevering from the posts in both directions—very dramatic,

The oceanfront view has a covered deck off the living room and open deck from the bedroom. The large rooftop deck is reached from the stair hall.

This framing shot from the ocean shows unique pinwheel post-and-beam framing and double cantilevers.

but difficult to execute for the first time. Between the crooked poles and the tricky framing system, the carpenters were only half finished with the frame when I returned from my trip. Both weather and tempers had turned ugly. We were experiencing very cold weather early in the fall, and the house site had sub-gale-force winds. To say that the client and the carpenters didn't get along is an understatement. The job limped along until Thanksgiving, when the crew went home, never to return. The contractor was nearly killed in a holiday automobile accident and was hospitalized for several months. In the meantime, the house was open to the weather. I did persuade some of

the workmen to return for a couple of weeks to enclose the shell. Although the contract was basically fulfilled, the house was still vulnerable to the very bad weather. Michael and Mona worked very hard and installed the Carlisle Rubber roofing themselves. We had left the roof out of the shell contract because we were having difficulties in locating enough material to complete it. The other major (and very critical) task that remained undone was the glazing of the 32-foot-high expanse of glass on the south wall. Michael tackled this job on his own. Glazing of this sort requires special techniques, materials, and skills. Michael

(continued on page 218)

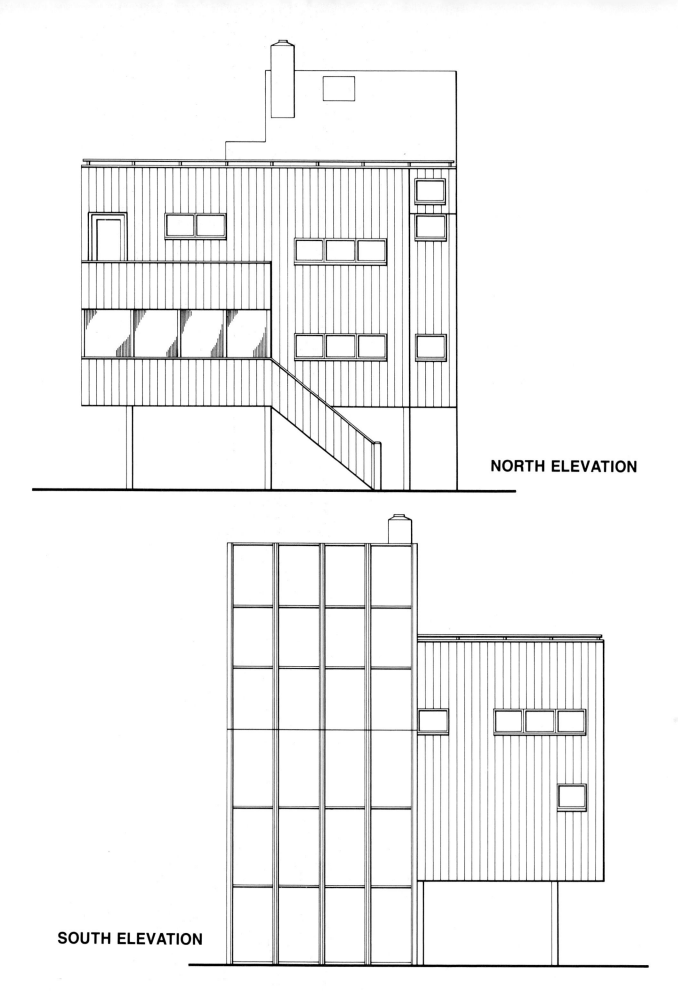

NORTH ELEVATION

SOUTH ELEVATION

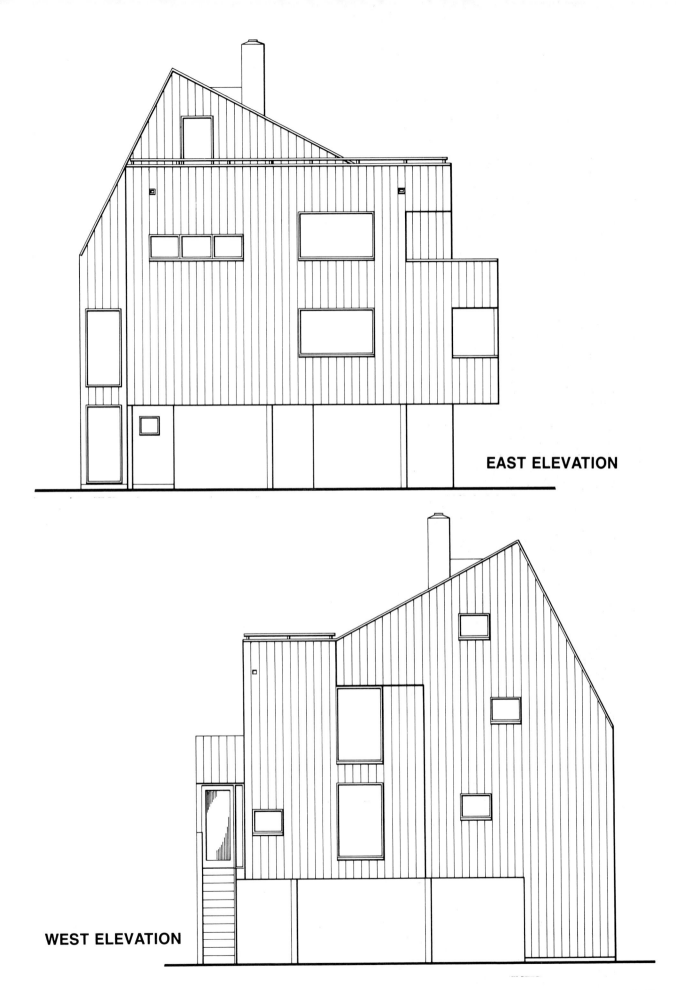

EAST ELEVATION

WEST ELEVATION

A homemade door leads to the open riser staircase in the greenhouse. Note the sloping wall at right.

did a splendid-looking job, but the glazing leaked. In fact, almost everything seemed to leak. When the wind blew from the right direction, commercial windows and doors leaked water very badly. After consulting the manufacturers, we discovered "they aren't designed for heavy winds like that." About the only place that didn't leak was that dandy rubber roof Michael and Mona had done themselves. In addition to the windows, doors, and south glazing, water leaked in through the joints in the shiplap siding at the parapet. The winds were so strong at the top of the house that water was actually driven through the joints and into the wall itself. Michael built a metal cap flashing for the parapet, but the winds peeled the flashing right off.

In analyzing the failures, one big mistake was the extensive use of silicone caulking. I always specify Tremco Mono acrylic caulking because it sticks well to roughsawn and damp wood. Silicone is extremely durable and very elastic, but it does not bond unless every surface is perfectly clean and dry. It is ideal for a glass-to-glass or glass-to-metal seal, but not for the wood-to-glass details on this house. Michael found that the carpenters had relied on silicone rather than proper flashings and that it was all peeling away from the rough-sawn wood. Another major disadvantage to silicone is that it is frequently diluted with oil-based compounds that can destroy the edge sealant in insulating glass. The Lowes found that the silicone was indeed creating edge sealant problems on their glass. Extra flashings have been installed on the windows and doors and the silicone has been laboriously removed and replaced with Mono. The wooden glazing system on the south wall will eventually be replaced with an all-metal system; it will be much more expensive, but it is guaranteed not to leak. We'll see, but I'll bet in high winds there'll be some leakage with that system, too. If the original system had had a metal flashing over the wood structural members, Tremco caulking, and clear cedar battens, I am sure that the leaks would have been minimal.

The heating and cooling systems for this house are also unique. The mechanical room is located at the top of the house just behind the sunspace. A small forced-air furnace provides backup heating as needed. A fan and duct system distribute the warm air from either the collector space or the furnace to the lower levels of the house through a small central light shaft that does double-duty as air return for the heating system. An exhaust fan is also located in the light shaft for summer ventilation. A battery of phase-change salts, designed by Michael, that store a great amount of heat in a relatively small mass helps smooth out the heat flow from the solar space.

I have gone into some detail on the difficulties encountered with this house in hopes that others can avoid some of the pitfalls. First, if you have a very limited budget, keep your design—and your site—simple. Although it eventually got built, the complexities of the house were a bit beyond both the professional contractors and the Lowes. Correcting the mistakes was expensive; it would have been much cheaper to do it right the first time. Second, if you are in a waterfront area subject to high winds, use only top-of-the-line windows and doors and pay extra attention to flashings and sealants. A really tight joint should have a neoprene or metal flashing which is then sealed with a high-quality sealant such as Mono. If you use silicone sealants with insulated glass, keep the sealant away from the rubber-edged seals.

Finally, work with your contractor, not against him. Workmen do not like to have someone watching and second-guessing all the time. If you really can't get along, it may be better to terminate a contract rather than continue with extremely hard feelings.

HOUSE A

Early in the planning stages of this book I reviewed my plan orders and correspondence and made a tally of the number of inquiries for each design. Much to my amazement, House A, which was featured almost 10 years ago in *30 Energy-Efficient Houses,* won hands-down as my most popular house. What was amazing to me was that this house was only mentioned briefly in the back of the book, in the plans for sale section. At the time, none of these houses had been built and I only published floor plans and a cross section of it. Nonetheless, my readers liked the house so much, even sight unseen, that they pushed the plan orders for this house into first place. Many people have sent me construction shots of House

A over the years, and I have selected one of the best examples to show here. This particular house was constructed in the Finger Lakes region of New York State in 1980.

House A shares its 24-foot-square, two-story configuration with my Civic house in the next chapter. Study these plans carefully; if you like them, as many do, they can be adapted directly to the Civic house's panelized system. The layout of House A is less conventional in that it relies upon built-in bed platforms to organize space in the sleeping areas more efficiently. The Civic plans are laid out with conventional bedroom spaces. The loft areas are larger in the House A scheme, allowing them to be used as separate rooms, if desired. Finally, the Civic design depends upon its attached greenhouse for much of its aesthetic appeal. If you don't want a greenhouse, I recommend using the plans for House A with the panelized structure for the Civic house.

(continued on page 227)

This 24-foot-square house was built from plans from my first book. It sits atop a bluff overlooking a bend in a stream to the west.

A deck, porch roof, and extra glass have been added to take advantage of the spectacular view to the west.

The house literally perches on the edge of a bluff, as can be seen from the angle of this photo. An elegantly simple railing provides security for small children. Many building codes require a railing with small openings such as this one.

The north side of the house has few windows. The large front entrance vestibule is at left.

The open living, dining, and kitchen area is flooded by southern sun. Brick pavers make a durable floor. A Defiant stove, out of view on the left, provides ample heat; so much so that the backup electric baseboard units have never been used.

SECOND FLOOR PLAN

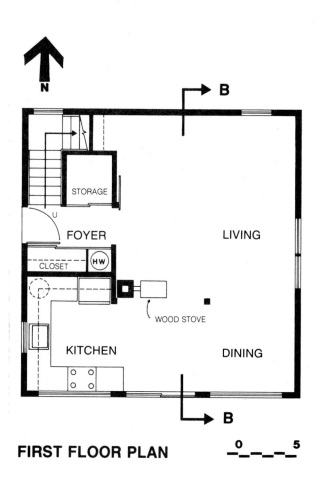

FIRST FLOOR PLAN

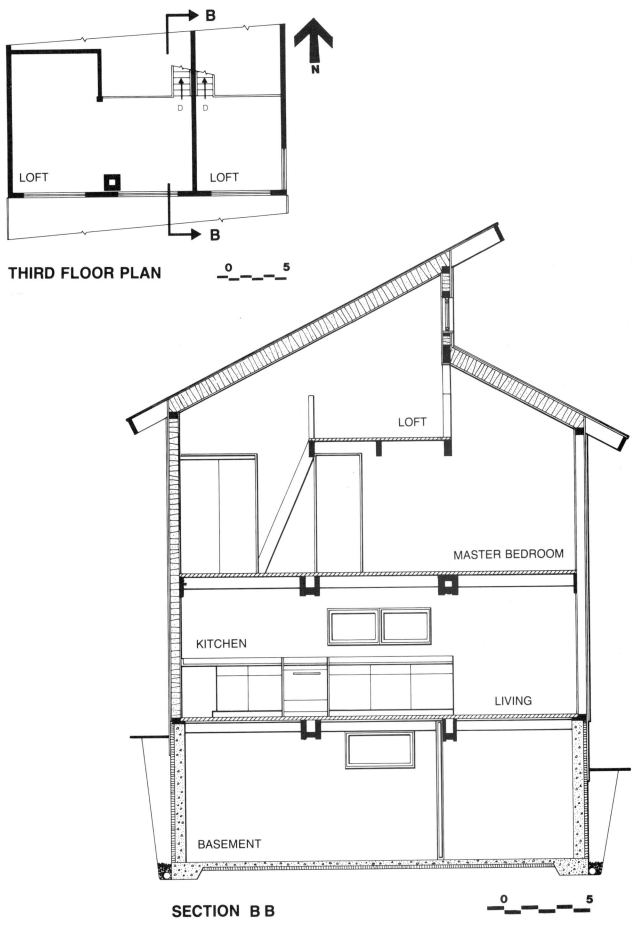

THIRD FLOOR PLAN

B

B

LOFT

LOFT

D D

N

0 5

LOFT

MASTER BEDROOM

KITCHEN

LIVING

BASEMENT

0 5

SECTION B B

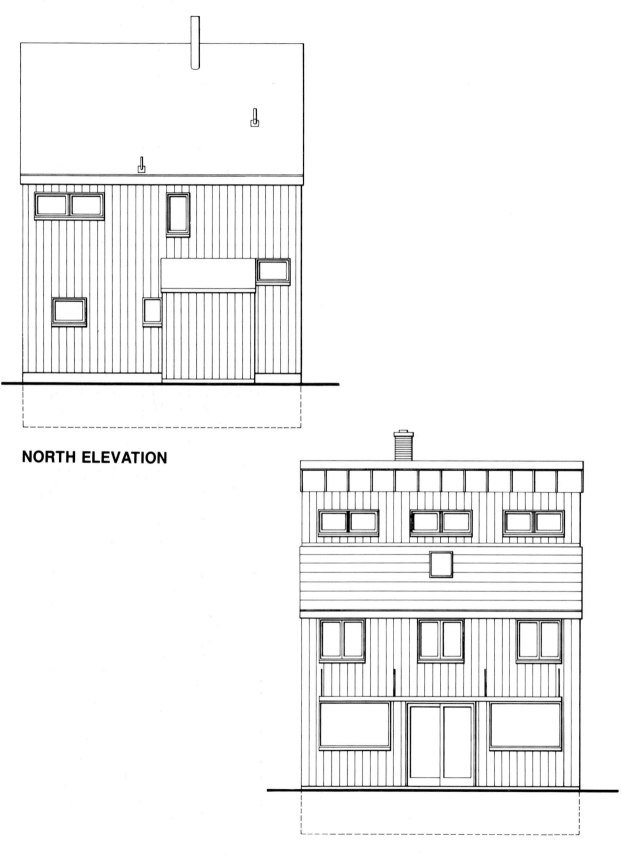

NORTH ELEVATION

SOUTH ELEVATION

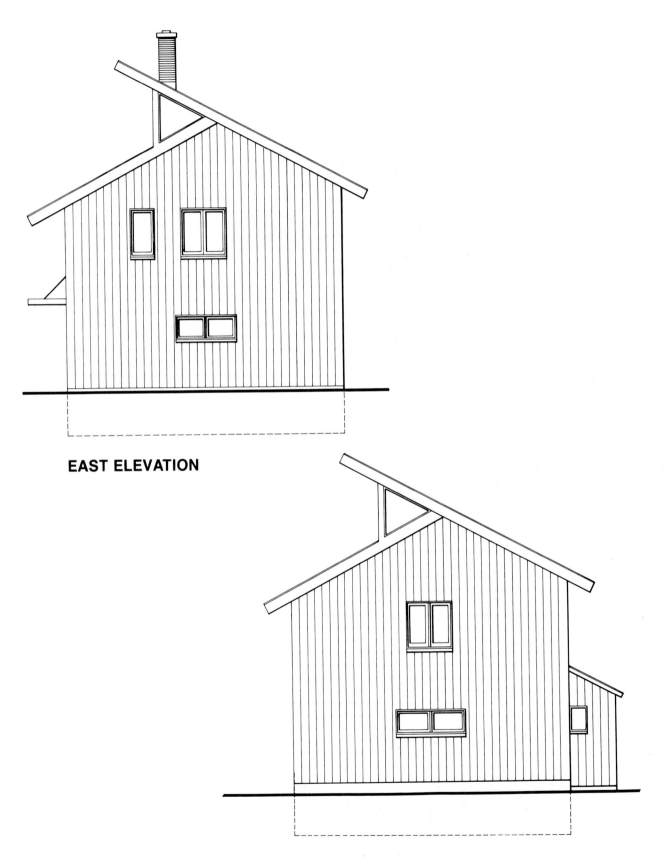

EAST ELEVATION

WEST ELEVATION

Light streams into the master bedroom from the loft above as well as from the window at the right. The exposed braced post-and-beam frame has walls built on the outside for maximum insulating value and to preserve the aesthetic integrity of the frame.

Al Green looks down from the sunny sleeping loft atop his house. More than 1400 square feet is packed into this compact house. It cost just a bit over $40,000, with the Greens doing some of the final finishing and all the subcontracting.

HOWARD HOUSE

This house has been designed to fill a specific niche in the housing market that has been completely ignored by commercial builders and plan services—a compact, detached living unit for a single person. Although almost 30% of the houses in this country are sold to single homeowners, virtually all houses are designed for a family of several people. Deborah Howard works for a county planning board near me. She asked me to design an attractive living unit for a single person that would be simple enough for her to build herself. She liked the idea of passive solar and particularly liked my Tompkins house with its graceful sloping south wall. This house was featured in my book, *A Design and Construction Handbook for Energy-Saving Houses* (Rodale Press, 1980). Her top budget figure was $5000 for materials, all to be purchased new from normal commercial sources; labor was to be provided by herself, family, and friends.

The resulting house contains less than 600 square feet, yet contains all essentials, and even a small greenhouse. The embedded-post foundation and simple laminated post-and-beam frame made the house quick and easy to erect. A small crew of wildly disorganized volunteers was able to get the shell enclosed in two weekends; two skilled carpenters could easily erect the shell in two days.

Deborah and her mother spent their spare time for the rest of the summer finishing the inside in time for winter occupancy. Finishes are simple; flagstone floors set in sand, white Sheetrock, and the natural wood plank-and-beam second-floor deck. A tiny Jøtul cookstove provides ample heat to supplement the sun. The main living area is flanked by the sunspace on the south and storage and vestibule areas on the north, so it is very easy to heat. The massive stone floor, combined with heavy insulation, permits the house to be left unattended for a couple of days, even in southern New York, without danger of freezing.

This tidy little house cost Deborah Howard less to build than her base-priced Toyota cost. Cedar-shingled exterior blends well with the remote forest site.

Although the original plan (and budget) did not make provision for running water, I have added a bath to the plans shown here. The building code that was in effect in the area at the time of construction permitted an outhouse, provided there was no existing source of running water and the plot of ground was larger than 10 acres. That code has since been changed so that such construction in this area would now be illegal. The final plans as shown should comply with most building codes, although some would outlaw the steep stairs to the sleeping loft. Many areas of the country have zoning ordinances that were designed to outlaw trailers without naming them specifically, and as a result, these ordinances frequently prevent the construction of detached small houses. If you are determined and really want a small place of your own, the vast majority of areas in our country are unfettered by such regulations.

After three years of living in her house, Deborah reports that it is spacious and comfortable. The house even attracted the attention of the U.S. Department of Housing and Urban Development, which has included it in a film on passive solar houses.

The three lower windows admit light into a solar greenhouse. The upper window lights up the whole house.

A cozy corner of the main living room. The snowshoes and manual sewing machine are purely functional in this remote house.

The dining table looks into the solar greenhouse. The oil lamp is the main light source.

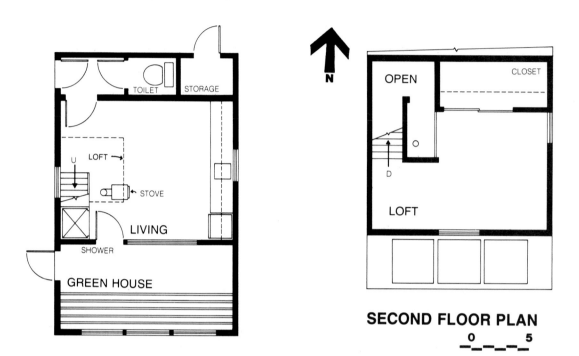

N

SECOND FLOOR PLAN

0   5

FIRST FLOOR PLAN

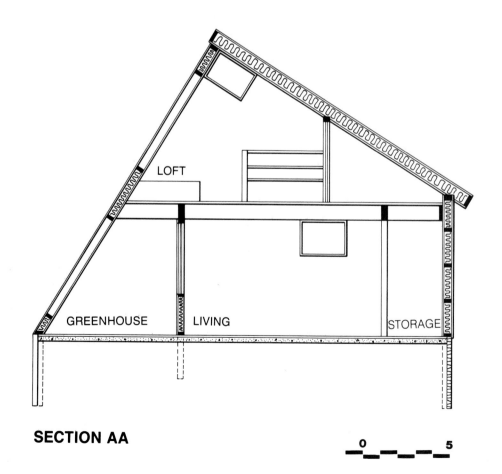

SECTION AA

0   5

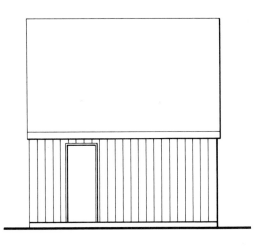

NORTH ELEVATION

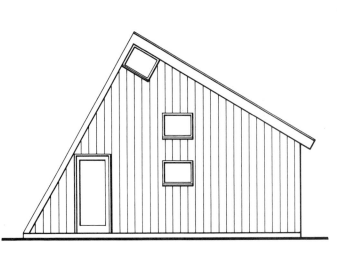

EAST ELEVATION

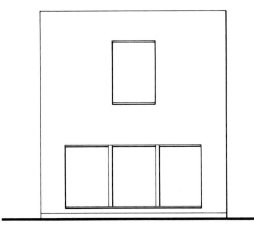

SOUTH ELEVATION

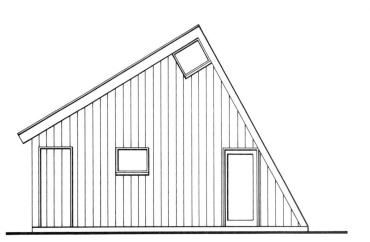

WEST ELEVATION

This beautiful Jøtul stove provides cooking and heating aplenty. The gas hot plate in the background is for summer use.

A view from the front door shows the two-story light well; it's surprisingly spacious for a small house.

The second-floor bedroom has extensive built-in cabinetwork—a must in a small house. The desk has a great view out the window.

Deborah figures her woodpile contains enough wood for two winters. In sunny winter weather, no supplemental heat is needed. Her slate floor sops up the excess for cold nights.

25 Panelized Houses

This chapter shows examples of houses that use the panelized construction techniques I've talked about throughout the book. I have made my selections as diverse as possible in order to show the flexibility of this system. Many of them are derivations of the custom houses shown in the last chapter. Most of these houses had the frame or shell erected by a contractor, with the owner supplying or supervising the balance of the construction. One of the houses was entirely contractor-built; two were entirely owner-built. Frames for the houses were furnished by four different contractors; panels for three of the houses were shop-fabricated by Vermont Frames; the others were job-fabricated by the contractor or the owners. Although there was considerable variation in the speed of construction, all these very diverse groups of workmen achieved entirely satisfactory results by using this new building technique.

CIVIC HOUSE

Three different clients have now constructed houses based upon my Civic plans for a 24-foot-square panelized house. Although all the houses use the same building system and the same 8-foot module, all the clients took advantage of the flexibility of the system to modify the plans. Two of these clients have requested anonymity, so I have not provided my usual degree of detail regarding clients and location. All three examples are located in the northeastern part of the United States where the winter climate exceeds 6000 degree-days.

The first version of the Civic house I show here was constructed for a young family with two children. It follows the basic Civic plans exactly, except for the addition of a basement and provision for a larger greenhouse, which is to be added when funds permit. Low first cost and high insulating value were prime considerations in the design of this house. Wall panels were site-constructed by the owner with a 3½-inch-thick polyurethane core. Exterior facing is ⅝-inch-thick Texture 1-11 plywood; interior is ½-inch-thick Sheetrock. In this house, the clients opted for the main living space on the top floor with three bedrooms on the ground floor. The two loft areas provide a guest space and a study.

Since the budget is quite limited, a contractor was hired for the block foundation and the post-and-beam frame only. All other work has been done by the owners and friends. Savings of $12,000 provided enough money to hire the contractors and purchase materials to complete the shell. The house is being completed on weekends and during vacation periods, so progress is slow. On the other hand, there is no bank loan nor mortgage payment.

Since this house does not have a masonry floor or other mass for heat storage in the main living space on the upper two floors, we have arranged a fan system to store excess heat in the basement area. We have also limited the glass area and have provided a continuous row of vents along the top of the south wall.

Here's the Civic, a small family house built on a very limited budget. This is a view from the southeast. Windows on the side walls and back will be installed as the budget permits. In the meantime, the shell is warm and dry and construction can proceed.

A continuous row of vent windows well sheltered by an overhang provides excellent ventilation for the whole house. A full basement has been added to the basic house design. A future greenhouse is planned for the east half of the south facade. The little boy sits in the opening for a future door to the greenhouse balcony.

This is the north wall of the enclosed shell minus windows. The finished grade will come just above the waterproofing line after the foundation insulation is completed.

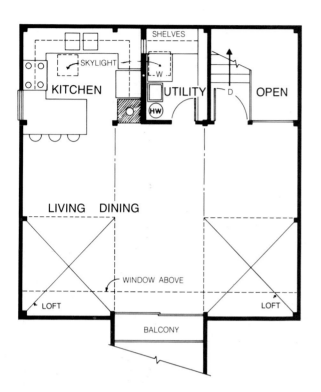

SECOND FLOOR PLAN

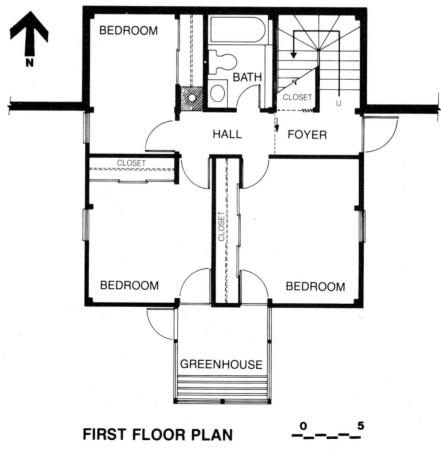

FIRST FLOOR PLAN

The second version of the Civic house is for a single man whose hobby is woodworking. He built his entire house, including frame and wall and roof panels, himself. Of course, other workmen helped with the heavy work, such as the fabrication and erection of the frame and panels, but all work was directed by the owner. He even had his own trees felled from the property and milled into posts, beams, and decking.

Again, the shell follows the basic Civic profile, but the owner has made significant changes. In this case, the roof has been extended 18 feet to the north to enclose a huge woodworking shop. This space was enclosed first and used as a work area for constructing the wall and roof panels. The main section of the house has full 4-inch-thick polyurethane wall panels with full 6-inch-thick roof panels of the same material. The house is so thoroughly insulated and has so much thermal mass that even without any supplemental heating or cooling its temperature never gets above 80°F in summer nor below 50°F in winter. In this version, the main living space is on the ground floor, open to the greenhouse. The second floor has been modified to provide one large master bedroom as well as a study, each with its own sleeping loft. The owner was so enthralled with the view from the sleeping lofts that he wrapped the glass around the corner on the east and west walls at loft level.

The panelized walls for the main house were left unsheathed on the exterior surface and then covered with Plekko stucco. This was not an entirely satisfactory finish, because it was difficult to get different batches of the Plekko uniform in color and thickness. I have used the same material extensively for exposed foundation walls with excellent results, so the problem may have been with the method of application or lack of uniformity in sand or other related materials.

As I noted, the house needs only a small amount of supplemental heat. A novel heating system was devised by the owner based upon an idea in one of my earlier books. An oversized propane-fired hot water heater provides both domestic hot water and hot water to a heat coil installed in a small forced-air distribution system. The carcass and fan from a discarded electric furnace are used to distribute and control the heat from the heating coil. Return ducts are located high on the east and west walls so that they feed the warmest air in the house back to the furnace. This heat distribution setup not only makes the house temperatures more uniform, but also reduces the heating requirements; in mild weather only the fan is necessary to provide uniform heat throughout the house.

(continued on page 244)

This second version of the Civic house used fixed glass at the top of the south wall to gather solar heat. A fan system at the peak exhausts hot air in the summertime. Even without this system in operation or the shading louvers in place, the house stays remarkably cool.

Job-fabricated panels leave the exterior face exposed for stucco installation. The owner had trouble locating satisfactory workmen to install the stucco uniformly and does not recommend the material. Others, with different workmen, have had very good success.

The greenhouse has been installed but the louvers are yet to be put in place on the outrigger beams above the windows.

The roof of the basic Civic design has been extended to the north to provide a large workshop for the owner.

An extra chimney
has been installed so
that the shop can be
converted to a
separate apartment.
The garage doors at
left permit occasional
shop work on auto-
mobiles.

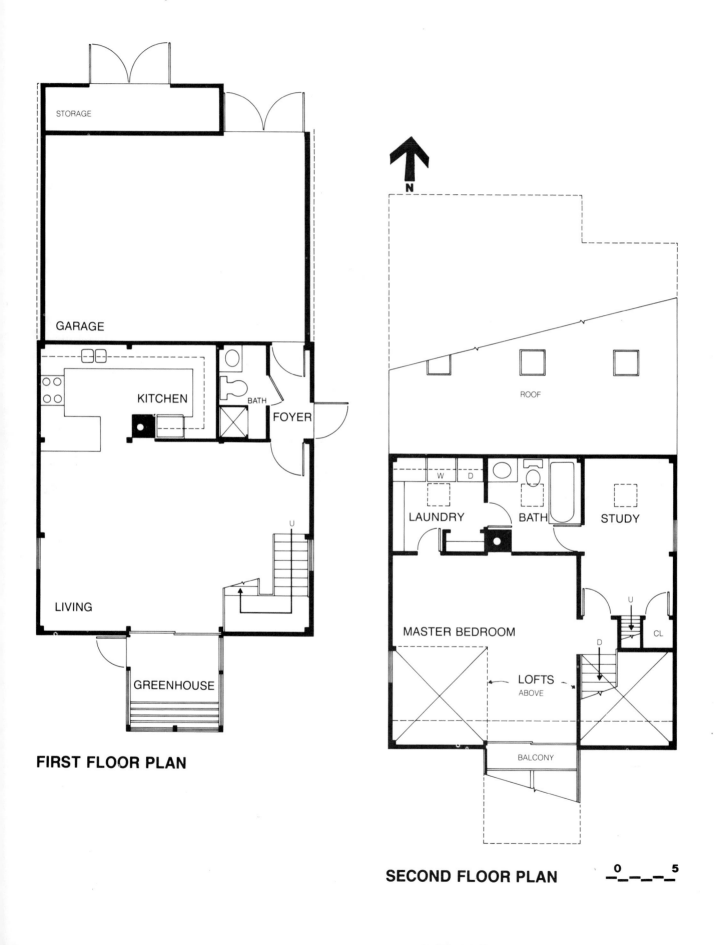

STORAGE

GARAGE

KITCHEN

BATH

FOYER

U

LIVING

GREENHOUSE

FIRST FLOOR PLAN

N

ROOF

LAUNDRY   W   D

BATH

STUDY

MASTER BEDROOM

LOFTS
ABOVE

U

CL

D

BALCONY

SECOND FLOOR PLAN

0 _ _ _ _ 5

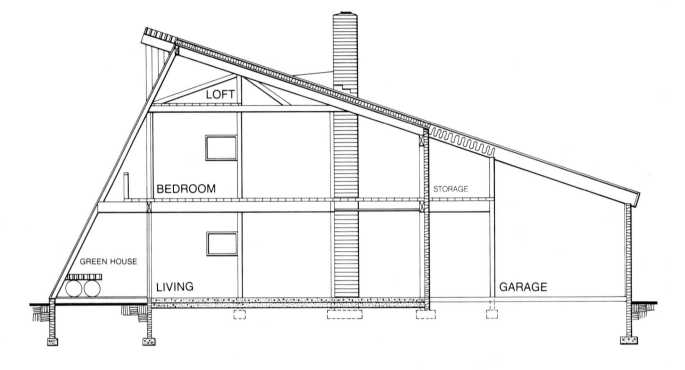

SECTION AA

0 _ _ _ _ 5

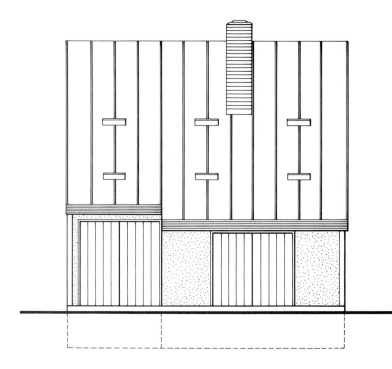

NORTH ELEVATION

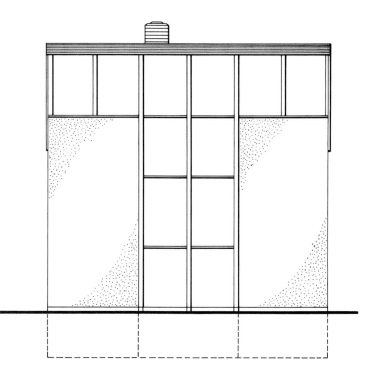

SOUTH ELEVATION

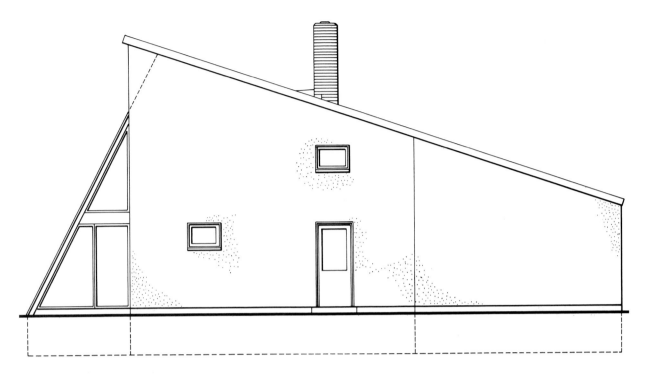

EAST ELEVATION

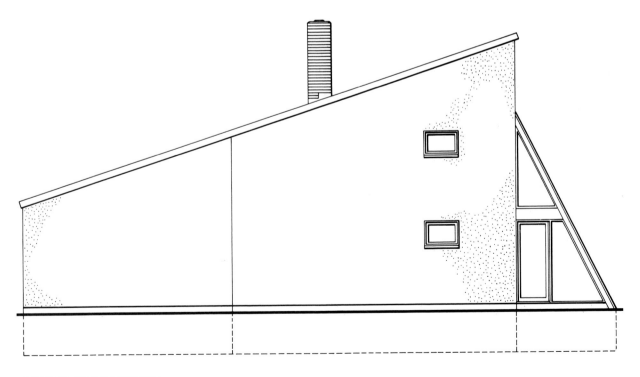

WEST ELEVATION

The third version of the Civic is designed for a plant lover. In this case, the house was made longer and lower to fit its site and its owner's requirements. The house was lengthened by 8 feet to allow a larger greenhouse and greater area on the first floor. The roof line was lowered to make a story-and-a-half profile with bedrooms along the south wall. A bridge connects the two bedrooms and leads to a stairwell. The greenhouse and a screened porch are on a half-level 4 feet below the first floor.

The site was extremely difficult in that it sloped in two directions and had previously been occupied by another house. The landscaping from the earlier house was mature and spectacular, and we tried to save as much as possible. This has resulted in a house that is angled too much to the west of south, which causes overheating in late afternoon in mild weather. In fact, it even overheated in cold weather before the window louvers were in place.

Comparing the three versions of the Civic house shows how seemingly slight changes in orientation, glass area, and masonry mass can adversely affect the performance of a structure. It is very important in all structures to have a masonry floor, if possible.

The original design scheme for this third version of the Civic house showed a concrete slab 2 feet below original grade. The building inspector vetoed this version before it was even presented

to the client; the first floor had to be at least 1 foot above original grade or he wouldn't approve the plans. Since the slab was vetoed, I substituted a quarry-tile floor over a suspended wood floor. I consider this a wasteful and expensive solution, and the tile mass is too thin for good heat storage. Furthermore, a useless space has been constructed below the floor which cost a good deal to build yet cannot serve any practical purpose. If time had permitted, the house would have been redesigned with half slab-on-grade and half basement, eliminating the crawl space.

This version of the Civic was completed entirely by a contractor. Although he is an experienced post-and-beam builder, he had not previously used panels to enclose a structure. Even so, he learned quickly. All the exterior wall panels were constructed and set in place in four working days; windows and doors took two additional days to install. Since construction was delayed until late fall, the instantly insulated shell was very welcome.

The large greenhouse was difficult to build and slowed construction considerably. Fortunately, the main structure of the house was enclosed and warm so that work could proceed on the interior. The heating system is a Kero-Sun Monitor 30 wall-mounted kerosene furnace; it takes only a couple of hours to install. The panelized wall system made the house tight; there is minimal heat loss and air infiltration, so this small furnace is all that's needed to heat the house. Also, the messy Sheetrock and insulation operations were

This third version of the Civic house has a screened porch with a sleeping loft appended to the west side. The original drawings show a full-height screened porch, which the architect thinks is a better design solution.

virtually eliminated. We took advantage of this heated, semifinished space to set up a wood-working shop to build interior doors, trim, and cabinetry. Even though this process took a bit longer than buying ready-built units, the custom units are far superior to competitively priced lumberyard products and are far more attractive. Finally, site-built units can be made to fit exactly, eliminating ugly, wasteful filler strips.

The panelized wall system is estimated to have saved three to four weeks of construction time on this project. If there had been a severe winter, the panels would have made the difference between building or not building. As it happened, we had one of the mildest winters on record, so construction could have continued regardless. Cost savings over conventional construction were only about 10 percent, primarily reflecting the time savings. Winter weather and a 100-mile-per-day commute for the contractor offset some of the savings inherent in this system.

(continued on page 254)

The plain shed shape of the house is nicely offset by the inclined plane of the greenhouse. Vents above the sloping glass were in the original design, but were omitted.

The greenhouse sweeps down and ties the house to the grade. It is nestled into a lush garden spot that is perpetually 10° warmer than the surrounding area.

The greenhouse floor is 4 feet below the main living level. A stair from the living room provides an exit through the greenhouse.

The entrance to the house is on the north. Windows have been minimized except in the kitchen.

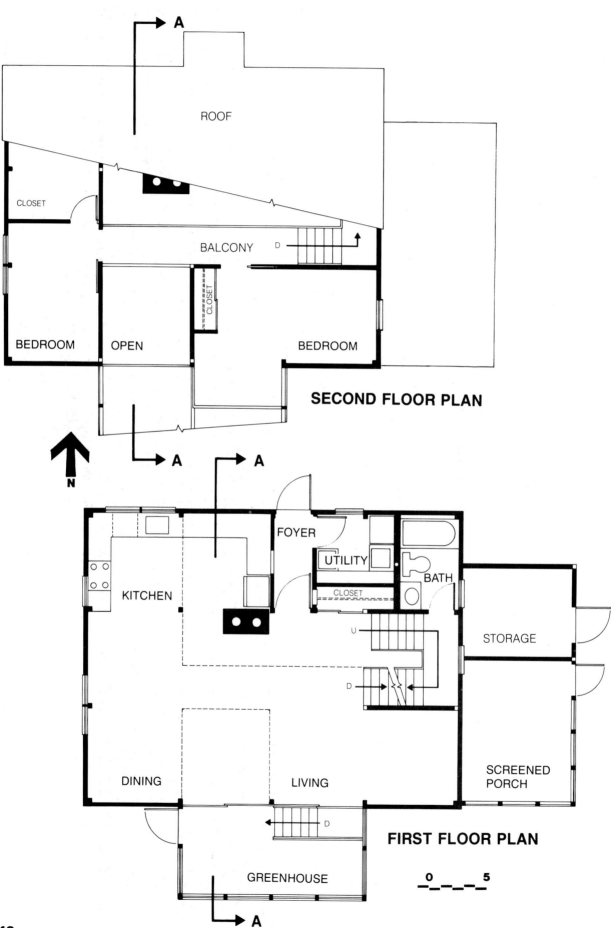

A

ROOF

CLOSET

BALCONY   D

CLOSET

BEDROOM   OPEN   BEDROOM

SECOND FLOOR PLAN

N

A   A

FOYER

UTILITY

KITCHEN   CLOSET   BATH

STORAGE

U

D

DINING   LIVING   SCREENED
                                          PORCH

D   **FIRST FLOOR PLAN**

GREENHOUSE   0 _ _ _ _ 5

A

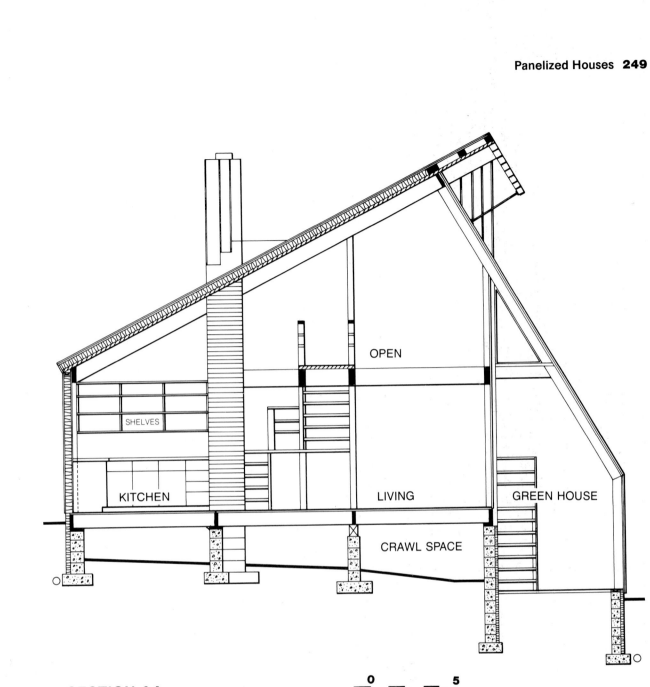

SHELVES

OPEN

KITCHEN

LIVING

GREEN HOUSE

CRAWL SPACE

SECTION AA

0   5

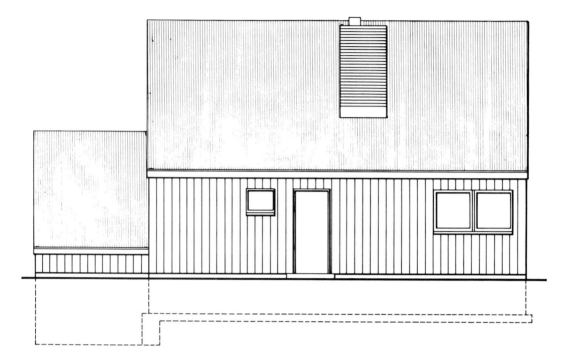

NORTH ELEVATION

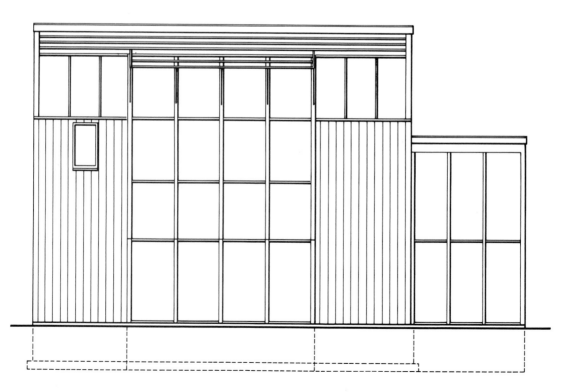

SOUTH ELEVATION

EAST ELEVATION

WEST ELEVATION

The main living area is open to the roof and spanned by a bridge. The greenhouse is at left.

A view from the bridge looking down into the living room.

Stairs at the side of
the living room lead
to suspended bridge.

The bridge itself. The greenhouse is at left.

The guest bedroom has a novel folding door, economically job-fabricated.

SOLAR SALTBOX

Jim Clark is a sculptor and an avid reader of my books. And he and his wife, Nanette, are close neighbors of one of my other clients. The Clarks' solar saltbox is entirely of Jim's own design, with some help and suggestions from me. The saltbox roof has been designed to accommodate solar collectors on the south face, so I call it a solar saltbox.

The Clarks took their plans for the house to Woodstock Barn Homes (now Kaatskill Post and Beam) and hired them to design and cut the frame. They supplied their own timbers; Barn Homes did the design and cutting for a mere $1500. Jim and Nanette's basic concept was to build entirely from savings and current income without resorting to borrowing. The 800-square-foot structure has cost a bit less than $20,000 for all expenditures, including a long driveway and electric line.

The house sits on a concrete block foundation with a concrete slab floor on the south side to absorb heat from the sun. The north side of the foundation is split between a small basement and a spring-fed cistern. A prolific spring was uncovered by the excavation and, rather than try to divert it or move the house, Jim incorporated a cistern into the foundation to capture spring water for their water source.

Wall insulation is 3½ inches of Styrofoam; the roof has 3 inches of Thermax for insulation. Ample backup heat is provided by a Vigilant wood stove. Since electricity wasn't installed right away, the principal power source was (and still is) propane gas, which is used for cooking, refrigeration, and water heating. While the house now has electricity, it uses so little that our friendly local utility company "rewards" the Clarks by charging them 46 cents per kilowatt-hour. The going rate is more like 10 cents per kilowatt-hour, and I have heard

Jim Clark's sculptures are nicely set off by the two buildings as one approaches the house.

A wood-fired Snorkel stove provides heat for a redwood hot tub.

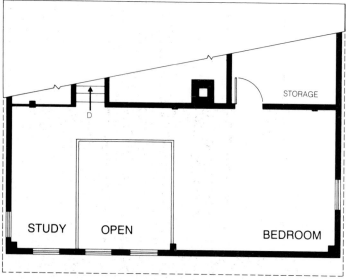

SECOND FLOOR PLAN

STUDY   OPEN   BEDROOM

STORAGE

D

N

FOYER   BATH   KITCHEN

U

LIVING   DINING

DECK

FIRST FLOOR PLAN

0   5

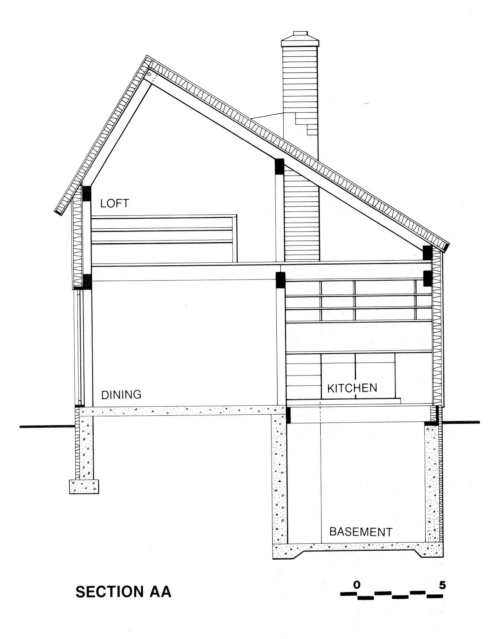

SECTION AA

0 _ _ _ _ 5

folks in other parts of the country complaining about paying a tenth that much.

By starting small and doing all their own work, Jim and Nanette have been able to add several amenities to the house and property. A studio-workshop-guest house has been constructed adjacent to the original house. A large deck has been added to the south side, and a wood-fired hot tub with Snorkel stove is now off the kitchen.

This house shows that with just a little help from professionals (the foundation and frame), a hard-working couple can still build their own house for a reasonable price without resorting to an expensive mortgage. *(continued on page 262)*

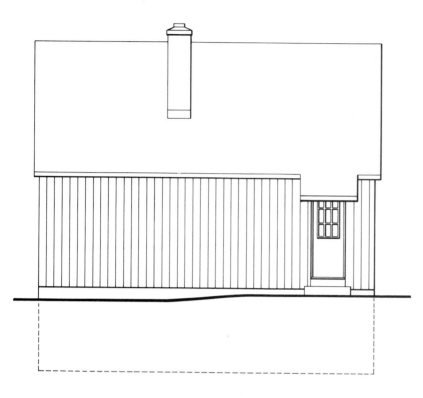

NORTH ELEVATION

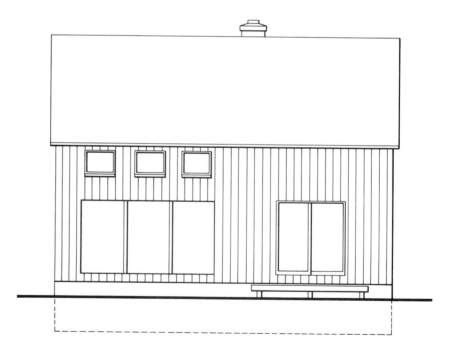

SOUTH ELEVATION

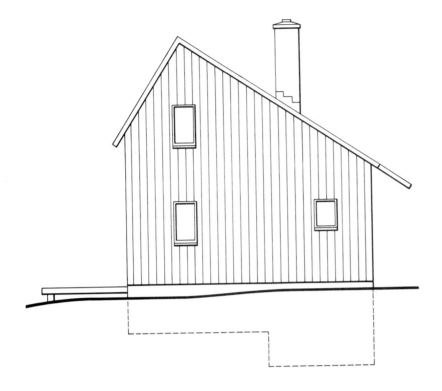

EAST ELEVATION

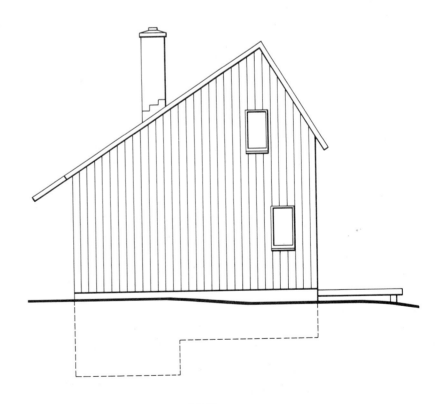

WEST ELEVATION

Passive solar saltbox is flanked by solar studio. A solar shower hangs near the corner of the deck.

Jim has put his sculpting skills to work in designing a kitchen pot rack.

The master bedroom is in the loft at the top of the picture.

The living room has a concrete floor to soak up the sun's heat. The wood stove is rarely used; there is no backup heating system. The tree grows up through a well in the second-story floor.

RETIREMENT HOUSE

One of the first panelized houses I personally knew of was built by Bruce Binger in northern Vermont. I was beginning my research for this book, and Bruce's parents had commissioned me to design a retirement house for them. Meanwhile, Bruce was just starting construction on his own house. I sent Bruce all the information I had on commercially available panels, and the next thing I knew he had built his house using them. Peter McNaull of Vermont Frames was just starting to experiment with panels of his own, so Bruce had a ready supply for raw materials. Peter fabricated and erected the frame, and Bruce built and erected his own panels.

In the meantime, it had occurred to me to send the Bingers to visit the Knopfs. Except for the swimming lane, the Knopf house (presented in Chapter 24) came very close to the Bingers' requirements. The other big challenge was budget; the Bingers wanted to spend considerably less money than the Knopfs. A final ingredient was those prefabricated wall panels; they were thoroughly sold on them. They handed me the task of redesigning and simplifying the original Knopf house to accommodate both the panel system and their budget.

Without all the design constraints of the original house, I was able to make considerable savings and many improvements. Although I still prefer the Knopf version, the Bingers got a lot more house for their money. I removed the projecting greenhouse and swimming lane and substituted a full-length greenhouse along the south wall of the basement. The garage was bumped out of the basement and took the place of the Knopfs' guest suite. We raised the roof line just a bit to accommodate two small bedrooms on the second floor behind the clerestory.

The cost reductions were extremely successful. The poured concrete foundation and the frame

each cost almost exactly half as much as the Knopf version. Part of this can be explained by simplification; there is no swimming lane, suspended concrete slab, nor complicated sloping glazing, but much of it has to do with geographical location and competition. Wage rates are lower in the far North, and there are many more skilled post-and-beam framers there. Whereas there was only one bidder for the Knopf frame, three contractors were interested in bidding the Binger job. Cost reductions and efficiencies were suggested by each of the interested parties. When all was said and done, Peter McNaull was the low bidder. Peter also furnished the laminated structural wall panels for the house.

Heating in the Binger house is Vermont traditional —wood stove with a bit of electrical backup to keep pipes from freezing. A sign of the times: a fallout shelter has replaced the hot water storage tank in the original house version. The Bingers have done much of the final construction work themselves, with occasional help from their son. The only serious construction snags were caused by a wet late spring, which caused a very late start for the excavator and foundation contractor. Peter was left with a fabricated frame and panels underfoot for much of the summer, waiting for the foundation to go in.

For those who like the idea of a swimming lane and greenhouse entrance but have a budget closer to the Bingers', you can order the original drawings for the 1100-square-foot Knopf house (see Appendix C). It is smaller and simpler than either the Knopf or the Binger version. It has no guest room on the north, but a higher roof does permit a second-floor loft space. There is a single garage space in the basement. It has been laid out to take advantage of the economy of panelized construction.

(continued on page 271)

The plants and rocker are already enjoying the view from the living room. The kitchen is at the far end of the room. Notice how the post-and-beam framing allows a completely open space without a bearing partition.

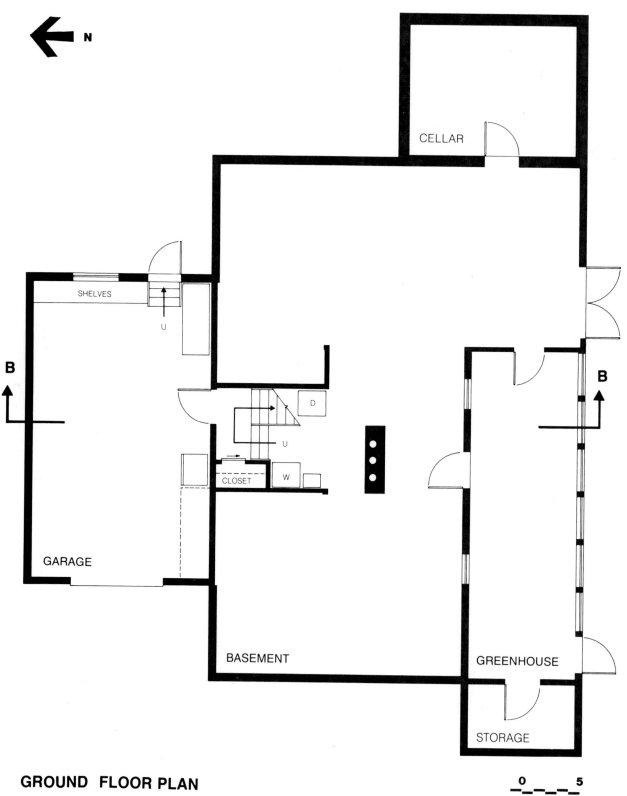

N

CELLAR

SHELVES

U

B

B

D

U

W

CLOSET

GARAGE

BASEMENT

GREENHOUSE

STORAGE

GROUND FLOOR PLAN

0 ___ 5

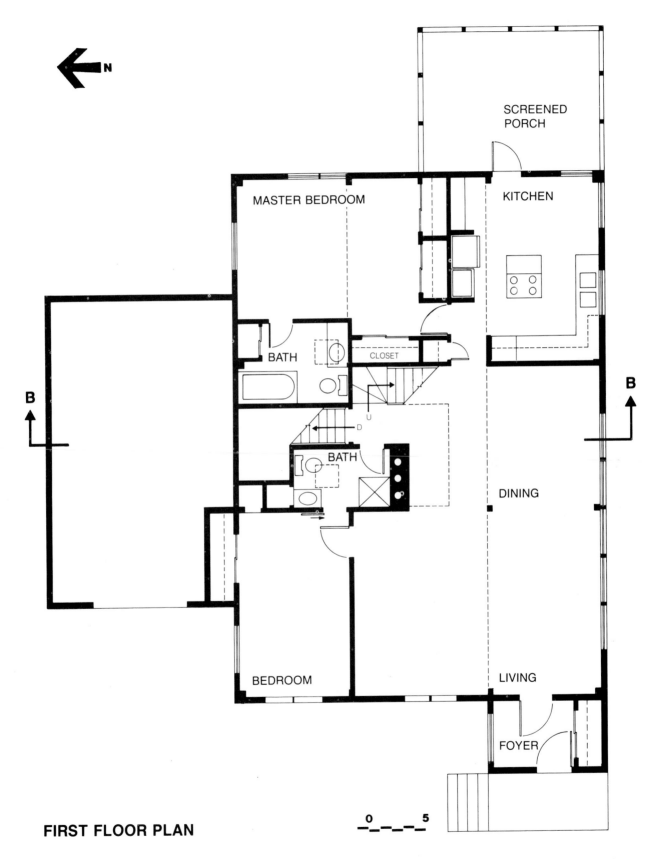

N

SCREENED
PORCH

MASTER BEDROOM

KITCHEN

B

BATH

CLOSET

U

D

BATH

B

DINING

BEDROOM

LIVING

FOYER

0 — — — 5

FIRST FLOOR PLAN

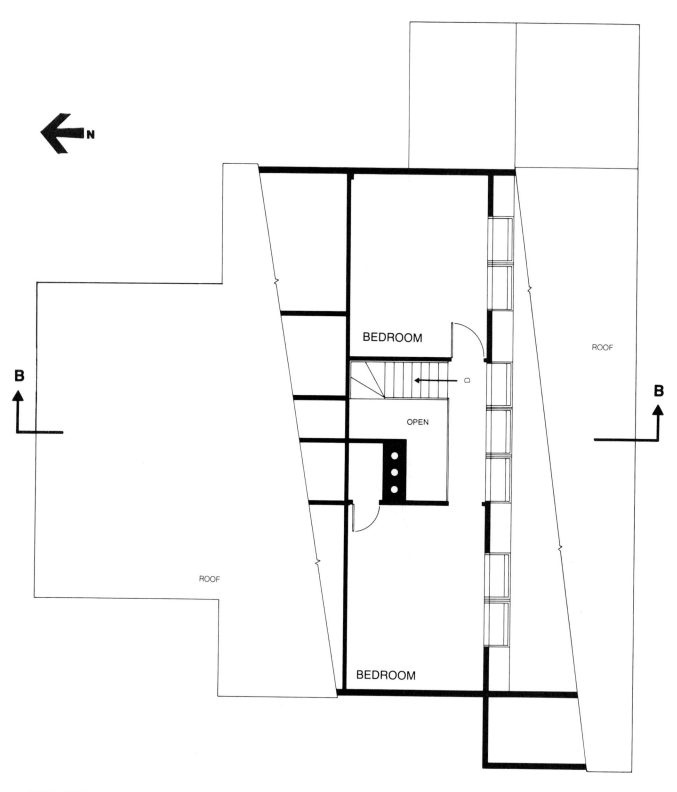

N

B

B

BEDROOM

OPEN

ROOF

ROOF

BEDROOM

SECOND FLOOR PLAN

0 _ _ _ 5

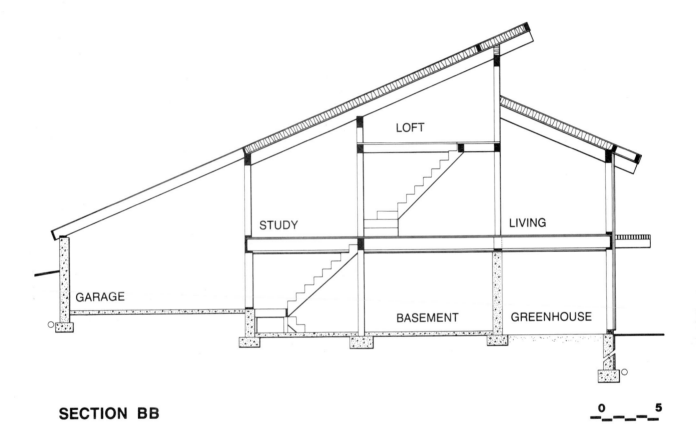

LOFT

STUDY

LIVING

GARAGE

BASEMENT

GREENHOUSE

SECTION BB

0 _ _ _ _ 5

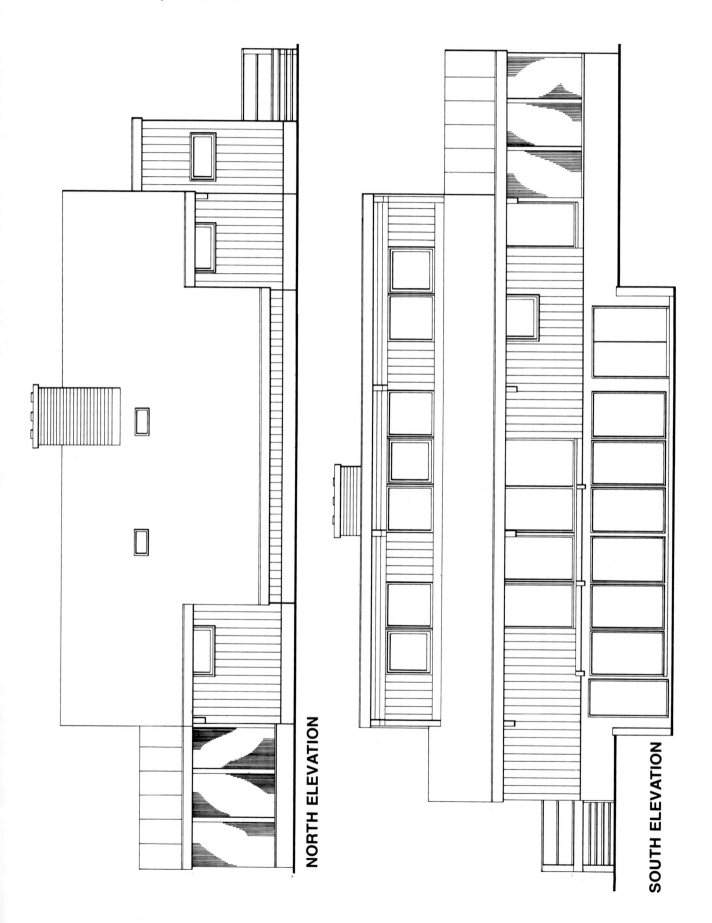

NORTH ELEVATION

SOUTH ELEVATION

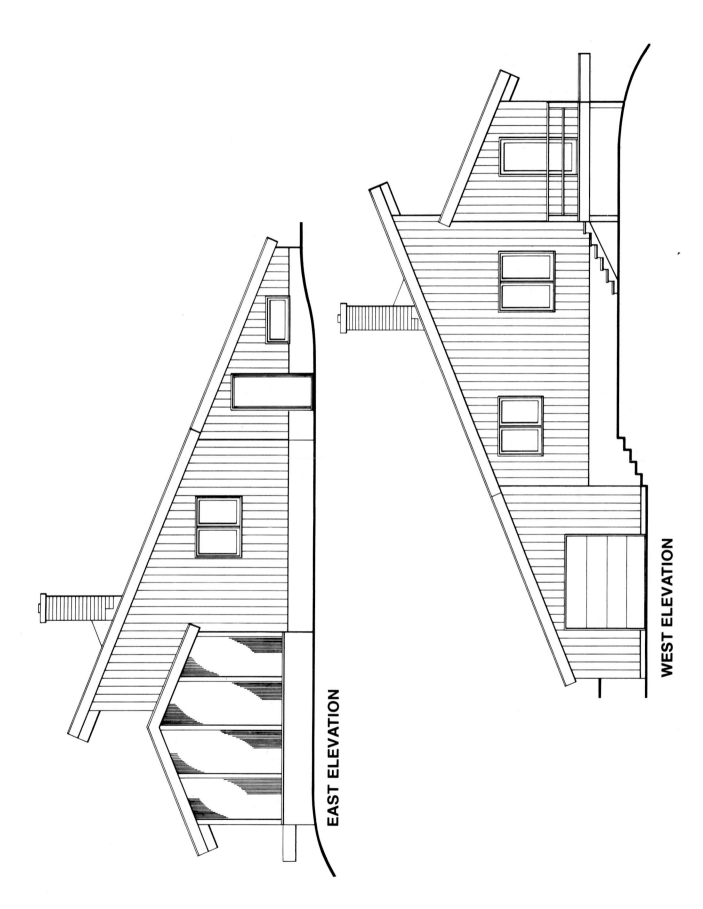

EAST ELEVATION

WEST ELEVATION

The entrance view from the southwest shows how much work remains. The greenhouse is on the lower level with the Xs on the glass.

The porch is a delightful braced frame structure.

Even though the exterior is far from complete, the panels and post-and-beam frame produce an almost instant interior. The second-floor loft at the upper right is missing a railing. It is open to the living room and enjoys a view down the valley through the south-facing glass.

BROOKHAVEN HOUSE

Mac and Cheryl Curry had searched for years for a house that fitted their needs. Finally, Cheryl took a course in solar energy and discovered the Brookhaven house, the result of a solar project sponsored by Brookhaven National Laboratories. Except for an awkwardly placed stairway and an extraneous entrance, the basic house was exactly what they wanted. One big problem—they both thought it was ugly, not in concept, but in final detailing. Engineers had tacked on a mishmash of greenhouses and Trombe walls that did not relate well to the basic farmhouse lines of the house.

Mac and Cheryl arrived with their sketches just as we were starting several of the panelized houses. I showed them some of my work. Would it be possible to convert the Brookhaven house to panelized post-and-beam construction and at the same time clean it up so that it would be acceptable in their traditional neighborhood? I eagerly accepted the challenge.

The Brookhaven house responded nicely to the discipline of a post-and-beam frame. Rotating the stairs 90 degrees solved the most glaring problems with the plan, and eliminating the extra entrance further smoothed the flow of traffic. A little further tweaking got all the plumbing efficiently arranged around a center core. The jumbled greenhouses were consolidated into one simple sun porch with three massive bow-top windows. Two large ventilating skylights provide top lighting. The heat storage capabilities of the Trombe wall were replaced by a concrete slab in the living-dining room and a Finnish contraflow fireplace similar to the one in the Grant house (see Chapter 24). We did lose a bit of heat gain capability compared to the original design, but the vastly superior panelized structure is much more weathertight than the heavily insulated conventional construction of the original house. Finally, the improvement in appearance is dramatic. Relatively simple changes have transformed an "ugly duckling" into a swan. Virtually all who have seen the design have been impressed by its beauty.

This aerial view of the Brookhaven house from the southeast shows how an integrated greenhouse with graceful bow-topped windows and skylights replaces the clutter of the original Brookhaven design.

The east view shows the double-car garage on the north to shelter the house.

A construction view from the northwest shows the oak frame with a few of the wall panels in place. The area wrapped in plastic contains all of the wall panels for the entire house.

The same view with cedar shingles being applied. Note how the house steps down the hillside.

I arranged for the frame to be constructed of red oak by Essex Timber Frames. Since this is a huge house (2800 square feet), they underestimated the amount of materials needed, and numerous delays were required to find enough material to complete the job. Due to a limited budget, the Currys and a local crew did most of the work. Bob Dakin of Essex went to the job with the frame and supervised its erection. Panels that have a 5½-inch-thick polysytrene core were purchased from Vermont Frames. Even with a novice crew, the entire frame and shell, including finished roofing, was complete in about three weeks.

Exterior finish for the house is natural cedar shingles. The windows are aluminum-clad Marvin Casemasters. The roof is heavy-weight asphalt shingles with #40 terne flashings; it was done by a professional roofer in order to enclose the house as rapidly as possible.

By using the panelization technique, the Currys have a weathertight warm shell in which to work over the winter, and the neighbors get an attractive house to look at rather than a messy construction site.

(continued on page 278)

The southwest corner of the house is fully finished except for fascia board.

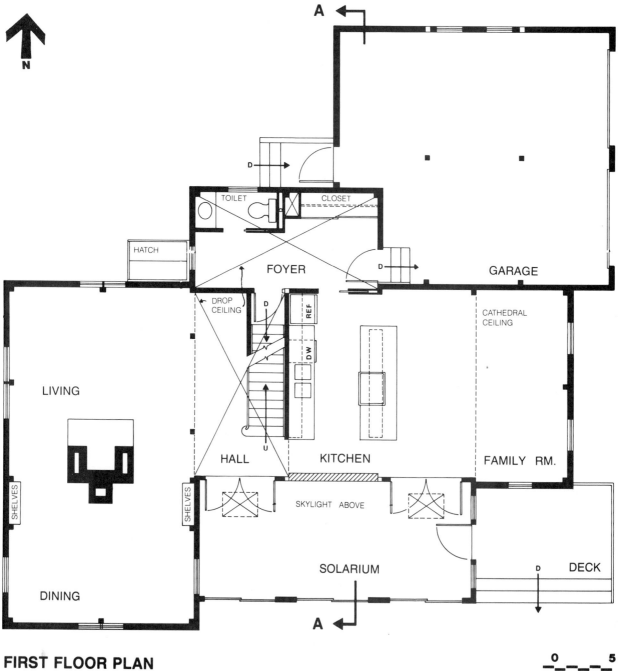

N

A

D

TOILET   CLOSET

HATCH

FOYER

GARAGE

DROP
CEILING

REF

D

DW

CATHEDRAL
CEILING

LIVING

SHELVES

SHELVES

HALL   KITCHEN   FAMILY RM.

U

SKYLIGHT ABOVE

DINING

SOLARIUM   DECK

D

A

FIRST FLOOR PLAN

0 — — — 5

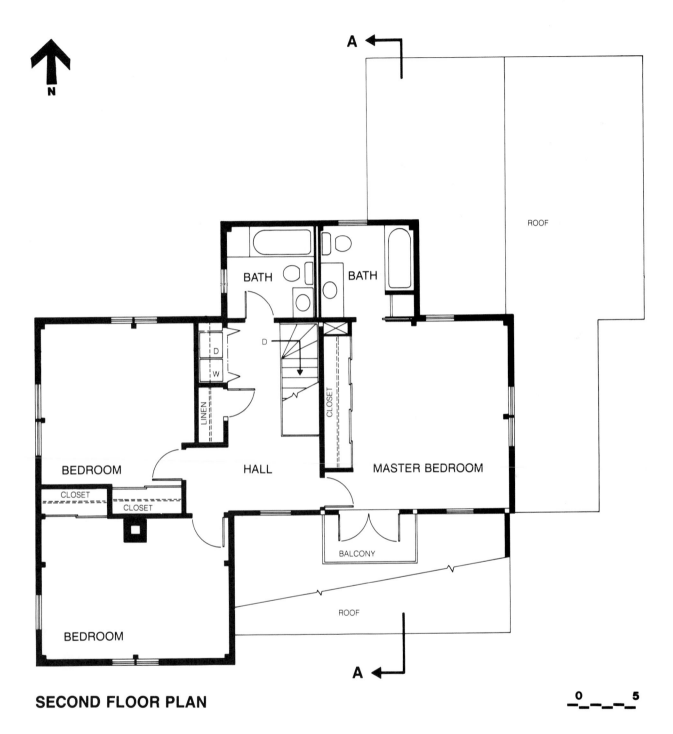

N

A

A

BATH

BATH

ROOF

D

W

LINEN

D

CLOSET

BEDROOM

CLOSET

CLOSET

HALL

MASTER BEDROOM

BALCONY

ROOF

BEDROOM

SECOND FLOOR PLAN

0 _ _ _ _ 5

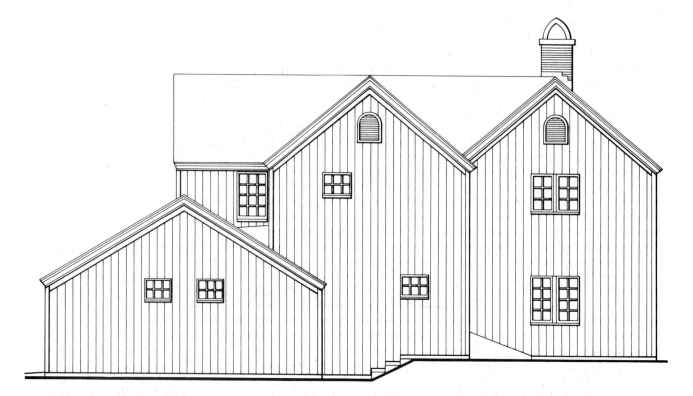

NORTH ELEVATION

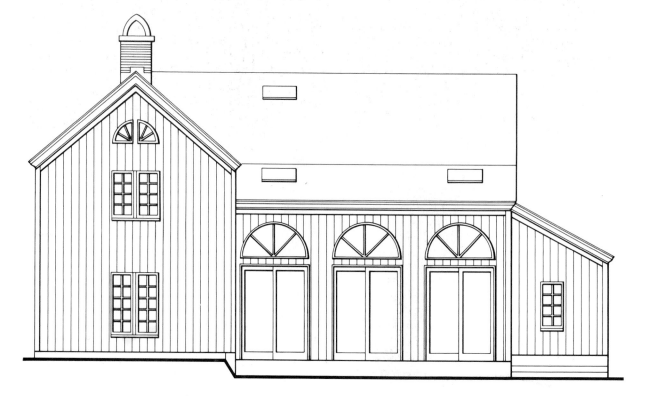

SOUTH ELEVATION

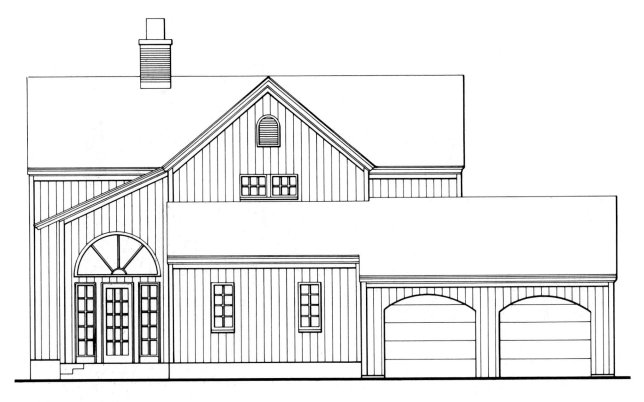

EAST ELEVATION

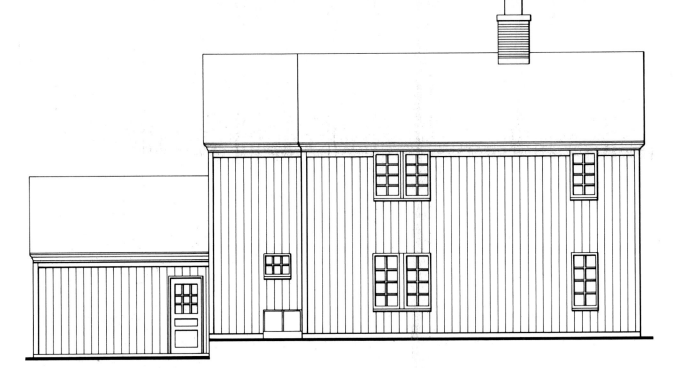

WEST ELEVATION

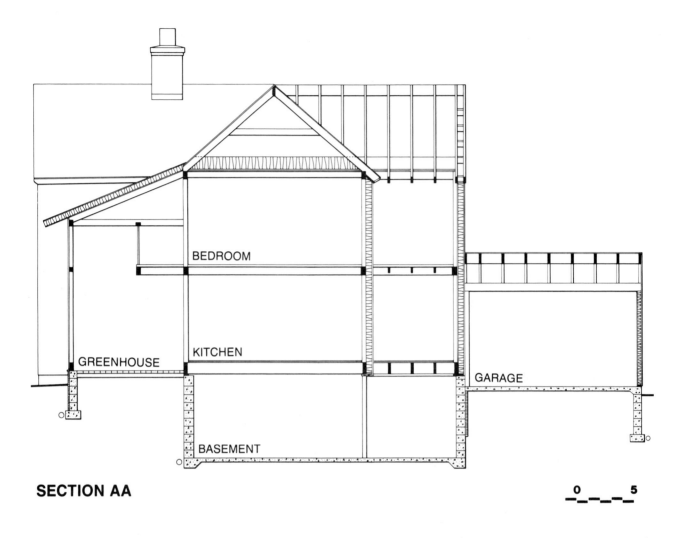

SECTION AA

0 _ _ _ 5

OCTAGON HOUSE

For the last house in the book I have saved a delightful, practical bit of whimsy, an octagonal house. Here in the Hudson River Valley, where I live, there is a long tradition of octagonal houses. They can be traced back all the way to the mid-1800s when Orson Fowler's book, *The Octagon House, A Home for All* influenced many local architects and builders. This book was reprinted in 1973 by Dover Press and has again inspired a great number of people to build octagon houses. Since the octagon is a very efficient shape in that it encloses a maximum amount of floor area with a minimum amount of exposed wall, it is not as whimsical as it may first appear in these energy-short and money-tight times.

Several years ago I designed a small octagon with 12-foot sides for the dean of a local college. Working drawings were completed, and he was

enthusiastically preparing to build when he discovered that he did not have clear title to his property. Attempts at finding alternate property and financing were futile, and the plans languished in my file drawer. Then, last year, I had two requests for an octagon house. One of them is now being constructed at each end of the country —in New York and in California. The California version has a full basement and is very slowly being crafted of native redwood (fallen timbers from the site). At this writing, only a skeletal framework exists, and the owner lives in the basement apartment.

The New York version shown here was revised for Andy and Sheryl Cline, who are doing most of the construction themselves. As the house is built on solid bedrock, we have omitted the basement apartment. Jeff Seeley of Kevin Berry

Builders did the bulk of the work of constructing the shell, and the Clines have finished off the balance of the work themselves. The roofing, siding, brick floor, and foundation insulation, as well as all subcontracting, were handled by the Clines. Since the Clines did most of their own work, they freely experimented with the layout. There have been several changes to the plans shown here. The primary changes involve omitting the partition between the two bedrooms to make one large room. Since many people would want both bedrooms, I have shown the original version. Another change involves the addition of a mud room-vestibule. The extremely exposed site on a remote road dictated this addition. Again, I like the original better and have shown the plans in their first version.

Even though octagons are supposed to be hard to construct, this one went up quickly without a hitch. One cost- and time-saving feature was the pressure-treated, direct-embedded posts that form the foundation and main supporting posts. With this post construction the complicated layout for the octagon only has to be made once, and there is no chance for a sloppy mason to make a mistake. Also, if a mistake is made, it is much easier to move a post than to chop out a masonry wall.

The Clines' budget for the project is $50,000 and it looks as though they'll make it with no trouble. The pole frame structure with floors and roof cost $14,000, and Peter McNaull bid just over $3000 for the 5½-inch-thick polystyrene-cored exterior wall panels (cupola walls not included).

Of course, the crowning feature of this house is the cupola. It is the favorite spot for kids of all ages. It is also the warmest spot in winter and the coolest in summer.

The greenhouse of the Octagon house was enlarged with a projection on the south side of the octagon. It is flanked by arch-topped windows.

This side view shows the Octagon's barnlike profile.

This framing shot shows clean lines of the octagonal framing. Posts are directly embedded in the ground.

The north side of the house has a projecting entrance vestibule with a custom-made insulating door.

A view of the master bedroom shows the balcony railings to the living room below. The ladder leads to the cupola.

The second floor of the greenhouse was incorporated into the master bedroom as a sitting area.

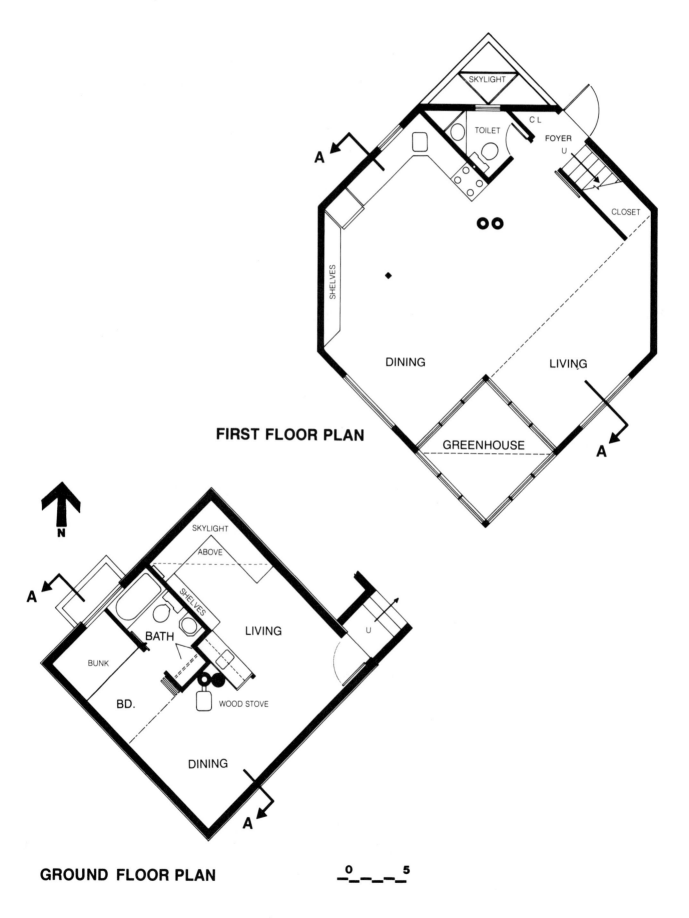

FIRST FLOOR PLAN

SKYLIGHT

TOILET

C L

FOYER
U

CLOSET

SHELVES

DINING

LIVING

GREENHOUSE

A

A

N

GROUND FLOOR PLAN

SKYLIGHT

ABOVE

SHELVES

BATH

LIVING

U

BUNK

BD.

WOOD STOVE

DINING

A

A

A

0 _ _ _ _ 5

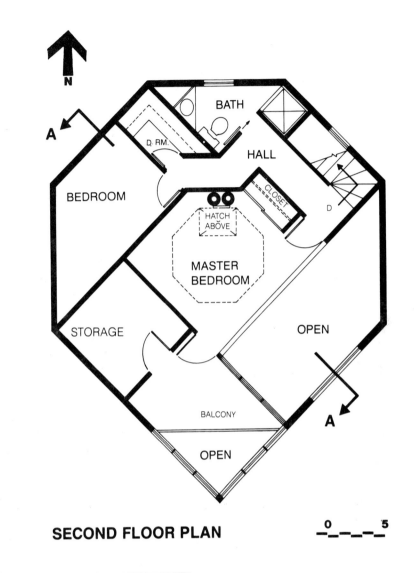

BATH

HALL

D. RM.

BEDROOM

CLOSET

D

HATCH
ABOVE

MASTER
BEDROOM

STORAGE

OPEN

BALCONY

OPEN

A

A

N

SECOND FLOOR PLAN

0 ____ 5

A side view of the house as seen from the road.

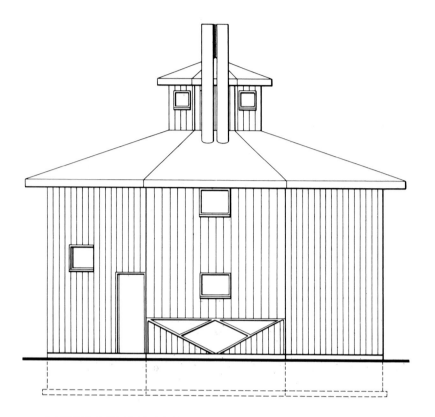

NORTH ELEVATION

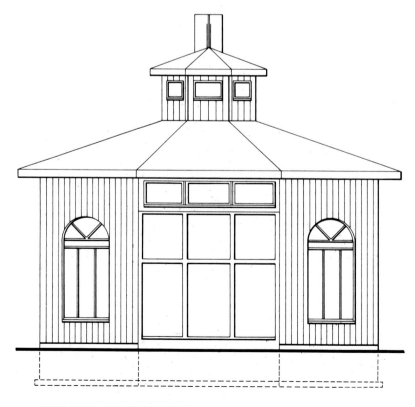

SOUTH ELEVATION

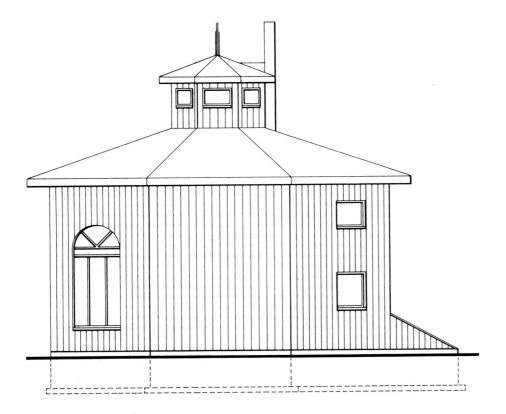

EAST ELEVATION

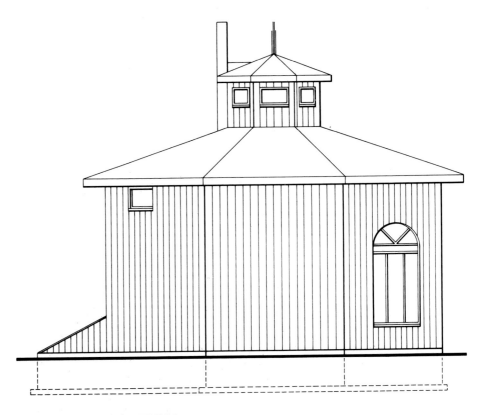

WEST ELEVATION

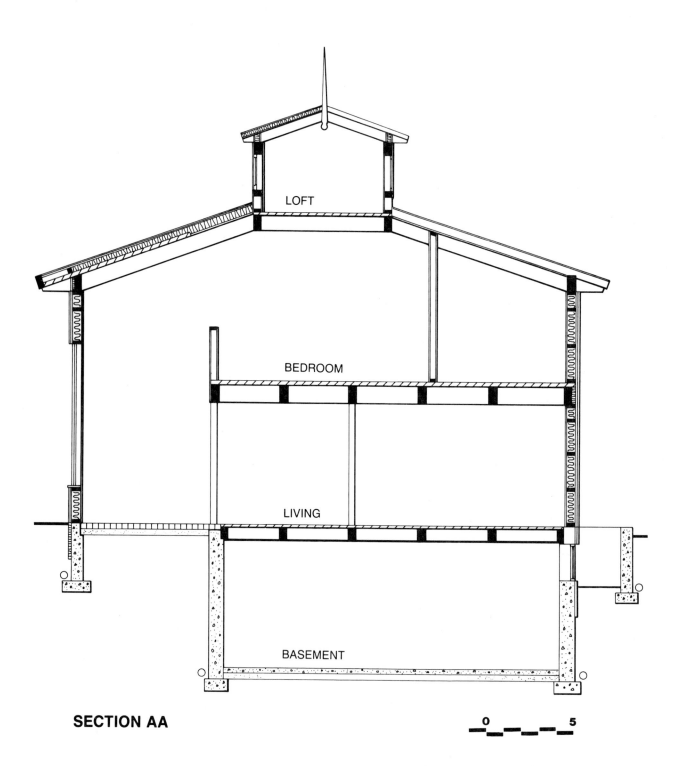

LOFT

BEDROOM

LIVING

BASEMENT

SECTION AA

0 ____ 5

Part V

Appendixes

Appendix A
Sources of Information and Materials

I've designed this last part of my book to provide you with some important specifics that will help you in designing and building your house. The first listing is that of individuals who have a sound track record in low-cost, environmentally sound construction. You'll also find a selection of books, magazines, and catalogs that I have found to be particularly good.

What follows then are several listings of supply sources for building materials that you'll need to construct the panelized post-and-beam houses featured throughout the book. Other materials, equipment, and furnishings that will help you build a high-quality, low-cost, energy-efficient house are also here. These product listings don't include readily available products that are carried by almost any lumberyard or hardware store, but rather sources for good products made by small or foreign companies that are not widely advertised in this country. In a few cases I have included highly desirable foreign products that are not imported to this country. If you're interested in getting any of them, you will either have to import the item yourself, with all the attendant red tape, or coax the manufacturer into importing the item for you.

Architects, Consultants, and Contractors

The usual architect in this country designs commercial buildings and is not interested in houses;

the usual contractor is interested in neither low cost nor energy efficiency. For these reasons, you won't find many conventional architects and contractors in this listing. What you will find is a select group of professionals who have been of great help to my clients.

In choosing any professional for a major project, first make sure that the two of you get along and think along the same lines. That might seem like an obvious suggestion, but you'd be surprised how often people just assume that they'll get along with the architect or contractor they hire. Too often—and too late—they find that their working style, sense of aesthetics, and manner of dealing with people is uncomfortably different. And this difference becomes more apparent as the pressures of budget and time build. And build they will. Once you think you see eye to eye on most matters, check several of his or her completed projects to make sure that the owners of these houses are satisfied with the work that was performed, and with the manner in which it was done.

John Averill
Box 33
Sandstone, WV 25985
A specialist in alternative waste disposal systems, John has done work on owner-built composting toilets for the National Center for Appropriate Technology.

John Barns
414 Abbott
East Lansing, MI 48823
A first-class builder recommended by Don Price.

Kevin Berry Builders
Rt. 2, Box 295
Catskill, NY 12414
Kevin has constructed the majority of the houses
shown in this book. He doesn't travel more than 75
miles and prefers to construct only the shell of a
house.

George Bogosian & Co.
Marlborough, NH 03455
George builds post-and-beam frame houses with
panelized exteriors and also does renovations.

Terry Brennan
Red Wing
RD 4, Box 62
Rome, NY 13440
Terry is a solar design consultant and contractor. He
is one of the top experts in the country on analyzing
cost/benefit ratios for various types of energy-
conserving construction. He is also a contractor, so
he is well versed in practical applications and knows
the actual costs, not the theoretical ones.

Linda Brock
Box 915
Bozeman, MT 59715
One of the winners in the Garden Way Small House
Competition, Linda has also designed another
winning small house for *Better Homes and
Gardens*. She is a top designer.

Doug Elliot
Sunspace Solar Design and Construction
Rt. 2
Worland, WY 82401
Doug retrofits old houses and occasionally builds
new ones. His specialty is sunspace additions.

Bruce Johnson
2528 15th Ave.
San Francisco, CA 94127
Bruce is an architect who has done work on
small, panelized, low-cost houses.

Akira Kawanabe
Alamosa, CO 81101
Akira is an architect who specializes in solar
applications for low-income families.

Keith Krolak
941 E. Polk St.
Morton, IL 61550
Another winner from the Garden Way competition,
Keith has a flair for making a simple house elegant.

Pat Manley
Washington, ME 04574
Pat is a mason who is expert at building Russian
and Finnish fireplaces. He also sells cast-iron
fireplace doors and decorative brickwork. He
constructed two Finnish contraflow fireplaces for
houses featured in this book. He travels widely.

Bruce Osen
818 S. Kanawha St.
Beckley, WV 25801
Bruce entered the most unusual house in the
Garden Way competition; in my opinion, the first-
place winner. His house is a takeoff on Japanese
design with post-and-beam framing, complete with
Japanese soaking tub, composting toilet, and an
integrated solar design.

Don Price
6792 Scio Church Rd.
Ann Arbor, MI 48103
Don has done considerable research on alternate
construction systems, as well as constructing
several post-and-beam houses, one of which has
been widely published.

Harry C. Rustad
1025 Rt. 32
Saugerties, NY 12477
"Rusty" builds insulated doors and staircase/
ladders of tulipwood and cedar. Reasonable prices
for beautiful work.

Woody Schempp
The Passive Solar Homes Co.
272 Newton Ave.
Norwalk, CT 06851
Woody specializes in passive solar design and
construction.

Greg Torchio
Jersey Devil
Box 145
Stockton, NJ 08559
Greg is an architect and a former assistant of mine
who has joined Jersey Devil, a firm that designs and
builds houses in all parts of the country.

Bennie Williams, Sr.
Box 409
Darien, GA 31305
Bennie designs houses for hot climates. He also
does mechanical and structural work.

For other builders, see the listing, Post-and-Beam
Frames and House Packages, that follows.

Books, Periodicals, and Catalogs

Ever-growing volumes of materials are sold by mail.
Rather than wasting time with local stores, many
people prefer to order directly. Books and
periodicals that I think should receive your
attention, but are not readily mentioned elsewhere
in this book, are also included here.

Alternative Sources of Energy
107 S. Central Ave.
Milaca, MN 56353
For those who want to be energy-independent but
still have all of the conveniences of home. A serious
publication for those of us who are concerned about
the coming shortages of energy. Published six times
a year.

Brookstone Tool Catalog
Brookstone Co.
127 Vose Farm Rd.
Peterborough, NH 03458

Building Stone Walls
by John Vivian
Garden Way Publishing, 1976

Building with Stone
by Charles McRaven
Lipencott-Crother, 1980

Build Your Own Stone House
by Karl and Sue Schwenke
Garden Way Publishing, 1975

Heating the Home Water Supply
by Larry Gay
Garden Way Publishing, 1984
Alternate means of heating water without paying the utility companies. Remember that this means you do the work, not the fuel company.

How to Build A Low Cost House of Stone
by Lewis and Sharon Watson
Stonehouse Publications, 1980

The Necessary Catalogue
New Castle, VA 24127
Anyone who has a home with a yard and garden needs to consult this catalog. The people connected with this catalog bill themselves as suppliers and consultants for biological agriculture. They perform soil audits and furnish everything imaginable for ecologically sound gardening. Recommended by John Averill as a source for biological compounds for breaking down human wastes.

Professional Timber Falling, a Procedural Approach
by D. Douglas Dent
Box 905
Beaverton, OR 97005
Privately published by the author
For those who may wish to cut their own timber, this book is a must. The book dwells heavily on safety procedures and techniques for harvesting timber to make sure that none is wasted.

Solar Catalog
Solar Components Corp.
Box 237
Manchester, NH 03105
This is an offshoot of the Kalwall Corporation. The catalog serves as a relatively complete source book for commonly used solar components.

The Solar Wonderbook
Energy Sciences
832 Rockville Pike
Rockville, MD 20852
This is a catalog of 12-volt power—photovoltaic cells and devices that can be used with them. If you are a long way from power lines, this catalog may help.

Stone Masonry
by Ken Kern and Steve Magers
Owner-Builder Publications, 1976

Stone Shelters
by Edward Allen
MIT Press, 1969

The Warming Trend
Box 1184
Manchester Center, VT 05255
An entire catalog of energy-saving devices and related goods. Many worthwhile items that are not usually available in retail stores.

Insulation Systems for Foundations and Masonry Walls

To take advantage of the thermal mass of masonry and to protect the masonry wall from the effects of freezing and thawing, insulation should always be placed on the outside surface, rather than the easier inside surface, of the wall. There are several systems now on the market, all imported from Europe, that do this job well. Most of these systems use a reinforced cement-base coating applied to an extruded polystyrene insulation board that adheres to the foundation wall. *Caution:* These systems have been known to hide termite infestations. Many lending agencies will require that you treat the ground around the house with a chemical to prevent termite infestation. If you do not treat the soil, run a termite shield through the wall at sill level to prevent hidden infestations.

Drivit
1 Energy Way
Box 1014
W. Warwick, RI 02983
The most common of the systems and the one that will be familiar to most masons. Unfortunately, the system is franchised to large contractors and will not be practical unless you have a large area such as an entire masonry building. For renovation work, these people do a fine job, but they are too expensive for foundation insulation.

Insulcrete
Cubic Structures, Inc.
4311 Triangle St.
McFarland, WI 53558
An American competitor to the imported systems. It does not appear to be quite as flexible, but the material is economical and readily available.

Insul-Guard
Trend Products
Box 327
Waupaca, WI 54981
Fiberglass rigid panels to protect foundation insulation. The panels have an L-shaped top configuration to cover the exposed edge of insulation board. This is ideal for renovations where the insulation cannot be installed flush with the wall above.

Plekko-Therm
Kern-Tac, Inc.
4421 Orchard St.
Tacoma, WA 98466
and
Super Steel Stud
4–57 26th Ave.
New York, NY 11102
Like Drivit, Plekko is an additive that is mixed fifty-fifty with portland cement to create a strong, flexible adhesive coating. All these systems are reinforced by a fiberglass mesh that is treated with an alkali-resistant coating. Do not use ordinary fiberglass mesh, because it will deteriorate quickly. Plekko is distributed by Kern-Tac and Super Steel Stud.

Rhodipor (Thorowall)
Standard Dry Wall Products
7800 N.W. 38th St.
Miami, FL 33166
Another well-known European import, this consists of an insulating plaster with a synthetic stucco top coat similar to the preceding products. This is a less expensive system that provides about half the insulating value of the other methods listed.

STO
STO Energy Conservation, Inc.
Box 219
Rutland, VT 04701
Another imported product, this one is a nonmasonry-based premixed stucco. Again, the material is reinforced with fiberglass mesh, but untreated mesh can be used. This is an extremely flexible, highly waterproof material that bonds to almost everything. You can literally wrap an entire building in the stuff. Expensive, but top quality. Again, the system is only available through franchised installers.

Post-and-Beam Frames and House Packages

Several companies now offer packages of post-and-beam frames with panelized exterior wall systems. Usually the firms offer either the frame alone or a complete package. All offer either hardwood or softwood frames.

American Restoration Trades
Box 255
Danville, OH 43014
This company offers high-quality, well-designed post-and-beam frames, frequently of recycled old timbers. Roy Tiede, the proprietor, also mills oak tongue-and-groove flooring specially made for exposed plank-and-beam ceilings. He is also a source for 1×7-inch cypress siding. Roy uses only oak for his frames.

Essex Timber Frames
Essex, NY 12936
Bob Dakin builds braced timber frames of hardwood and softwood and travels extensively. He has constructed many of my frames in various parts of the country.

Kaatskill Post and Beam
(formerly Woodstock Barn Homes)
Zabel Hill Rd., Box 128A
Feura Bush, NY 12067
Kaatskill offers a wide range of sizes and styles. Packages of Neilsen-Winter panels are available for walls and roof.

Riverbend Timber Framing, Inc.
Box 26
Blissfield, MI 49228
Another early mover in the panelized post-and-beam trend. Excellent house designs at reasonable prices. Emphasis is on passive solar designs.

Sawmill River Post and Beam
Box 227
Leverett, MA 01054
Excellent floor plans for a small house. Frames are fabricated on a water-powered sawmill. Wall and roof panels by Neilsen-Winter are also available for these houses.

Vermont Frames
Box 100
Hinesburg, VT 05461
Peter McNaull of Vermont Frames has been instrumental in the development of panelized post-and-beam houses. Peter furnished wall panels for some of the houses shown in this book and constructed the frame for the Binger house.

Concrete and Masonry Specialty Products

Various methods have been devised to make concrete walls lighter and provide insulation within the wall. Surface finishes are also a constant problem, and various molds and pattern-making devices can help provide a solution.

Forton
518 Academy Ave.
Sewickley, PA 15143
Forton manufactures a glass fiber–reinforced, polymer-modified cement that can be economically fabricated into building panels. This is a Dutch company that has recently introduced the system to the United States. The material shows great promise for facing for insulated building panels such as those we use to enclose post-and-beam houses.

Precision Stamped Concrete Tools
562 S. Greenwood Ave.
Montebello, CA 90640
and
Lasting Impressions in Concrete, Inc.
9900 San Fernando Rd.
Pacoima, CA 91331
Both companies market floor pattern tools for embossing various tile patterns in a poured concrete floor. If a pigmented concrete is also used, this results in an inexpensive, good-looking concrete floor without the time or expense of a layer of tile.

Scott System, Inc.

4575 Joliet St.
Denver, CO 80239

Scott uses a system of 2-inch-thick concrete panels with a textured 1- by 3-foot exposed face to construct a cavity wall that is then pumped full of urethane foam. The molds for the panels are available either for rent or purchase from the manufacturer. A wide choice of face patterns is available. Without the benefits of mass production, the system is relatively expensive; this is an ideal construction method for do-it-yourselfers, however.

Standard Dry Wall Products

7800 N.W. 38th St.
Miami, FL 33166

Standard Dry Wall makes Thermocurve, an undulating Styrofoam (polystyrene) insulation board that is cast into place in a concrete wall to provide insulation. The curved shape, along with dimples on the face, holds the insulation in the center of the wall while the concrete is poured. By using this insulation board, no expensive external insulation systems are required for the wall. It is one of the most effective and least expensive methods for insulating poured concrete walls.

Stramit International

Yaxley, EYE
Sufold, England 1P23 8 BW

While not technically masonry, Stramit's building panels are used in similar fashion to masonry panels, so I have included them here. Stramit presses ground straw in molds at a high temperature to produce a dense, masonrylike building material with excellent insulating qualities. Five tons of straw are required to make a typical house.

Stressed-Skin Building Panels

Stressed-skin building panels are usually made with a polystyrene or polyurethane foam core with laminated faces of Sheetrock and particle board or plywood. Polystyrene cores are usually high-density, expanded polystyrene (EPS); that is, made from pellets compressed together. Extruded polystyrene (blueboard) can also be used, but is rare because of the limited range of thicknesses that are readily available. Before purchasing foam or fabricated panels, check carefully for the insulating value of the installed material. A complete directory of EPS distributors is available from The Society of the Plastics Industry, Inc., 3150 Des Plaines Ave., Des Plaines, IL 60018. A listing of those companies with which I am familiar is included below. Upjohn and Mobay Chemical Divisions of Pittsburgh Plate Glass Industries are the two principal raw material suppliers for polyurethane foam. Dow Chemical makes extruded polystyrene that is available at commercial lumberyards.

Raw Materials Suppliers

Avilite Industries

Box 367
Marlborough, NH 03455

Big Sky Insulations Unlimited

Box 838
Belgrade Industrial Park
Belgrade, MT 59714

Contour Packaging Inc.

8930 Rosehill Rd.
Box 5337
Lenexa, KS 66215

Elliott Company

9200 Zionsville Rd.
Indianapolis, IN 46268

Foam Plastics of New England

Rt. 69
Prospect, CT 06712   *2" EPS Not a Dealer*

French Creek Products

Reading RR Plaza, First Ave.
Royersford, PA 19464

French Creek is a full-line supplier of foams and adhesives.

Adhesives

The adhesive of choice is 3M Mastic Adhesive 4289. 3M Fastbond 30 can also be used, but needs two coats, and drying time. Both are readily available from 3M dealers.

Isoset

Ashland Chemical Co.
Box 2219
Columbus, OH 43218

Isoset is a urethane-type adhesive for structural purposes.

Mor-Ad 336

Morton Chemical Co.
110 N. Wacker Dr.
Chicago, IL 60606

Mor-Ad is a urethane laminating adhesive approved by ICBO as a structural adhesive.

Panel Suppliers

Most of the panel suppliers in this list make foam-cored panels by gluing Sheetrock and waferboard or plywood to the core with a variety of adhesives. The Neilsen-Winter panels are an exception—they are fabricated with a foamed-in-place polyurethane core. The core is self-bonding. David Howard is the sole manufacturer to use extruded polystyrene, and his panels have no outer skin. They are fabricated by laminating 2-inch and 1½-inch layers of blueboard together to make long horizontal panels. Two by sixes are inserted into the outer layer of blueboard at 2-foot intervals to give the panels strength. Patents are pending for this novel system.

Atlas Industries

(formerly ICP, Inc.)
6 Willows Rd.
Ayer, MA 01432

Atlas also supplies raw materials.

Chase Panels

16608 W. Rogers
New Berlin, WI 53151

David Howard
Box 295
Alstead, NH 03602

Delta Industries, Inc.
Galasie St.
Columbus, OH 43207

Drew Foam of Colorado, Inc.
1450 W. Colfax Ave.
Denver, CO 80204
Drew also supplies raw materials.

J-Deck, Inc.
2587 Harrison Rd.
Columbus, OH 43204

Neilsen-Winter
Main St.
West Groton, MA 01474

NRG Barriers, Inc.
61 Emory St.
Sanford, ME 04073
NRG also supplies raw materials.

324-7745

Riverbend Timber Framing, Inc.
Box 26
Blissfield, MI 49228

Texcon Products, Inc.
2301 Commerce St.
Houston, TX 77002

Vermont Laminates, Inc.
Box 102
Hinesburg, VT 05461

Soil Additives

For construction in remote areas, it is frequently difficult to transport masonry materials or machinery. There are products that can be used for stabilizing earth for use as a construction material.

Pecks' Products, Inc.
945 Sunset Dr.
Costa Mesa, CA 92627
Pecks manufactures a variety of useful materials for this purpose. Geo Tec C-50 can be added to native soils to make roadways, walks, or bricks and blocks. The manufacturer claims that any type of soil or water can be used. The C-50 compound is a liquid that is diluted with water and applied to tilled soil. Pecks also markets a full line of waterproofing compounds.

Vapor Barriers and Moistureproofing

Attempts to tighten construction by conventional techniques have resulted in widespread disaster stories. If you are renovating an old house or building a new one using conventional construction techniques, make sure that you provide a good vapor barrier on the *warm side* of the insulation. Don't let any well-meaning, uninformed carpenter or "old-timer" tell you "the house has to breathe." It does have to breathe, but it must do it from outside. Warm, moist air from the house proper must be kept out of your insulation. The January 1984 issue of

Solar Age magazine has several excellent articles addressing the problems of moisture in tightly insulated houses.

Vapor barriers should be as nearly continuous as possible. Use 6-mil polyethylene or one of the new high-density vapor barriers.

Super Sampson Poly Vapor Barrier
Poly Plastic and Design Corp.
Springfield, OH 45501
and

Tu-Tuf Poly Vapor Barrier
Sto-Cote Products
Richmond, IL 60071
Both of these companies offer high-density vapor barriers. Joints in the vapor barrier must be lapped a minimum of 2 inches and sealed.

Tremco Acoustical Sealant
Tremco Co.
1130 Hwy. 202
Raritan, NJ 08869
This adhesive is used to seal the joints in the vapor barrier. If you are ordering this sealant, you should also order a case of Mono caulking for use throughout your house.

Tyvek
Spunbonded Products Div.
Du Pont Co.
Center Rd. Building
Wilmington, DE 19898
An exterior air barrier that breathes moisture, but will not admit air or water. Excellent for remodelings or new houses with fiberglass insulation. This is a fine, temporary waterproof covering for walls or roof. This product is beginning to be available at retail lumberyards.

Air/Vapor Barriers for Electrical Boxes

The most likely break in your vapor barrier is at electrical boxes. Do not use recessed ceiling outlets or fans. Minimize all other electrical devices on exterior walls. If you must have outlets in outside walls, use special plastic vapor boxes by Mold Processors Ltd.

Energy Conservation Equipment Co.
Box 161
Worcester, VT 05682
This company distributes Mold Processors' vapor boxes. These boxes enclose a standard outlet box and make sealing the wires and vapor barrier easy.

Air Vents

Roof cavities should be carefully ventilated. Shed-type roofs can pose a problem and may require special ventilating flashings for shed roofs abutting vertical walls.

Cor-a-vent
16250 Petro Dr.
Mishawaka, IN 46544
A good-looking, extruded polyethylene vent cap for gable roofs. Maintains uniform roof appearance without the usual projecting profile.

H. C. Products Co.
Box 68
Princeville, IL 61559
This company has shed-roof flashings available.

Vapor-Resistant Paint

While not a substitute for a good vapor barrier, two coats of a good vapor-retarding paint such as Glidden Insulaid (available at most Glidden dealers) will considerably slow the movement of vapor through the walls. This paint is a good layer of extra protection in new construction and may be the only possible solution for existing houses.

Thermo-Paint
Enterprise Co.
1191 S. Wheeling Rd.
Wheeling, IL 60090

Skylights

Skylights add light and warmth to interiors and can be obtained in a wide variety of sizes, both fixed and operable. For an economical fixed skylight, a sheet of ⅝-inch, tempered, insulating sliding-door glass can be glazed right into the roof. Detailed plans are available from Charles Haynes (see order blank in Appendix C). Excellent instructions for this type of glazing are also given in Issue No. 18 of *Fine Homebuilding* magazine. Commercial skylights vary greatly in price, quality, and features. Most are obtrusive and project above the roof; many are of an ugly bubble-dome configuration. For a nonventilating skylight, the flush, glazed, tempered-glass unit is your best buy.

Fox Lites
Fox Marketing, Inc.
Skylight Div.
4518 Taylorsville Rd.
Dayton, OH 45424
Of the commercially available fixed skylights, this one is the best buy for the money and one that I have used. It is triple glazed and molded in one piece with no moldings or gaskets to leak. It is anchored from inside, so no one can take out a few screws and break into your house. If you live in a very cold climate, the triple glazing is recommended; the glazing also has an ultraviolet barrier.

Insula-Dome Skylights
80 Horseblock Rd.
Yaphank, NY 11980
This company offers fixed and ventilating skylights made of high-quality materials, and at a moderate price.

Thermalized Skywindow
Wasco Products, Inc.
Pioneer Ave., Box 351
Sanford, ME 04073
Wasco is the originator of modern skylights. They are available in glass and plastic, fixed and ventilating, and prices are moderate.

Velux
Velux America
155 West St.
Wilmington, MA 01887
Velux is the imported standard of quality for operable skylights. Velux makes double- and triple-insulated glass units with a wide variety of shades, shutters, and tints. These skylights are top quality at top price.

Sloping Glass

Tilting glazing so that it is normal to the angle of the sun's rays (about 55 to 60 degrees in the northern United States) considerably increases the amount of heat transferred to your house by the sun. It is quite elegant and, if properly executed, can function very well. If adequate heat storage is not provided, heat will be reradiated or vented and lost. You are now building a roof, not a wall; it must be completely watertight. Considerable criticism has been published on sloping glass, written largely by those who have made mistakes. Rather than try to see where they went wrong, they senselessly attack the concept of sloping glass.

Glazing material should always be installed on top of your framing members, never between them; that's a guaranteed leak situation. Glass can be installed directly over the framing members; use Tremco glazing tape on both faces of the glass and cover with redwood or cedar battens fastened with stainless steel or brass screws. Follow the details shown in the working drawings in Appendix B. If the glass is more than one panel high, use an aluminum H-channel, ¾ inch wide. This must usually be special-ordered by a glass dealer.

Thermal storage of sufficient size to absorb the sun's heat is vital if sloped glass is to perform properly. Ideally, the mass should be located between the house and a sunspace that has the sloped glass. Masonry and water are the two traditional choices for thermal storage. Phase-change salts are encapsulated in containers and take up much less space than masonry or water. They are still fairly expensive.

Abundant Energy, Inc.
116 Newport Bridge Rd.
Warwick, NY 10990
I recommend this company's ready-made metal-gasketed system for installing glazing. It is of high quality and reasonable price, and is easy to install.

Boardman Energy Systems, Inc.
Box 4299
Wilmington, DE 19807
and

Enerphase
(a div. of Dow Chemical Co.)
Box 1206
Midland, MI 48640
Both of these companies market phase-change materials.

C. R. Laurence Co., Inc.
1501 Ton Rd.
Elk Grove Village, IL 60007
C. R. Laurence stocks the ¾-inch H-channels. The company has additional warehouses in Los Angeles, Dallas, and Atlanta. The H-channel is a very important item, well worth ordering. Without it, it is virtually impossible to construct a leakproof mullion.

Heating Systems

Up-to-date furnaces don't require big chimneys to waste heat these days. Reputable manufacturers have redesigned their units so that they burn more efficiently and condense their waste heat instead of discharging it. Most of these units just require a small pipe through the wall for discharging a bit of water. The pipe doesn't even get hot.

Condensing Furnaces

Amana
Amana, IA 52204

Arkala Industries, Inc.
Box 534
Evansville, IN 44704

Clare Brothers, Ltd.
223 King St.
Cambridge, ON N3H 4T5

Magic Chef
851 Third Ave.
Columbus, OH 43212

Condensing Boilers

Hydrotherm
Rockland Ave.
Northvale, NJ 07647

Weil-McLain
Blaine St.
Michigan City, IN 46360

Stoves and Accessories

Vermont Castings' Vigilant stove, which can burn coal or wood, is my pick of the domestics. The entire Jøtul line is well designed and finely crafted, but a bit overpriced. For cooking and heating here are my favorites.

Chill Chaser
Turbonics
11200 Madison Ave.
Cleveland, OH 44102
I recommend this for remote rooms. Hook it up to a source of hot water and a small pump and you have an extra heating circuit.

Findlay Oval
Elmira Stove Works
22 Church St., W
Elmira, ON N3B 1M3
Fine-quality, expensive re-creation of the famous original. Cast-iron, airtight, with many options. This stove is primarily for cooking, but has a 50,000-Btu output, enough for most houses.

Pro-Former Z
Pro-Former Engineering Corp.
14 Hanover St.
Hanover, MA 02339
and
Rupert Grover, Inc.
Fireline Products
147 Portland St.
Fryeburg, ME 04037
Both companies market waterbacks for wood stoves. Pro-Former also markets pumps, controls, and all accessories to hook up the waterback. The Pro-Former Z is marketed in Canada under the name Canadian Thermal Water Jacket.

Ram Stove
Ram Dis Ticaret A.S.
Istanbul, Turkey
High-quality, Turkish, reasonably priced coal/wood stove for cooking and heating. Enameled cast iron with lift-up cover for cook top. Approximate heat output—25,000 Btu.

Sotz, Inc.
13639 Station Rd.
Columbia Station, OH 44028
For those on a low budget, I heartily recommend Sotz's barrel stove kits. Sotz also carries a full line of stove accessories including Corning catalytic combustors.

Heat Exchangers

Heat exchangers are absolutely essential for a tight house in a very cold climate; hence, there are several Canadian makes.

Air Charger
34 King St.
Toronto, ON M5A 1K8

Berner, Inc.
12 Sixth Rd.
Woburn, MA 01801

Conservation Energy System
Box 8280
Saskatoon, SK S7K 6C6

Des Champs Laboratories
Box 348
East Hanover, NJ 07936

Ener-Corp Management Ltd.
2 Donald St.
Winnipeg, MN R3L 0K5

Family Homes Cooperative ✗ Kit
P.O. Box C
Lanark, WV 25866

Memphremagog Heat Exchangers
Box 456
Newport, VT 05855

Mitsubishi Electric Sales America ✗
3030 E. Victoria St.
Compton, CA 90221

Water Heaters

Fuel for heating water can consume up to one-third of home energy costs, so these fuel savers are important. They use gas unless noted.

Instantaneous

Heats water only when the faucet is turned on. Originally developed in the United States, but now most units are imported. Available in gas and electric models. Gas is preferable because it is much cheaper per Btu.

Instant-Flow
Cronomite Laboratories
21011 S. Figueroa
Carson, CA 90745
This heater is available in an electric model only.

Junkers
Walter Bosch Corp.
Box 4601
North Suburban, IL 60196
A high-priced heater of good, German quality.

Little Giant
Little Giant Manufacturing Co., Inc.
Box 518
Orange, TX 77630
This heater comes in gas and electric models.

Paloma
Paloma Industries, Inc.
241 James St.
Bensonville, IL 60106
The leading Japanese contender.

Thorn
Tankless Heater Corp.
20 Melrose Ave.
Greenwich, CT 06830
A British heater, it comes in gas and electric models.

Wood-Fired

Aquaheater
Anchor Tools and Woodstoves, Inc.
618 N.W. Davis
Portland, OR 97209
Good for solar backup heater, hot tub heater, or domestic hot water in remote areas.

Solar Batch Heaters

After a period of virtual absence from the market, there is a sudden flood of these simple, potentially inexpensive heaters. Batch heaters have the storage capacity mounted right on the roof, integral with the collector. Some are designed to be built flush with the roof. Check to make sure that your roof is strong enough; they are heavy.

In my selection of the following heaters, reasonable price was the prime consideration. All of these heaters cost less than $1500. If the price of a water heater is much more than that figure, you would be better off using an instantaneous-type heater. If first cost is a consideration, an electric instantaneous heater is your best bet.

Conservation Concepts, Inc.
484 Middletown Rd.
Hummelstown, PA 17036
This heater holds 50 gallons and is available as a kit.

Cornell Energy, Inc.
4175 S. Fremont Ave.
Tucson, AZ 85714
The heater is a 32-gallon tank enclosed in an insulated reflective box that is set on the roof.

Nature's Way Energy Systems
P.O. Route 8
Old Homestead Hwy.
Keene, NH 03431
The collector is attached directly to the tank. It is designed to be mounted within the roof structure and has a 36-gallon capacity.

Environment One Corp.
2773 Balltown Rd.
Schenectady, NY 12309
A thermosiphon-type heater with a 40-gallon storage tank. This company has a fine reputation and is one of my favorites.

Hasco
Hasco Solar Industries
214–22 14th Ave.
Bayside, NY 11360
This award-winning Israeli heater has a 35-gallon capacity, but it is poorly insulated and cools rapidly at night in cold climates.

Hitachi Chemical Co. Ltd.
437 Madison Ave.
New York, NY 10022
This is a very low-cost heater. It has a 55-gallon integral collector and storage. See Chapter 5 for a photograph of the unit.

Nature's Way Energy Systems
Rt. 8, Old Hempstead Highway
Keene, NH 03431
A 40-gallon unit designed for flush installation with the roof of the house. Manual insulating shutters cover the tank at night. (These can be automated at extra cost.)

Prime Energy Products, Inc.
7669 Washington Ave. S.
Edina, MN 55435
A low-cost unit for vacation houses; it must be drained in winter. The unit has a 30-gallon capacity.

Solcoor, Inc.
849 S. Broadway, Suite 208
Los Angeles, CA 90014
A top-selling Israeli heater. It has only a 28-gallon capacity, but has a highly efficient collector and insulation.

TEF Manufacturing
1550 N. Clark
Fresno, CA 93703
A 40-gallon-capacity unit with a very cleverly designed, foolproof sliding shutter arrangement to insulate the tank at night.

Yazaki Sola-Ace Solar Water Heater

American Yazaki Corp.
32700 Capitol
Livonia, MI 48150
A heater of highly efficient Japanese design, with 50-gallon storage capacity and a stainless steel collector.

Owner-Built Collectors

Commercial active hot-water systems are typically priced at $3000 to $4000 installed. If glazing is built right into the building shell, such as in the Knopf house, it is possible to install a fine system for around $1000; less if you do the work yourself. The well-known product, Solaroll, can be fabricated into a collector quite easily. Although the collector is not quite as efficient as a metal one, there are none of the problems with stress cracking and the like that have plagued metal collectors. Stainless steel makes for very durable collectors, but those are usually imported from Japan. Since the Solaroll collector is inside the envelope of the house where it can't freeze, no antifreeze solution or heat exchanger is required. A simple insulated tank is all that is needed for storage.

Metalplate Galvanizing-Jacksonville, Inc.

Box 2368
Jacksonville, FL 32203
This company specializes in solar hot-water storage tanks ranging in size from 30 to 1500 gallons.

Windows and Window Insulation Systems

Once you have thoroughly insulated and sealed your house, you are faced with the windows as your major source of heat loss or gain. Ideally, the windows should have maximum gain on cold, sunlit days, with minimal losses at night. Triple and quadruple glazing is very expensive and still does only a moderate insulating job. Various systems of insulating shutters and shades have been devised to allow the insulating value of the windows to be changed to meet heat flow conditions. The best, most cost-effective window insulating system for my money is a Thermax-type insulating board panel covered with fabric, which is simply set into the window cavity at night. Roll-type shades are also a solution for insulating windows, although they don't seal as well as shutters.

Aerius Design Group

RFD 1, Box 394B
Kingston, NY 12401
Aerius produces a fine kit of adhesives, foam edge strips, and detailed instructions for making insulating panels. Clever people can make their own, but one of these kits will start you on your way with no hassles.

Beckhoff Gesellschaft

Messingstrabe 16
Postfach 1126
D-4837 Verl 1
West Germany
Beckhoff Gesellschaft offers a foam-insulated, aluminum rolling exterior shutter.

Halu-Rollscreen

2340 Gold River Rd.
Rancho Cordova, CA 95670
This company makes exterior rolling shutters for security as well as energy savings.

ÖLSS

2352 Market St. Dr.
Portland, OR 97201
This company makes magnetic stainless steel strips for holding fabrics to window frames.

Solaroll Shade and Shutter Corp.

915 S. Dixie Highway E.
Pompano Beach, FL 33060
Solaroll makes high-quality exterior shades at moderate prices.

Solar Systems Design

RD 1, Box 426A
Voorheesville, NY 12186
This company markets a kit for use with Thermax-type board. This kit consists of plastic framing extrusions, weatherstripping, and plastic hinges for making bifold shutters. This is one of the best solutions for window insulation that I have seen. An extra track is provided on the framing extrusion for a solid facing material if desired.

SRC Solar Roller Corp.

709 Spruce St.
Aspen, CO 81611
The company makes heavy-duty rollers with a built-in motor, and you make your own shades. The cost for the rollers is low.

Sunflake

P.O. Box 28
Bayfield, CO 81122
Sunflake markets windows with built-in sliding insulating shutters. The shutters are arranged so they slide into a pocket in the wall next to the window, eliminating problems of storage for the insulating panels. The windows are single glazed with optional removable double-glazed panels. These windows are available in a wide variety of awning, fixed, and casement types at reasonable prices.

Solar Radiation Films

Reflective films can be applied to the inside of glass areas and to the structure itself to control solar radiation gain. This is usually done in hot climates or to correct excessive areas of improperly shaded south-facing glass. Sometimes you may have a view to the south or west that results in problem glass areas; these films can be the answer.

Energy Control Products/3M

220–8E 3M Center
St. Paul, MN 55144
This company markets Scotchtint Sun Control Film, which reduces solar heat transmission, glare, and ultraviolet transmission.

Gila River Products, Inc.
6615 W. Boxton St.
Chandler, AZ 85224
Gila River Products markets similar films with multiple coatings that reduce the heat transmission even more than the 3M product.

Parsec, Inc.
Box 38534
Dallas, TX 75238
Parsec makes a nontransparent foil film for roof insulation in southern climates. The material is installed under the roof sheathing to reflect the sun's heat. Its effectiveness in northern climates has not been tested.

Lumber Mills

Rather than pay for commercial lumber companies to mill and transport lumber across the country, many homeowners are cutting their own timber into lumber.

Granberg Alaska Mark III
Granberg Industries, Inc.
200 S. Garrard Blvd.
Richmond, CA 94804
The old standby lumber maker. To use this mill, you need a good, heavy-duty chain saw equipped with a ripping chain and auxiliary oiler. Finished lumber is serviceable, but accuracy can vary.

Mobile Dimension Saw
Mobile Manufacturing Co.
Troutdale, OR 97060
The industry standard in portable sawmills. A bit expensive, but the company will furnish an owners' list if you want to hire someone to come to your property to mill lumber. Several of my clients have used this machine; all rave about its performance. The carriage for the machine comes in sections; it can make very long cuts.

Wood Mizer Band Mill
Dupli-Carver
4004 W. 10th St.
Indianapolis, IN 46222
An inexpensive portable mill that runs along a carriage. Smooth, accurate cuts are obtained. The unit is relatively lightweight, so I question long-term durability.

Hardware

Unless you pay a great deal of money and special-order from a commercial hardware firm, most readily available commercial hardware, so-called builders hardware, is of mediocre quality. Schlage and Russwin are two quality manufacturers.

Baldwin Hardware Manufacturing Corp.
841 Wyomissing Blvd., Box 82
Reading, PA 19603
Baldwin offers museum-quality, surface-mounted locksets.

Sturbridge Yankee Workshop
Brimfield Tnpk.
Sturbridge, MA 01566
Sturbridge has reasonably priced authentic reproductions of surface hinges and cabinet hardware.

Water-Saving Toilets

Water shortages have brought forth a wide variety of water-saving toilets.

Carousel
Enviroscope Corp.
711 W. 17th St. F8
Costa Mesa, CA 92627
A composting toilet that uses no water at all, although it does require a small amount of electricity. This unit has been the most successful one for my clients who have tried composting toilets.

IFÖ Sanitar AB
Western Builders Co-Op
2150 Pine Dr.
Prescott, AZ 86301
A top-quality china fixture, but expensive.

Nepon, Inc.
John Averill
Box 33
Sandstone, WV 25985
A china toilet that uses a chemical foam and air compressor that mixes with 1 cup of water per flush.

Royal Flush-o-matic
Sanitation Equipment Ltd.
1081 Alness St.
Downsview, ON M3J 2J1
The Royal unit is made of plastic but priced competitively with conventional toilets.

Seiche One
Patrick Creet Corp.
Box 135
Hinesburg, VT 05461
Another moderately priced plastic toilet in the 1 quart-or-less water category.

Japanese Furnishings

The Japanese make much better use of space than Americans do by utilizing sliding screens and portable furniture. These furnishings are hard to find in the United States, but well worth the look. Shoji sliding screens are usually very expensive.

Blue Horizons
1716 Ocean Ave., Box 123
San Francisco, CA 94112
Blue Horizons offers Shoji sliding screen kits.

Miya Shoji & Interiors, Inc.
107 W. 17th St.
New York, NY 10011
This company offers ready-made Shoji screens.

Woodworks
William Brouwer
9 Montague St.
Cambridge, MA 02139
Brouwer was the cabinetmaker for the legendary Shinera and makes bed frames for futons, tables, stools, and other items at reasonable prices. My bed from Shinera is one of my most prized possessions.

Appendix B
Working Drawings

The working drawings on the following pages include two sets of floor plans and two sets of elevations for the Civic house. These plans and elevations are completely interchangeable; either roof design can be combined with either set of floor plans. Between them, the two sets of plans offer complete flexibility of site and entrance placement. Since both designs are square in plan, they can be reversed or turned at will to fit your site. The shed-roofed version of the house is designed to have the high side of the roof faced south, but the gable-roofed house can be faced in any direction that the site may dictate. If possible, locate as many windows as you can on the south and eliminate unnecessary north-facing windows. My suggested window layout assumes a southern orientation for the house. Using this layout as a guide, try for a similar orientation of windows if you rotate the house.

Plans, but not complete working drawings, are also shown for Bob Dakin's Japanese house. This story-and-a-half house is designed on an 8-foot-square structural grid so that it can use lightweight, delicate members in Japanese tradition. Sliding screens placed at the grid lines allow for great flexibility of interior space.

All plans are available reproduced on 17 × 22-inch blackline print paper. See the order blank in Appendix C.

These plans are exempted from the copyright of this book and may be freely reproduced. In return, the author and publisher are absolved from any liability in conjunction with their use.

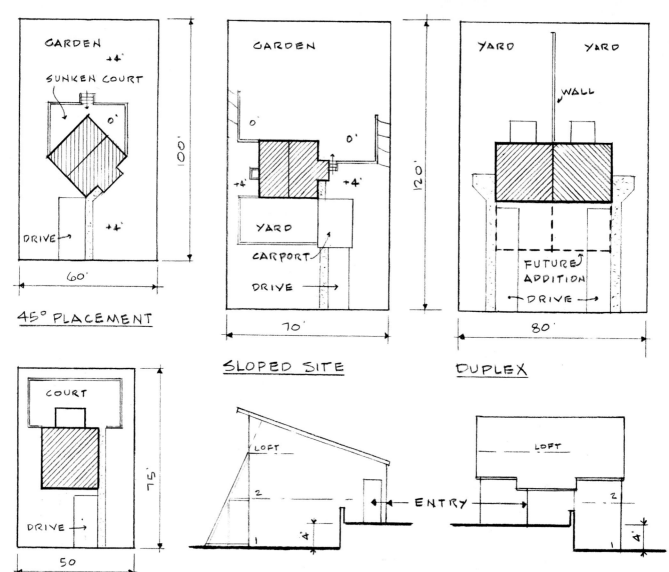

45° PLACEMENT

SLOPED SITE

DUPLEX

MINIMUM LOT

SHED ROOF

GABLE ROOF

SECTIONS THRU SLOPED SITES

(NORTH SIDE OF HOUSES IS SHOWN FACING STREET)

SUGGESTED SITE PLANS

SCALE 1" = 40'·0"

▥	INSULATED PANEL
▨	STUD WALL
▤	RIGID INSULATION
– –	SHELF OR CABINET ABOVE
₵	CENTER LINE
○50W	ELEC. FIXTURE (INC.)
⊏20W⊐	ELEC. FIXTURE (FLOUR)
⊕ –	SINGLE POLE SWITCH
⊕³ –	3-WAY SWITCH
⊖	DUPLEX OUTLET
⊖GFI	GROUND FAULT OUTLET
⊙	FLOOR OUTLET OR 220V
Ⓜ	SPEC. CONNECTION (MOTOR)
○SD	SMOKE DETECTOR

LEGEND FOR PLANS

GENERAL NOTES

THESE HOUSES ARE DESIGNED FOR 40 PSF FLOOR LOADS AND 50 PSF SNOW LOADS. FOUNDATIONS ARE DESIGNED FOR 3,000 PSF SOIL BEARING. FOR UNUSUAL CONDITIONS, SUCH AS CLAY SOILS, HEAVY WINDS AND EARTHQUAKE ZONES, A LOCAL PROFESSIONAL SHOULD BE CONSULTED. THESE PLANS ARE EXEMPTED FROM THE COPYRIGHT OF THIS BOOK AND MAY BE FREELY MODIFIED.

- BEDROOMS HAVE BEEN SHOWN ON FIRST FLOOR FOR SAFETY AND COOLER TEMPERATURES. FLOOR LAYOUTS MAY BE REVERSED IF DESIRED. SEE CHAPTER 14 FOR LAYOUT WITH BEDROOMS ON SECOND FLOOR.
- POST & BEAM FRAMING AND WALL PANELS ALLOW COMPLETE FLEXIBILITY IN WINDOW, DOOR AND PARTITION PLACEMENT. SINCE ALL LOADS ARE CARRIED BY FRAME, OTHER ELEMENTS CAN BE REARRANGED AT WILL.

1

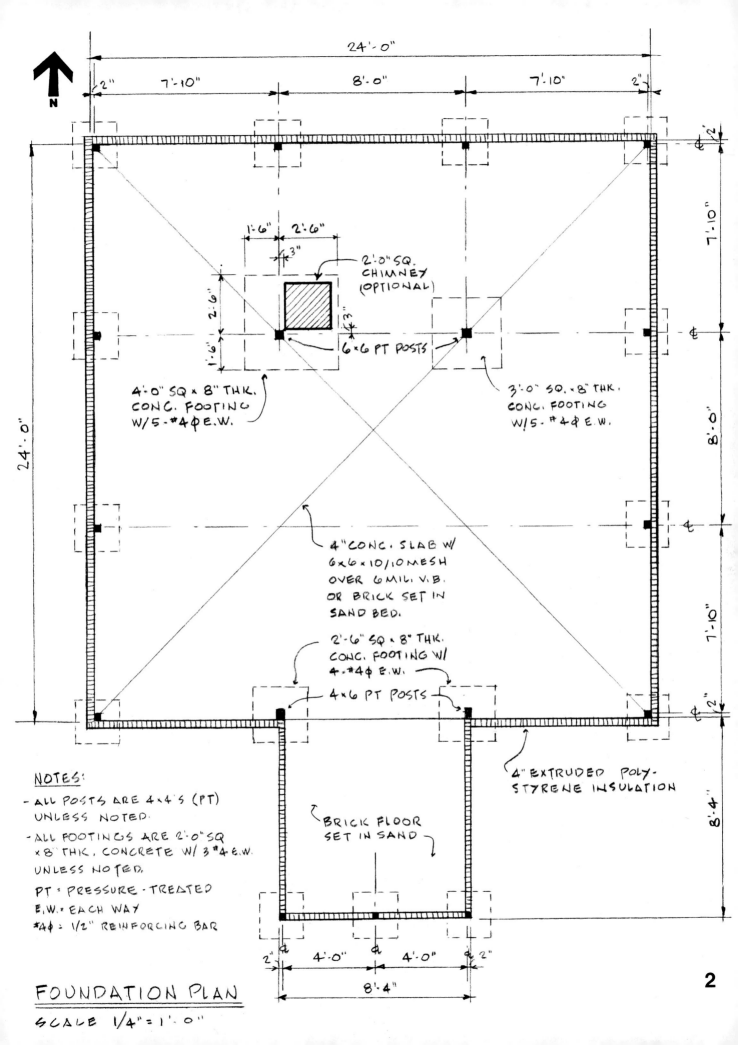

N

24'-0"

2" 7'-10" 8'-0" 7'-10" 2"

2"
7'-10"
8'-0"
7'-10"
8'-4"

24'-0"

1'-6" 2'-6"
3"

2'-6"
3"
2'-6"
1'-6"

2'-0" SQ.
CHIMNEY
(OPTIONAL)

6×6 PT POSTS

4'-0" SQ × 8" THK.
CONC. FOOTING
W/ 5-#4∅ E.W.

3'-0" SQ. × 8" THK.
CONC. FOOTING
W/ 5-#4∅ E.W.

4" CONC. SLAB W/
6×6×10/10 MESH
OVER 6 MIL V.B.
OR BRICK SET IN
SAND BED.

2'-6" SQ × 8" THK.
CONC. FOOTING W/
4-#4∅ E.W.

4×6 PT POSTS

4" EXTRUDED POLY-
STYRENE INSULATION

BRICK FLOOR
SET IN SAND

NOTES:
- ALL POSTS ARE 4×4'S (PT)
  UNLESS NOTED.
- ALL FOOTINGS ARE 2'-0" SQ
  × 8" THK. CONCRETE W/ 3 #4 E.W.
  UNLESS NOTED.
PT = PRESSURE-TREATED
E.W. = EACH WAY
#4∅ = 1/2" REINFORCING BAR

2" 4'-0" 4'-0" 2"
8'-4"

FOUNDATION PLAN
SCALE 1/4" = 1'-0"

2

N

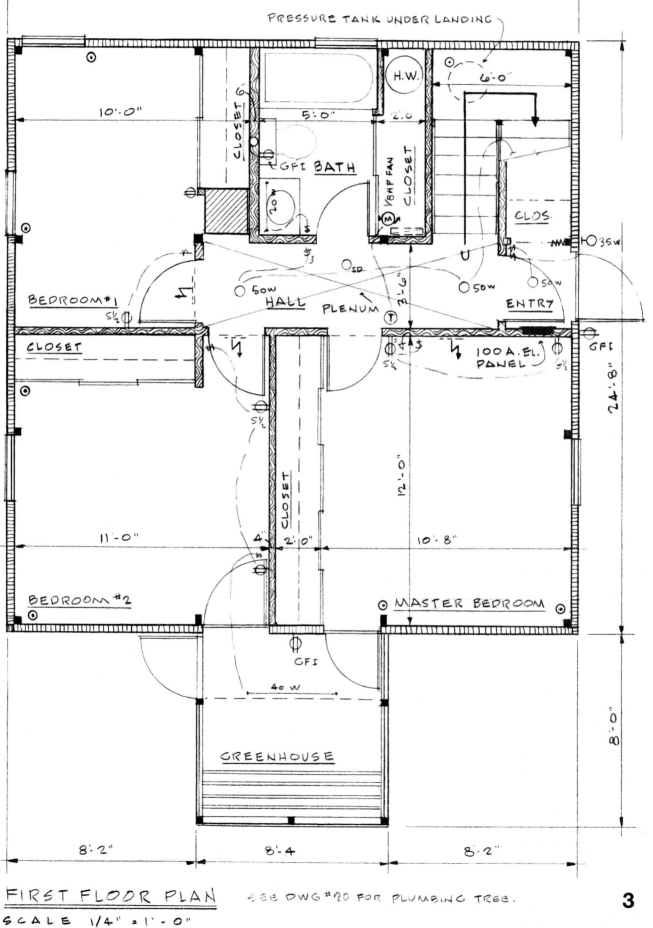

24'-8"

PRESSURE TANK UNDER LANDING

10'-0"

H.W.

6'-0"

CLOSET 6'

5'-0"   2'-0

BATH

GFI

1/8 HP FAN

CLOSET

20 w

M

CLOS.

35 w

BEDROOM #1

S D

50w

50w

50w

5 1/2

HALL

PLENUM

ENTRY

CLOSET

T

100 A. EL. PANEL

GFI

5 1/2

5 1/2

24'-8"

12'-0"

CLOSET

11'-0"

4'

2'-0"

10'-8"

BEDROOM #2

MASTER BEDROOM

GFI

40 W

GREENHOUSE

8'-0"

8'-2"   8'-4   8'-2"

FIRST FLOOR PLAN   SEE DWG #20 FOR PLUMBING TREE.   3

SCALE 1/4" = 1'-0"

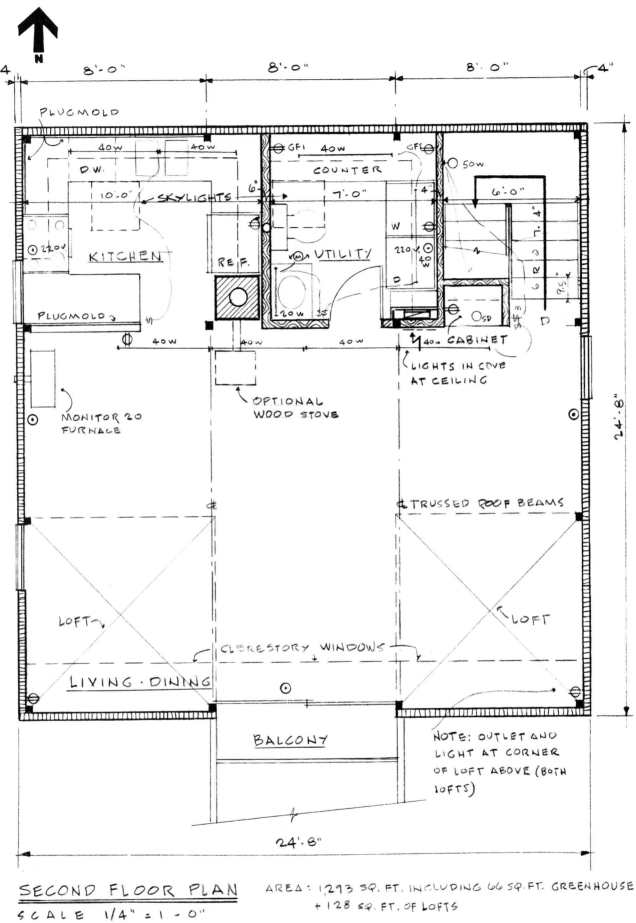

N

8'-0"   8'-0"   8'-0"   4"

PLUGMOLD

40W   40W
D.W.
10'-0"   SKYLIGHTS
220V
KITCHEN
PLUGMOLD

MONITOR 20
FURNACE

REF.

GFI   40W   GFI
COUNTER   50W
6"   7'-0"   4"   6'-0"
W
UTILITY   220V
40W
D   220V
40W
20W

40W   40W   40W   40W   CABINET
OPTIONAL   LIGHTS IN COVE
WOOD STOVE   AT CEILING

TRUSSED ROOF BEAMS

LOFT   LOFT
CLERESTORY WINDOWS
LIVING · DINING

24'-8"

BALCONY   NOTE: OUTLET AND
LIGHT AT CORNER
OF LOFT ABOVE (BOTH
LOFTS)

24'-8"

SECOND FLOOR PLAN   AREA: 1293 SQ. FT. INCLUDING 66 SQ. FT. GREENHOUSE
SCALE 1/4" = 1'-0"   + 128 SQ. FT. OF LOFTS

NOTE: 220V. OUTLETS ARE SHOWN FOR ELECTRIC STOVE & DRYER.
DELETE IF GAS IS USED. WASHER AND DRYER CAN BE INSTALLED
IN CLOSET SPACE IN FIRST FLOOR BATH.

4

HEATING REQUIREMENTS THESE HOUSES REQUIRE VERY SMALL AMOUNTS OF SUPPLEMENTAL HEAT BECAUSE OF THEIR TIGHT CONSTRUCTION. FOR AREAS WITH LESS THAN 5,000 DEGREE-DAYS, ELECTRIC HEAT IS ECONOMICAL. USE 2,000 WATTS FOR MAIN LIVING SPACE AND 500 WATTS EACH FOR BEDROOMS, 250 WATTS WILL HEAT BATH & UTILITY SPACES. VENTED CATALYIC GAS HEATERS CAN BE USED AS AN ALTERNATE TO ELECTRIC. ONE 6,000 BTU "CAT" HEATER FOR THE MAIN LIVING SPACE CAN BE COMBINED WITH ELECTRICITY FOR SMALLER SPACES.

FOR AREAS OF 5-7,000 DEGREE-DAYS, SMALL HEATERS PRODUCING 20-30000 BTU'S ARE RECOMMENDED. EXAMPLES ARE KERO-SUN MONITOR 20 & 30 VENTED KEROSENE WALL FURNACES AND EMPIRE 30,000 BTU GAS WALL FURNACE, A SMALL WOOD COOKSTOVE WILL ALSO BE SUITABLE FOR SPACE HEATING. I RECOMMEND SMALL WOOD-COAL COMBINATION HEATERS SUCH AS THE RAM STOVE OR THE SMALL FEDERAL BOX HEATER (CONSOLIDATED DUTCHWEST, BOX 1109, PLYMOUTH, MA. 02360.)

FOR 7,000 DEGREE-DAYS PLUS, USE A MONITOR 30, VERMONT CASTINGS VIGILANT OR SMALL FEDERAL CONVECTION HEATER WITH OUTSIDE AIR INTAKE.

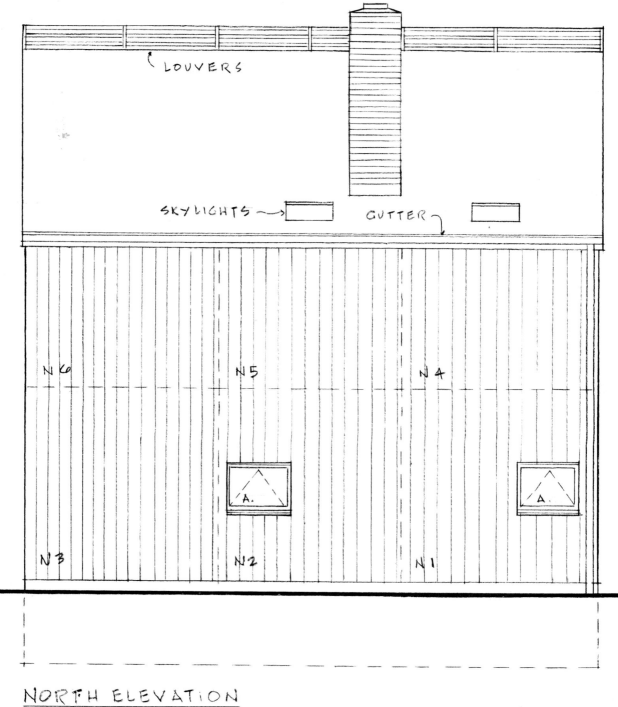

NORTH ELEVATION

SCALE 1/4" = 1'-0"

5

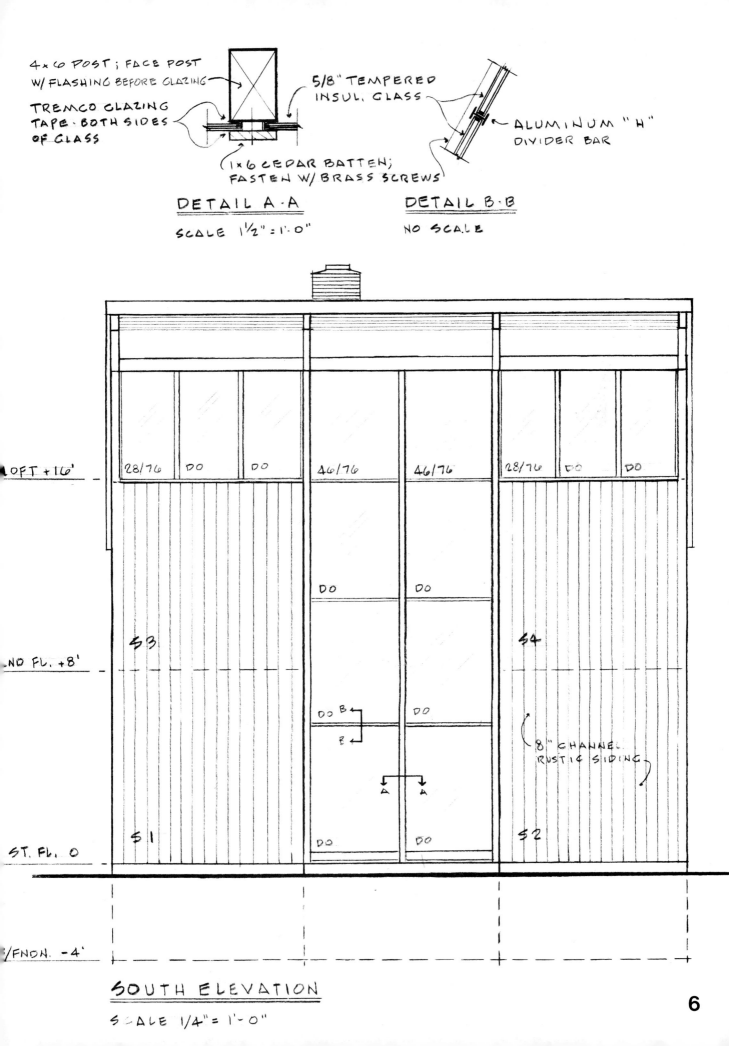

4 x 6 POST; FACE POST
W/ FLASHING BEFORE GLAZING

5/8" TEMPERED
INSUL. GLASS

TREMCO GLAZING
TAPE. BOTH SIDES
OF GLASS

ALUMINUM "H"
DIVIDER BAR

1 x 6 CEDAR BATTEN;
FASTEN W/ BRASS SCREWS

DETAIL A·A
SCALE 1½" = 1'-0"

DETAIL B·B
NO SCALE

OFT + 16'

28/76   DO   DO   46/76   46/76   28/76   DO   DO

DO   DO

S3   S4

ND FL. +8'

DO B   DO

8" CHANNEL
RUSTIC SIDING

A   A

S1   DO   DO   S2

ST. FL. 0

/FNDN. -4'

SOUTH ELEVATION
SCALE 1/4" = 1'-0"

6

WINDOW SCHEDULE

A 8 · 2028 HOPPER TYPE (INSWINGING)
   6 · 28×76 × 5/8" TEMPERED FIXED LITES
   8 · 46×76 × 5/8"   "   "   "
 * 2 · CUSTOM TRIANGLES (2ND. FL. G.H)
 * 2 · CUSTOM TRAPEZOIDS (1ST. FL. G.H)
   2 · 24×24 TRIPLE-GLAZED SKYLIGHTS

 * CUSTOM GLAZING CAN BE SINGLE 1/4"
   PLEXIGLAS OR CUSTOM DOUBLE GLAZING.
   FIRST FLOOR GLAZING MUST BE TEMPERED

DOOR SCHEDULE

4 · 2'·4" 6'·8" × 1 3/8" INT.
4 · 2·8" × 6'·8" × 1 3/8" INT
1 · 2·8" × 6·8" × 1 5/8 EXT. (GL.)
1 · 3·0" × 6·8" × 1 5/8 EXT (1/2 GL)
1 · 8·0" × 6·8" SLIDING GLASS
1 · 2'·6" × 6·8" FOLDING CLOSET
1 SET 12'·0" × 6·8" SLIDING CLOSET
1 SET 8·0" × 6·8"   "   "
1 SET 6·0" × 6·8"   "   "
(CLOSET DOORS MAY BE 1 1/8" OR 1 3/8" THK.)

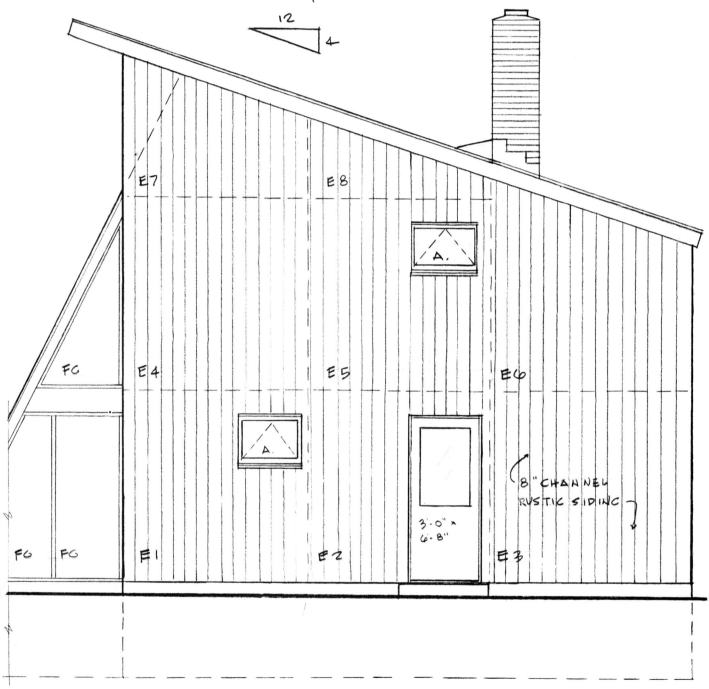

EAST ELEVATION
SCALE 1/4" = 1'- 0"

FRAME MEMBERS SHOULD BE ACCURATELY CUT TO DIMENSIONS SHOWN ON DWGS. #11 & 12. SPECIAL DRILLS, CHISELS, SAWS AND MALLETS ARE AVAILABLE FROM: FOX MAPLE TOOLS, SNOWVILLE ROAD, W. BROWNFIELD, ME 04010. SEE DWG #13 FOR MATERIALS LIST & FRAMING SECTION. ANCHOR FRAME MEMBERS W/ 8" ANNULAR RING BARN SPIKES. IF NOT AVAILABLE LOCALLY, ORDER DIRECT FROM: VERMONT FRAMES, BOX 100, HINESBURG, VT 05461. THESE SPIKES SHOULD ALSO BE USED TO ANCHOR THE LAMINATED PANELS TO THE FRAME. SPACE NAILS 2' 8" O.C. USE 4 NAILS FOR 2 MEMBER FRAME JOINT; 6 NAILS FOR 3 MEMBER JOINT.

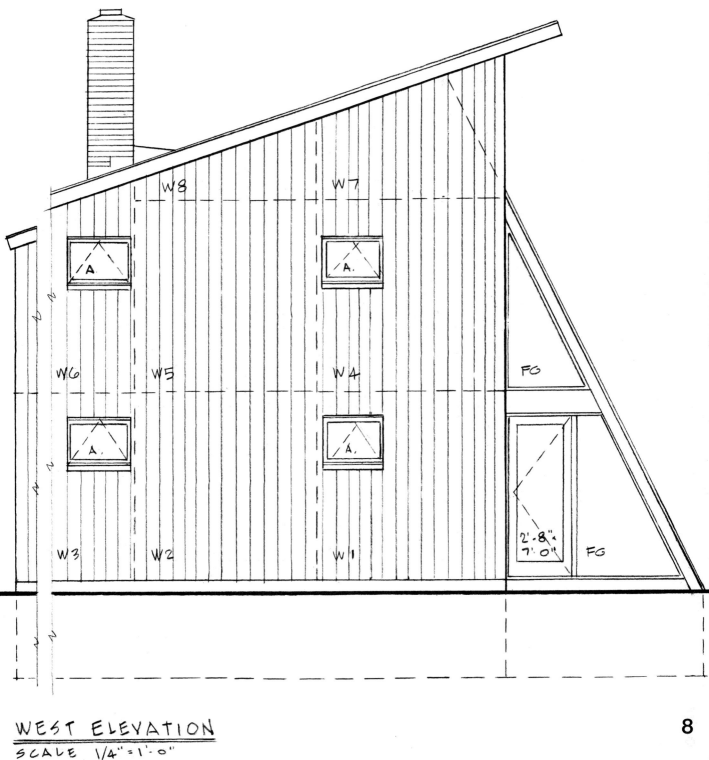

WEST ELEVATION
SCALE 1/4" = 1'-0"

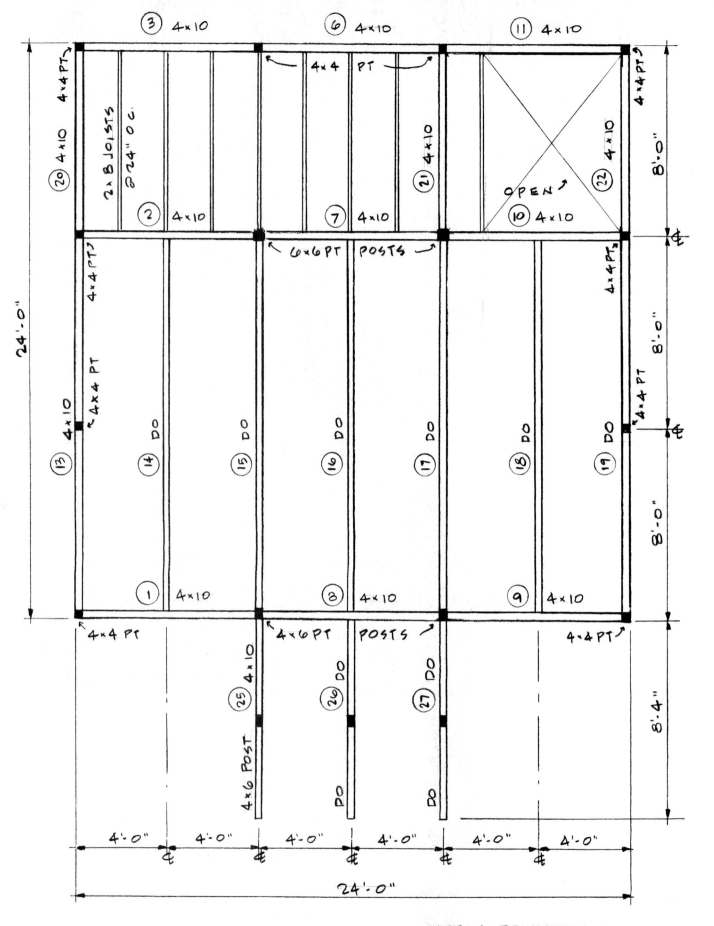

SECOND FLOOR FRAMING PLAN

SCALE 1/4" = 1'-0"

NOTES: PT = PRESSURE-TREATED
RS = ROUGHSAWN
DO = DUPLICATE ORDER

9

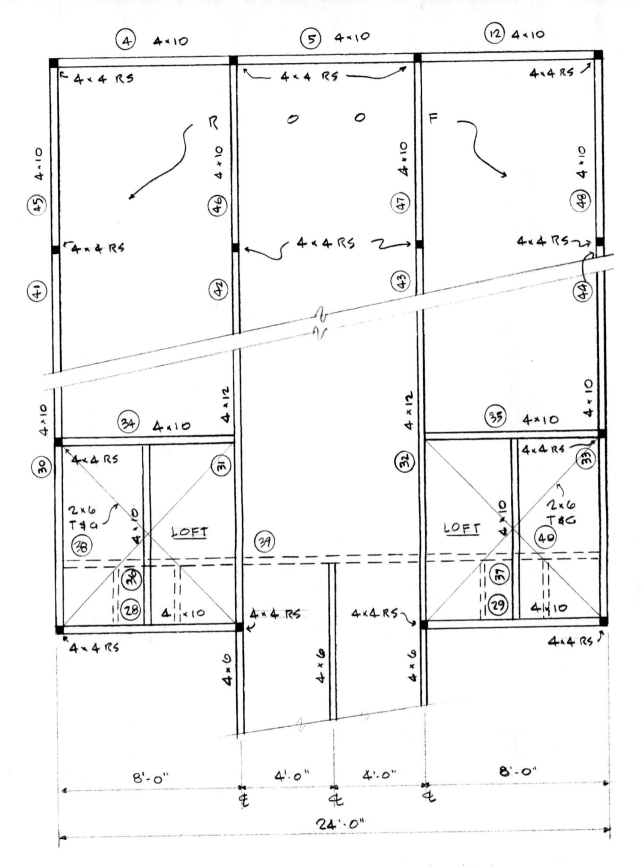

NOTE: DASHED LINE SHOWS BEAMS 38,39,&40 AT RIDGE

LOFT & ROOF FRAMING PLAN

SCALE 1/4"=1'-0"

#12,9 MADE FROM 4×10-8'

#7,8 MADE FROM 4×10-8'

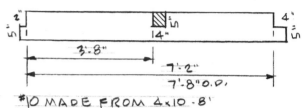

#3,4 MADE FROM 4×10-8'

#10 MADE FROM 4×10-8'

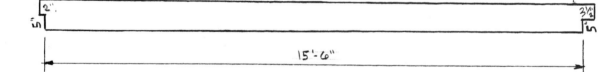

#5,6 MADE FROM 4×10-8'

#11,12 MADE FROM 4×10-8'

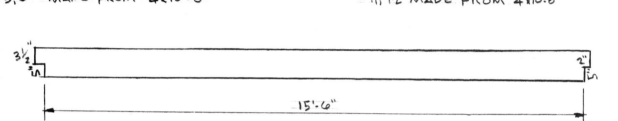

#13,18 & 19 MADE FROM 4×10-16'

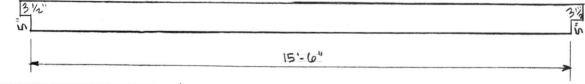

#15,16 MADE FROM 4×10-16'

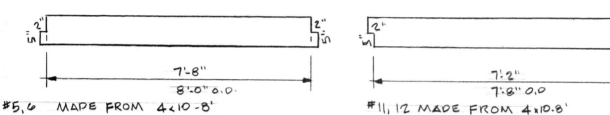

#14 MADE FROM 4×10-16'

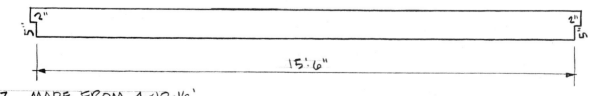

#17 MADE FROM 4×10-16'

FRAME PARTS I NO SCALE

11

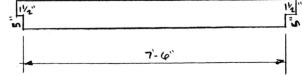

1½" 1½"
5" 5"
7'-6"

#20,22 MADE FROM 4×10-8'

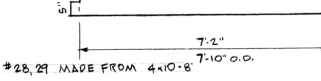

4" 4"
5" 1 1 5"
7'-2"
7'-10" O.D.

#28,29 MADE FROM 4×10-8'

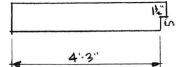

1½" 1½"
5" 5"
7'-6"

#21 MADE FROM 4×10-8'

#23 & 24 NOT USED

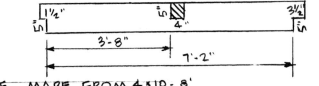

3½" 5" 1½"
5" 4" 5"
3'-2"
7'-2"

#34 MADE FROM 4×10-8'

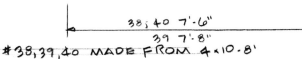

1½"
5"
4'-3"

#25,26,27 MADE FROM 4×10-16' CUT @ SITE

1½" 5" 3½"
5" 4" 5"
3'-8"
7'-2"

#35 MADE FROM 4×10-8'

4"

38; 40 7'-6"
39 7'-8"

#38,39,40 MADE FROM 4×10-8'

3½" 1½"
5" 5"
7'-6"

#36,37 MADE FROM 4×10-8'

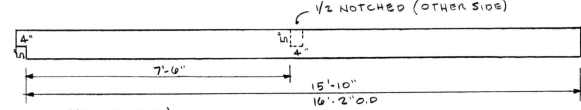

4" 5"
5" 4"
7'-6"
15'-10"
16'-2" O.D.

#30,33 MADE FROM 4×10-16'

½ NOTCHED (OTHER SIDE)

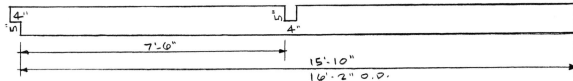

4" 5"
5" 4"
7'-6"
15'-10"
16'-2" O.D.

#31 MADE FROM 4×10-16'

½ NOTCHED (THIS SIDE)

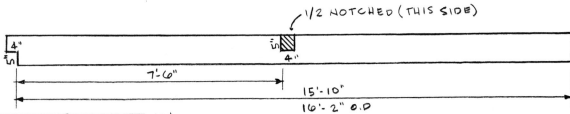

4" 5"
5" 4"
7'-6"
15'-10"
16'-2" O.D

#32 MADE FROM 4×10-16'

12

<u>FRAME PARTS II</u> NO SCALE

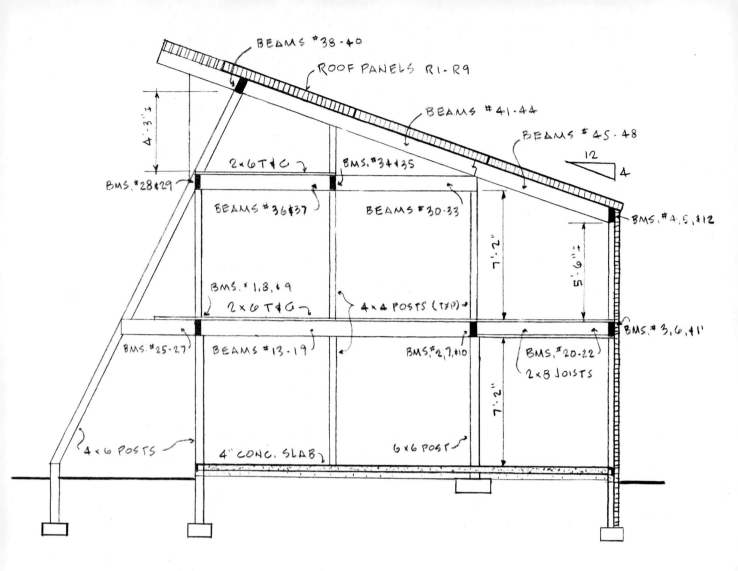

FRAMING SECTION SCALE 3/16" = 1'-0"

ROOF BMS. #41, 42, 43, 44 CUT FROM 4-4×10'S @ 18'
          #45, 46, 47, 48 CUT FROM 4-4×10'S @ 10'
          TO BE CUT AT SITE.

BEAMS	20 - 4×10'S @ 8' RS
	1 - 4×10 @ 12' RS
	11 - 4×10'S @ 16' RS
JOISTS	7 - 2×8'S @ 8' SPF
POSTS	10 - 4×4'S @ 12' PT (EXT)
	4 - 4×6'S @ 12' PT (EXT) 3 PCS @ 4'-0" + 2 @ 12'
	2 - 6×6'S @ 8' PT (INT.)
	10 - 4×4'S @ 8' RS (INT)
	2 - 4×4'S @ 12' RS (INT) 4 PCS @ 5'-6"
	5 - 4×6'S @ 10' RS (GNHSE)
	1 - 4×6 @ 16' RS (GNHSE)
	4 - 4×6'S @ 12' RS (CLERESTORY) 8 PCS @ 6'
	1 - 4×4 @ 12' RS (LOFT POSTS) 4 PCS @ 3'

SILL PLATES
15 - 2×4'S @ 8' PT)
15 - 2×6'S @ 8' (PT)

MATERIALS LIST FOR FRAME

RS = ROUGHSAWN
PT = PRESSURE TREATED
SPF = SPRUCE, PINE, FIR

SEE DWG. #15 FOR LARGE SCALE DETAILS **13**

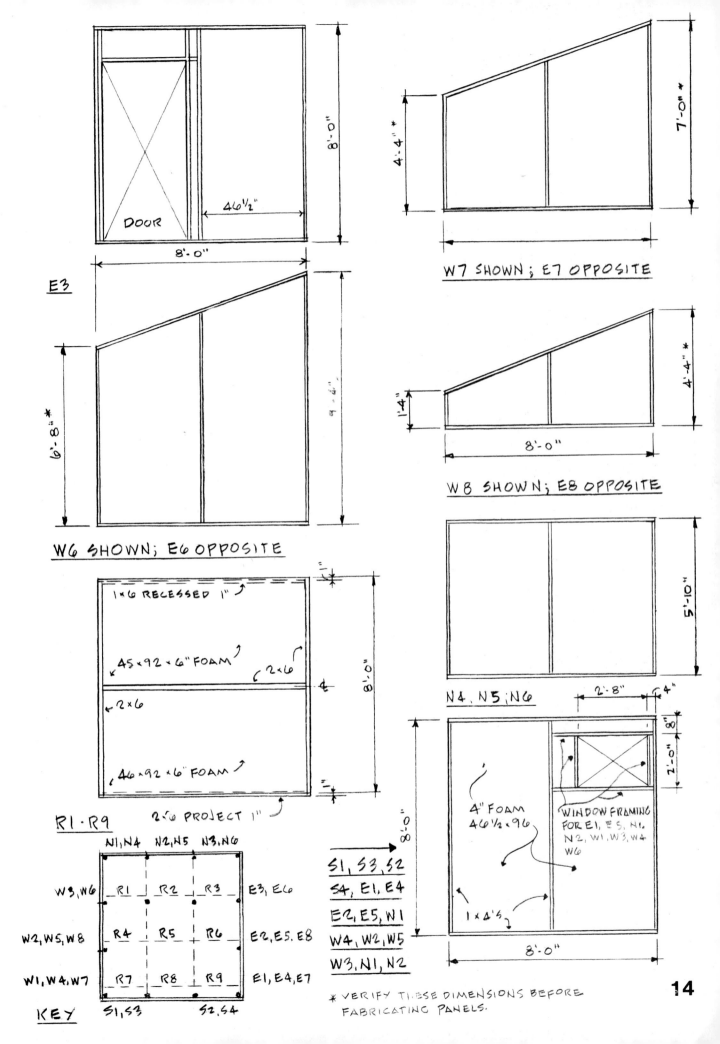

E3

8'-0"
8'-0"
46½"
DOOR

W6 SHOWN; E6 OPPOSITE

6'-8"*
9'-6"*

W7 SHOWN; E7 OPPOSITE

4'-4"*
7'-0"*

W8 SHOWN; E8 OPPOSITE

1'-4"
4'-4"*
8'-0"

1" 1×6 RECESSED 1"
45×92×6" FOAM
2×6
2×6
46×92×6" FOAM
2×6 PROJECT 1"
8'-0"
1"

R1-R9

N4, N5, N6

5'-10"
2'-8"
4"

4" FOAM
46½×96
WINDOW FRAMING
FOR E1, E5, N1,
N2, W1, W3, W4,
W6
1×4'S
8'-0"
8'-0"
8"
2'-0"

KEY

	N1,N4	N2,N5	N3,N6	
W3,W6	R1	R2	R3	E3, E6
W2,W5,W8	R4	R5	R6	E2,E5.E8
W1,W4,W7	R7	R8	R9	E1,E4,E7
	S1,S3		S2,S4	

S1, S3, S2
S4, E1, E4
E2, E5, W1
W4, W2, W5
W3, N1, N2

* VERIFY THESE DIMENSIONS BEFORE
FABRICATING PANELS.

14

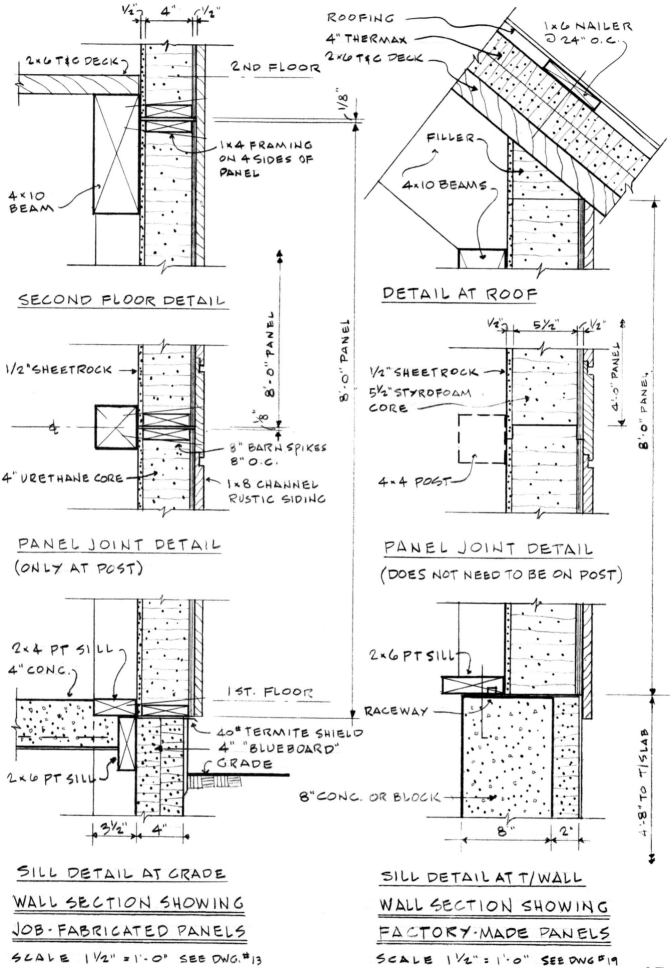

SECOND FLOOR DETAIL

2×6 T&G DECK

4×10 BEAM

2ND FLOOR

1×4 FRAMING ON 4 SIDES OF PANEL

½" 4" ½"

DETAIL AT ROOF

ROOFING

4" THERMAX

2×6 T&G DECK

1×6 NAILER @ 24" O.C.

FILLER

4×10 BEAMS

⅛"

PANEL JOINT DETAIL
(ONLY AT POST)

½" SHEETROCK

4" URETHANE CORE

8" BARN SPIKES 8" O.C.

1×8 CHANNEL RUSTIC SIDING

8'-0" PANEL

8'-0" PANEL

8"

PANEL JOINT DETAIL
(DOES NOT NEED TO BE ON POST)

½" SHEETROCK

5½" STYROFOAM CORE

4×4 POST

½" 5½" ½"

4'-0" PANEL

8'-0" PANEL

SILL DETAIL AT GRADE

2×4 PT SILL

4" CONC.

1ST. FLOOR

40# TERMITE SHIELD

4" "BLUEBOARD"

GRADE

2×6 PT SILL

3½" 4"

SILL DETAIL AT T/WALL

2×6 PT SILL

RACEWAY

8" CONC. OR BLOCK

8" 2"

4'-8" TO T/SLAB

WALL SECTION SHOWING JOB-FABRICATED PANELS

SCALE 1½" = 1'-0" SEE DWG. #13

WALL SECTION SHOWING FACTORY-MADE PANELS

SCALE 1½" = 1'-0" SEE DWG #19

15

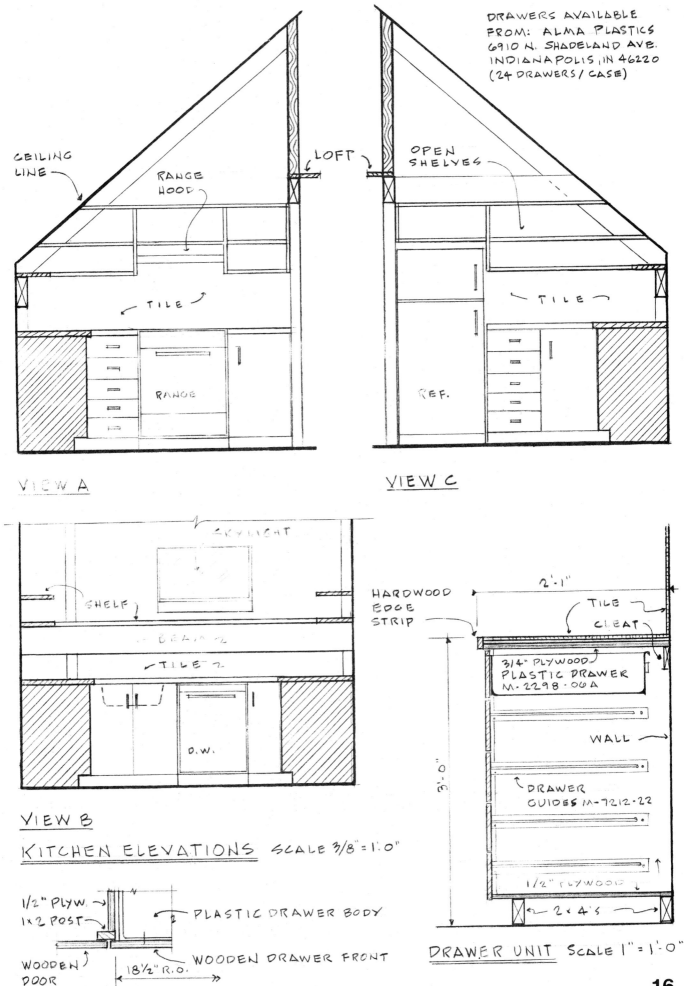

DRAWERS AVAILABLE
FROM: ALMA PLASTICS
6910 N. SHADELAND AVE.
INDIANAPOLIS, IN 46220
(24 DRAWERS / CASE)

CEILING LINE

RANGE HOOD

LOFT

OPEN SHELVES

TILE

TILE

RANGE

REF.

VIEW A

VIEW C

SKYLIGHT

SHELF

BEAM

TILE

D.W.

HARDWOOD EDGE STRIP

TILE

CLEAT

2'-1"

3/4" PLYWOOD
PLASTIC DRAWER
M-2298-06A

WALL

3'-0"

DRAWER GUIDES M-7212-22

1/2" PLYWOOD

2 × 4's

VIEW B

KITCHEN ELEVATIONS SCALE 3/8"=1'-0"

1/2" PLYW.
1×2 POST

WOODEN DOOR

PLASTIC DRAWER BODY

WOODEN DRAWER FRONT

18½" R.O.

CABINET DIVIDER DETAIL SCALE 3"=1'-0"

DRAWER UNIT SCALE 1"=1'-0"

16

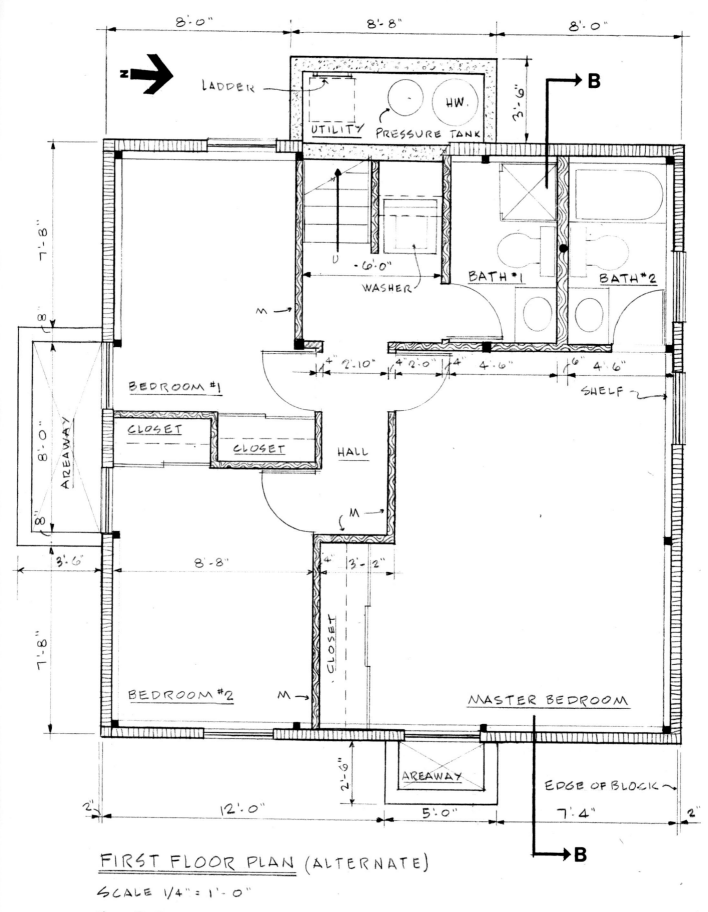

FIRST FLOOR PLAN (ALTERNATE)

SCALE 1/4" = 1'-0"

- M - PARTITIONS THUS MARKED MAY BE MASONRY FOR HEAT STORAGE.
- SECOND FLOOR FRAME IS AS SHOWN ON DWG #9 EXCEPT THAT OPENING FOR STAIRS MOVES TO CENTER BAY.
- AREA: 1,306 SQ. FT. + 128 SQ. FT. LOFT

17

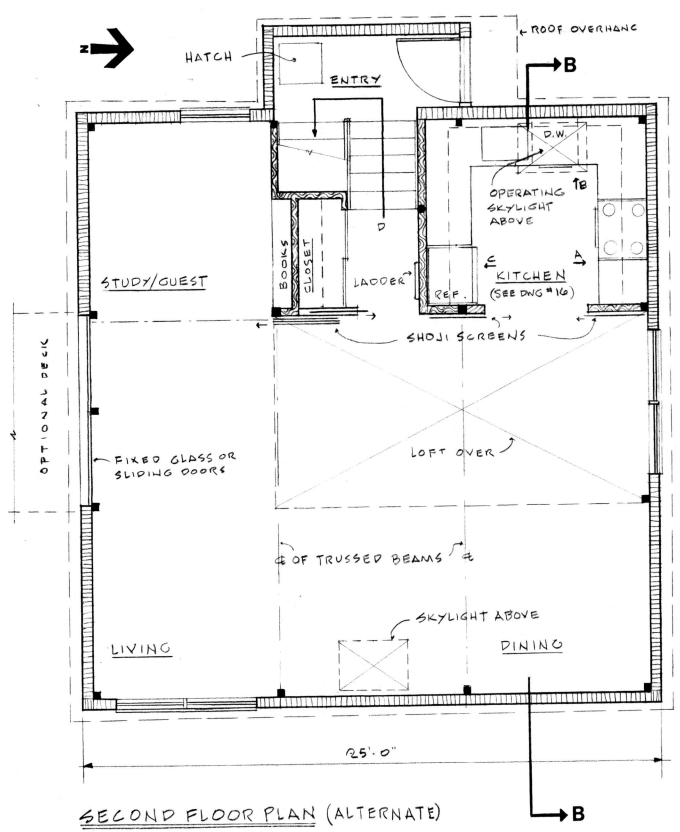

N →

HATCH

ROOF OVERHANG

→ B

ENTRY

D.W.

OPERATING
SKYLIGHT
ABOVE

B ↑

STUDY/GUEST

BOOKS

CLOSET

LADDER

REF.

KITCHEN
(SEE DWG #16)

C ← → A

SHOJI SCREENS

OPTIONAL DECK

FIXED GLASS OR
SLIDING DOORS

LOFT OVER ↗

₵ OF TRUSSED BEAMS ↗ ₵

SKYLIGHT ABOVE

LIVING

DINING

25'·0"

SECOND FLOOR PLAN (ALTERNATE)

SCALE 1/4"=1'-0"

NOTE: SOME CODES WILL REQUIRE 2 EXITS FROM SECOND FLOOR, OPTIONAL
DECK W/ SLIDING GLASS DOORS AND STEPS TO GROUND SHOULD BE PROVIDED
IN SUCH CASES.

→ B

18

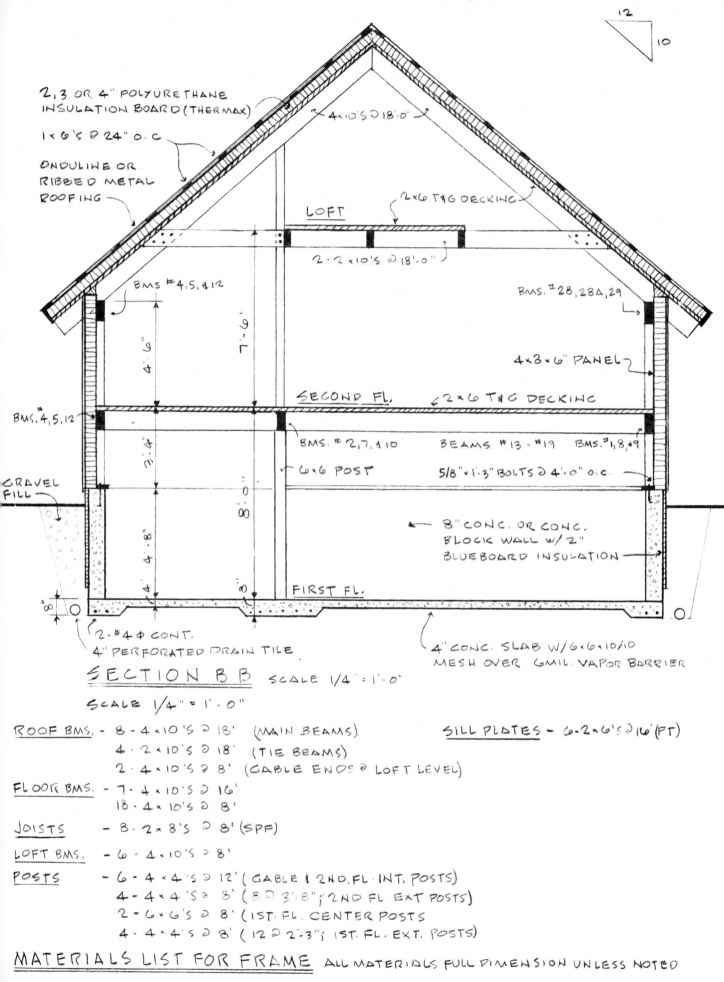

12
10

2, 3, OR 4" POLYURETHANE
INSULATION BOARD (THERMAX)

1 × 6'S @ 24" O.C.

ONDULINE OR
RIBBED METAL
ROOFING

4×10'S @ 18'·0"

2×6 T&G DECKING

LOFT

2-2×10'S @ 18'·0"

BMS #4, 5, &12

BMS. #28, 28A, 29

4×8×6" PANEL

9'·6"
4'·9"

SECOND FL.

2×6 T&G DECKING

BMS. #4, 5, 12

3'·4"

BMS. #2, 7, & 10   BEAMS #13 - #19   BMS. #1, 8, &9

6×6 POST   5/8" × 1·3" BOLTS @ 4'·0" O.C.

GRAVEL
FILL

8"·0"

4'·8"

8" CONC. OR CONC.
BLOCK WALL W/ 2"
BLUEBOARD INSULATION

8'·0"

FIRST FL.

8"

2 - #4∅ CONT.
4" PERFORATED DRAIN TILE

4" CONC. SLAB W/ 6×6×10/10
MESH OVER 6MIL. VAPOR BARRIER

SECTION BB   SCALE 1/4" = 1'-0'

SCALE 1/4" = 1'·0"

ROOF BMS. - 8 - 4×10'S @ 18'   (MAIN BEAMS)
            4 - 2×10'S @ 18'   (TIE BEAMS)
            2 - 4×10'S @ 8'   (GABLE ENDS @ LOFT LEVEL)

SILL PLATES - 6 - 2×6'S @ 16' (PT)

FLOOR BMS. - 7 - 4×10'S @ 16'
             18 - 4×10'S @ 8'

JOISTS   - 8 - 2×8'S @ 8' (SPF)

LOFT BMS. - 6 - 4×10'S @ 8'

POSTS   - 6 - 4×4'S @ 12' (GABLE & 2ND. FL. INT. POSTS)
             4 - 4×4'S @ 8' (8 @ 3'·8"; 2ND FL. EXT POSTS)
             2 - 6×6'S @ 8' (1ST. FL. CENTER POSTS
             4 - 4×4'S @ 8' (12 @ 2'·3"; 1ST. FL. EXT. POSTS)

MATERIALS LIST FOR FRAME   ALL MATERIALS FULL DIMENSION UNLESS NOTED

WALL PANELS - 28 - 4'×8'×6" PANELS   SEE DWG. #15 FOR LARGE SCALE DETAILS   **19**

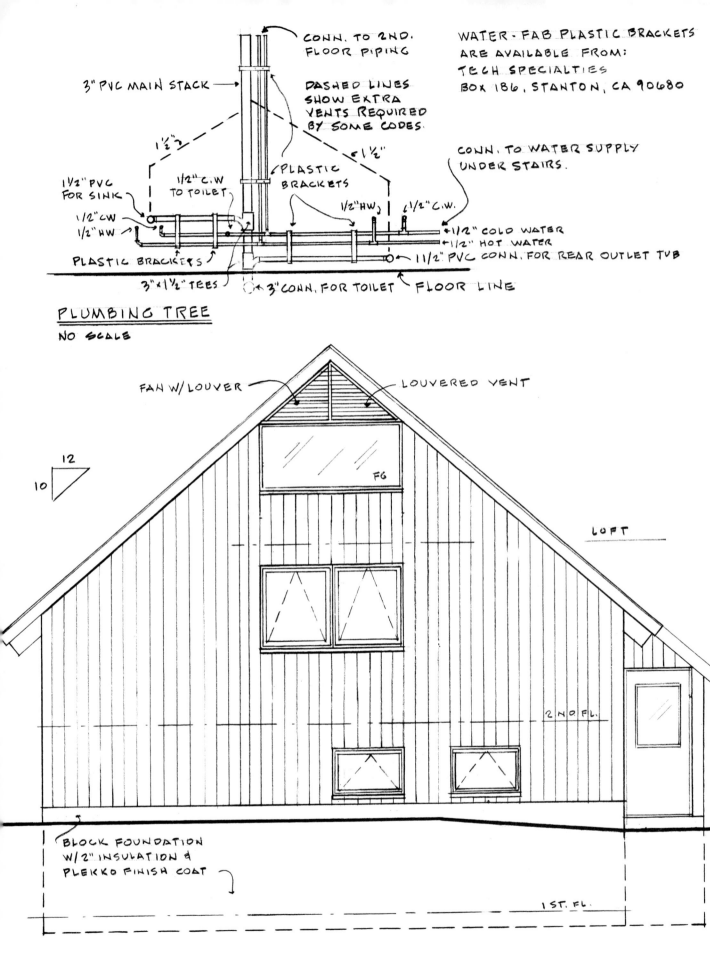

CONN. TO 2ND.
FLOOR PIPING

3" PVC MAIN STACK

WATER-FAB PLASTIC BRACKETS
ARE AVAILABLE FROM:
TECH SPECIALTIES
BOX 186, STANTON, CA 90680

DASHED LINES
SHOW EXTRA
VENTS REQUIRED
BY SOME CODES.

1½"

1½"

CONN. TO WATER SUPPLY
UNDER STAIRS.

1½" PVC
FOR SINK

1/2" C.W
TO TOILET

PLASTIC
BRACKETS

1/2" HW

1/2" C.W.

1/2" C.W
1/2" HW

1/2" COLD WATER
1/2" HOT WATER

PLASTIC BRACKETS

1 1/2" PVC CONN. FOR REAR OUTLET TUB

3"×1½" TEES

3" CONN. FOR TOILET

FLOOR LINE

PLUMBING TREE
NO SCALE

FAN W/LOUVER

LOUVERED VENT

12
10

FG

LOFT

2ND FL.

BLOCK FOUNDATION
W/2" INSULATION &
PLEKKO FINISH COAT

1 ST. FL.

NORTH ELEVATION
SCALE 1/4" = 1'-0"

20

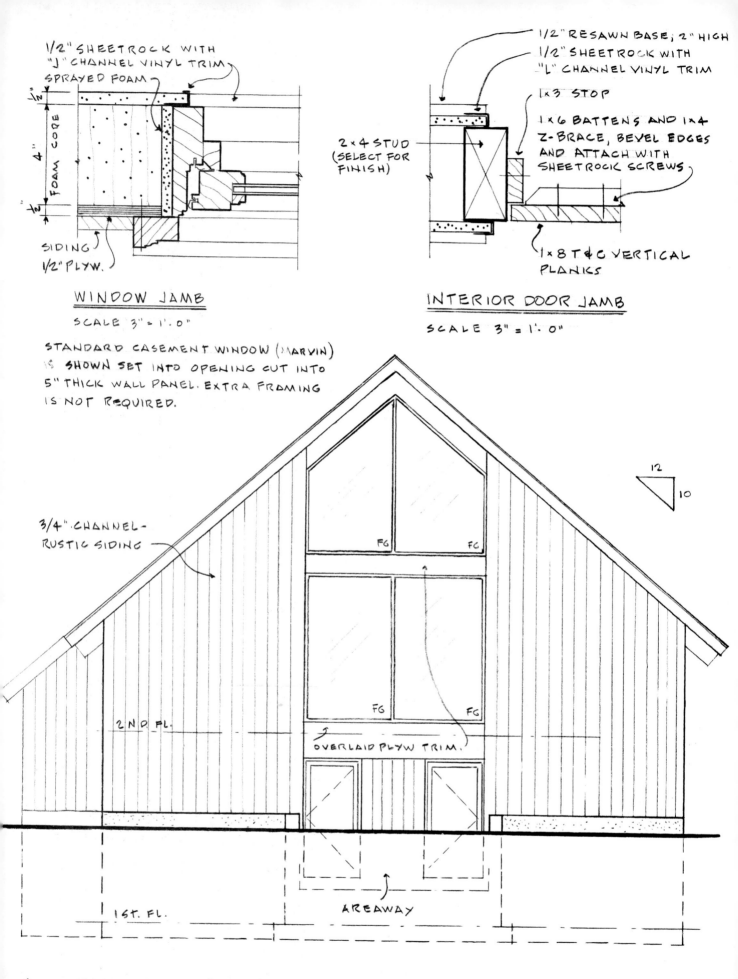

1/2" SHEETROCK WITH
"J" CHANNEL VINYL TRIM
SPRAYED FOAM

FOAM CORE

4"

SIDING
1/2" PLYW.

WINDOW JAMB

SCALE 3" = 1'-0"

STANDARD CASEMENT WINDOW (MARVIN)
IS SHOWN SET INTO OPENING CUT INTO
5" THICK WALL PANEL. EXTRA FRAMING
IS NOT REQUIRED.

1/2" RESAWN BASE; 2" HIGH
1/2" SHEETROCK WITH
"L" CHANNEL VINYL TRIM

1x3 STOP

1x6 BATTENS AND 1x4
Z-BRACE, BEVEL EDGES
AND ATTACH WITH
SHEETROCK SCREWS

2x4 STUD
(SELECT FOR
FINISH)

1x8 T&G VERTICAL
PLANKS

INTERIOR DOOR JAMB

SCALE 3" = 1'-0"

12
10

3/4" CHANNEL-
RUSTIC SIDING

FG   FG

FG   FG

OVERLAID PLYW TRIM.

2ND FL.

1st. FL.

AREAWAY

SOUTH ELEVATION

SCALE 1/4" = 1'-0"

21

WINDOW SCHEDULE

7 - 3625 AWNING WINDOWS
2 - 2456 CASEMENT WINDOWS
3 - 3638 AWNING WINDOWS
2 - 46 x 76 x 5/8" TEMPERED FIXED GL.
1 - 33 x 76 x 5/8"   "   "   "
2 - DOUBLE GLAZED CUSTOM TRAPEZOIDS
2 - 36 x 36 DG SKYLIGHTS; ONE VENTING

NUMBERS FOR ALL OPERATING
WINDOWS ARE MARVIN

DOOR SCHEDULE

1 - 2'-8 x 6'-8" x 1¾" EXT.
2 - 2'-4" - 6'-8" x 1⅜" INT.
3 - 2'-6" x 6'-8" x 1⅜" INT.
1 - 2'-8" x 6'-8" x 1⅜" POCKET DOOR
5 - 2'-6" x 6'-8" x 1⅛" SHOJI SCREENS
3 SETS 4'-0" x 1⅜" SLIDING CLOSET DOORS
1 SET 8'-0" x 1⅜"   "   "   "

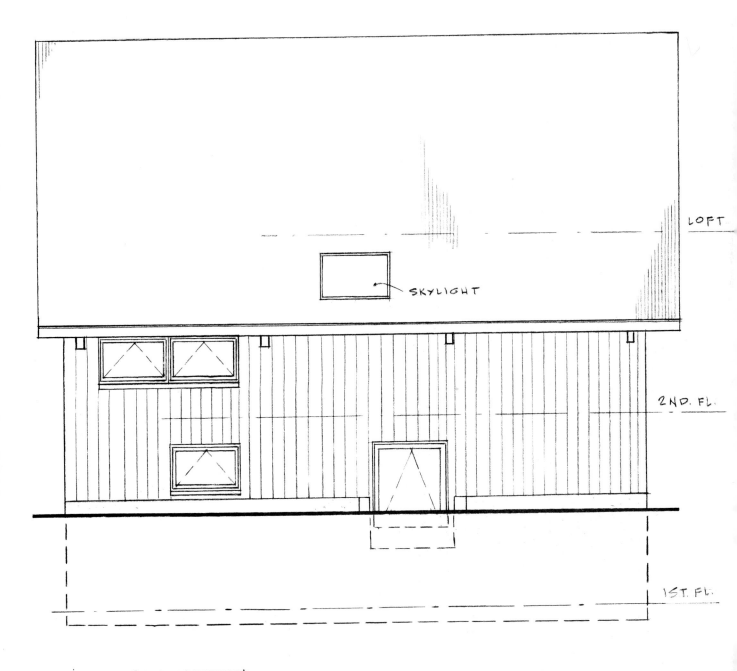

LOFT

SKYLIGHT

2ND. FL.

1ST. FL.

EAST ELEVATION
SCALE 1/4" = 1'- 0"

22

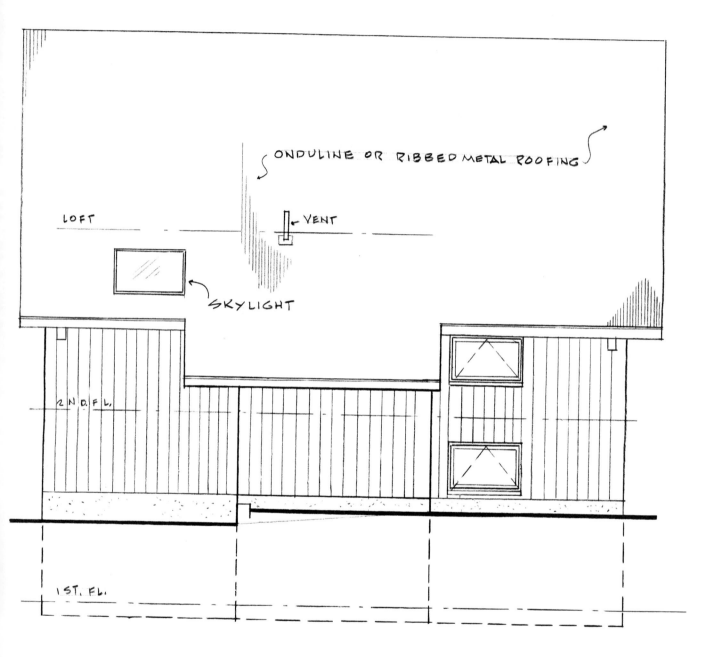

ONDULINE OR RIBBED METAL ROOFING

LOFT

VENT

SKYLIGHT

2ND. FL.

1ST. FL.

WEST ELEVATION
SCALE 1/4" = 1'-0"

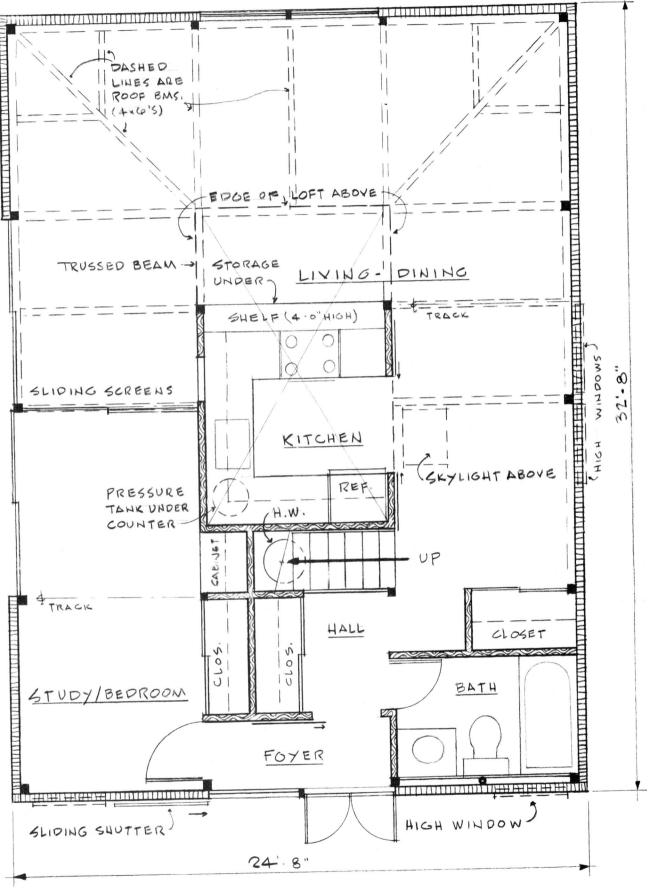

FIRST FLOOR PLAN OF "JAPANESE" HOUSE

SCALE 1/4" = 1'-0"   768 S.F. + 108 S.F. LOFT

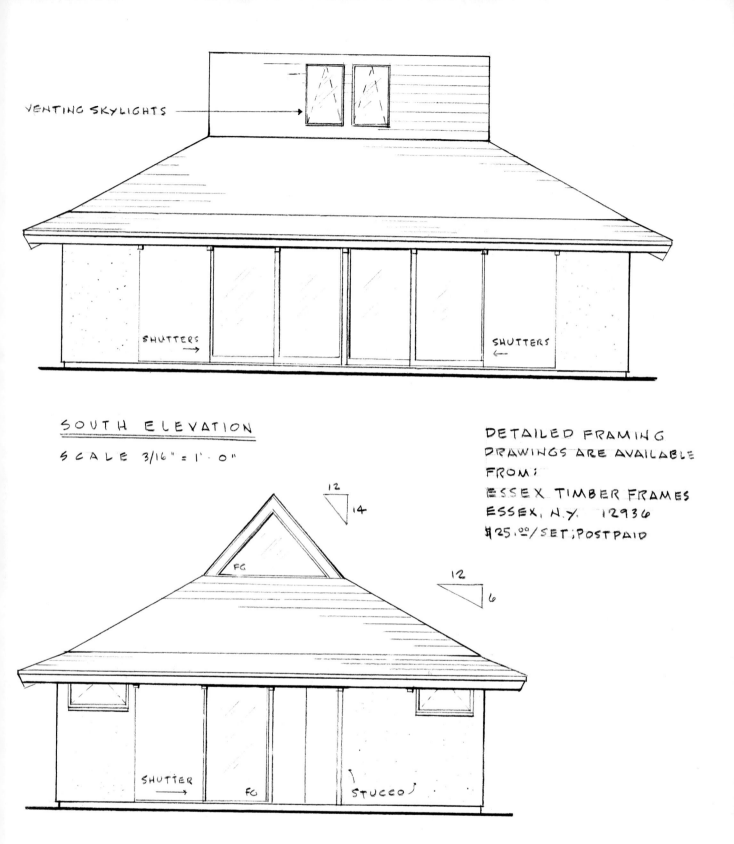

VENTING SKYLIGHTS

SHUTTERS →

← SHUTTERS

SOUTH ELEVATION

SCALE 3/16" = 1'- 0"

DETAILED FRAMING
DRAWINGS ARE AVAILABLE
FROM:
ESSEX TIMBER FRAMES
ESSEX, N.Y. 12936
$25.00/SET; POSTPAID

12
14

12
6

FG

SHUTTER →

FG

STUCCO

EAST ELEVATION

SCALE 3/16" = 1'- 0"

NORTH AND WEST ELEVATIONS ARE SIMILAR TO SOUTH
AND EAST EXCEPT FOR WINDOWS. SEE PLAN FOR WINDOW NOS.

25

Appendix C
Order Form for Plans

The following plans from Part IV are available from Smallplan for immediate delivery. Plans are $30 for the first set and $15 for each additional set included in the initial order, except where noted otherwise.

NO. OF SETS   PLAN NAME

_____   **House A.** Plans show both conventional and panelized construction and include an optional basement, or a pole foundation.

_____   **Howard house.** Plans show conventional construction with embedded-post foundation.

_____   **Gummere house.** Plans show pole-type house for rugged terrain. Conventional or panelized construction can be used. Alternate slab-on-grade details are provided.

_____   **Civic house with shed roof.** Reprint of plans bound into this book. These plans are $15 per set regardless of number ordered.

_____   **Civic house with gable roof.** Reprint of plans bound into this book. These plans are $15 per set regardless of number ordered.

_____   **Brookhaven house.** This house is designed for panelized construction over a braced post-and-beam frame. Garage is of conventional construction.

_____   **Retirement house.** Smaller version of the house shown in this book. This house is designed for panelized construction over a braced post-and-beam frame. Design shows swimming lane that may be omitted to allow an expanded plant-growing area or basement.

_____   **Solar Saltbox.** This house is designed for panelized construction over a braced post-and-beam frame. Foundations are slab-on-grade or embedded-post type.

Other plans from Part II and Part IV may be made available if interest warrants. Please cite page number of the plan in which you are interested.

In addition to my plans, Smallplan is acting as the U.S. distributor for plans by Charles Haynes. A set includes the following:

Three sets of permit and finance drawings
One set of detailed construction plans
One set of expansion options (30 pages)
Price of the above package is $75 (U.S.).

Detailed drawings are also available for each of the expansion versions of the plans at $20 (U.S.) each. Expansion drawing sets include the following:

Three sets of permit and finance drawings
One set of detailed construction drawings

Excellent detailed drawings for flush glazing a standard, tempered 34×76 glass skylight are also available for $5 (U.S.).

Canadian readers may order all of the above directly from:

Charles Haynes
Architecture Shop Ltd.
210–2182 W. 12th Ave.
Vancouver, BC V6K 2N4

Smallplan orders should include check or money order in U.S. dollars. Order from:

Smallplan
Box 43
Barrytown, NY 12507

For inquiries about other plans, contact:

Alex Wade
Mount Marion, NY 12456

For additional copies of photographs of houses in this book, contact:

Michael Saporito
4584 Esopus Creek Rd.
Saugerties, NY 12477

Photo Credits

Since the majority of the photographs for this book were taken by the author, you can assume that those not otherwise credited were taken by Alex Wade.

IDA System Housing photo courtesy of Tomomasa Hayashida of ABC Development Corporation, Tokyo.

Photos of solid polystyrene house courtesy of Cubic Structures, Inc.

Photos of David Easton's rammed-earth house courtesy of Magnus Berglund.

Photo of Rotunda house courtesy of Northern Counties.

Photo of Family Homes Cooperative house courtesy of FHC.

Photos of Acadia and Canadian Conserver houses courtesy of Charles Haynes.

Construction sequences, the before and after photos of the Weiss house, and the energy-saving products in Chapters 18 and 19 were taken by Howard Dratch. Dratch also shot the Howard house and interiors of the Knopf, Solar Saltbox, and Civic houses.

Peter McNaull shot the photos of the Retirement house.

Kevin Berry shot the photo of the roof insulation system.

Dick Kellum shot the photos of his expanded version of the Gummere house.

Sheryl Cline shot the photos of the Brookhaven house.

Cheryl Curry shot the photos of the Octagon house.

Michael Saporito shot the Japanese soaking tub, Swedish toilet, and homemade light fixtures. He also processed and printed most of my photos for the book.

Henry Peach shot the photos of the Bow House.

Index

Page numbers in **boldface** type indicate tables.